Get Connected With Your Dog

Emphasizing the Relationship While Training Your Dog

Brenda Aloff

Brenda Aloff can be reached at:
1711 Karat Road
Midland MI 48640
989.631.8217
www.brendaaloff.com

This book is available at:
Dogwise
701B Poplar
Box 2778
Wenatchee, WA 98807-2778
Orders: 1.800.776.2665
www.dogwise.com

First Edition
First Printing

Also by Brenda Aloff:

Positive Reinforcement - Training Dogs In The Real World
(2001). New Jersey: TFH Publications, Inc.
Aggression In Dogs: Practical Management, Prevention and Behaviour Modification
(2003). Tennessee: Fundcraft Publishing, Inc.
DVD: *Foundation Behaviours for Every Dog*
(2005). Michigan: Pix Elegance
Canine Body Language: A Photographic Guide
(2005) Wenatchee:Dogwise.

Maeve

When I was with you I felt like I was so much more and now that I have been left behind I feel like so much less. Indeed, it is my hope, that I can become the person you believed me to be.

Acknowledgments

It would be impossible to list all of the clients and dogs that made my learning experiences possible. There are some, in particular, whose involvement and dedication made this book a reality and improved the quality markedly. To all the lovely people who trusted me to help them with their dogs, I am so grateful. Thanks especially to those of you who contributed Case Histories and for all of the work you donated so that your dog's story can be told. These people and their dogs are very special to me, not just on a working basis, but in the friendships we form while working together.

As always Betty Owen has been by my side through thick and thin. I would never have gotten this done without her constant pressure on! - I mean gentle persuasion and support. Like the Monday she finally said to me: "You must have this book to the editor by Wednesday." When I started my typical whining and moaning and "poor, pitiful me" act, she merely fixed me with a steely eye and said in an ominous tone, "Wednesday." I crawled off, spent two really late nights (or rather early mornings) after working all day (see, poor me!) and the manuscript was, in fact, to the editor by Wednesday. Without Betty's gentle persuasion and support this book would still be languishing on my computer, unfinished.

My daughter, Abbey, who is working on a creative writing degree, did a lot of reading and helped me to get many of my thoughts in articulate order. On her first read, after about 15 seconds, she looked up and with a straight face said, "Mom, how do you structure your paragraphs?" After a small pause, as I looked at her with a blank expression on my face (righto - I do not structure my paragraphs and have never given it a thought...), she said in that bright voice reserved for small children and idiots, "Well, perhaps we could start there..."

Steve, as always, brought nourishment to me in the form of tasty cooking and fed the sheep, dogs and horse when I was too beside myself to get it all done. He also puts up with an amazing amount of impatience and bad temper on my part (writing is fun!) while I am struggling with the frustration of putting the words on the paper.

To the unbelievable crew at Dogwise, Charlene & Larry, I must add Nate. Patience IS a virtue and thank you all for exhibiting so much virtue. Nate, thank you for all the extra help with the layout. I was really bogged down...You are a life-saver! Charlene, the endless emotional and moral support was more valuable than you could ever know. Larry, the read-throughs and editing improved this book immensely. I am grateful to all of you.

My friend Mary Wilmoth, who always has words of encouragement like, "Good God, you haven't finished this yet! What is wrong with you?"

Dave & Marguerite Schrader were very devoted in helping me with the visuals. They worked as a team to get video and photographic footage. Without the accompanying film, the exercises would be virtually impossible to explain to someone (at least with my writing skill set!). The photographs add depth to the text and increase understanding in ways that words cannot.

I would like to thank Victoria Craig of New Brunswick. The chapter in which I discuss Newton's Laws of Physics and dog behaviour is an idea which gets credited to Victoria Craig. She and I had many rousing discussions about the topic of this book and she always gave me ever new ways to look at my work. Lovely mind, super direction!

Dr. Jason Jones, a neurobiologist at Vassar College, gets my undying gratitude. I met his wife, Jenn, at an IAABC symposium. We were discussing dog training (what else is there?) and I was telling her of a chapter I was having particular difficulty with due to the fact that I am not a neurobiologist. She quite generously volunteered her husband to aid me. Jason, even more generously, agreed to help me with the "Brain Stuff" chapter. Without him, I am afraid it would have been outdated and erroneous. I am so grateful to him for his patience. He is also an excellent teacher. In this book I endlessly talk about outlasting the dog to provide her with information in the most non-confrontational way possible. When training a dog, I do my best to make my idea her idea, then she will quickly comply. Jason helped me to realize just how very effective this technique can be. In the first draft I sent him, he sent back an edited version, and mildly suggested that I change some of my analogies with viable reasons why I should do so. I, of course, had decided that my analogies were sensational, (who doesn't love the statement: "Behaviour is like snot"?) and should not, under any circumstances be altered. So I made the changes he suggested (the ones that were technical in nature) and cheekily left in my analogies. The dear Dr. Jones immediately sent the draft back with a few more (a list of about 26 this time) minor corrections and another suggestion that I should change my anaologies, however, he sent a different list of reasons. By the third reading, surely he was getting bored with my idiocy by this point, but he never said so. He became so convincing, was so persistent and came up with so many valid reasons, that, in time, I decided my analogies were quite stupid and wondered why he had not mentioned how insipid they were upon the first reading. Jason, thank you so much! I appreciate the help with the chapter and for using my own techniques on me.

I would like to thank Barb Kahn for letting me present this new material for the first time at her facility, Wonderdogs. Presenting new material is always very scary to me, and it was nice to be able to do that among friends. I would like to also thank Valerie & Mia (Valerie's German Shorthair), and the dear Marlene, whom I met at the clinic in New Jersey at Wonderdogs. Valerie, thank you for keeping in touch and keeping me up to date on Mia's progress. Marlene, your words of encouragement meant more than you will ever know. Good luck with those huge Fila's, and I am so glad that you found my meagre tips helpful with your big guy.

Another hostess with the mostest was Sharon West, who also allowed me to present this new material at her training facility in Wentzville, Missouri, Everything Under One Woof. Sharon takes good care of me and we had some very invigorating conversations about the Get Connected exercises. Sharon is not just a great instructor, she was also a fabulous student, open-minded and curious. I cannot pay anyone a higher compliment than that.

I must thank Priscilla Walker, especially. What a woman! I told her I would send the manuscript a million times and then I didn't have it done. She never, ever got crabby about my lack of organization and always, with her editing, makes my work so much better. My work, in fact, appears to be done by a literate person when she is done with it, no small task, let me tell you! Priscilla, I enjoy your company and your help so much. Thanks!

Kendall Justiano also did one of the first read-throughs. He came back to me with pages of notes and a real outline (an item I usually bypass in my enthusiasm to be disorganized). This feedback was invaluable and helped me get out of a "stuck" spot.

If there are any errors or omissions, they are mine alone, and cannot be placed at the doorstep of anyone else!

Get Connected With Your Dog

Emphasizing the Relationship
While Training Your Dog

Brenda Aloff

Table Of Contents

Table Of Contents

Table Of Contents

Table Of Contents

Table Of Contents

Table Of Contents

Table Of Tables

Table Of Photographs & Photo Essays

Table Of Photographs & Photo Essays

Foreword

Jean Piaget, the world-renowned Swiss psychologist, taught that the optimum state for learning is one of dis-equilibrium. There must be a reason, a *need*, to learn something new. Learning something new involves change, and change is difficult even when the change is desirable; even when the change is our own idea. In order to learn something new (change our behavior) we must be motivated to do so, since change is always stressful.

The pre-adolescent is willing to be uncomfortable (hungry) and deprive herself of pleasure (pie), because she is motivated to lose ten pounds so she can wear her new school clothes, feel good about herself and be considered "cool."

Jean Piaget developed his theory of learning by observing children. Children learn by doing, by watching and by listening, *in that order*, so we can learn about training dogs from Piaget's research, since they learn in much the same way. Obviously, children and dogs are different, since we educate children and we train dogs, but as any teacher will tell you: It's much easier to educate a trained child!

Piaget taught that children are highly egocentric. They tend to think and care only about those behaviors that feel good to them, without regard to others. They are self-centered, not other-centered. They must learn to be other-centered because it is not their natural way. Children learn new behaviors that those in authority (others) think are important when those in authority are responsive to their actions. When the new behaviors are exhibited or approximated, those in authority show approval. When undesirable (old) behaviors are exhibited, those in authority show disapproval. Children learn to pay attention to others, because it is necessary to do so, not because they want to.

Another reason that children learn to pay attention to others is by developing satisfying relationships with those in authority. Children depend on adults for safety and problem-solving, for comfort and affection. Children are motivated to bend to authority when they have satisfying relationships with those in authority. The pre-adolescent is unwilling to be uncomfortable (hungry) and deprive herself of pleasure (pie), just because her father wants her to lose ten pounds so she can wear the new school clothes. She may be motivated to reach for the salad, instead of the pie, if when her father is present, he shows approval when she reaches for the salad and disapproval when she reaches for the pie and holds her accountable for her choices by agreeing to pay only for salad. (He refuses to pay for pie.)

These signals must be very obvious and consistent, since children are called upon to learn new behaviors that they don't necessarily want to learn: the new learning is someone else's idea and is likely to make them uncomfortable in the short-term. Over time, the new behaviors become assimilated and the results become their own reward.

The pre-adolescent is willing to be uncomfortable (hungry) and deprive herself of pleasure (pie), because even though it was originally her father's idea for her to lose weight, she has noticed that she feels better when she eats healthy, her clothes fit better, she is included in the peer group, and she doesn't even care that he has refused to pay for pie.

Conforming to outside approval, disapproval and accountability helps children integrate new learning into their repertoire. New behaviors are usually uncomfortable, because they cause us to inhibit immediate wants and desires. We become comfortable once new behaviors are integrated into our schema, our framework of understanding, through practice and consistent accountability.

Learning, for children or dogs, takes place in what Piaget called a "state of disequilibrium." This is a state of heightened awareness. We want the learner off-balance, but not too stressed to learn. Stress is counter-productive to learning, because it creates distraction, fear and anger. These negative feeling states prevent thinking and may create resentment, resistance, rebellion or rebellious compliance.

The pre-adolescent was once shamed for eating pie, so now she "loses it" and makes a scene in the restaurant or she eats the salad sullenly and sneaks off to buy candy bars to eat when dad is not around.

On the other hand, complacency is just as counter-productive to learning as is stress, because with no pressure to change behavior, there is no reason, no motivation, to learn.

The pre-adolescent knows that her dad wants her to eat the salad, but she orders the pie, because dad doesn't say anything about her order and willingly pays for the pie.

The important thing to realize is that stress, like everything else, exists on a continuum and that stress, like everything else, becomes negative only when there is too much or not enough. Too little stress ("I love you just the way you are!") precludes learning. Too much stress ("I don't like anything about you!") precludes learning. A new job is stressful, but considered positive. So is a new husband or wife, a new baby or a new puppy. Stress can make life interesting, motivating, challenging, exciting. The idea is not to avoid stress, but to make it manageable and to use it for enhancing our lives.

Piaget's theory was a constructivist theory, meaning that each child creates (constructs) her own ways of behaving, based on her own experiences of what works well and what doesn't. Beyond, simple behaviorist theory of learning as reaction to reward and punishment, Piaget understood the role of planning and problem-solving.

The pre-adolescent's father helps her create for herself a healthy, rewarding lifestyle by holding her accountable for unhelpful behaviors and by rewarding her for helpful behaviors until the behaviors themselves (and their logical results) become the reward.

The father is willing to make the effort to say no and to follow though, because he is able to see that minor, immediate discomfort can give his daughter larger, long-term rewards. His brain has developed to the point where he can see the "big picture," in ways that his daughter's brain is unable. He understands that to help her to a rewarding life, he must sometimes do her thinking for her until she is able to construct helpful habits that will be second nature to her.

Protocols for dogs work the same way by helping the dog to construct a framework for living in the world of humans that will work well and be personally rewarding. An effective protocol is firm and quiet and consistent. The trainer does the dog's thinking for him until he is able to construct helpful habits that will become second nature.

Effective protocols put the dog into a state of disequilibrium, of heightened awareness, that will help the dog become aware of the demands of living in an other-centered world.

Effective protocols create discomfort by their very nature, because they are asking for new learning – for change. Effective protocols are not unduly stressful, but they MUST create internal turmoil if the dog is to be motivated to see a need to change.

Effective protocols are not emotional, but thoughtful. The trainer is doing the dog's thinking for him. Setting physical limits on a dog's emotional reaction is not negative; it is teaching the dog in kinesthetic terms – the dog's own language.

It is always ineffective, with children or with dogs, to be mean. There is a big difference between hitting a child and restraining a child.

A two-year-old runs into the road. The mother rushes out into the road and scoops the child up, rushing her from the road.

The mother executes the discipline with great drama, because she wants to make a big impression on the child about running into the road and she understands that the child does not have the brain development to understand a conversation about running into the road. The mother removes the child from the road and restrains her from running back. At the same time, the mother gives visual (frowning, shaking her head) and verbal (NO!) cues. She uses physical cues, visual cues and verbal cues, in that order, because that is how learning takes place at this stage of development. The mother doesn't slap or spank or yell, because that will put the child into an emotional state (stress) about the spanking and circumvent learning. However, if the mother doesn't physically restrain the child, he or she will not learn to stay out of the road, because there will be no reason to learn the lesson.

Effective protocols are implemented by trainers who understand that it is not mean to set limits, because the brain development of the dogs requires trainers to do dogs' thinking for them, until they build effective habits that will help them co-exist peaceably and effectively with humans.

A child or a dog learns best in an atmosphere of kindness and consistence in an environment where each has lots of opportunities to make limited choices within firm guidelines; where those in authority have no qualms about setting limits in the short-term, so their charges will function successfully in the long run. The adult who abdicates his responsibility to be in charge, because of some misunderstood idea that it is mean to set limits, sets up his child and his dog for a lifetime of misery, because life has all kinds of limits and only those who respect the limits can negotiate life happily and successfully.

Effective protocols are implemented with very firm kindness and the understanding that being firm and being mean are different experiences altogether, and that overindulgence is as irresponsible as meanness.

Effective protocols are implemented with a willingness to be in charge and an understanding that immediate discomfort in exchange for a lifetime of reward is worth the effort. It is the type of kindness that our children and our canine companions deserve.

I first became aware of Brenda Aloff when I was feeling "stuck" with the level of dog training that was available to me. My husband and I own a pack of hounds that we use for hunting, showing, competition and companionship. Dog trainers didn't seem to understand the difference between a working companion and a lap dog. Assumptions were constantly made about the kind of lives my dogs live, their usefulness and their intelligence. I have always demanded that my dogs are well-behaved and obedient, whether they are walking in the neighborhood, competing in a swimming race, or running bears, *even though they're hounds*. I have always believed that my dogs are capable of understanding appropriate behaviors in disparate situations, *even though they're hounds*. For example, hounds are barkers by nature, but there are appropriate times and places to bark and they are capable of making appropriate choices. Another of my hobbies, raising rabbits, constantly causes consternation among people, because my rabbitry is adjacent to my kennel. They want to know how I am able to keeps rabbits and hounds together. The answer is simple – the dogs have been taught the difference between domestic bunnies (off limits) and wild rabbits (fair game). They have learned appropriate behaviors.

When my friend first took me to Brenda's class, I felt a connection and a sense of relief within minutes as I realized that Brenda taught canine management, not just simple training. Her protocols don't pertain to the show dog, the lap dog, the guard dog, the hound dog, but to every dog. The protocols are universal; they are sensible and sensitive responses to how dogs are likely to think and act and react in any situation. When handlers behave in certain ways that include an understanding of the dog's brain development and motivation, they invite the dog to respond in a natural, logical way. When handlers behave in certain ways, they develop solid, hierarchical relationships with their dogs that motivate dogs to want to learn and behave.

No more dog trainers who can't let their own dogs off the leash!

Brenda's techniques encompass all theories of learning and methods of training. Instead of eliminating accepted dog-training methods, she integrates them into a sensible, sensitive framework of *when* and *why*. Brenda Aloff has developed, through experience and science, the thinking person's guide to training dogs.

Nancy Weber Taylor, MA

(Nancy Taylor is a former classroom teacher with over 25 years of experience. Nancy has done over 2000 keynote speeches and workshops in the USA, Canada and the Bahamas since 1987. Nancy is co-author of *Teacher Talk: What It Really Means* and author of "A Simple Touch" in the bestseller *A Second Helping Of Chicken Soup For The Soul* and the lead chapter in the National Association For The Education Of Young Children's, *The Power Of Guidance*. Nancy has also been a film consultant for Disney Educational Productions. In addition to all of this, she breeds and trains Black and Tan Coonhounds and Plott Hounds.)

What Is This Get Connected Stuff?

The Get Connected protocol is, fundamentally, a program I developed to help humans understand dogs and dogs to understand humans. The animal-human bond was uppermost in my thoughts when I designed this series of exercises. I love to see dogs who are happy and getting their doggy needs met paired with humans who are happy and getting their human needs met.

Improving the relationship between people and dogs has consumed my life for many years, and, utilized correctly, the Get Connected protocol will improve the relationship you have with your dog. Better communication, mutual understanding and clear interactions always enhances a relationship, and this is what the Get Connected protocol is all about.

The key to better communication is developing what I call a communication loop between handler and dog. When I talk about the training process, I am always thinking of ways I can communicate clearly and emphasize telling the dog when she is right and when she is wrong. Dogs need to be told they are wrong. At some point we all do. This means you need to have established penalties that the dog understands ahead of time, will work to avoid, but that do not cause fear and are humane.

The protocol requires that you can read what your dog is trying to express and have effective means of letting your dog know what you are trying to communicate. That is the where the emphasis of all your training should be: that all important communication Loop.

Since daily living with your dog means that you will be asking the dog to do things other than what she might choose to do on her own, the Get Connected protocol will help you to find your dog's areas of discomfort and stress and will help your dog to develop good coping skills. Instead of ignoring stress, we will hand the dog stress in controlled "small packages" to help her work through it effectively. This is fantastic for fearful dogs, as well as rescue dogs and performance dogs. The formation of good coping skills is also the best way to prevent problem behaviours from developing.

Learning how to effectively control your dog's movement will help you to guide your dog's priorities and gain relevance. It is also possible to gain an animal's trust and alleviate fearful responses when you have the ability to direct or redirect the dog's movement. You do this by teaching the animal to be acquiescent and sensitive to cues regarding movement. You will work with the dog's movement by developing specific cues to:

- Cause Movement
- Change Direction
- Inhibit Movement

Thresholds, the application of pressure on vs. pressure off, and consistent body language are the main teaching tools used. Thresholds are landmarks. Like physical landmarks which change over time, thresholds change drastically with training. A threshold is like a marker for tolerance or comfort zones.

While learning how to use thresholds and pressure, you will learn to present your body language effectively and consistently to the dog. This is great news for both of you because body language is the dog's natural mode of communication. If you are unaware of how you are placing and using your body it is difficult to communicate clear intentions, so confusion results. Trust me on this one: your dog is very aware of body language. Because of this, it is important for you to know what you are conveying with yours.

You will learn to use the dog's body language as accurate feedback. This allows you to train in a sensitive, considerate way that promotes respect for the dog and increases understanding between the two of you.

In order to be successful, you must have a plan. A plan that is coherent and systematic. You will learn to be more tolerant of your dog and your dog will learn to be more tolerant of you. Husbandry behaviours, like nail clipping and everyday occurrences, like bending over your dog, or walking through the house without tripping over her are things that people do not often approach logically. They just expect the dog to "get it." Well, lots of dogs don't and this protocol will provide a way to achieve harmony in the home.

Using the Get Connected protocol eventually results in a paradigm shift. This comes about as you begin to work with, understand and eventually negotiate change regarding your dog's Fixed Action Patterns (instinctive behaviours) - most specifically impulse control mechanisms and the opposition reflex - which are the two biggest reasons that dogs get into trouble. Your dog will learn, with you as her guide, that she indeed has choices about her behaviour. This is what I call the Magic Switch, the point at which the dog switches from predominantly using her Hindbrain (the part of the brain which controls instinctive behaviours) to using her Frontbrain (the part of the brain involved in responsive, thinking behaviour).

The ultimate goal is a dog who thinks and responds, rather than one who just reacts instinctively or fearfully. The Get Connected protocol is wonderful for teaching a dog to think and then do. The exercises are straight forward, which is good, because dogs, above all, need really easy to understand explanations in black and white. This work improves communication, respect, and trust, all at the same time. It just doesn't get any better than this!

Improve Your Relationship.

This program is all about the big "R" - the relationship. As I gain age (and I hope wisdom) the relationship becomes ever more dear to me and ever less taken for granted. I have had some excellent teachers in this area, animals that taught me valuable lessons about how to negotiate and carry on a relationship. I am excited to share this program with you, knowing that it will help you and your dog, just as it has helped many others. I know the efficacy of these exercises because I do not publish protocols until I have used them for a number of years with a wide variety of dogs and handlers. You will get to read just a very few of those stories in the Case History section at the end of this book.

The Get Connected protocol is just a part of the training I do, but it has come to be more and more important as I discover the far-reaching influence that this specific technique has on the animals I work with. I see so very many fearful and uncomfortable dogs, or dogs who are stressed by performance events. I really wish to give both dogs and handlers some ease and provide a strategy for increasing comfort zones of dogs and the understanding of the people who live with them.

Who Am I Talking To?

The type of person who would neglect or physically abuse a dog is not the type of person who would pick this book up to read it, so I am not talking to them. I am not usually concerned that my clients would ever physically abuse a dog, but I am more concerned about the inadvertent mental stress that many dogs are put under by their well intentioned owners. I am talking to the kind of dog owner the rest of us are: people who love our dogs and want the best for them. The clients who bring me dogs, for the most part, have problems with providing structure, boundaries and clear communication in ways that they feel are humane. They care about their pets deeply and want their dog to love them back. One of their main concerns is, if they make the dog behave, the dog will be angry with them and won't love them anymore. At the same time, they want techniques that are effective and possible to do. Clients who have not trained legions of dogs often have serious communication problems which create confusion and frustration for both partners, resulting in adverse effects on the relationship.

Therefore, the main audience for this work will be people who are intensely involved with dogs: dog owners who are training their dogs, dog trainers, both professional and amateur, and behaviour specialists. If you love dogs and train dogs - or one dog - this book will give you valuable insight into training, which I define specifically as the development of a communication loop between handler and dog.

Get Connected Adds To A Positive Reinforcement Program.

There is no one way to develop a communication loop. When I think about the training process, I am always thinking of ways I can communicate clearly and emphasize telling the dog she is right. *That is where the primary emphasis of all your training should be.*

I use a variety of reinforcement-based techniques rooted in behaviorism and cognitive psychology. I started Clicker training on the very first wave, many years ago now, and still carry on a love affair with clicker-based training and ideas. The lovely thing

about this protocol is that it adds a wonderful facet to my first love - Positive Reinforcement techniques.

Another favorite methodology is Tellington Touch work. TTouch has a wonderful philosophy based on mental comfort for the animal - and gives you practical applications that work. This philosophy understands the mind-body connection exquisitely. If you are not familiar with TTouch work, you absolutely must research it. Linda Tellington-Jones has several excellent books and videos available, as well as hands-on clinics and training.

What has influenced my philosophy?

Working with and living with aggressive and reactive dogs has shaped my thinking in a way that no other experience possibly could have. Some of the dogs that fall into this category are incredibly cheeky and confident, others are fearful and possibly paranoid and still others seem to be a bizarre combination of the two. Just as important are the gracious, kind and friendly dogs: in them one can find a particular kind of joy and a faith in the species.

I have been greatly influenced in my training methodology by training other species. My daughter's Sun Conure parrot has taught me a few lessons. Birds place many limitations on a trainer and learning about these have made me a better dog handler. For instance, birds are extremely literal in their interpretations of your training efforts. One of the first things we taught our bird was to bite us, then shriek "Ow. No." Of course this was not intentional, the bird was merely mimicking our own behaviour. Fortunately, we have installed alternative behaviours to biting us, like sitting quietly and waiting for attention or treats.

Keeping sheep and watching how they interact with each other, as well as getting involved in herding, have had a tremendous impact on how I view the space between any two beings. (Indeed, even inanimate objects such as trees, fences and walls can impose a "pressure" that will influence behaviour.) Seeing a kind and skillful sheep shearer work is a thing of beauty and wonderment. He keeps panicky, untrained animals quite calm with his manner and how he touches their bodies, using his own body language as effective communication: thus preventing injury and excessive stress to the sheep.

Watching my Border Collie communicate with the sheep is fascinating. Both the sheep and the Collie are extremely aware of and manipulating personal space at warp speed. The most lovely dogs communicate with a finesse that is breathtaking. I once watched a dog work ducks with such consideration, that if the duck ruffled a feather, the dog would immediately release the pressure of movement by lying down until the duck showed less stress and had settled back into a sedate waddle. The dog knew (and this trait had been enhanced through careful training) that it is easier to communicate clearly when you reduce stress and use clear and deliberate signals. There is much for dog trainers to learn from this exchange that skillful Border Collies use all the time. Moving slowly, thoughtfully and deliberately can enhance communication. Use the least amount of enough pressure to get the job done.

Of equal importance is the horse training I have done. I ride in dressage competitions and have also explored Natural Horsemanship philosophies extensively. Dressage is all about the mental and physical development of a partnership with the mental well-being of the horse held as the utmost concern. Reading classical dressage texts is like reading love letters that master horsemen and horsewomen have written about horses. Some of my favorites are books by authors Walter Zettl, Reiner Klimke, Charles DeKunffy and Paul Belasik.

My current dressage coach tells me that learning dressage is "learning to speak the language of the horse." (quoted from Cameo Miller, American Riding Instructor's Association certified riding instructor.) The idea is to be so in balance with your mount, mentally and physically, that you do not disturb the horse in his way of going or cause him undue stress.

Natural Horsemanship practitioners are absolute masters of respect and trust in a relationship. They also use the native language of the horse as feedback during the training process: a communication loop. Because horses are big, potentially dangerous, and prone to flight, people who count on the horse as a work partner need to be able to have a trusting relationship based on cooperation, so jobs can be accomplished safely. Imagine you, a horse and several hundred cattle. You need to be able to count heavily on your working partner in this situation, because the horse can help you or, quite literally, get you killed. This situation is not as romantic as television shows would lead one to believe. Respect and trust are crucial to riding a horse, the ultimate flight animal.

Every time you communicate with or observe another species, there are opportunities to learn of different ways you can communicate. This gives you ever more tools to talk to your dog. One of the things that I love is when I feel that my partner and I are of one accord. That *connection* is so gratifying. Time changes, and for a few moments the whole world goes away except for me and my dog. A specific kind of a bond is formed when this happens, that moment in which we are two creatures with one thought, one goal. This is that all important communication loop.

This book is about helping people create the most effective communication loop possible and to help trainers identify missing pieces in a dog's education. To get the most from this book it will also help if you have at least a basic understanding of Reinforcement-based training methodology. The Get Connected exercises have already helped many dogs. Fearful dogs become more confident. Pushy dogs become more compliant. Owners enjoy their dogs more. Everybody is happier!

That Sub Title Is Kind Of Long. What Does It Mean?

The sub title "Using Body Work, Sensitization, Desensitization And Habituation Techniques In A Systematic Way To Bring About A Paradigm Shift In Canines" is long and sounds stuffy and complex. But there are a variety of reasons why each component of the sub title is important. Dogs are uncomfortable in a variety of situations that people expect them to accept. This problem is so severe that many dogs lose their homes over reasons that would be ridiculous if the results were not so tragic. A dog may bite someone who reaches for her collar abruptly. A dog may become frightened or reactive when joggers or skateboarders roar by. These are just a couple of circumstances that irritate people mightily and cause rifts in the relationship between people and dogs. Teaching dogs about being comfortable being touched, bent over and restrained are things that people wish to take for granted. Teaching your dog to override her instinctive behaviour to chase things in motion, or to be attentive when interesting (to dogs) environments are present are necessary to living peacefully with dogs. Because your dog does not speak your language and is not a human it is unfair to expect her to respond as a human would. On the other hand, we expect dogs to accept things that a person would not even accept without an understandable explanation. Halloween, for instance, terrifies many of our own young children until they become accustomed to it!

Body Work
Body work is my euphemism for teaching a dog about different kinds of touch and massage with the express purpose of creating a confident, comfortable companion. This body work is used to desensitize the dog to touch and approaches. You will be introduced to new ways to think about personal space, both his and yours.

Sensitization, Desensitization and Habituation
Sensitization, desensitization and habituation techniques all concern identifying and manipulating thresholds with a definite purpose and to generate a predictable outcome. Remember, a threshold is a marker that indicates a tolerance or comfort zones. Thresholds are all important and affect every aspect of your training and relationship with your dog.

- Sometimes the dog's thresholds are just fine: she is tolerant of those things she needs to be tolerant of, and she is comfortable in a variety of social situations. Sometimes the dog has low thresholds of tolerance in some areas, say, for example, when she cannot resist chasing anything that moves. This dog is too sensitized to motion. Sometimes the dog's tolerances are too high, as in the dog who body slams you and doesn't even seem to notice the fact that he just knocked you to the ground. This dog is insensitive (too desensitized) to personal space.

The use of pressure is integral to the specific techniques I will be covering in this text to teach you how to use sensitization, desensisitization or habituation. I use pressure as information. Pressure is a means to influence a dog's threshold level for comfort, to make an event memorable and to control movement (and therefore the dog's thoughts).

- Pressure may be applied using your hand in a rubbing motion using no more pressure than slightly more than the weight of your hand, or by using your body to "take up space" to move the dog. It is important to understand that the amount or the force of the pressure used in this technique is not nearly as important as the persistence with which it is applied. You will learn to become water dripping on stone.

- Pressure may be a steady physical pressure (never jerking or harshly done) applied in a deliberate and gradually increasing technique which is explained in detail in the *Get Connected Exercises* Section.

- Pressure eventually becomes the *suggestion* of physical pressure and involves how you "take up the airspace." If you do not understand this, watch a good Border Collie in action. They know how to take up space without ever touching the sheep. Sheep are not necessarily the fluffy and timid creatures you might have in mind, and it takes a lot of power and application of just the right amount of pressure applied in exactly the right way to control a flock of untrained or slightly trained sheep - that is, sheep who are not "dog broke." Pressure off is even more crucial, because the moment of the *release of pressure*, whether physical or social, is very salient to dogs. I think of the release of pressure as being Mother Nature's clicker: a built in, intuitively understood Memory Marker.

- As you work with pressure you will use the dog's body language as feedback. This is the beginning of understanding your dog on an entirely different and more intuitive level. This is training using the dog's own language, opening doors for both you and your dog.

My worst fear is that this work, specifically the application of pressure, will be misinterpreted as "forceful." Nothing could be farther from the truth, and, in fact, if you are forceful with pressure the technique will not be effective. I wish to also point out that used inappropriately, any tool, *including your attitude*, can be abusive. A nasty, mean attitude does obvious damage, but so can an over-emotional attitude. I have worked with dogs that have been neglected and physically abused - and dogs whose owners are literally killing them with kindness and passivity, unintentionally perpetrating willful, fearful or aggressive behaviour. In other cases the handler is not clear about communicating what they want in a way the dog can easily understand it, then when they do not get the desired behaviour, the interactions become laced with frustration and irritation. Lisa Lit says it beautifully: "However, there is no substitution for empathy. A handler who views his dog as simply a tool to be used and discarded when no longer necessary will not, as a rule, get the same results as a handler who treats his dog with respect, as a partner. Handlers who are simply trying to muscle results from their dogs generally do not get the same results as handlers who recognize that their dogs can think, and spend a little brain time trying to figure out how to get

their dogs thinking in a way that benefits working goals." (Lit, 2002)

Systematic

Systematic means using a plan to work toward a definable pre-determined goal. Do not mistake this for rigidity in thinking, or inflexible training plans. Nothing could be farther from the truth. Good approximations are truly teaching steps. Each step is built firmly on the preceding one. Subsequent steps are determined by a communication loop, with the dog actively participating, telling you when he is ready for the raise in criteria. You will systematically develop a Ready To Learn dog - ready to learn anything! Ready To Learn is a very big deal. A dog who is Ready To Learn is cooperative and easy to teach.

Paradigm Shift

A paradigm provides us useful ways to classify and think about complex subjects. Paradigms give you a way to try out a belief system, containing basic preconceptions that are held to be true and taken for granted. Paradigms are useful for organization, but can lead to a rigidity in thinking and over-generalization. If some of the truths are based on a lack of knowledge as opposed to a wealth of knowledge, the paradigm becomes an excuse for faulty thinking. *At its best, a paradigm provides a concrete organizational system that can be used to provide structure for a safe place to learn and grow in knowledge.*

Paradigm shift, in this instance, has a discrete meaning. I want to take into account the dog's natural tendencies. The paradigm shift occurs when we work with a dogs' fixed action patterns (instinctive behaviours) - most specifically impulse control mechanisms and the opposition reflex - and teach dogs that they have choices about their behaviour. Wouldn't you love to be able to say to your dog: "When you watch another dog run agility you do not have to begin fussing, barking and acting out your frustration. You can lie quietly and give me eye contact to emotionally anchor, so we can have a focused, fast, clean run at the Agility Trial." Or, "When we walk down the street, you do not have to frantically pull and bark at each approaching dog. You can walk quietly by with me. You do not have to engage your opposition reflex and pull on the leash. Instead you can respond to the lightest touch on the collar and "follow the feel" of the pressure, thereby loosening the leash."

With the paradigm shift comes different ways of think-ing for the dog across the board. Some of that thinking will involve making that switch from Hindbrain to Frontbrain quick and easy. That is, the dog will allow you to control the "magic switch." This isn't just a magic switch: that moment in which you are allowed to guide the dog's thinking becomes a magic moment, because you and your dog are "in it together" instead of being at odds with one another.

Sheep Aggression & The Application Of Pressure

Yup. This is what the sheep look like when they first see the dog. They close ranks, lower their head and threaten the predator. Definitely not behavin' in a cute & fluffy way. If the dog looks indecisive at this moment or turns slightly, equivalent to "releasing pressure," the sheep will move toward the dog with the intent of intimidating the dog. How the dog "takes up the airspace" between her and the sheep determines success.

What Is This Get Connected Stuff?

With the application of just the right amount of "pressure" at just the right time and at the proper angle, Rylie achieves the "lift," that moment when the sheep turn their heads and move in the direction the dog indicates. A skillful dog will move the sheep carefully and confidently and will not panic the sheep. Getting the job done with the least amount of pressure and force while still being decisive and in charge is a delicate task.

Photo essay by Dave Schrader

Why Get Connected With Your Dog?

Because the "connection" is why you got a dog in the first place, isn't it?

Photograph by Dave Schrader.

Get Ready To Enhance Your Training Program

The Get Connected protocol is used to enhance any training program. It sets the stage for the predictable results all trainers long for. It helps to make dogs safe, a major concern for trainers and behaviorists. It will also help dogs become more confident.

Are You Ready To Learn?

Before anyone, you included, can learn anything, you must be *Ready To Learn*. This means you are attentive, that you are able to concentrate. If you are rigid with preconceived notions (that may or may not be based on fact), you will constantly be resistant to learning instead of open to learning. If you cannot agree that there is more than one way to accomplish a task, you will forever be trapped in your own mind. You don't have to agree with everything a teacher tells you, you just have to give it a try, and give yourself a chance to assimilate the material. This process involves critical thinking skills and determining what works best for you. It means that you are not competing with the learning process or the teacher because of preconceived notions, but rather approach the learning situation with curiosity and wonder. It's called an open mind for good reason! It is easier to put stuff in an open container.

Your Dog Must Be Ready To Learn, Too

The same is true for your dog. If you have never taught your dog how to concentrate, it will be difficult for her to maintain attention long enough to learn anything. If she is competing with you by leaping all over you to get at the cookies, she is not Ready To Learn. If your attempts to punish the dog have frightened her or confused her she is not learning what you intended. If you have not noticed and rewarded your dog for trying, she will believe that trying for you is a dead end. The Get Connected protocol teaches you to prepare your dog so she is in a state of readiness: Ready To Learn.

Get Connected Promotes Team Work

The Get Connected protocol actively reinforces the dog for using submission and cooperation as a working pattern, and for interacting with you as a thinking participating and obedient partner. The word "submission" is used in this sentence in the way that a horse trainer would. Dog trainers seem to picture a groveling, down-trodden dog when this word is used. That picture is not the one I wish to convey. For the dressage trainer, "submission" indicates a partner who is light, willing, engaged with you, responsive and cooperative - taking direction from you without resentment or fear. Submission, as used by horse trainers, means you have gained the respect and trust of your partner, and that you have accepted the responsibility of being a fair and educated leader. It's called Team Work.

There is a bit of wisdom in the dressage world that epitomizes this concept of team work: "You whisper the cue and the horse shouts the answer." This means that the rider is able to give a subtle, nearly invisible, cue and the horse answers with 110% effort and a willing attitude. This subtle exchange occurs because the horse and the rider are so aware of and so in concert with each other, so connected, that communication flows effortlessly between the two. In this scenario both team members are the absolute best they can be in body, concentration, and soul.

Don't Just Leave It To Chance

When I train a dog, instead of just "letting it happen," I carefully control the process to educate the dog so he isn't frightened of boundaries or any kind of human movements. I also do not want to give the dog an excuse to misunderstand boundaries. If I am unclear about boundaries, it can cause fearful or pushy behaviour, depending on the temperament of the individual dog. Having clear ways to communicate desired vs. undesired behaviour is essential to providing good boundaries.

Wrong Should Not Be A Moral Judgment

Learned behaviour, or learning through experience, is often referred to as the "school of hard knocks," because in nature, punishment contingencies are the most frequent teachers. With our domestic animals this process doesn't have to consist of literal and physical Hard Knocks. We can make the training process kinder by using Positive Reinforcement. Of course for minor errors, such as mistaking a Sit Cue for a Down Cue, a No Reward Mark is sufficient. A NRM (No Reward Mark) is part of a necessary communication system developed using Positive Reinforcement training. In a nutshell, you install a cue that tells the dog "your current behaviour is not what I am looking for. Offer me another." In Learning Theory this is technically considered a conditioned aversive. In the case of dog trainers, we specifically pair a word (the conditioning part) with the removal of the treat (the aversive part). There are many great texts on basic Positive Reinforcement training. See the Appendix for a list of them.

Sometimes your dog is not merely making a minor error, but is engaged in an activity that is life-threatening or so irritating and naughty that it is intolerable. To be effective, you need a way to provide humane consequences, which tell the dog "No! Don't Ever Do That Again!" and "Your current behaviour is over the top - Stop It." This is strong language and is intended to be, because it is your responsibility to keep your dog safe. If your dog is running toward the road or counter surfing or eating someone's socks, it is imperative that you have a way to tell him that certain behaviours are not allowed. This is necessary in order to keep the dog safe. Running toward the road is obviously dangerous, but counter surfing is irritating and potentially dangerous and eating socks is irritating and can result in surgery. In short, you need to be able to tell a dog she is wrong. *I am using the word "wrong" to describe undesired behaviours, not as a moral judgement.* There are several degrees of "wrong" and these need degrees of consequences that match the "wrong" thing as well as taking into consideration the temperament of the dog. What you don't want to see when you tell your dog she is wrong is that she feels it is an earth-shattering experience that sends her weeping to a specialist for years of therapy. Both timid, cautious, over-sensitive dogs and pushy, assertive, I-don't-care-if-I-make-you-uncomfortable dogs need us to use effective and humane ways to give them information about personal space, respect, trust and just plain old good manners.

Dealing With Dogs Who Have Low Tolerance For Stress And Stop Working

I want to promote training techniques that create a dog who is able to withstand stress. If the dog gets an accidental correction (such as, when setting your dog up in Heel position, you accidentally step on her tail) you want her to be able to deal with it matter-of-factly and not randomly avoid Heel position for a month of Sundays. It is important to develop a dog who can "take a correction." By this terminology I don't mean you are preparing your dog to take a beating, tolerate being whacked on or screamed at. There is a difference between abuse and giving a dog information in the form of a correction. Taking a correction means you are developing a dog who can be told she is wrong, and she understands this for the information it is, not as a trauma. I have seen a fair number of dogs who fold and shut down (cease to work, will not return to work) as soon as you tell them that you wish to see an alternative behaviour (sit instead of down) or if the cookie feeding schedule is too thin. Some dogs refuse to work as soon as they determine cookies are not available. Often this shutting down is not due to the dog being over-disciplined, but quite the opposite. The dog has not been prepared to be told "you are wrong." Therefore, she has no coping skills when she is told she is wrong and exhibits stress-related behaviours. The owner has never allowed the dog to work through problems. This does the dog a disservice and promotes "shutting down" behaviours. Then, when the dog is placed in a position where he must problem solve, he becomes confused and waits for the owner to "help," or to do the job for him. Want to help your over-stressed dog? Teach her how to engage in an information exchange, so confusion does not develop.

Grey Isn't Good Enough. Dogs Need To Have A Way To Distinguish Black From White

Confusion is the death knell to any conversation. When information is inconsistent or boundaries are non-existent, confusion is the result. Confusion causes a great deal of stress. Confusion develops because communications are grey, instead of black and white.

In some instances, the dog has been corrected, but has absolutely no idea why, so is very confused. Perhaps the correction was too harsh or so mild the dog didn't even notice it was a correction at all. I have lots of clients who tell their dogs in a mild, sweet tone of voice, "Stop jumping now. You know you are not supposed to do that." Not only is it obvious that the dog has no idea that jumping is rude, it is clear he has no idea what you are saying either. You don't have to scream or beat the dog here, but you do need a system in which the dog can distinguish approval vs. disapproval. It is just as unfair to correct a dog using too much force. That is not teaching: it is just graceless and heavy-handed.

A Fair System, Understanding Of The Correction And No Resistance

Dogs need feedback about appropriate behaviour, and this might entail telling the dog she is "wrong." Dogs need to be told they are wrong. At some point, we all do. Knowing the rules about how to behave makes any individual more confident and secure. I want a fair system that promotes understanding. This means I have established penalties that the dog understands ahead of time, will work to avoid, do not cause fear and are humane. Unfortunately, sometimes withholding a cookie, the use of a NRM or ignoring an unwanted behaviour do not work. I want to have the same results my male Smooth Fox Terrier, Sherman, used to get: with a Look, he could send another dog out of the room. The other dogs weren't afraid of him, he'd never been in a fight with anyone (unbelievable, I know, and I didn't have many like him), and there was absolutely no resistance on the part of the other dog or any defensive or nervous behaviour, only willingness to comply. That is grace and power in a social situation: presence. I want to follow Sherman's example of clear communication that is easily understood by the recipient.

Competing Reinforcers

There are times when you are training a dog who has an understanding of what you want and she still makes a deliberate choice to be inattentive, such as, when the handler calls her and she chooses to continue going her own way because she is on the scent of something interesting. Or, because someone else has thrown a ball for their dog, she thinks she should go after it instead of holding a Stay. I do not wish to punish my dog in such cases, I just want her to pay attention and work with me. Once you teach a dog what you want, the problem is not that she does not understand what you want, the problem is that the dog is not engaged and committed to working with you. This choice then becomes an issue of prioritizing. The Get Connected protocol provides a humane way to enforce attention without begging, bribing or correcting. Because you are educating the dog about the enforcement procedure ahead of time, the dog understands and is not frightened or intimidated. *This technique uses the method the animals themselves use, a ritualized procedure that* is predictable and uses increasing increments. Therefore, the animal is allowed endless choice in the process. That is, the individual can "choose" the degree of pressure she wishes to respond to. It also means this technique lends itself beautifully to "individualization," allowing the trainer to easily adapt to each individual. Remember: the amount of pressure used in this technique is not nearly as importance as the persistence with which it is applied and timing of the release.

Part of what is learned during the learning process is how to prioritize. That is, when a certain cue is present that cue takes priority over all else. Even though there might be many reinforcers present in the environment: other dogs to be played with, people to be petted by, rabbit turds to be eaten; when a cue of "By Me" is given, all other factors are ignored, and staying close to the trainer takes priority. That is how a dog learns to put your cue on the top of his To Do List.

This is what we all want. Happy dogs who comply with joy and no resistance. They are confident that the communication lines are open and have no need to become defensive. When corrected, they understand that it is *information*, not avengement.

Photographs by Dave Schrader.

The cues given by the trainer are prioritized at the top of the dog's To Do List, even though the environment is distracting and holds potentially more reinforcement than I have available. (We are in a field chock full of scenting and chasing opportunities and I have no treats or toys, only past training and the relationship we have developed.)

Maeve is busy doing her own thing. When I call her I want her to go from this...

...to this: an immediate response and intense concentration with a single cue. The best part is the attitude of happy compliance. No resistance. No fear. Just calm confidence and acceptance.

...but mostly this is what we live for! It's the relationship.

Photographs Mary Wilmoth

35

What Kind Of Dogs Benefit From This Work?

I have used the Get Connected protocol successfully - actually success beyond my wildest dreams - with fearful dogs, rescue dogs, reactive dogs, pushy, in-your-face dogs, well-trained dogs and new puppy dogs. The Get Connected protocol has improved the responsiveness of every dog/handler team which takes the time to develop it properly. There are always two considerations when I am working: one of them is the client and the other is the dog.

Here is one of the common situations I see with the people and dogs who come to me for help with their problems. The person doesn't have a plan and has poor mechanical skills. The dog is not Ready To Learn, does not know how to learn and is competing with his owner. The dog and owner are in conflict and have no skills to negotiate their way out. This is sad. The relationship is worn ragged with frustration on the part of both the owner and the dog. Both are desperately trying to communicate with each other, but in vain. How does this happen? Poor communication and a poor understanding of the species.

A bit trickier is the following situation: some people have a great understanding of dogs, are experienced trainers and competing in dog sports, and yet they are still having trouble. In these cases, the problem is not that the dog isn't trained. But there is obviously a missing piece. There are two possibilities in this instance:

1. In rare cases, the dog is "not misbehaving, he is abnormal." (Overall, 1975). If this is the case, you need to seek professional help. If you suspect but lack the experience to know if your dog is abnormal, and your current trainer or behaviour specialist cannot discern if the dog is abnormal, seek a second opinion from a qualified person. This is not your neighbor or your dog-training buddy. This is a person who has had extensive experience and knowledge of abnormal dogs specifically. Abnormal means the dog has abnormal learning patterns and is a discrete category. Think of the dyslexic child or the ADHD child or the autistic child. These are discrete, describable conditions. Abnormality can range from relatively mild conditions, such as dyslexia; to severe conditions, rendering the individual dysfunctional for normal life, such as extreme cases of autism.

2. The most common occurrence is that the dog is highly trained, but within a very narrow band of circumstances, all revolving around competition work. These dogs have competition Heel work or Agility skills to die for, but you cannot walk them on a loose leash without being dragged. In other words they are book smart and sophisticated learners in one respect, but their owners haven't taught them daily life skills. In some cases, the owner places high priority on performance skills and is willing to tolerate the dog's poor life skills. The other class of trainers in this category are doing the same thing but for different reasons. They think that they are "making a deal" with their dog by trading. This trade consists of "you do really good in the performance event for me and I will let you do what you want the rest of the time." This is faulty thinking: making this kind of deal with a dog indicates a lack of understanding of the species. The issue here is that the fundamental inconsistency of operating this way is confusing for dogs.

The normal, well-trained dog owned by the experienced trainer, but who is lacking in daily life skills - that is, he still jumps on the trainer at the door, mobs guests when they come over, will not cease putting the slimy tennis ball in the lap of whoever is trying to watch television and walks on the leash okay if there isn't anything distracting then pulls like a freight train - will benefit from learning about personal space and respect. Surprisingly, in a way these people have the same problem as the inexperienced, frustrated dog trainer. They are just no longer frustrated about the dog's behaviour. These trainers are better at management and generally more tolerant and because they are accustomed to the species their expectations have changed drastically. Experienced dog people anthropomorphize in much more subtle ways. Their expectations tend to be really high in some areas and very low in others. Unlike the first time pet owner, who is stunned beyond belief if their dog isn't house-broken by twelve weeks of age but cannot imagine their dog doing a simple task like "Stay," the seasoned trainer will put up with the dog vomiting on the sofa (or even on guests) with practiced ease (not the first time, won't be the last), but will be shocked beyond belief if their dog misses a single subtle cue when Obedience training. This problem the experienced share with the inexperienced or first-time dog owner is the lack of a quick and easy, humane way to communicate basic ideas to the dog about personal space and polite manners.

Dogs that are mannerly in daily life skills as well as "well-read" in their field are allowed many more opportunities for environmental enrichment, and are more of a joy to have around. Non-dog people can enjoy these dogs as well as your not-so-dog-tolerant family members.

Other people have just gotten their third or fourth dog, or they might even have a multiple dog household. They love dogs, so have decided to bring home a carefully chosen puppy, or they did the noble thing and brought home a rescue dog in need of a loving home. Either way, they are shocked because they just got their first "real" dog. Unlike their previous pets, who were relatively well-behaved with whatever technique was used, THIS animal is a nightmare. He is active, in fact active is a ridiculous understatement for this perpetual motion machine that is disguised as a dog. "No" does not exist for this animal. "Leave It" incites the dog to eat whatever he has (that he shouldn't have) faster, including your Victoria's Secret underwear. Your clothes all have tears in them from this animal's claws. You go everywhere covered with sticky dog saliva from his loving kisses. He is friendly, too friendly, in fact. Your friends won't come in unless he is sequestered because he is so obnoxiously friendly. You think it is possible the obedience class instructors graduated you just to get you out of their class. How do you go about teaching this dog anything? This dog is far from stupid. The biggest problem here is the dog is

out-smarting you at every turn. He understands the communications just fine, but has decided that he can overlook your pitiful attempts to teach him civilized manners. Once again, you need an effective technique and a teaching system the dog can relate to and cannot selectively ignore.

Keep in mind the perfect dog. This dog is polite to guests and the owner has off-leash control, including calling the dog off squirrels, to which the dog turns on a dime in response to the first cue and happily complies. This dog gets along well with other dogs and adores children. He is gentle with elderly people, does therapy work in Nursing homes and runs clean and fast at Agility Trials. He gets high scores in the Obedience Ring and has a Tracking Title. He barks when strangers come to the door, but quickly ceases when you appear to take care of the territory entry matter. He never dashes out into the street or bites the UPS delivery person. He does occasionally get into the trash. Your dog can be closer to this dog than you might imagine. What you need is an organized training method and a way to create a relationship which contains not only love, but trust and respect, too.

Effective For All Levels Of Students and Interest Levels.

Over the years, we have many times reorganized our puppy class and beginner level class material and format. My instructors and I are constantly reassessing these classes and working to meet the needs of this group of pet owners. For a few years I taught exclusively clicker training in puppy and beginner classes. As time went on and in response to feedback from students, I have constantly searched for new ways to help this group, representative of "the general dog owner." These are the people who most desperately need reasonable information and exercises that they can manage to do. The exercises need to be more than manageable though, they must also be palatable. If you do not take your antibiotics for ten days they will not be effective. So when we give these entry level people training help, it must be something that they will do. You can give the best training advice in the world, but if the client does not do the exercises, no help was received. (Some of the responsibility, of course, must sensibly be placed on the shoulders of the client.) Sometimes clients do not follow instructions because they do not listen and sometimes they do not follow instructions because the tasks look overwhelming to them. Often, I find, the student is confused or the exercise does not make sense, or the student cannot understand "why" one would do this exercise.

In addition, these entry level classes, such as Puppy and Beginners are one of my testing grounds. This is because these handlers have the least experience and, in general, the most unruly dogs. It is also a group lesson, meaning participants get less individual instruction than a private lesson. I figure if these students, who are, for the most part, inexperienced, can use a technique competently, then most handlers, no matter what their level of experience is, will be effective using that technique under a variety of circumstances. My beginner level classes include many of the Get Connected exercises listed in this book. Specifically the Be Still Switch and Follow The Feel. In the second tier of classes I begin to teach the students the Move Into exercises. I have found these to be quickly assimilated by the students and they are motivated to practice the exercises because they get immediate results. My personal, ulterior motive is to get the students aware of the dog's body language and feedback. I want the dog to be able to have a "voice" in the training process. These exercises teach entry level dog owners to watch closely for the dog's feedback.

While teaching these exercises we have lots of opportunities to point out to people when they are "coming in too strong" and causing their dog to feel uncomfortable. Likewise, those people who are wishy-washy and ambivalent can be directed to be clearer with their communication so they are less confusing to their dog.

Brain Stuff

It is time to have a bit of a chat about the brain and it's function. Don't worry, I am not going to bore you with a dry and meaningless anatomy lesson complete with psycho-babble. This is wondrous and fun stuff! A basic understanding of the physiology of the brain is the cornerstone of making sense of "why" dogs do what they do. I am going to make it easy for you, as I have organized the material to be useful in daily interactions. Then I will follow with my super-duper-easy-to-understand model to use for daily training.

Photogragh by Cherish DeWitt. The super brainy looking dog is Rix, a stray we found lying in the middle of the street. She was just as brainy as she looks in this photograph.

Forebrain, Hindbrain, Midbrain

Lordy, How Many Brains Do We Need? And The Darn Dog Still Keeps Outsmarting Us...

Recent discoveries provide, and will continue to provide, us with an ever changing view of this little gloppy mess of grey matter, or "wet ware" as computer programmers graphically call the brain to distinguish it from computer hardware and software. Not so neatly compartmentalized as a computer binary system, the brain weaves a dance of learning, fixed action patterns, habit and memory in a very complex and inter-woven dance, indeed. The different parts of the brain are in constant communication with each other, creating a constantly changing and delicately balanced landscape.

With brains, it's all about surface area - how many folds and convolutions there are in the brain. Your brain has more of these folds and convolutions than a dog's brain, allowing you to think in more complex ways that a dog can. Your dog is not a person, and there are some basic biological reasons for that. It is obvious that we look different, but it doesn't end there. Dogs think both like we do and differently than we do. We have developed different native languages, based on our physical skills. That's why dogs sniff butts to greet, and we shake hands. Expecting your dog to develop human moral codes is unreasonable, as is expecting him to be able to use fractions or design a quantum physics theory. For dog training purposes, what is important for you to understand is that dogs and people have physiologically slightly different brains.

The Hindbrain. Some scientists used to refer to this brain region as the "lizard brain." The brain stem regulates basic life functions: respiration, circulation, digestion and reproduction. The cerebellum helps control movement by integrating the timing of sensory-motor functions. For instance, when you touch something hot your hand jerks away from it. This is not a "conscious" thought process, it is a hindbrain reaction. If the information had to travel all the way into the

forebrain, and you had to take the time to "think" about the sensation, the damage would be much worse because your finger would have been held to the heat for a longer period of time. When your dog recoils from a physical stimulus, such as being stung by a wasp or stepping on a sharp stone, he isn't thinking; it is an instant reaction, integrated between the midbrain and the hindbrain by the cerebellum.

The Midbrain. It's purpose is to "relay specific sensory information from sense organs to the brain." (Carey, 2006) The midbrain, extending out from the brain stem, contains the limbic system. This part of the brain is where strong, overwhelming emotions reside. I humorously tell clients this is where the 7 Deadly Sins reside. The Midbrain is the control center of the General Adaptation Syndrome. The General Adaptation Syndrom is a basic survival response, designed to keep an organism safe. Everyone has heard of the Fight or Flight response, which is actually only the *first* stage of the General Adaptation Syndrome. The second stage is either resistance or adaptation, which develops if the stress that generated the alarm itself does not go away. The third stage is exhaustion, which can occur if there is no relief from the stressor, and neither resistance or adaptation bring about any discernible results. The most important idea is that the limbic system is the seat of emotional reactions to external stimuli. These reactions are often unconscious, that is, not always under control of the forebrain thinking centers. For the rest of this book, when I am referring to an emotional, unconscious limbic-based response, I will label it "reactive." What I wish to emphasize here is that some behaviour you see is a result of thoughtful action (responsive), whereas other behaviour is not a result of executive function at all: the dog is not thinking and is instead "reacting" in a knee-jerk manner to the incoming stimulus.

When you are experiencing raw grief, rage or fear, you are in the grip of your limbic system functions. When you are having trouble with "logic overrides" and cannot think beyond the emotion you are currently feeling, your limbic system is in control. When your dog slams himself against the window, barking uncontrollably, because someone passed by on the sidewalk, your dog's brain makes significant changes. Brain segments are activated by an internal process of chemicals which is generated by the visual cue of the passer-by. This causes a mix of reactive emotions: frustration (not being able to greet or repel the intruder onto your dog's territory) and excitement (possible opportunities for socialization or predation) are outwardly observed as body slamming the window and barking. All the outer signs of reactivity. If your dog has not been well socialized and has had a traumatic event with another dog, when he sees another dog while on your daily walk, the immediate reaction is to enter a Fight or Flight state. This internal state will be outwardly observable as defensive barking, lunging against the restraint of the leash and general uncontrollable mayhem. These are examples of dogs who are currently under the control of their limbic system. This behaviour, to the dog's owner, appears to be out of control.

For other dogs, a behaviour occurs because the first time the dog was presented with a particular stimuli, no matter the "reason," the dog used lunging, barking, etc. as the reaction to the stimuli. Therefore, that specific behaviour becomes the one practiced and that particular neural pathway is the one accessed as soon as the visual or auditory cue is presented.

From a biological and evolutionary point of view though, this type of behaviour makes perfect sense. In addition, the dog's behaviour makes perfect sense to that individual, on some level, or the dog wouldn't be doing it. That this kind of reactive behaviour is obviously self-reinforcing for many dogs, is evident because habits of this type are so difficult to interrupt and modify.

The Forebrain. The forebrain "is credited with the highest intellectual functions - thinking, planning, and problem-solving." (Carey, revised 2006) The cerebral cortex provides the ability to solve problems and develop memory. This is where executive decision making processes (neurobiologists terminology) occur. What sets the primate brain apart from other mammalian brains is all the extra "folds" in the neocortex. This extra surface area is what gives humans some extra ability to develop extremely complex language skills,

use numbers and have imagination. (Although there is now some research being done about whether animals may use rudimentary methods of numbering: "It may therefore be that dogs only represent numbers of objects as 'one', 'two', and 'lots'." (Animal Behaviour, Cognition and Welfare Research Group, UK) An increase in the surface area of the brain allows the brain to specialize because it has the extra room to do so.

Dogs and people problem-solve and think. We might not think about the same things, but we do consider and mull over things that are relevant to us. Dogs think about how to "get that cookie" by offering behaviours that have been reinforced in the past or by experimenting with behaviours to see if they "work" to gain resources. People think about how to gain more money or more vacation time and about how to please people that are important to them. We all have numerous examples of our dogs' problem-solving. Many of the solutions dogs come up with are very clever, and some are surprisingly complex and circuitous. Jet, a little schnauzer mix we had years ago, knew she was not capable of moving the Fox Terriers off her favorite spot on the sofa. She didn't have the status within the group nor the physical strength. Since I always had several dogs, like all social groups, there were rules that were agreed upon by the residents. Possession was an observed rule: if you currently had it you owned it. In light of what Jet knew about the social group she lived with, she developed an ingenious plan to move the Fox Terriers. Jet would begin to alarm bark and would run toward the door. All of the other terriers would leap from the furniture in a state of keen anticipation and excitement and run toward the door. Jet would pass them at a calm trot, going the opposite direction, her little tail waving in triumph, as she jumped up onto the sofa, curved her body into a "C" shape, turned around twice and laid down with a contented sigh. By the time the terriers returned from their mission, she was firmly ensconced in her place, and the terriers would respect her "possession" of the area she was currently lying in. This is just one small example of the millions of solutions I have watched dogs create.

Masters of Yoga and the martial arts are examples of people who have integrated forebrain and hindbrain functions to such an advanced state that most of us cannot even imagine it. Controlling hindbrain processes like breathing and heartbeat is difficult to do! Most of us are quite content with being able to keep the emotions of daily irritations (like dropping the eggs onto the floor when getting them out of the refrigerator) under reasonable control. Dogs have trouble doing logic overrides, too. However, just as I have had to work for many years to learn to do logic overrides on my red-headed temper, dogs can be taught to do logic over rides on their reactivity.

Behaviour Is Like Body Odor

More relevant to us dog trainers than the anatomy of the brain itself is what happens inside it and how that affects the outside of us and dogs. I am fond of saying that behaviour is like body odor. Behaviour that you can observe is an indication of the physiological processes going on in the brain. What we can see is a product of what we cannot see. In the same way, when you begin to smell like sweat, it is just the tangible (observable) symptom of processes that are the root, but not readily visible, cause of your odor. As in sweating, internal chemical changes are involved in the behavioural process, but remember this is just one part of the story. Behaviours have both anatomical and physiological components. That is, there is the structure of the brain itself, and the chemical and electrical components of the inner workings of the brain.

The Garden In Your Head.

This is just a memorable way of saying that you are the representation of what is happening, chemically and electrically, in your brain. Think of the brain and neurotransmitter system as a garden. In the context of my flower beds, I am a rhododendron failure. Every time I plant a rhododendron (a flowering shrub which I dearly love), it dies on me. While I take this quite personally, the fact is it is not dying just to spite me. The real problem is that rhododendrons require a very acidic soil, and the soil I kept planting them in was too alkaline. To make the soil acidic enough to support a rhododendron, I must add the right kind of chemicals and organic matter to the soil so that the rhododendron can thrive instead of die. So must it be for learning to take place: the chemical state in your head must be in a state of balance such that learning and thinking can take place. Some of this balance has to do with the physical construction of the brain, some with the communication between neurons and some with the balance of the neurotransmitters.

Neurons

The hod-carrier[1] of the brain is a specialized cell that transmits information to other cells: the neuron. These are really cute little guys who reach little tentacled arms toward each other, like people in a romantic novel. One kind of tentacle, the receiving end of the little arms, are called dendrites. At the other side of the cell body are another set of tentacles sending out-going information which are called axons. Between the axons and the dendrites are little contact points called synapses. Synapses are like the space between your lips and your dog's nose, just before you kiss her. When neurons talk to one another, it is sort of like a fire brigade. Electrical charges build up on both sides of the cell membrane of the neuron. In a neuron at rest, the outside of the cell is negative relative to the inside, as the membrane is selectively permeable to certain ions. These specific ions passing through the cell membrane cause an electrical signal to flow through the neuron. When this electrical signal reaches the axon it keeps on going until there it is: at the synapse. There this electrical charge is transmitted to a chemical signal - the neurotransmitter. The neurotransmitter crosses the synaptic cleft to the neighboring neuron's dendrites where it's influence starts a new electrical wave. Using our fire brigade analogy, this electrical change cues an axon to "pass the bucket" via the neurotransmitter across the synapse to a dendrite, enabling the message to keep going.

Neurotransmitters

Neurotransmitters are the brain's chemical messengers. Like couriers in an office, they madly race through the wavy hallways, dodge office traffic and try not to get sucked into gossip at the water cooler. Okay, I added a little drama. Although the neurotransmitters have to find their way across the synaptic cleft, it is not too difficult because the synaptic cleft is quite tiny. Once across the synaptic cleft, the courier must not only find the right address, he must also know who the package goes to at that address. Being a neurotransmitter is tricky, because neurotransmitters must deliver their message to the right "address," the proper receptor site on the surface of another neuron.

This is where the biology becomes really amazing and elegant. At this cellular level, the proper delivery by the neurotransmitter to the proper receptor site becomes a geometry rather than a geography problem. The neurotransmitter has to find the right door (receptor site), and that door will have a lock in it. But wait - there's more! Once the correct receptor site is found, the neurotransmitter must be the right "shape,"

---

1. A brick-layer's assistant: the person who carries the bricks.

because the neurotransmitter *is the key* that will unlock the door and wa-la! The neurotransmitter can hold the door open and deliver the message. This causes a change in the next neuron cell so the cycle begins again. And this is going on in your head so fast you couldn't even think about it if you tried to.

What I described here was only one kind of informational transfer, chemical synaptic transmission. When you combine this one tiny, basic process and think about all of the other processes that must happen for information to travel around in our brain, then add the higher-order brain processes to this, it is no wonder stuff gets lost in the shuffle occasionally! If you want to know more about neurotransmitters and dendrites and more detailed brain anatomy, the best source is a university library, which will have current books on neurobiology.

I hope this helps you to think of behaviour as the manifestation of a *physiological* process, just as certainly as developing your abdominal muscles. For dog training purposes, I think it is enough that you are aware that all this stuff is happening and that you can have an effect on this process to the extent that you can help your dog exist and learn in an appropriate emotional state and mind-set. It is vitally important to understand that different animals have different skills, and some of that has to do with the anatomy and physiological processes that go on in the brain.

Something Old, Something New...

What makes up each individual's brain is the result of a vast array of elements. Behaviours are highly adaptive and liable to change. Some behaviours have evolved over generations and are shaped by changes in the environment or other selection pressures. On top of all that, the brain is a highly adaptable organ and it makes changes in response on an individual level to environmental and experiential factors. It is safe to say that all behaviours involve choice on some level, either a conscious (thinking) choice or an unconscious choice.

- There are ethological (species-related) components that have an effect on the brain. Species-related behaviour and inherited tendencies from that individuals immediate ancestors (parents and grandparents) are just a couple of those. The individual's brain is also shaped and changed by personal experience.

- There are natural and sexual selection pressures that could come into play that might cause changes to the brain. These would come under the heading of evolution: how a species, as a whole, adapts. The way that dogs choose to live in groups and raise a family, is one example of these kinds of pressures.

- In addition, for our dogs, there are artificial selection pressures resulting from domestication. Domestication means selective breeding programs that Mother Nature did not design. Humans will selectively breed animals for a very specific task or even for frivolity, which results in dogs that have a certain "look," for instance, or distinctly specialized behaviours. When you breed dogs for hunting a specific prey animal, or for speed, or to be a great lap dog, it is not merely the obvious physical characteristics that make the dog a specialist, but also the mental characteristics that come along that make a dog better at a certain job, too.

- Just because a behaviour was once useful or adaptive for the species does not mean that it is still useful or adaptive for today's canine, who is often living under relatively artificial circumstances. While the brain is capable of changing and adapting continually, both to benefit the species as well as the individual, at the same time, the brain will hold on to behaviours that were once useful to the species, but might not fit in with an individual's current lifestyle. Humans crave salt and sugar because they were, at one time, not widely available. Today, people can go to the grocery and pick up all the salt and sugar they would ever need and more. Our "old" craving for salt and sugar creates health problems for us today, because our lifestyle is vastly different than it was, say, even 100 years ago. Even though it is not as useful as it once was, there that behaviour still is, affecting us down through the ages. For dogs, car chasing is really NOT a good pastime, mostly because cars do not "behave" like prey animals. Motion activates triggers that are very "old" behaviours that were developed long before cars entered the scene. Ditto on skateboarders and bicyclists - all situations that activate predatory sequences in the dog that cannot have a happy ending in today's society.

Behaviour is the result of a blend of both old and new patterns, constantly adapting to new circumstances.

Behaviour is not a disembodied or random entity. It is dynamic and follows a predictable progression of development.

Nature vs. Nurture

There is no doubt that genetics plays a front-stage role in behaviour. It is just as valid to say that the experiences that are catalogued by an individual play a co-starring role. Genetics, environment and experience all combine to make each one of us - and our dogs - the individuals that we are at any given point in time. How the animal is cared for physically can have an effect on the hardware of the brain, too. Items like malnutrition can have a deleterious effect on the normal development of an organism. When a puppy leaves his mother too young or he is not exposed to novel stimuli at young ages the hard-wiring development of his brain will suffer. Even though the circuits were normal at birth, the brain may not develop normally (altering the brain physically) when the puppy does not have particular types of stimulation and learning experiences.

Even if all things are perfect, that is the dog has good genetics, stayed with his mother until he was *at least* 8 weeks of age (the mother teaches the puppy certain social lessons and some of the important ones occur up until this time frame), and got good training, you will still be addressing individual temperament. How an animal handles stress is defined primarily by the hardware and the hard wiring the dog comes with. Some dogs are able to concentrate for relatively long periods of time, even with no prior training. Other dogs will require extensive training in order to be able to concentrate on certain tasks. For instance, my Smooth Fox Terriers can concentrate on hunting or prey-related tasks from a very young age and with incredible intensity. It is entirely another matter to teach that same dog to "stay" in one place enduring distractions with the same dedication they bring to hunting. I am certain I could have taught my Basset Hound to herd sheep, (I admit it, I am an optimist at heart) because he was a really bright and cooperative dog. But my Border Collie didn't need to be taught to herd sheep at all, I just had to learn how to place instinctive behaviours on cue and learn where I needed to position myself. It was much more about training me than her. What I wish to emphasize is that different dogs will indeed learn certain behaviours quickly and will struggle with others. Just like we do. We all bring strengths and weaknesses with us when we learn a new task, and so it will be for your dog.

As you are training, keep in mind that you cannot remove the brain or the physiological aspects of the brain from your training program. Your dog's brain and your brain will be working constantly behind the scenes to produce results of one kind or another. Remember, too, that many factors have a say in those results: some of them will be species related, some of them may be breed-related and some of them will be on an individual level.

Expect your dog to be a dog. He is very good at that, and very poor at being human. Thank God. Remember, what humans have over dogs is that we can use fractions, build rockets to fly to the moon and are excellent at deceit.

Brenda's Brain Model

For my students, I loosely classify the brain into two parts, so it is easy for them to remember and easy for us to talk about during training sessions. I know that the brain is much more complex than this model, but if you have to consider all those neurotransmitters bicycling frantically around in there and the dendrites and axons constantly kissing each other and giving each other "charges," and the neurotransmitters fumbling for tiny keys to fit into little locks...well, you'll just be too crazy thinking about all that to get any training at all done. So here is how I divide the brain into a useful model for everyday use by my students:

- My **Hindbrain** model is the Hindbrain and the Midbrain System schlepped together. These brain parts are involved in reactive behaviour.

- My **Frontbrain** model is the forebrain - the Learning Brain. The brain parts that are involved in responsive, thinking behaviour. These brain parts are involved in responsive behaviour.

Keep in mind, my brain model is not so accurate if you want to pinpoint where behaviours are truly originating from and what places would fire in the brain if you did an MRI. But this model works very well for me (a lay person as far as neurobiology goes) and for my clients, who are often lay people in two ways: as neurobiologists and as dog trainers. With this model, my only goal is to help people to be aware of the fact that behaviour is the result of a series of complex internal processes and to identify whether a dog is in a learning state or not. My clients love this model and use it daily and tell me it helps them to be more understanding in the training process.

Hindbrain Behaviour Looks Like

Hindbrain behaviour is *Reactive* behaviour that originates in the limbic system and is characterized by a variety of observable, tangible actions on the part of the dog:

• Reflexive.

• Difficult-to-interrupt behaviour. (The dog feels as if she is on a tractor beam. You know, like in the *Star Wars* movies when your spaceship gets too close to an enemy spaceship and they capture your ship by sucking you in on a tractor beam. Dogs get sucked in by tractor beams, too: scents, eye contact from another dog, the list is endless.)

• Difficult to impossible to communicate with the dog. (The dog has "hung up the phone" or there is "static on the line.")

• Hectic. Overactive or hyperactive. Emotionally overwhelmed in response to stressors. This can include agitated behaviour and frustration.

• This behaviour is associated with neurotransmitters like adrenaline.

You know what your dog looks like when he is Hindbrain. He is leaping around, pupils dilated and acting like "an idiot," as many of my clients express it. He doesn't seem to recognize known cues and will maddeningly persist in unruly and sometimes life-threatening behaviours. He may display dangerous behaviour, such as intensely and arbitrarily guarding a dirty sock, and biting you when you reach for it; all the while acting as if he doesn't even know who you are. Lunging and snarling at approaching dogs, even though the approacher is displaying friendly body language, is attributable to Hindbrain oriented behaviour. When all that is done and said, don't get too down on the Hindbrain, it is also the part of the brain that takes really good care of you in situations where it would take too long for logic to be useful. Remember that jerk that pulled out in front of your car? Your Hindbrain is the one who slammed on the brakes, saving you from a fender-bender.

Zoey Switches From Frontbrain To Hindbrain

Here is that moment in time when Zoey makes that switch from Frontbrain to Hindbrain. This is early in her Stay work and before she learned to do a logic override and resist distraction. At this stage in her training the decision to move rather than remain in the requested Stay is not a conscious one. She goes with the Hindbrain: chase that ball! The motion of the ball rolling triggers the reaction: movement towards the ball.

The Frontbrain decision, less emotional, more involving executive decision making skills, would have been to hold the Stay behaviour even though the ball is very tempting. That resisting temptation thing gets all of us at some time or another!

Photograph by Dave Schrader

Frontbrain Behaviour Looks Like

Frontbrain behaviour is *Responsive* behaviour that is characterized by being discernible (from *reactive* behaviour) as originating from the Learning center of the brain being in primary control. We can tell this because the behaviour reflects:

- Reflects cognition.
- Demonstrates thoughtful Action.
- Is easy to redirect.
- Shows communication is flowing in a circle - from you to the dog and back around. This can happen because the dog is capable of thoughtfully responding instead of survival-based reacting. The good old communication loop made possible because of thoughtful actions (conscious decisions).

- Looks to the handler for inclusion in decision-making process (once trained to do so!).

- Accurate response to cues.

- The dog is not hectic or agitated; instead her actions are deliberate. For instance, the dog will try a behaviour, look at the handler for feedback, then try another behaviour.

- Frontbrain behaviour is associated with neurotransmitters like serotonin, dopamine and amino acids that can act as neurotransmitters, like GABA and glutamate.

You also know what your dog looks like when he is Frontbrain. He is calm and able to concentrate. He can problem-solve and reason when you are shaping behaviours. (Shaping is the development of a new behaviour by reinforcing small steps toward the final response to attain the final response.) I love Frontbrain dogs. They are fun to be around and captivating. The Frontbrain dog deliberately charms your socks off; he doesn't have to steal them. The Frontbrain dog can turn intensity on and then lie down on a dime from a full run. Frontbrain dog makes you look very good in performance events and during a walk on the street. Frontbrain dog is a joy because the lines of communication between the two of you are accessible.

For performance dogs, the absolute ideal is a mix of the intensity of Hindbrain behaviour balanced perfectly with the precision and responsiveness of Frontbrain behaviour. This is a very delicate balance indeed and requires a very clever and thinking trainer. People love to watch dogs who are "on the edge," with intense, but responsive behaviour. As a handler, I love to be teamed up with a dog who I have trained to be in this state. It's quite a rush!

Frontbrain Behaviour Looks Like...

Both of these dogs are engaged in a thinking state. Even though the Border Collie in the top photograph is moving fast, she is also taking direction from her handler. Sports like Agility, Herding and Protection work require a balancing act between the Hindbrain and Frontbrain.

Photograph on the left: Dave Schrader   Photograph above: Brenda Aloff

Writing: A Frontbrain Behaviour...

Writing is clearly a Frontbrain activity...Okay, really someone just stuck a pen in the puppy's paw. However, the puppy is not reacting or worried. Instead, she is remaining calmly in place. For a dog, whose natural reaction would be to dislodge the pen, this is clearly thoughtful, rather than reflexive, behaviour.

Photograph by Joanne Weber

Frontbrain/Hindbrain Do Not Pull As A Double Team.

It is of vital importance to develop awareness of this Frontbrain/Hindbrain model during training sessions because of the next important fact I am going to tell you: The Frontbrain and the Hindbrain don't pull as a double team. They work more like a Unicorn hitch. For those of you who are not familiar with draft animal hitches, a double team is the familiar one: two horses or oxen hitched up side-by-side, pulling together. A Unicorn team is one animal placed in front of the other, (similar to some dog-sled teams) - in a single file. This little gem of knowledge has huge ramifications on how behaviour is displayed. While the Hindbrain and Frontbrain definitely work together, one leads while the other follows or vice-versa. The brain

"hitch," to the outside observer, sometimes seems to most resemble that bizarre cartoon character, CatDog, the animal who is the front half of a cat on one end and the front half of a dog on the other end. They are hooked together and they communicate and, at times, cooperate, but one leads and the other follows. As one would imagine, there is occasional conflict about the direction that will be taken first because of different "ways of thinking."

Responsive Vs. Reacting - A Pearl Of Wisdom From Clinton Anderson.

You want your dog to be thinking and responding, not reacting. Clinton Anderson is talking about horses, but I love his sense of humor as he expresses this: "The reacting section tells the horse that whenever anything might be a predator, "Run!" The problem is, after the running is over, horses never start thinking. They usually start eating. We want to change that. We want to teach our horses to use the thinking side of their brains before the reacting side." (Anderson, 2004) With horses, dogs, dolphins or birds, whatever we are training, we want a thinking and responsive, not a reacting, animal.

You Must Be The Reliably Frontbrained Partner.

Easy guess where you want your dog to be. Now let's figure out how to get that switch from Hindbrain to Frontbrain on cue. To develop and promote team work you need to set yourself up as relevant and reliable to your dog. This involves you being consistent in your actions and fair in your thoughts. Part of fairness is knowing which parts of your training program are grounded in reality and which parts are free-floating in space. Keep in mind, if you do the right "thing," but with an over-emotional or reactive attitude and countenance, you will get "wrong" results. In other words, when you are with your dog, ONE OF YOU MUST ALWAYS BE FRONTBRAIN. Ideally, both of you are always Frontbrain! Since this isn't possible, and since you must be the one in charge, the onus is on you to remain Frontbrain and keep the team on track and out of trouble. This responsibility is YOURS!

Why Do I See So Many Hindbrainers?

Since we all love Frontbrain dog, why is it people have dogs who never seem to leave their Hindbrain? The natural tendency of some dogs is to be primarily Hindbrainers. (We know some people like that, too, don't we?) These dogs are easily stimulated and display a tendency to act impulsively.

When dogs do not get enough physical exercise and do not get stimulation sufficient to work their Frontbrain, Hindbrain states, by default, are encouraged. When a dog is exercised, you cannot just run him to death or throw a ball or frisbee until he is panting. That doesn't create Frontbrain neural pathways: it just creates tired muscles and Hindbrain patterns. Rest that dog 10 minutes, and he is ready for another vigorous bout of exercise. You must provide Frontbrain exercise to get a dog who is calm and tired - ready to relax. Throw the ball, ask the dog to fetch, then ask the dog to place the ball in your hand. Now ask for a Down. Cue the dog to get into Heel position. Ask the dog to back up three or four steps in Heel position. Throw the ball again and send the dog to fetch. Repeat this sequence, inserting different exercises each time. Now you are working the dog properly. The dog will be tired and relaxed. He will rest for a few hours and you will have developed a better relationship with the dog as an added bonus!

Owners encourage their dog to be Hindbrainers when they do not offer adequate structure. For instance, if your dog is slamming his body against the window sixty times a day and barking at people walking outside the window, and you do not stop him, he is practicing impulsive, reactive behaviour. Other owners idiotically encourage the dog to blast out of the door and "get'em" at the squirrels on a daily basis. These very same owners are puzzled when their dog blasts through the door, runs madly down the street and won't allow himself to be caught until he is finished squirrel hunting. The owner does not make the connection between encouraging and allowing the dog to chase squirrels in the back yard in an out-of-control manner and not being able to control the dog on a walk, and just cannot believe it when the dog charges an innocent cyclist or skate-boarder. While predation is a very natural behaviour, by practicing controlling the dog in other arousing circumstances it is possible to gain a great deal of control over fixed action (instinctive) behaviour patterns. Since I can call my dogs off running cats and deer I know I have adequate control to keep them and others safe. I start with more controllable Switching exercises with easily controlled prey objects (balls, tug toys) first, managed with fervor so that my dogs do not get chances to make mistakes and form bad habits as puppies, and train a recall systematically and meticulously. Two years of work, but satisfying - and safe - for the lifetime of the dog.

Dogs who are frustrated and have no way to get rid of the frustration are very Hindbrain. This type of frustration occurs because there is no escape. You see this especially in the case of dogs who are tied on chains to dog houses and left there endlessly. Some dog pounds or shelters are not able to provide environmental stimulation or adequate exercise for dogs, and these types of environments can create this kind of frustration.

There are many very caring people in the world of animal shelters and pounds and humane societies. Some of them are able to find funding and have enough caring people to provide adequate care for the animals under their jurisdiction. Other animal shelters or pounds simply do not have the funding or personnel and do the best they can with what they have. All shelter, animal control officers and volunteers deserve the support of all of us who are in dogs. It is indeed a big challenge to properly meet the needs of a rescue or fos-

Brenda's Brain Model

ter dog. It is an uphill battle because there are significant gaps in the education of the general public, which is directly at the root of the problem.

Some boarding kennels and dog day care institutions also unwittingly and unintentionally provide an over-stimulating-with-no-relief type of environment. In these kinds of environments, the General Adaptation Syndrome becomes a trap for the dog. Fight or Flight do not work because this type of environment does not allow for flight and fighting with walls, fences or dogs on the other sides of fences becomes one of the only outlets for the anger and frustration the dog is feeling. Resistance doesn't work because concrete walls and adequate containment systems prevent it. Some dogs are not capable of adapting to this kind of environment and sensitize instead of adapting or desensitizing to it. This kind of frustration can occur in any dog who is constantly placed under the pressure of too much chaos in the environment. Places where dogs are barking endlessly and where there is inadequate exercise or Frontbrain stimulation are very stressful for dogs.

I meet the occasional dog who is a real intellectual and has naturally beautiful communication skills both with dogs and people - a real Frontbrainer. The wonderful thing is that you can easily create, from 98% of the raw material of the dog population, a dog who is reliable, confident and thinking: a real joy to have a relationship with. Of course, to do this, you must be at least reliable and thinking yourself. If you find a Frontbrainer in a shelter setting, now that is an incredible dog. He's like the under-privileged child that beats all the odds and rises above his early experiences. If that dog ended up in a shelter or dog pound in the first place, it is unlikely that the person who would relinquish an animal to a shelter is the type of person who was concerned about environmental enrichment and thoughtful training in the first place. Stack that on top of the dog having a very sudden change to his environment that probably does not resemble anything he has ever experienced before; and it is a very sound animal that retains the ability to think and problem-solve efficiently under those circumstances. For the most part, it is up to you to encourage your dog's Frontbrain abilities, by teaching her good impulse control and concentration skills. You cannot teach her these things unless you can do them yourself.

The Magic Switch

A very good question to ask right now is: What is it that controls which "brain" is currently leading? Not only can I tell you that answer, better yet, I am going to tell you how to manipulate the controls!

The Reticular Activating System

The Reticular Activating System (RAS) is a switch that controls whether the Frontbrain (responding, thinking brain) or the Hindbrain (reactive, reflexive brain) is currently in charge. Think of a toggle switch that controls lighting and is equipped with a dimmer function. This RAS is located in the brain stem and reaches into the cerebral cortex. This system is at work in you as well as in your dog! When your dog becomes extremely emotionally aroused, the RAS switches control to the Hindbrain, and Instinct Rules. Reactivity is the name of the game. As soon as arousal subsides, the RAS switches control back to the Frontbrain and allows Good Thinking to return. Responsive, thoughtful action and calm concentration are the resulting behaviours. The "zen" feeling we want our dogs to have, and the "zen" feeling we want to have when we are working with our dogs, is acquired through a Frontbrain state.

Why Control Of The RAS Is Important.

For some dogs, a trip to the Frontbrain requires a month of planning on our part! The single most important facet of training, in my book (ha, bad pun award), is the ability of the trainer to manipulate this RAS. How fast can you get your dog to go from Hindbrain to Frontbrain? This has real meaning: How fast can you stop your dog when she is chasing a squirrel into the street? How quickly can I get my Border Collie to lie down when she is herding sheep? How chop-chop can I stop my German Shepherd (she is armed and dangerous and fits the discrete diagnosis for territorial aggression) when she is in mid-spring toward someone who wanders into my yard unexpectedly?

Because I have had so many reactive and down-right aggressive dogs of my own, it became painfully apparent early on that I needed to get control of this switching system. I could see that when dogs were engaged in certain activities it was difficult to impossible to interrupt them. But if I didn't figure out a way, they were going to be dead dogs. Identifying what a dog looked like when she was Hindbrain and being able to cue her to Switch to a Frontbrain, listening state seemed to be the key. But how to flip this Switch? How do you take a reactive dog and manufacture calm, reliable behaviour that holds up under fire?

You Cannot Solve A Hindbrain Problem With A Frontbrain Solution.

The reactive and aggressive dogs I work with have generously taught me a very crucial lesson: once you are in the midst of a hindbrain problem you cannot apply a frontbrain solution. This is my expression of the dog's inability to "listen" and perform learned behaviours when they are in the grip of extreme arousal.

When you are in Fight Or Flight mode it is not so much that you *cannot* think, but you *do not* think. I was delighted to discover this: the fact that it is not so much that it is impossible to think when aroused; instead it is difficult and not the natural choice of the brain. The fact that you "do not think" rather than "cannot think" is a glorious thing because it means you can teach the dog - and yourself! - how to do a logic override in arousing circumstances.

In Fight or Flight mode, you do not think because as far as the brain is concerned, once that RAS is flipped, thinking becomes of secondary importance. Reacting is more useful for survival. This may happen even though survival is not the immediate issue, and the arousal or switch into "survival mode" merely happens out of habit. For instance, your dog has become aroused when other dogs pass by your living room window. The sight of another dog causes an adrenaline dump, and the dog exhibits reactive behaviour. The dog on the street isn't really threatening and this isn't really a matter of survival, but the brain does not necessarily recognize that. The neural pathways for reactive behaviour are already burned for the visual cue of another dog. The only way to modify the behaviour is to change the behaviour cycle and help the dog burn a new neural pathway in response to the visual cue of another dog passing by.

There are 3 E's that you should be aware of. These processes create new neural pathways, vital to the learning process. In fact, it *is* the learning process. The dog will not create a new neural pathway unless the old one is inadequate: it no longer works to bring about a result that makes the dog more comfortable or feel safer. Crucial to note is there is no conscious thought involved at the neurological level, which is where the

E's operate. For a new neural pathway to be burned the information must be:

- Engraphy: It must be encoded into memory - physically "transferred" from short term into long term memory.

- Engram: There must be neuroanatomical changes. That is, an enduring change in the nervous system which conserves the effects of this experience across time.

- Ecphory: The memory must be able to be retrievable, or it isn't much use at all.

Often, I see trainers trying to get executive thinking decisions from a dog who is in a high arousal mode and has not been educated to easily Switch from a reactive, non-thinking, Hindbrain state to a responsive, Frontbrain state. The fact that this becomes frustrating for both parties does not prevent trainers from trying, because they do not have any other tools. You must address the problem FIRST from the same level it is occurring. One of the basic operating systems to take into account when you are training is described by Maslow's Hierarchy: If you are hungry, your social and intellectual needs become a secondary priority. Once you feed the starving person, he can begin to think about something other than his physical suffering again. To the mother who is watching her children starve, funding for space exploration must seem like insanity. You cannot even begin to open a conversation with her about anything, no matter how trivial, until her immediate needs are met.

For instance, let's say you are driving down the street and some jerk pulls his car out in front of you, and you must slam on the brakes to avoid a car accident. At the moment the danger has been averted and you realize you will probably live through this after all, I turn to you and say, "What is the cube root of 64?" Even if you know the answer to this question under normal circumstances, the question is clearly ludicrous in this context. Clearly, the cube root of 64 is the farthest thing from your mind at this time. Actually, the cube root of 64 is the farthest thing from your limbic system at this time, tucked away in the file cabinets of your frontal cortex, and not horribly accessible at this moment due to the reticular activating system switch is thrown to the limbic system side. And rightly so, figuring that the cube root of 64 is not survival oriented. It is clear as well that *emotionally* the question asker doesn't have a clue at this moment. Animals get this, too. Asking for a "sit," when the dog feels his life is in danger from an approaching dog is just as inaccessible

as the cube root of 64. Furthermore, from the dog's point of view, his handler is clueless.

All dogs have moments of extreme arousal, no matter what their temperament. What I know from experience is that when a dog was lunging and screaming at the end of the leash, whether the reason was to murder the approacher or the more innocent reason of desiring another's tennis ball - "sit" didn't work. Name Recognition didn't work. As a matter of fact, almost nothing worked at these moments. Now, we can say, disapprovingly, hands on our hips, "You should never let your dog act this way!" This is a true statement, but the judgment is invalid. While I can honestly say that my very own dogs do not act this way (even the ones who are reactive and aggressive look like angels) because I am exquisite at management, and we have already had that discussion about who is making decisions for our little team. However, it is a fact of life that my students will have these moments. Heck, the occasional untrained, reactive dog even takes me by surprise occasionally the first time I work with her. The point is, at this pinnacle of Hindbrain display, you need to have some technique that provides adequate damage control. I hand you the short-term solution in the Back Away combined with Move Into Exercise detailed in the *Exercises* section of this book. The long-term solution is behaviour modification. But until that has been completed, these exercises will offer you sustenance in your moment of desperation. In fact, with a minimum of training, they successfully switch the dog into a thinking, Frontbrain state.

The bottom line is that you may not be able to change a dog's neurochemistry, but you can teach your old dog - or young dog, or reactive dog - new tricks. You will be most efficient in your teaching if you are constantly aware of which emotional state your dog is in and can determine whether that state is conducive to learning. You can also have a great effect on yourself by applying exactly the same principles to yourself as you would to your dog. Training techniques can help people and dogs be more Frontbrain, thoughtful individuals. It is not that all arousal or emotion prevents learning: the exact opposite is true. But arousal, for the most part, causes and creates nothing but a vicious circle of undesired behaviour that feeds on itself. Controlling and preparing for a state of arousal is what I am advocating, so both you and your dog can have a more satisfying relationship.

?'s To Ask When You Are Training.

Manipulation of the RAS became a sort of obsession with me, and I developed an entire protocol during the process of figuring it out. The first training question I am always asking myself:

- Is the dog Hindbrain right now?

Leads to two other questions:

- If he is, how do I get him to use his Frontbrain?

- How do I get him Frontbrain most effectively?

If you are really clever and pro-active, ideally you become a bio-feedback machine for your dog. Once you do this, you will be effective and successful. If you take nothing else away from this chapter please take this: *You must be constantly aware of the emotional state your dog is in and whether that state is conducive to learning.* This doesn't mean you never stress your dog, it means you get good at determining Frontbrain vs. Hindbrain behaviours, and you install habits such that you can switch the dog into a Frontbrain, learning state on cue. If you are really good, your dog will be able to maintain concentration and impulse control for extended periods of time.

The Get Connected work is wonderful for teaching a dog to Switch over to Frontbrain. It is simple work, which is good, because dogs, above all, need really simple explanations in black & white. This work improves communication, respect and trust, all at the same time. Whoo Hoo!!! That's Good Stuff!

What Switching Looks Like

I play a game with Rylie where I offer to be a substitute sheep. This is her favorite game and, once taught, is used as a high value reward. This game sends her into glaze-eyed, reactive Hindbrain within a second. She will treat me exactly as she would a sheep. Notice I keep my hands together and close to my body so I don't contact her unintentionally AND so she doesn't bite my hands accidentally. The cue to begin is my body posture and movements.

I use this game to practice switching Rylie from Hindbrain to Frontbrain. See the following photographs to see how I use this game to practice switching (and have fun at the same time!).

Rylie is so caught up in the game (and her Hindbrain!) that she is rushing in to muzzle punch me. If I continue, she will hit me harder and bite, albeit in an inhibited open mouth correction style bite as she would use on sheep.

In this photograph she is doing something she would never, ever do if she was in a Frontbrain state: violate my personal space in an aggressive way and use her teeth on me. This is exactly the type of behaviour I want to be able to absolutely control. I don't ignore her instincts, I help her learn when to use them.

I can play this dangerous game with her because trained, well-bred (good genetics) Border Collies have amazing bite inhibition, even when aroused, and use just enough force to "get the job done," a lesson humans would be wise to learn. I did suffer some minor bruises and tooth scrapes and had some of my clothing ripped in the process of teaching her enough self-control so this game could be turned "on" and "off" on my cue. I always decide when this game will be played. Rylie NEVER EVER gets to initiate this game.

I originally learned the importance of working with arousal levels in high-in-drive dogs from my terriers. Dogs who are easily aroused need handlers who understand the arousal levels and can control them, in order to keep terriers safe and out of trouble.

Two seconds later, in the amount of time it takes to straighten my body and say "Rylie, Heel," this photograph is taken. "Heel" is a Frontbrain task. Immediately she responds, stepping into Heel position perfectly. It sure didn't look this way at first! The transition was slow and ragged (taking up to 5 seconds and lacking precision). Rylie would fall into Heel position but would require extra cues. Even at that, she might Heel a couple of steps and then get out of position, to see if she could get me to be a sheep "just one more time." We are a slick team now, though!

It takes practice and a deliberate, well-thought out program to get your dog to switch this quickly, effortlessly and precisely. But oh, how handy this is! I consider this training requisite for all dogs. Especially if your dog is anxious, hyper or reactive, this ability is priceless!

Photo essay by Mary Wilmoth.

Frontbrain

Responsive

Cognitive

Conscious, Thoughtful
Action

Problem-Solving

Good Impulse Control

Hindbrain

Reactive

Reflexive

Unconscious Action

Not "Thinking"

Poor Impulse Control

For a Behaviour to be "Put On Cue" 3 things must occur.
This is a physiological process that creates new neural pathways.

- Engraphy (short term into long term memory)

    Encoding information into memory.

- Engram (neuroanatomical changes that must take place for learning to occur)

    An enduring change in the nervous system that conserves the effects of experience across time.

- Ecphory (cue system)

    The process of activating or retrieval of information or memory.

First Training Question to ask:
Is my dog in a Front-brain or Hindbrain state?

If she is in a Hindbrain state, how do I switch her to her Frontbrain?

And remember: It's all about gaining control of the switch:

Dogs, Humans & Paradigm Shifts

Toys are not just for playing with. When people think of dog toys, they think of watching their dog play or making their dog happy by buying cute toys that have an appearance that appeals to them (humans). When people look at this photograph, they think: "Aw, how cute." This might have nothing whatsoever to do with a dog's perception of the toy. This dog obviously feels that toys make good pillows. My experience tells me that this dog could also be using his position as a strategy: lying on your toy is a great way to safeguard it from being taken! In essence, this position could just as likely be a guarding position as not.

Photograph by Lesley Ashworth

Do You Really Understand Who Your Dog Is?

When you do will you still love her? Most people would rather think of their dog as the imaginary dog they have in their head rather than the individual the dog really is. If you wish to have a great relationship with your dog, realistically look at her and yourself. Understand who she is and what she needs. Keep her safe and do not expect things of her that she cannot provide. In order to train your dog effectively you may need to shift your paradigm. This means you may have to give up some faulty ideas and start thinking in new ways.

Changing Your Belief System

A first rule of training is KNOW THE SPECIES you are working with! This is a bigger order of business than most people realize, because it means you may have to think in new ways about dogs. To communicate effectively, it is only fair to understand just who it is you are communicating with. It is not the scope of this book to give you an ethological view of dogs, so I have suggested a couple of excellent texts in the bulleted list below. What I would like to mention are the primary mind blockers that contribute to people not being knowledgeable about dogs as a species. I call this: The Killer Of Realistic Expectations List

- Do not anthropomorphize (except as a fun and humorous exercise in frivolity.) Anthropomorphizing is attributing human characteristics onto animals. Do not assume animals think like people. Just because they sometimes do does not mean they always do. The much repeated "Dogs are not Little People in fur suits" is not a joke, it is true.

- Do not transfer your own bizarre neuroses ('fess up, we all have one or two...), when training, onto your dog, human student or any other species that crosses your path. The rest of the time you can drip your bizarre neuroses all over anyone sluggish enough to put up with it.

- Stay Out Of Your Own Way: The moment you become emotionally reactive your efficacy level begins to circle the drain. This means you may have to step out of your own comfort zone and look through the eyes of the dog, on a very basic and unadorned-by-*your*-emotions level. Continually ask yourself: What *information* is the dog getting from what I am doing right now? Training is about an exchange of information, not about projecting your emotional state of frustra-

tion, confusion and irritation onto the dog. Love is not enough.

- You will have to take a real look at the species and leave the Lassie Myth behind. (Credit for this term goes to Jean Donaldson, author of *The Culture Clash*.)

- Your pre-determined thinking about what dogs are may be entirely wrong. oops! A couple of excellent books will help you with this. *The Culture Clash* by Jean Donaldson. *Dogs* by Ray and Laura Coppinger. Read them. Patricia McConnell, PhD. has several excellent texts available. Two of my favorites are *The Other End Of The Leash* and *For The Love Of A Dog.*

Hey, Everybody Is An Individual, Too
Assessing The Individual Dog

In this chapter I am not trying to pigeon-hole (rigidly place in a category) any individual dog. Nor am I attempting to divulge the "personality" of the dog. I am speaking about a specific context: how the dog approaches a learning experience. The broad descriptions are meant to help you determine a general "starting point." An individual may certainly fit a niche, but you might find that over time, as the dog learns, he changes and therefore might change from one description to another. Just as likely, he might stay put, depending on how that learning style was most strongly influenced, from within (genetically) or from without (life experiences).

Every time I get near an animal, I immediately engage in determining the best way to appeal to and communicate with that individual. Without staring at him, I surreptitiously regard the dog. I notice how he watches me and the expressions that flit across his face and body as I observe him. What does he do as I initially ignore him? What happens when I give brief, but direct eye contact? Does he try to get closer to me? If so, does he push into my space or stand warily just outside arm's length? Do I see overwhelmingly friendly signals or caution? If any unfriendly signals are apparent are they subtle or overt?

This initial assessment has much to do with intuition and a "feel" and less to do with hard observations that are easily related and scientific. The only way to be able to assess a dog is through experience. It takes literally years of observation and field work to be able to assess a dog you have never seen before handily and instantaneously. I want to determine very rapidly what this dog needs from me to thrive and grow, and I need to ascertain what the problems are between the human and the dog. Then I try to close the gap in the relationship and foster understanding between the dog and owner. With no drama intended, in some cases the

dog's life may depend on my ability to assess their behaviour accurately. In other cases, this same ability will prevent me from being bitten.

If I am sweet and over-tolerant with a strong, assertive dog, he will take advantage of me. If I come on too strong with a timid dog, I will frighten him. In either case, misjudgment on the trainer's part creates emotional baggage and resistance. This resistance on the part of the dog is why the human does not get the desired result and why the dog is left unsatisfied with the relationship and continues to act out and seek balance.

You may never develop this particular skill of being able to accurately and immediately assess a dog you do not know well. Do not let your lack of experience intimidate you, because you do know your own dog well. Just by living with him on a day-to-day basis you have much knowledge of what makes him tick. Some of it may certainly puzzle you, but you are familiar with your dog's mannerisms and you certainly do know what you like about him, as well as the things about him that make you want to moan with despair. No one knows better where the communication breakdowns are, even if you do not know at this moment how to fix them.

The most difficult part of dog training is teaching students when to do what. The what itself isn't all that difficult, really. You begin with a behaviour you want to develop and plan, with approximations, exactly how you are going to get there. No, the difficult task is trying to hand a student the judgment required about just when to do what and with what sort of attitude.

A timid dog needs structure, just as the assertive dog does. You can use the same array of mechanical skills for each personality type of dog. That is the science of dog training. The mechanical skills are not difficult to learn if you work at it a little bit. Then there is the art of dog training, and this is the part where frustration first becomes evident. How you apply the mechanical skills according to each personality type and your attitude can make all the difference in the world. A friendly, neutral approach and calm, concise movement are crucial to good communication skills when working with dogs. Clear communication must always be our guiding beacon and the pure goal. With this in mind, your temper will be well in check, and your intellect active so you will not lose objectivity.

Clinton Anderson says it with his typical simplicity: Whatever you do, "do it as gentle as possible and as firm as necessary." "Firm" in this sentence does not mean forcefully, it means apply your firm intent in a thoughtful way, appropriate to the individual.

Michael Peace, a British horse trainer known for his kind ways and reliance upon learning theory, says, "In *Think Like Your Horse* I explained in detail the importance of balance: not being too hard and not being too soft. If you are too hard a horse will resent you, on the other hand, if you are too soft, he'll exploit you. It's the principle of using as little as you need at every second. Never use less than you need to get the job done and never use more than you need to get the job done. Just as little as you need." (Peace, 2005)

Any initial assessment of the animal will change as you move along through the training steps. You might begin with a pushy, annoying in-your-face-type, and, with a little work find that this dog is actually quite anxious and feeling a wee bit defensive. You might begin with a dog who, on the first impression, looks to be very timid, but discover that he is actually a very bright and manipulative creature, who is taking advantage of his handler's passivity and sympathy. Sometimes it is the dog who appears to be the "hardened case," a real tough guy, who becomes a slobbering mush-ball with a bit of empathy. I have had the pleasure of a few of these latter types; one was my Smooth Fox Terrier bitch, Breanna, another was my Shepherd bitch, Maeve, and a third was my dear Morgan mare, Sally. All of these girls were happy to negotiate with you, but they demanded to see what you had to bring to the table as well. All were assertive, confident and very, very mentally tough animals. Breanna and Sally, in particular, were quite exacting in what was expected of the relationship. Breanna was ever ready to point out the slightest error in your training method. Sally

would work her heart out for you as long as you were never, ever intimidated by her (she had marvelous powers of intimidation) and never used excessive force. Maeve chose me and was very cooperative if I approached her with a workmanlike and powerful (not overbearing! confident) manner. For Maeve and I it was only later into the relationship that it became affectionate, once I had proven that I was a good working partner.

At it's very epitome that is what training is: the trainer helps the dog to be the very best he can be. At the same time the dog, in turn, helps the trainer to develop her very best character. It's a communication loop that becomes a relationship loop.

The Silver Spoon Dog

This is the puppy that the owner researched for a year. The parents were carefully chosen, the breeding eagerly awaited. This owner has usually trained at least one or two dogs for competition already. This dog is elevated to a pedestal: he will be the "perfect" agility dog, obedience dog, breed ring special...just fill in the appropriate blank and add "if I just don't do anything wrong." He is loved indeed, and is treated as if he is a bit better than "others." In some cases, this dog is treated as more important than a spouse or a child. Some people even brag about how the dog is more important than other family members. (I am not going there - that is the job for a human therapist...) As long as this dog does well in his chosen sport, the owner makes endless allowances for this dog's behaviour. If he runs clean in agility and fast, it doesn't really matter that he spins and barks in his crate and maniacally continues to tug on the leash, even if told to stop. This owner is so concerned about the dog's "drive" and whether he will perform that all other considerations pale in comparison. As long as his competition heel work is beautiful, who really cares that he hauls on the leash like the handler is the sled and the race is the Iditorod? If he looks perky in the breed ring, does it really matter if he launches himself at guests and humps them? All problems are surmounted for this dog by the doting owner. Excuses are fast and furious or the handler proclaims, "That (whatever manners are being discussed) just isn't important. Besides, he doesn't *like* that."

This animal is arrogant and cannot believe it when you do not "bow down" to his wishes as he is accustomed to. When you insist that he display good manners and

Hey, Everybody Is An Individual, Too

not run roughshod all over you, he does one of several things: he either pouts and shuts down (stops working); acts nervous and insecure; gets defensive and snappy or tries to escalate assertiveness right up to the point of being nasty. His "how dare you...Do you know who I am?" attitude smacks of relatively harmless indignation in most dogs, but in a few dogs can range to overt hostility. So, while this superior attitude can be a temporary and relatively harmless behaviour in the majority of dogs, it can extend to biting a person, attacking a dog or redirecting aggression to the handler, by the rare character who has been taught to take himself much, much too seriously. Because of how he has been handled, this type of dog sees no reason to try to see himself in context with others at all. These dogs usually have a rather indifferent air about them, expecting the way to be made smooth for them. They are the rock stars of the dog world.

- This dog needs to cease being the center of attention. This will be much harder on the owner than it will the dog, and may, in fact, be impossible. The owner will have to wish to make these changes. Many of these owners, on some level, understand their role and have become irritated enough with the dog's behaviour to make the necessary changes to make the dog more comfortable and improve the relationship.

- In the beginning stages, this dog's behaviour will get worse. After all, the "How dare you...Do you know who I am?" attitude did not come about over night. The dog was carefully taught this attitude. Because a great deal of this dog's attention probably comes from "acting out," he will use that old strategy and become frustrated when it does not work. The dog has few other coping mechanisms at his disposal and will have to build some new ones. When the dog feels a bit vulnerable, he will finally turn to you for help. This is when you want to give him consideration, soften to him immediately and teach. In fact, this feeling of "needing someone" is your teaching moment.

- Once these dogs learn that "behaviour has consequences," they are good to go - and much happier and more balanced individuals. Since they have learned that good manners gets them results, they will feel contentment.

- This dog will always try force and bullying first. Then, if you area calm and endlessly persistent, he will, as a last ditch effort, try negotiation and

cooperation. Take advantage of this and reinforce this change in attitude, to foster it. He will soon come round.

The Rescue Dog

Plenty bad has happened to this dog. The most damaging is a lack of stability in the environment and a lack of consistency in handling from the humans this dog has encountered. The rescue dog may be suffering from a variety of traumas or very little trauma other than being shuffled around. Neglect of the dog's mental and physical needs is a given. Dog shelters are hectic places. Well-meaning rescue personnel and humane society folks are doing their best, but when you are involved in rescue work, you are overwhelmed. No one could handle the sheer crushing number of dogs in need. That said, this rescue dog, *your* rescue dog, is not suffering anymore. The bad stuff is not happening now. When someone is over-sympathetic and constantly feeling sorry for this animal, they are perpetrating the prior abuse. It is time to help the dog become mentally and physically healthy again. Normal dogs, like normal humans, are remarkably resilient - amazingly so. And, although I know it is sentimental and perhaps not backed up by scientific facts, I swear that my rescue dogs are way more grateful than my silver spoon dogs. It is radiated in everything we do together, and makes the relationship just that much more special.

- Give your rescue dog time. You will see quite a difference in two weeks, and he will smell better, too, after a bath! In six months there will be such a change that you will think you are "there." But I find it is closer to a year before this dog finally trusts the fact that he is home at last.

- Your rescue dog may be suffering from the human-equivalent of Post Traumatic Stress Disorder. Consistency and stability will go a long way towards helping the dog "find his way back" to normalcy.

- Give your rescue dog structure and rules from day one. No matter how much he protests, he will settle much more quickly and feel that his world is stable right away.

- Train, but make sure your rescue dog is physically ready for what you are asking. Some dogs just need a couple of days of rest from the bedlam of a kennel situation, others may require extensive veterinary care. Most of these dogs, unless they have been in a good foster home, will

Hey, Everybody Is An Individual, Too 61

have been eating less than top-drawer food and will often be undergoing a physical metamorphosis: losing the old nasty coat to be replaced with a shiny, new one or recovering from parasite infestation, heart worm or any one of a number of health issues.

The Confused Dog

People just aren't very clear when they communicate to animals. When a dog has decided that learning and trying to communicate with people is just too maddening, he does not just "give up." He adapts. He learns that people are confusing and it is futile to try to figure them out. He begins by trying to discern a pattern, so he can figure out what the human wants. Because the person is inconsistent, it is virtually impossible to discern a pattern. So his adaptation is to give up. Then when you try to teach him something, he doesn't try very hard, figuring that it is a waste of time anyhow. This dog approaches learning with a hectic idiocy sometimes, convincing you that he is much too stupid to learn. Other times he will shut down and stop working as soon as you tell him he is not getting it right. He is suspicious of your motives during learning experiences and will not expend much effort in trying to figure out what you want.

If you have been confusing your dog, or you have gotten a dog second-hand, do not be discouraged. You can turn this situation around in a heartbeat - well about two weeks actually - just by changing your own behaviour so you become consistent, clear and relevant. The Get Connected protocol will rescue you with no further effort on your part.

- As soon as you begin to have consistency in your behaviour and mannerisms, this dog will, after a brief period of, "Oh, yeah, I've heard that before..." come right around.

- When this dog gets sort of squishy, and acts like he is shutting down, immediately cue him for a known behaviour and then reinforce that. This helps him succeed.

- Be quietly persistent when he is hectic and acting like he has an IQ of 2. He doesn't, you know. You just need to be calm and keep presenting the cue in the same way, clearly showing him what behaviour you want.

The confused dog is such a common occurrence that there is a lot of material in this very book regarding this subject. Under the following headings you will find more information and suggestions about working with the confused dog:

Your Dog Must Be Ready To Learn, Too on page 31.

Dealing With Dogs Who Have Low Tolerance For Stress And Stop Working on page 32.

Grey Isn't Good Enough. Dogs Need To Have A Way To Distinguish Black From White on page 32.

Dogs Are Resistant For A Variety Of Reasons. Still, Approach Each Dog As If She Is Pure Of Heart. on page 75.

Unfairness Of Emotional Communication on page 78.

You Must Have An Effective Technique. Talking Isn't It. on page 80.

When you wish to change (modify) already learned or instinctive behaviour, what are the first knee-jerk reactions you often get? Resistance. Confusion. on page 177.

When Resistance And Confusion Aren't Temporary And What You Can Do About It on page 178.

Clarity counts - Reducing Confusion on page 179.

Normal Stuff Happens on page 117.

The Capitalist

It is my humble opinion that I shouldn't require a clicker and treats, or "better" food to get *already learned* behaviours that have been generalized (performed repeatedly and correctly in several different locations and situations). I do not think I should have to have six weeks of planning and an arsenal of goodies to obtain the real basic, day-to-day-living-with-me-behaviours that must be resolved so that my dog and I can live in a functional and peaceful way. Stuff like "don't jump all over me without permission," or "do not apply 600 foot/lbs of pressure with your nose each time you see the door crack and in the process of running over me to get through the door, do not break my toes, fingers or nose." Training isn't just about "paying for what you get" or "trading." It's about doing activities together, forming a relationship and working, if not as a well-oiled machine, at least bumbling through daily life with an absence of excessive irritation with each other. Because I believe that dogs and other animals are thinking, feeling and social creatures, I know that pay isn't enough. Appreciation counts. *In order for an animal to appreciate your appreciation, he must first appreciate you.* There are a few dogs that just hand this to you with no effort on your part (and often no awareness that it is being done for you). Other dogs do not. It isn't all about manipulation and whether you can out-manipulate your dog. (Truly, some people are really not up to that task. The only way to survive it is if you like each other, and the dog is generous and doesn't point out your small intellect too frequently.) You are dealing with a cognitive creature, who is adaptive and working to make his world comfortable for him. If you do not insert yourself in as a teammate, your dog will work his best to get around you and still get his needs met. Some dogs are quite benign in the way they do business, the equivalent of a successful, liberal boss. Others are quite ruthless in their quest for "what I want" and will cheerfully walk right over top of you - as long as you will put up with it. In fact, you are the only one that can change this dynamic.

- Have good mechanical skills. Use treats by all means, use a clicker and all the science at your disposal.

- A clicker is a wonderful, magical tool. But not the only tool.

- Treats are the best thing to hit town in dog training and have been used successfully by all kinds of animal trainers for years. The history of using treats to train animals is extensive. Treats are just one more tool in your toolbox. Alongside the voice, the clicker, your touch, the leash, fences and collars - all are used in the proper context to manage and train the dog.

- Using clickers and other Markers (such as a verbal "yes") as a way to enhance clear communication is mandatory in a training program. There is no better way to pinpoint behaviour when a dog is first learning the behaviour. Developing consistent cues is equally important.

- Some clients get so "hooked" on the clicker that I find them clicking and treating when they are not even aware of what they are reinforcing! Or they will mindlessly feed the dog treats for doing a behaviour that the dog obviously already understands and finds easy to do. This is a sign of clicker addiction (not in a good way.) Think before you click. Think before you feed. Use the clicker, the Marker and the treats as information, not as *your* knee-jerk habit.

- Work entire sessions without your clicker or your treats. It will do both you and your dog good. After all, you won't always have a clicker and treats with you.

- Develop the cooperative spirit and sociable nature that most dogs are born with.

- Remember, at the end of the day, you and your dog are bound by a relationship. If the clicker and the treats are the only way to convince your dog to comply with your wishes, you've got problems.

The Anxious Dog

Sure, people do plenty to make dogs anxious, but dogs who are constant, *chronic* "worriers" were probably born worriers. This dog tries too hard and gets upset even if he thinks he might possibly not have it "just right." This dog is easily confused, but that is mostly because he is worrying so much about getting it wrong that he isn't making good decisions. He tends to leap frantically from one choice to the next and, in the end, just cannot make any choices at all and stops working. This dog also tends to have poor rebound, and once upset over the task at hand, has a hard time re-focusing and going back to work. The most tragic part of this tale is that these dogs are usually the dearest, sweetest creatures. Gentle and "pleasers" by nature, it hurts to watch them try so hard and make such a mess of learning a simple task. But it doesn't have to be this way. A few considerations for the dog's learning style and true effort on the part of the trainer to be clear and not confusing will make this dog into a gem.

- Don't be cross with this dog.

- Proceed slowly, using miniscule approximations (teaching steps) so he can tuck some success under his belt.

- Show indifference to error, rather than show your own frustration. If you are like me and have a low tolerance for frustration and show it, do what I do. When I got my Border Collie, after years of terriers, it was yet another culture shock. The terriers require a bit of assertive handling and after years of them training me, I am up for that. However, I found if I said a cross word to the terriers (which bothered them not in the least) or even sounded a bit disgruntled, my Border Collie would fling herself to the floor in an apologetic fit. The sad thing about this scenario is that the Collie was not in trouble, inevitably I was giving one of the terriers a piece of my mind. This was not going to do at all. The house was chock-full of terriers, and some of them were young, so attrition was not going to solve my problem. I have habits, too, and some of them

were not going to go away. The occasional outburst is excellent for my mental health. I wasn't going to suddenly turn into Miss Merry Sunshine. When Rylie was a puppy, there were seven or eight terriers in the house, as well as my Shepherd, a teen-age daughter and a husband. I love them all more than life itself, but it is not all goodness and light in such a household. Cross words were spoken and were going to continue to be spoken. I developed a rather convoluted way of dealing with the dilemma. When I was keeping the terriers toeing the line or "discussing" things with Abbey (daughter) or Steve (husband), I would run for the treat jar, call Rylie over and feed her treats for as long as the tone of voice wasn't all brightness and light. After a couple of days of this, she was very excited when I became temperamental and would eagerly rush over to me, tail wagging, as I upbraided a member of the family. My family found it a bit unnerving and distracting to the matter at hand, and I often forgot what I was chastising the chastisee for; but the Border Collie toughened up nicely under my tutelage.

• Once you establish a good communication system and have "predictable" body language, this dog can become surprisingly tough and is an absolute joy to work with once confidence has been gained.

• Avoid confusing the worrier. He has enough to worry about without being confused, too. In fact, a great deal of anxiety is caused by confusion. If you work on the confusion, perhaps the anxiety will take care of itself.

• Do not let the dog's anxiety cause you to "feel sorry" for her and stop training her, or (the death knell) show her how bad you feel that she is exhibiting anxiety. This will quickly create an anxious, manipulative neurotic.

• Be consistent, persistent and quietly insistent when he has anxious moments during training. To prevent anxiety during training make your approximations smaller.

For more about approximations:

Refer to *Clear Criteria* on page 104.

Refer to *Successive Approximations* on page 105.

The Real Deal Neal: A True Alpha

Normally the word "alpha" would never pass my lips. This word has been ridiculously over-used to explain dog behaviour by many who do not have a clue of the true meaning of the word. However, I have occasionally come across dogs who do rather fill this bill. This is not a learning style. This is a state of being. This dog, if dropped into a wild dog pack, would be either on top of the heap or gladly die trying. This is not something the dog "chooses" to do: it is a fire that burns from within. Usually a calm, confident and clear-headed type, this type of dog can also display tendencies that humans misinterpret as "bullying." (I think of the true bully as a dog who lacks self-confidence, more of an alpha-wannabe than the real deal.) As long as other dogs are cooperative, have excellent social manners and never cross the line, this dog is polite, mildly aloof and will play when it is her own idea. She is happy to engage in mutual grooming and is confidently friendly with other dogs. However, if a dog crosses the line, ignores signals or - heaven forbid - challenges this dog, there will be swift and terrible action. Some dogs of this type are quite capable of killing another dog over status-related disagreement.

I am not talking alpha in the context of dog to human relationships. I don't even think about alpha in the context of dog-to-human relationships. I am speaking of dog-to-dog relationships. It is possible for a dog to be very dominating and even murderous with other dogs and yet be kind and not at all aggressive with people. Still, the dog who is very commanding around other dogs has an air about him that will be evident in all that he does. The confidence level on this dog is very high and she is not the type to give in or give up easily.

This kind of dog is powerful and aware. In the hands of a passive or hesitant handler, this dog is dangerous, as his drive to be in charge of his environment can easily get him into trouble if he does not have someone he will look to for guidance.

• This is a super dog if managed beautifully and will be one of the most notable dogs you will ever have the pleasure to be associated with. Owning two of these animals simultaneously is not at all recommended. I speak from personal experience.

• Handle this dog in a workmanlike manner and do not be patronizing. Allow this dog to work and problem solve.

- Once a working partnership is formed, this dog is dependable and predictable as long as he has the type of person who is capable of providing strong leadership. This dog is looking for a competent partner, otherwise she will tend to "take care of" the owner. This can lead to problematic behaviour, because dogs do not have human judgment.

- This type of dog is not all that common.

The Predatory Dog

This is another category in which the genetic component is strong and has great impact upon the dog's learning style. The predatory dog is one who is described as "drive-y" and is sometimes insanely so. The more predatory the dog is the more he will exhibit the following traits:

- Hyper aware of environment.

- Bred to be "high-in-drive."

- Easily switches from playful behaviour to a more intense, serious behaviour.

- Obsessive behaviour over objects or watching motion.

- Easily aroused by the environment, particularly motion.

- Extremely interested in scenting and tracking, hard to break off scent.

- Possibly higher incidences of possessive aggression.

There is an edge to this dog's play, whether it is with other dogs or with people. In fact, for this dog, what people might commonly be thinking of as playful contexts really are not. This dog takes each encounter very seriously. I have had Smooth Fox Terriers that would kill another dog over a hose or sprinkler that was spewing water. This was a prey object, and it was *her* prey object. When Zasu "plays" with the hose I don't allow any other dogs near her, and the same holds true for the Wiggly Giggly™ ball. Zasu isn't playing with these items, she is hunting, and she takes her hunting very seriously. With all other toys, she plays fine with others, it is just these two items that she will guard fiercely. In predatory behaviour you often see tendencies towards possessive aggression as well. The average dog is not nearly so extreme, thank goodness. The dog that tugs fiercely and obsessively or the dog that goes entirely Hindbrain when he sees his ball, is exhibiting predatory behaviours. Predation is a great trait, as

long as it is tempered with training and impulse control. This dog is a fantastic performance dog, but is less desirable as a pet, as he tends to be much too high-powered and require too much management for the average dog owner.

- I begin these dogs with Mirror & Switch games (described in the DVD and also refer to *Mirror & Switch Games* on page 284.) as soon as possible. Switching games are all about teaching the dog to come from Hindbrain to Frontbrain, and they all involve using exciting prey objects, obtaining calm work while in the presence of the prey object and then rewarding with the prey object.

- Since predatory dogs tend to be real Hindbrainers, the more you practice gaining control of the dog around prey objects and motion, the better off you will be. Do not encourage this dog to engage in predatory behaviours that do not include you (like squirrel chasing). The only possible way you will ever get a handle on this dog is if the dog believes that he needs you to provide him with prey opportunities.

- I do not allow other people to play ball or roughhouse with this dog. I do not trust others to have the kind of judgment required to keep a good balance with this dog. I do not like this dog to think that he can access prey activities with just anyone, because others will not provide the structure and will encourage this dog to behave in a wild and uncontrollable manner.

For more information about predatory behaviour see: *Prey/Predator Paradigms and How They Affect You* on page 67..

The Normal Dog

A dog of sound temperament, raised by normal human beings who understand the species. When I meet these dogs and their handlers, I want to weep with joy. I do not come across this sort often because I work with problem dogs much of the time. This dog is well socialized and has no neuroses. He recovers easily and quickly from stressful situations. This dog sees himself in context with other dogs and people in a cooperative and social way. He seeks advice from his handler, is confident enough to have an opinion, but also open to suggestion. I always hope these glorious dogs have owners who appreciate them, because there just aren't that many about.

- All you have to do with this dog is not screw it up. This is difficult if the handler is competitive.

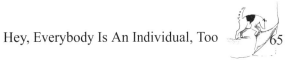

Because this dog is so cooperative and will try hard for you, it is easy to push him too far, too fast. This can lead to mental stress and physical injuries.

- This dog is surprisingly easy to be cross with. Because the dog is such a saint - the picture of sanity - and takes such good care of the owner, when the dog shows any signs of being mortal, the owner becomes disgruntled. Make sure you do not develop unreasonable expectations of this excellent dog.

I have had a couple of dogs who learned so quickly that when they did struggle with an exercise it made me feel impatient. One of them was my dearest dog, Maeve. Maeve learned the entire Competition Obedience retrieve exercise, start to finish, in about ten minutes. No exaggeration. I don't mean just putting together the components - I mean I taught her a Stay at Heel, Fetch, Front presentation with the dumbbell, Deliver, and Return to Heel in ten minutes. Before we started she knew where Heel position was and where Front position was. The multi-tasking of carrying and coming to Front and so on, as well as the fact that she had never seen a dumbbell before, was all included in that whirlwind ten minutes. She chewed on the dumbbell once on the first Front, and I touched her chin gently and said in a soft voice, "Don't chew." That was it. Perfect every time. Well, sure, we needed a bit of generalization, but the Acquisition phase of the behaviour was behind us. She learned most of her work this quickly. When I began teaching her footstep tracking, she made it clear that she preferred to quarter and mix air and ground scent instead of carefully moving slowly from footstep to footstep. I found myself getting impatient with her progress on occasion, feeling as if she should be "getting it" much sooner than she was.

In contrast, Breanna required meticulous planning and execution of each task. The approximations had to be small, each separate helper cue carefully faded. She did not generalize for nothin'. She was a tedious learner, with one advantage: once she had it, she had it. That, of course, is just the learning part; there was still no guarantee about the performance part. She was the type of dog, who, after learning a behaviour well would still come up with, "Silly. You *know* we don't Heel with *those* shoe-laces." I had endless patience with Breanna, because I began the task of teaching her with her learning style in mind. I was used to Maeve learning quickly and intuitively, and, on the one or two occasions when she didn't, I would feel impatient.

Breanna required ten times the effort, and when she would make even a tiny leap in understanding that I wasn't expecting, I would feel jubilant. Perception is a funny thing and is sometimes based on relativity, which can make for a bit of backwards thinking. I would urge you to keep your perspective and to have realistic expectations. Maeve didn't deserve one second of my impatience, and yet I would have to periodically remind myself of that - it should have been obvious to me.

Hey, Everybody Is An Individual, Too

Prey/Predator Paradigms and How They Affect You

(Oh, By The Way: Training Transcends Species)

My Fascination With Different Species

I have spent countless hours just sitting and watching animals. All kinds. I have been fascinated by animal behaviour since I was a small child. I would sit and watch the animals on the farm, the chickens, cats, and horses, for hours. Donning gloves, I took my dad's hunting hounds and upland game dogs out on a line and watched their hunting behaviour as they dragged me through the field, my child's body airborne more often than not. As an adult and after I got my Border Collie, I added sheep to our menagerie. Of course, I adore sheep and find them to be intriguing and amusing creatures with unexpected and delightful behavioural traits.

Prey Vs. Predator

Because I train across species, I have thought a lot about how many differences, and yet how many similarities, exist between species. One useful paradigm for training is to look at the predominant characteristics of major groups, then compare and contrast. For our immediate purposes, let us split mammals into two very basic categories - Prey or Predator. When people think of these two categories they tend to over-generalize. This leads to thinking that those classified as "predators" only exhibit one class of behaviour and that "prey animals" exhibit a polarized class of behaviour. In reality animals are much more complex and resist such pigeon-holing. When you are training, this type of narrow thinking can lead you into dead-end paths. Sheep, chickens and horses are classified as prey animals. Dogs are classified primarily as "predators." They are sometimes called social predators, and many ethologists quite correctly classify dogs as scavengers. But the most common way the average person on the street thinks about dogs is as predators. Indulge me in a bit of politically-incorrect stereotyping to illustrate. Timid, insecure people, people who are bullies, or

women who are worried about danger, are just some reasons why a person might like the thought of a "predator" by their side. I like having my German Shepherd around my house at night when I am alone. Some adolescent men, predator-like themselves, like the thought of a bad-ass predator on the end of the leash. We don't think of young toughs as carrying kittens around, or walking a fluffy lamb around the 'hood to be cool. Nor do we usually recommend that women living alone get a Guard Rabbit. So let's list some basic, general facts. Then explore them with curiosity, seeing where the process takes us.

Characteristics Of Prey Vs. Predator

Prey animals are those such as sheep, horses, rabbits: those animals who are hunted and consumed by carnivores. They do not consume other animals as a protein source.

Predators are those such as wolves, tigers, cheetahs: those animals who hunt and eat other animals. These animals eat other animals as a protein source.

When you discuss prey vs. predator it is important to keep in mind that these classifications involve behaviour patterns that evolved over time as basic survival strategies for a species. These traits help the prey animal survive hunters and aid hunters in getting a meal.

Prey animals have some basic hard-wired characteristics:

- Cautious, with flight and avoidance used as prevalent strategies.

- Almost never approach something directly; usually use an indirect and cautious approach, referred to as Approach And Retreat. Basically, the animal will approach the object of curiosity. Then she will re-approach, and repeat this process until she feels safe. In many cases prey animals depend on avoidance, leaving the area if something bothers them even slightly, or is novel (new).

Predators have some basic hard-wired characteristics:
- Bold, likely to move towards objects of curiosity and begin to poke, paw and bite it. Fight is the prevalent strategy.

- Direct approaches. Predators, if they are interested in something, walk right up to it and get it. Predators may charge or run up to others and immediately initiate social interaction. Some individuals exhibit greeting behaviour that is status-related rather than friendly.

Nature.

If we take those two very different behavioural tendencies, you can easily see that all animals do a little bit of each. The behaviour predominantly displayed - whether prey or predator - has a lot to do with *nature* - hard-wired, inherited behaviours that are typical to the entire species. You could also loosely relegate genetic behaviours to this category, at least for our purposes. A propensity towards the trait of being reactive, predatory or cautious - all have a strong genetic component.

Nurture

Then there is *nurture*. Nurture has to do with learning. Much of learning depends upon context: how a specific environment impacts learning and behaviour. "What is going on RIGHT NOW in THIS particular environment and how will I react/respond to it?" is a question that has multiple answers depending upon an individual's experiences. Nurture has to do with what that individual animal's experiences have taught her about consequences, establishing patterns and cause and effect. These items influence learned behaviour.

"Take an acorn, put it in the ground, it grows and becomes an oak. That is man. Man develops from an egg, and grows into the whole man, and that is the law that is in him. . . As each plant, each tree grows from a seed and becomes in the end, say, an oak tree, so man becomes what he is meant to be. At least he ought to get there. But most get stuck by unfavourable external conditions, by all sorts of hindrances or pathological distortions, wrong education - no end of reasons why one shouldn't get there where one belongs."

C.G. Jung in an interview with Stephen Blake.

Prey Animals Exhibiting Predator Behaviour

My observations and field experience led me to refine the Prey/Predator paradigm and think about it in a specific way: both prey and predator strategies are hard-wired. I have seen prey animals, like my sheep and my horse, chase animals that come into the pasture, just as my dog would. Chasing is something you would normally think of as "predator" behaviour; but it is commonly observable in prey animals. I have three sheep that love to chase cats. In fact, Katherine is so keen to chase cats that, when she was a small enough sheep to do so, she would wiggle her fat bottom underneath the gate when she spotted a cat and tear off across the yard after her hapless victim until she'd tree'd the cat. I had a Morgan mare, Sally, that delighted in chasing birds out of her pasture, snorting and posturing, pleased with her territorial aggression.

Predators Exhibiting Prey Behaviour

Dogs that are frightened of something act less like the predator they are most often thought to be, and a lot more like a prey animal. They use an Approach And Retreat strategy, or they just plain old retreat. Dogs are often cautious about novel objects or circumstances and spook away from objects just as a horse would. When anxious, like all the other animals I work with, dogs move *into* pressure, leaning on their owner when they are anxious, much as sheep lean on each other (an aspect of the flocking instinct) or people they know when they feel anxious or threatened. I have had sheep pick me up and carry me about when I am standing in the middle of my flock when they have gotten startled, because they press so tightly together in that circumstance. I have had dogs nearly knock me over in reaction to anxiety. When you are leading a horse and he becomes anxious, oddly enough, he will often press into you, as if he would like to get on your lap. This is disconcerting in an animal so large. Dogs will climb right up your poor little body, clawing and pressing into you. The point I am trying to make is that animals convey a wide range of behaviour and that thinking with an open mind about this topic can aid us in our understanding. Just because you own a dog does not mean that other species do not have valuable lessons to teach you.

Training Transcends Species

The premier trainers of domestic prey (flight strategy) animals are horse trainers and bird trainers. Much of this program is based on work I have used successfully with animals you would consider prey animals - horses and sheep - as well as limited, but satisfactory (although occasionally violent), experience with my daughter's Sun Conure parrot (birds can bite hard). So why would you want to do this stuff with a dog? Because, if you follow my line of thinking, dogs can benefit from the same kinds of paradigm shift that we commonly use with horses. Spooky, reactive dogs are unpleasant and unhappy, not to mention that they can be dangerous. For horse trainers, when 1000+ pounds becomes reactive it can be quite alarming. Safety for horse and handler is crucial, not just for successful training outcomes, but for survival of the training process at all. Therefore, horse trainers take Hindbrain, flight behaviours very seriously. It is already well accepted amongst dog trainers that techniques developed for working with marine mammals work great across species: from dogs to cats to llamas. You make allowances for each species, taking that specie's traits into account as you adapt the training system to the species and the individual animal you are training. For instance, I don't even try to teach my dog to go to an underwater target and hover there as a marine mammal trainer might do with a porpoise. However, I Clicker trained my dog to run to a target, sit and face me; and I Clicker trained my horse to trot out to a soccer ball, station there and wait. I used liver bits with the dog and carrots with the horse. The horse was more cautious in his initial approach to the target, but by golly, with allowances for the species, the grand result was the same: I got a Send Away and Wait There.

This information is relevant because when an animal is frightened, no matter their classification, they behave in a predominantly "prey-like" way. A scared or nervous dog behaves very similarly to my scared or nervous sheep or horse. I started to wonder if techniques that worked really well with horses, a sceptical and cautious species that displays predominantly flight-based behaviour, would work well with dogs. I travelled down this path because I saw so many spooky, cautious and panicky dogs and there seemed to be so few techniques available. Most of the techniques relied heavily upon treats. The problem was, some of the dogs I work with are so stressed they will not accept a treat, particularly some of the boarding dogs that came to stay and had never been boarded before, or dogs who were in rescue or shelter situations. In order to help these dogs I had to find ways to work with them that did not rely entirely upon the dog being hungry and relaxed enough to take a treat. I wanted to be able to reassure these dogs that the environment was safe so they could relax. Five years later I felt I had adapted a series of techniques that are tried and true in the horse world to a different species: our friend the dog. The better I understood the "prey animal" pattern of thought, the more effective I became in working with anxious dogs, spooky dogs, nervous dogs and insecure dogs.

Prey/Predator Paradigms and How They Affect You

Prey Animals Acting Like Predators

When the hunter becomes the hunted...Arthur, one of my lambs, spots an intruder in his realm. He checks the cat for prey potential by running towards it at a fast clip. Then he chases Mosley, the cat, across the pasture, hippity-hop. In the bottom photograph, Mosley has run up an old fence post in search of a safe harbour away from the wicked predacious sheep!

Prey/Predator Paradigms and How They Affect You

Here Arthur, the predator sheep, holds his ground as the cat glares at him from her safe perch. He may not have the wicked tools a "predator" has, but he's got the attitude!

Photo essay by Mary Wilmoth.

Sheep Moving Into Pressure

Sheep press into the shepherd in reaction to an anxiety-producing stimulus.

These sheep and the dogs in the photographs that follow are exhibiting aspects of the opposition reflex.

Photograph by Dave Schrader

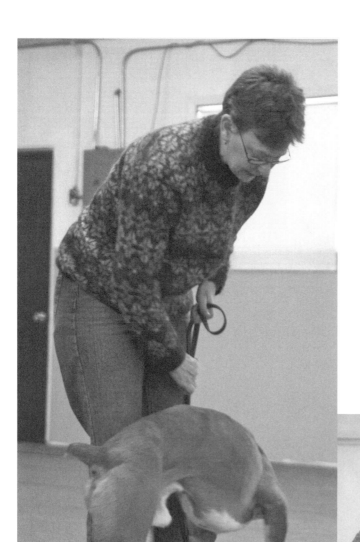

Dog Moving Into Pressure In Response To Anxiety

Just as the sheep in the previous photograph, these dogs exhibit the same "moving into pressure" behaviour when they are anxious.

This Boxer has just been picked up from a dog shelter and came to me for an evaluation. All of this change is very stress-producing. In this photograph he is in a very agitated state. He seems excited about greeting a person, yet uneasy about it at the same time. His body is very tense and he is "moving into pressure" just as the sheep do when they are uneasy and worried.

This puppy is worried about people approaching him. When approached he does not retreat, but instead "moves into" the pressure. His body tension is great, so he is not leaning into me in an affectionate way. You can tell this also by his forward commissure (shortened lips) and the puckered tension around his lips. In fact, in this photograph, he is opening his mouth to bite at my hands.

Photographs by Dave Schrader

Why Do I Want My Dog To Have A Paradigm Shift?

Isn't His Current Paradigm Just Fine?

Why Dogs Need A Paradigm Shift

If it were possible for dogs to have human judgment, the hard-wired paradigm they come with would be just fine. Since dogs do not have human judgment sometimes their fixed action patterns (instinctive behaviour) are the cause of problems in their relationships with people. Dogs wouldn't need different judgment than what they were born with, except for the fact they are living mostly in a human world, rather than among native speakers of their own language - other dogs. Yet, we expect dogs to function in our human environment. The fact that they are living with people in relatively artificial circumstances than genetically prepared for, means that they need different judgement than what they were born with.

If we really loved dogs as a species, why bother training them? Just let them mark (urinate on) the sofa (and the Christmas Tree). Allow your dog to play tug-of-war with your clothing. Let your dog growl and chase you away from your plate at the dinner table. Don't be unreasonable: be sure to let your dog bite guests to repel them away from the yard and house. The real truth is we don't love dogs, we love well-trained dogs that are fun to live with and provide companionship.

Training dogs has less to do with dogs than it does with people. Animals who live a totally natural life do not require training by humans at all. Training has to do with making dogs comfortable with the inevitable requests that humans will make and generating obedient responses so that we can keep our dogs safe in the world of humans in which they live.

Dogs Do Not Necessarily Feel Safe With Human Greetings

Because all of those things dogs will naturally do are most emphatically *not* okay in human world, you have to train your dog. The first naive assumptions people make are that dogs love to be touched and that, because they know "we love them," are never made uneasy by our touch or our approaches. The truth is, touch and other human greeting behaviours are frequently perceived by a dog as threatening, intrusive or frightening. People expect dogs to "just get it" in regards to touch and approaches. People misinterpret anxiety as excitement, because it would never enter their thoughts that the dog doesn't see the world the same way they do. After all, "dogs are man's best friend," "we are soul-mates," and "my dog understands every word I say." Unfortunately this kind of thinking, while very romantic, may blind people to their dog's needs. Just as in child-rearing, love is not enough. A well-adjusted and happy dog requires much more than love, she requires training by an understanding owner who is well-grounded in the real world.

Very few people use a systematic desensitization program to make certain that their dog is comfortable with all kinds of touches and petting or feels safe when people bend over, stare and reach for her. When we do train dogs, we assume that dogs are comfortable with the way humans interact with them while being trained way too much of the time. Because people do not recognize what dogs are telling them, they are not proactive and prepared for undesirable behaviour. Then when the dog lets us know, with reactivity, fear and aggression, that we neglected her education, we get all bent out of shape. I know there are many dogs out there that love to be touched. I also absolutely know that there is a much higher percentage of dogs than people suspect who detest touch or who are made anxious by touch and common human greeting rituals. They hang back or are particularly hectic during greetings. This misperception that dogs are okay with touch is perpetrated because the vast majority of dog owners have no idea how to read a dog: that is they do not have a very extensive understanding of the dog's native language and viewpoints.

How Dogs See The World

The Get Connected protocol makes some assumptions, too. These are based on a dog paradigm, not on a human's personal view of the world. The dog paradigm is:

- Dogs do not like to be touched - unless it is their idea.

- Dogs find primate greeting behaviours to be threatening and to contain easily misinterpreted and confusing body language.

- Dogs assume eye contact is dangerous or disrespectful, because dog-to-dog, it is.

- Dogs will try to "converse" with you as if you are a dog.

- Dogs have a strong opposition reflex.

    The opposition reflex (technically, positive thigmotaxis) is a reflexive behaviour wherein the animal *moves into a source of pressure*. This is a very complex behavioural phenomenon which shows itself in many different ways, one of which is the dog pulling on the leash when walked.

- Dogs *move into pressure* (physical pressure) when they:

    are anxious
    are defensive
    are frightened
    are panicky
    wish to get attention
    wish to check social organization or gain status
    are frustrated

Dogs also might press against you, in an entirely different way than I am describing above, to show affection. An example of this is when your dog rests his head lightly on your leg and looks at you in a loving way. Another example is a dog who comes over and presses her face lightly into your leg, perhaps in a way reminding herself of the comfort of being next to her mother while nursing. The difference and the way you can distinguish the two is the amount of body tension accompanying the pressure.

Get Connected Protocol Uses A Dog's Point Of View

Therefore, the Get Connected protocol is designed to take the dog's natural assumptions and native language into account. Through various proven techniques, we will ask the dog to take their basic precepts that "come hard-wired," and look at them differently. That is, we will teach the dog that:

- human touch is safe, not dangerous.

- Primate greeting behaviour is different than canine greetings, but it is friendly - not threatening.

- Eye Contact with humans will be used as an *emotional anchor* and is a signal to people of respect and attention. Eye Contact is, above all, safe.

- Human body language can be understood. This is virtually impossible if your body language is inconsistently presented to the dog. This program helps to teach YOU to use your body language in a consistent way so your dog can learn the correct interpretation. For instance, if you look relaxed, your dog should be able to say (Yikes, the anthropomorphizing meter is on High) "I feel a little nervous, but my mom's body language looks like this is a safe person approaching, so it is safe. I can relax."

- The opposition reflex can be thought about in a different way. One reason dogs pull on the leash and leap on you is because of their opposition reflex. By teaching your dog to move away from pressure on certain cues (overcoming her natural reactions) and to approach you when requested, the dog gets the benefit of avoiding your irritation and you get a well-behaved dog.

- A spooky, cautious dog can learn to feel comfortable and more confident in any environment. The exact same exercises will teach pushy, assertive dogs or physically insensitive dogs (like Larry Labrador) about personal space and how to be more respectful and sensitive to humans.

- Attention seeking dogs can learn to ask politely to get what they want instead of being rude, irritating and annoying to get their needs met.

- All dogs can feel more comfortable because they know and understand the rules.

Dogs Need To Learn Spatial Awareness. People Need To Learn "The Game."

Dogs do not necessarily understand that others occupy space and have matter. Some dogs are much too sensitive and spooky. Others act as if you do not exist at all. Still others use their powerful body to intimidate and hurt other dogs and humans. The work in this protocol is the equivalent of providing some simple physics lessons to the dog so she understands that humans occupy space and matter and have personal space boundaries. It teaches humans a lot about how the dog perceives social maneuvering and trust. It teaches dogs to have spatial awareness. It teaches humans how to be consistent with body language messages given to dogs. One of the most gratifying results of this work is to observe the instant awareness and regard that pushy dogs show to you when you show them you can play "The Game." Sometimes dogs have been allowed to take advantage of people to the extent that the dogs are injuring people. The dog does not understand that she is causing harm, it is up to people to teach the dog manners so that she does not knock guests over or flatten toddlers to the floor. The Game involves understanding that the dog has feelings and opinions and a language. The Game also involves understanding how to negotiate in a way the dog understands instinctively, because you are using teaching tools that dogs know about and use with each other. This does not involve violence, alpha-rolls, yelling or collar corrections. It does involve learning more about how your dog perceives his world and perhaps about leaving some of your own preconvceived notions out of the picture.

You see, most people don't know how to play "The Game." Heck, they don't even know there is a game going on, let alone have an understanding of any of the rules! Understanding "The Game" will teach you how to read dogs better. And dogs are gratified that you made the effort to understand their language. Dogs will also learn how to read humans better, which improves the relationship between the two of you and makes your dog a safer and more polite citizen. It makes you more aware of your dogs needs and better able to meet them.

If you and your dog are playing the same game it will be easier to be in concert with each other. And if you are going to play a new game, the first question people always ask is," What are the rules?" The Get Connected protocol provides a set of rules for people and dogs to follow, so that cooperation, instead of resistance, becomes the common thread throughout your communications.

Do Not Leave Safety To Chance

To accomplish these lofty goals, you must set out, in a systematic and logical way, to educate the dog. If the dog learns the lesson in one trial, great. If the dog already seems to know the lesson, fantastic! He figured it out on his own. But, no longer are you going to "leave it to chance" - only to discover that your dog doesn't like people to do things like, grab him by collar, and, Surprise! Your neighbor visits the emergency room and you get to pay the bill and the legal fees!

Dogs Are Resistant For A Variety Of Reasons. Still, Approach Each Dog As If She Is Pure Of Heart.

For all dogs, I first give them the benefit of the doubt, and approach them as if they have a pure heart, a willing mind and hold cooperation foremost in their thoughts. This is quite true of most dogs. *When presented with material in a way that makes sense to them, they learn quickly and are dependable.* Even the "hard to train breeds" become more compliant when the material is presented clearly and their communication needs are met. Dogs are resistant, hyper and uncooperative because humans communicate so poorly and, out of ignorance, encourage, tolerate and actively reinforce Hindbrain behaviour patterns. These dogs are merely confused and have given up talking to humans because it is a sad waste of their time. Some dogs have been given the wrong idea, again out of ignorance on the part of their human handlers. They think they are the boss of you instead of you being the boss of them. The Get Connected protocol can right this "wrong" thinking on the part of the dog. People need to be the boss of dogs, because dogs are not capable of human judgment. Not being the boss of your dog is the height of irresponsibility. Bosses should be fair, strong, trusted resources for their employees. You should be a fair, strong, trusted and wonderfully loving boss of your dog. Dog owners make the same mistakes that some parents make: they want to be friends with their toddlers. You need to be the parent of the toddler, so the toddler can grow up to be your friend. You need to be the boss of your dog to keep your dog safe and secure, so you can have your dog as a loving and well-mannered companion.

Love is enhanced by respect. A respectful and trusting relationship is evident in a million satisfying ways. I know you want your dog to like you and love you. The safest and most loving way to live with your dog is to take the responsibility and the time to gain her respect in a way that she understands. Become relevant to your dog by using language she understands.

How Dogs Determine Who Has Authority

In the animal world, who moves whose feet is a big deal. This will be outlined as we do the exercises. You want to be directing your dog's movements so you can keep him safe and help him to feel secure. Leaders in the canine world control two very important resources:

- Food. You do this by using a scheduled feed and by using treats to train and using Positive Reinforcement correctly. Food is a tool to further information, not a random hand out. The type of treats you use to train, the reinforcement schedule (Refer to "Engineering Reinforcement Schedules" on page 99.) and good timing all convey information.

- Locations. By directing the dog's movement with your body language, precise cue systems (how you present and teach the cue) and using Stays. This is what the Get Connected protocol is designed to do: control movement, therefore, by extension, you are controlling locations.

Horse trainers have a philosophy about this "moving of the feet." It cannot be a random act: it has to be deliberate and systematic. Natural horsemanship trainers have promoted this philosophy and made it attainable by giving the rest of us recipes. "Control the feet to control the mind," they say. Dressage trainers say the same thing, albeit using very different words. This is grossly oversimplified, but basically everything you do in dressage is pretty much about precisely placing the horse's inside hind foot where you want it using primarily your balance and your seat bones.

All riders want to control the horse so he is safe and a joy to ride; otherwise his natural tendency to run from everything and to get "predators" off his back will end up getting the rider injured or killed. The Olympic rider, Lendon Gray, expresses this concept in an appealing down-to-earth way: "I can talk half-halts and engagement and "classical" riding from back to front until I am blue in the face, but that critter won't lighten up until you find a system for separating his big, strong, uneducated body into smaller parts - hind end, middle, front end - that you can talk to and control individually (and, therefore, more easily)." (Gray, 2003) She is saying that you can talk philosophy and perfection until the cows come home, but what you really need to do is get control of the engine (hind quarters) and steering (front quarters).

Control the feet to control the mind. The universal wish to partner up with an animal and "feel as one" crosses species, too. An animal who is bigger than you, like a horse, is a challenge, but so is the dog who is faster than you are and more nimble! The common thread among animal trainers is that wish to communicate so effectively with another species that we feel a bond: a lifting of our heart as we connect.

The Function Of Subordinates

Years ago I read a lovely statement and apologize for not remembering the source. The premise was that followers give leaders authority. This is a very effective way to look at the balance of authority in a relationship and how the needs of the participants are different and how elegantly social structure can meet those needs.

While at a seminar, GaWaNi Pony Boy, a Native American horse trainer, was speaking to us of groups of animals and how individuals learn to function within a group. His comment was, loosely quoted,

"The subordinate members of a social group have a very important function." I was fascinated by this comment. It was looking at the world upsidedown, if you will, since we tend to emphasize the function of the leaders of groups. He continued on to tell us what that very important function is: to test the leadership. If the group doesn't have a good leader, then all the members suffer. This is food for thought, and his discourse helped me to make a paradigm shift. It helped me to overcome the feelings of frustration and, yes indeedy, resentment when a "student," canine, equine, ovine or human, questions my judgment, resists instead of cooperates and just is generally pig-headed. Now I figure the student is just trying to test if I am a good enough leader. This paradigm really helped me to think about leaders and followers in a non-confrontational way. I think about negotiation skills and good communication instead of frustration.

This paradigm is handy when I am speaking in front of people at clinics and I get a "heckler." You know, one of those who is really not interested in the learning process, but is there to "prove" something about themselves and are using me to do it. Or when my students, who are much less experienced that I am, argue with me about how to train a behaviour that I have seen more permutations of than they ever will. And, of course, when I am working with a dog who does not agree with my point of view, nor I with hers. (Yes, dogs quite definitely have opinions and may not share my point of view! I am pretty convinced that when I scoop cat feces out of the litter box and bag them up for the trash, the dogs think I am selfishly keeping all the "tootsie rolls" for myself.) This really helps me to keep my temper in check and my mind in a thinking state, so I can help the dog or a beloved student. Quite honestly, the heckler is on her/his own.

I never wanted to have to be a leader. It is a lot more work. Thinking of myself as a leader, I thought, meant my dog and I weren't "partners." I felt it had to be a 50/50 deal, or we weren't really partners. I wanted to be working partners, but when the dog didn't partner up it was truly frustrating. How could I have this much work into a dog and still not get the behaviour that I wanted, indeed, had trained extensively for? How could I find this missing link? How could I satisfy my vision of the relationship and get what I wanted from the dog and have a happy, willing dog? Well, the bottom line is, if you are going to be able to walk your dog down the street, convince her to participate in dog sports, and accept territory violations (allow guests in your home), somebody has to take the role of being in charge. When a dog respects and trusts you, you have earned the right to be in charge. Your dog will happily follow your suggestions and your lead. It was my delightful Breanna, the original "Lead, Follow or Get The Hell Out Of My Way" dog that taught me you can stop a lot of chaos by being in charge, and that everyone was happier when you did.

The biggest concern that all of us have is: how do we establish this humanely and with humility and understanding and yet still convey the right message to the dog?

Respect Helps A Dog Prioritize Paying Attention To You

Respect is important in other ways, too. If you are teaching a group who is talking amongst themselves while you are talking, gazing out the window, or constantly arguing with you; you just are not going to be effective in getting your ideas across. You must be relevant to your student, or they simply won't pay attention to you. Prioritizing is a learned skill.

Use Clear Communication To Establish Boundaries First

When Abbey was little, I was a room-mother for the class room parties. After I missed a party, the majority of the other mothers came to me and wanted to reassure themselves that I would be at the rest of the parties that year: "It just went so much smoother with you there." Why? Well, the biggest reason is I got the attention and respect of the children and eliminated confusion by setting boundaries FIRST! Then we had fun. I was not going to assume that a bunch of first graders will make workable rules for a party. Common sense tells me that way lies disaster! I walked into the noisy classroom full of excited, party-obsessed children, and said in a firm voice just loud enough to be heard: "Sit down and be quiet! Two Eyes and Two Ears on me!" The children, surprised into cooperation, all sat down. Any stragglers, I hustled into their seat with further individual instructions, "Where is your seat? Let's find it shall we? We cannot begin until you are seated." I wasn't rude, just authoritative. When I had everyone's attention, I set down the rules for the party. "We are all going to have a great time, and there are rules so all of us can enjoy ourselves. If it gets too noisy, I will ask you to quiet down. If you do not, the party will change, and I will make more rules, and they will not be fun ones. You can eat sitting down at your

desk. If you spill something, let us know right away so we can help you clean up." And so on...whatever I felt was applicable. I asked if the children wanted to add any rules or comments. A couple of the kids had great suggestions. Then we all had a fun party. Of course, the children always had be reminded to quiet down once or twice, and there were the inevitable spills, but with the rules set ahead of time the kids were very cooperative. I got their respect first. I established myself as an authority figure. Then, within a defined structure, the children were free to have fun. I was able to praise them for appropriate behaviour instead of nagging them ineffectually. It worked out great. If you frame yourself as a pushover with no boundaries, and then in the middle of the party, try to establish boundaries and rules, it just plain doesn't work. When you do this, the kids feel "betrayed": "Hey, we were having a great time, then suddenly we are doing everything wrong..." I didn't assume the kids knew the rules that I, personally, had in mind. I used clear communication to establish the boundaries.

Unfairness Of Emotional Communication

The same must be done for your dog. Establish boundaries FIRST. You can be ooey-gooey once that item of business has been established and the dog understands the rules. The biggest problem with ooey-gooey is not that it is bad (I am very ooey-gooey with my own dogs), but that people misplace its use. They place the emphasis on their own emotional state. They bribe and beg and nag, then wonder why their dog takes advantage of them. Dogs take advantage of humans because they can! Worse yet, people set themselves up to be taken advantage of, but then get wrathful with the dog when he does! People tend to try to emotionally manipulate dogs using morals, kindness, guilt - and the most mis-used of all - *words* and verbal communications that convey morals, kindness and guilt. This may work for humans, but it confuses animals desperately. It makes communication grey instead of black and white. It makes boundaries unclear. It makes rules fuzzy. *It is unfair to have unclear boundaries or to not make rules, and then get upset when the dog doesn't miraculously follow those rules or crosses the hazy boundary.*

Entrapment

People do not seem to realize that when they do not take responsibility to be the leader (or at least the CEO if you are more comfortable with that lingo) they are placing undue pressure on their dog. Lack of guidance, unclear boundaries and inconsistent, changing rules make dogs horribly uncomfortable. In my mind, this is a form of abuse: you are setting the dog up to make judgment calls that he cannot possibly make, not being human. Then you get emotional (angry, disappointed, tense) when he doesn't make the right decision. When humans treat other humans that way it is called entrapment. People do not do these things on purpose. They do these things because they do not know how to communicate more effectively.

Excuse Making For Drive-y Dogs

Just as cruel are those who "love" drive-y dogs, so they encourage the dog to be hyper-active and in a Hindbrain state. These handlers usually got involved in competition work. After watching experienced handlers with high-drive performance dogs they trot right out and get themselves way too much dog. Most of us in dog sports have done this. Problems occur when owners do not know how to meet the needs of the high-drive dog, so this dog is incredibly frustrated a good deal of the time. The owner permits barking and other neurotic behaviours by ignoring them. She does not know what else to do. She mistakenly believes the dog "needs to express himself;" and if the dog is not allowed to do this, she will "ruin the drive." The intimation is that placing boundaries on the dog will ruin him for competition. These people admire their dog when he is communicating anxiety and discomfort and they misinterpret this as "in drive." Dogs that are barking uncontrollably, pulling against restraints and leaping around are not necessarily excited, happy dogs. They are incredibly frustrated dogs. These people excuse all of this by saying things like: "Oh, he's just such a Border Collie." Or insert any other breed you like. Guarding and defensive behaviour is excused the same way: "Oh, he's a German Shepherd Dog." Insert any other breed you like. Over-friendly, obnoxious dogs are excused by saying in a proud voice, "You know how Labs are..." Basically, these people excuse poor manners, anxiety, defensive behaviour and aggression by making excuses for their training program and their misinterpretation of frustration, anxiety, predation and lack of impulse control for other things. This creates astronomical amounts of stress for the dog. If you are one of these people, face it, your dog is a Hindbrainer, and you got work to do.

Excuse Making For Spooky Dogs

Then there are the over-solicitous owners of a rescue dog. They too excuse poor behaviour. By doing so, they perpetuate any abuse and neglect the dog ever faced by making too many allowances and comforting the dog whenever the dog exhibits any shyness or discomfort. If the dog runs and hides when they get out a flyswatter, abuse is assumed to be the cause of the dog's spooky behaviour. While it may be true, it is often simply not true. The dog is the victim of a neglected education, which the current owner is continuing to carry on. The timid, cautious dog can be made, certainly, but can also be born with those tendencies. Many of these dogs have genetics that predispose them to be over-cautious and frightened, then they are inadvertently reinforced for spooky behaviour. The spooky dog benefits greatly from desensitization protocols designed to help her out of the dark, scary and stifling caves of her mind where she is going to reside unless you assist her out of it. This dog is a Hindbrainer, too, and is suffering. You wouldn't like to live consumed by fear of simple, every day occurrences, and neither does your dog like this. She doesn't know she has any choices. It is your job to show her the way to confidence.

You Don't Destroy Drive With Structure And Manners

I, too have high-drive dogs that display intense behaviours. I, too own and have owned human aggressive and dog aggressive dogs. I have been dismayed when my dogs are spooky. What I do not do is avoid training these dogs by making excuses. I understand the breed and I understand the individual. I know all the triggers and practice careful management. Did I make errors? You darn betcha. Do I have the scars on my body to prove it? Yup. Because when you make training errors with reactive dogs and aggressive dogs and fearful rescue dogs, they bite. They bite each other, and they bite you. Worse yet, my dogs sometimes paid the price in stitches and injuries incurred while fighting amongst themselves because my learning curve was slow. I hate that.

After years of terriers and being blissfully unaware of typical dog behaviours like developmental fear periods," I acquired my first Border Collie. I knew all about dog fights, but had no personal experience with fear periods. You can read about fear periods, you can help clients with it, but there is nothing like living through what you've read about. In addition, I didn't really "get" how intense herding behaviour could be. As a terrier owner, I thought I had seen it all. My own sweet little Border Collie, as a youngster of four and five months old, developed an unfortunate habit. When I was running her on an agility course, if I stopped (lost, I am always lost on agility courses....) she would

come racing to me and hit me in the shoulder or face with an open-mouth correction bite. She was just "being a Border Collie." It was obviously a misplaced herding behaviour: "Move, you sticky sheep!" Understanding "why" doesn't mean that I allowed this behaviour to persist, even though she was being true to her genetics. On one level I was even quite pleased to see this indication of her instinctive need to move and manage livestock. I just needed to redirect her drive into the proper channels and let her know that I wasn't livestock. Using Positive Reinforcement first, then at an opportune time, combined with some judicial and carefully timed Move Into maneuvers (The Move Into exercises are detailed in the section *Get Connected Exercises*), she quickly learned that if mom is lost, give her a second, Lie Down and wait for further instructions. She still has plenty of drive to burn, but now she knows when that kind of intensity is appropriate. Not allowing the behaviour to be used inappropriately did not destroy her drive. She runs agility with single-minded intensity, herds sheep wonderfully (considering her handler handicap) and heels with joy and precision.

The point here is that the best working dogs, whether that means a great lap dog or a top-of-the-line performance dog or a working farm dog, does her very best work when she has excellent concentration and impulse control skills. The wild and fast, but impulsive, Hindbrain dog cannot offer you the excellent performance that a quick-thinking, responsive Frontbrain dog can. She cannot even come close. The best performance comes from the dog who is able to switch quickly back and forth from Hindbrain to Frontbrain, offering everything they are.

Dogs Need Ways To Learn That Make Sense To Them.

You Must Have An Effective Technique. Talking Isn't It.

You cannot teach a dog a task using the same methods that you would use with a person. Sure, the learning theory itself crosses over, but when you teach a person a task, the most commonly used tool is the spoken or written word. Even all people cannot learn the same task the same way. Think of teaching a child to read. Then try to teach a dyslexic child using the same method. It just doesn't work. You can certainly teach a dyslexic child to read: there is nothing wrong with their *ability* to learn or their IQ. You just need to use the right methodology. Dogs are not out to get it wrong and be frustrating to you any more than the dyslexic child is trying to get it wrong. Dogs come with relatively cooperative natures. No doubt, some individuals are more cooperative than others! Still, the biggest single problem with cooperation is caused by humans, not dogs. *Humans are excellent at teaching their dog to ignore them.*

In Learning Theory this is called Learned Irrelevance. Learned Irrelevance happens when you are inconsistent. It happens when you threaten and complain, but never actually get your lazy bum off the sofa to "make it so." It happens when you do not have good ways to communicate what you want, so your dog becomes confused and frustrated. It happens when you fail to reward naturally occurring desired behaviour. So, get a plan, *then be consistent in word and deed.* Before you can cue for a behaviour, it must be learned, and once it is, don't ask for it unless you plan to make it so. Be a good consequence provider, be consistent and be aware of opportunities to reward your dog for making desired decisions.

People do not teach their dogs to ignore them intentionally, but they do a great job at it all the same!

How? Instead of teaching the dog in clear, concise methodology, people tend to attempt to "talk" their dogs into minding. This doesn't work because dogs do not speak any human native tongues. They lack a speech center in their brain that would correspond to the human brain, so human language acquisition in the dog is much more limited than with a human student. To target the right population, it helps to use the right method.

Good Training Transcends Philosophies

The scientific fields of behaviorism and cognition both have information that is relevant to dog training. Nancy Taylor, a clinician who works with teachers on a national level, says it beautifully, "Tell your students they first must 'Memorize the Recipe.' Then, when they are proficient, they will become creative."

In order to make really good pies, first you have to follow the recipe religiously to establish a "control. Then you can begin to tweak your "proven" recipe so as to make it sweeter or more spicy, the crust thinner or thicker or more flaky. To return to dog training, it took me about ten years of using Skinner-based techniques to get fluent at it. Since then, I've been tweaking...

One of the strengths of behaviorism-based Positive Reinforcement training are the great recipes. In addition:

- Animals learn from associations, and this technique recognizes that animals are good at picking out patterns. Dogs get ahead of people because they are considerably better at discerning patterns than people are at establishing deliberate, intended patterns.

- Animals learn from consequences. Trainers must learn how to provide appropriate and meaningful consequences so the dog has the opportunity to learn from them. The emphasis is on providing information and classically conditioning the emotional state that is bound to each behaviour.

- Trainers become really aware of their timing. This has value beyond belief.

- It gives great recipes for how to manipulate cause & effect.

- By emphasizing approximations - deliberate teaching steps - trainers are encouraged to *think* about the process and to establish goals and recognize criteria.

It is a given in my training paradigm that we are ALWAYS & FOREVER approximating behaviours: that is, one always uses tiny approximations (teaching steps) to get from unknowing-ness to the end goal.

- *When Frontbrain states are emphasized and that is what is reinforced*, it is humane. Unfortunately, this discrimination often falls by the wayside.

- Positive Reinforcement creates the beginnings of a good communication system, requisite for a satisfying relationship.

- If you are clever enough to shape behaviour and manipulate reinforcement schedules (which takes perseverance, skill and experience to do really well), you get to see out-of-this-world cool stuff. You get to see the "wheels turn" in your dog's cute little head. It doesn't get any more fun than this! Free-shaping behaviours is a hoot. This is a method whereby the handler allows the dog to lavishly experiment with behaviour and skillfully Marks *voluntary, spontaneously offered behaviours only,* that are "a step in the right direction."

- Attention is practically a by-product. This is magic!

- You get happy, creative working dogs. This is very important to me; more important than the ribbons or titles gained at a competition. Because of what I emphasize in training, my dogs tend to be very creative. If the ribbons or titles are more important to you, you may not want the creative part...Creative dogs can, in fact, be quite annoying in many circumstances. Most of my clients do not really want creative dogs, they want well-behaved dogs. You can have a creative and well-behaved dog, but quite honestly, many people do not wish to invest the time in keeping that balance. Neither preference is right or wrong: it is a personal decision.

- I love the paradigm of the "radical" behaviorist: You don't have to have a history, just work with the behaviour that you see in front of you right now. This is a particularly useful paradigm for rescue work.

- There is no better technique for acquiring behaviour. Each behaviour morphs from an infant (Acquisition - the dog doesn't even know the behaviour exists) to childhood (Generalization - performing the behaviour under gradually raising criteria) to adolescence (Fluency - automatic responses) to adulthood (Maintenance - ongoing use and repetition). Positive Reinforcement works fantastically for Acquisition and Generalization. There is nothing better.

- On a personal level, I learned to get organized, but also to enjoy the journey and to be aware of and open to suggestions made by the animal. This is valuable and enriching for me. Positive Reinforcement also fosters an upbeat attitude, and at it's best provides a safe environment for learning.

Respect Is A Crucial Part Of The Puzzle, And It Is Not Systematically Installed In Most Training Programs

If a boat is missed by trainers, this is often the one that pulls away from the dock while they are standing there watching the gap widen. When I first started with Positive Reinforcement training I was sick to death of hearing about dominance and authority. These words were so over-used by force-based training techniques that I rejected both of these ideas entirely. I took the view that it didn't matter if the dog thought she was "dominant" or not; as long as I got the behaviour I wanted, what was the problem? Years later, I see that this wasn't an issue for me because I have been working with animals my entire life and figured that taking responsibility to get the desired behaviour was my job. Getting this job done meant that I had a plan and that I took charge of the situation. I've also done this job enough times that I am confident of the outcome. This attitude gives one an authoritative demeanor, one that I developed as a child and honed as an adult - most of the time not even very aware it was happening. The animals themselves taught me the most efficient way to interact with them.

Many of my clients have not had this kind of extensive interaction with a wide variety of personality-types in animals. I do have to say that working with livestock such as cattle, sheep and horses, does give one a different patina. One develops a decisive air and learns the priceless lesson that force and physical battles are fruitless. Losing your temper with horses makes them flighty and dangerous, and if you have ever lost your temper with a cow or sheep...let's just say there is nothing more humbling than having an animal stare at you, cud-chewing and placid, then amble away while you are furious and still telling them about it. Worse yet, when you jump up and down and shake your fist, they may look at you with mild interest, but either way do not display the "respect" and validity you are longing for at that moment of frustration. Another common choice for livestock you are chastising, is to leave the area entirely, which is equally maddening. When you frighten livestock they have a tendency to leave the area at a very high rate of speed and over top your body if you happen to get in the way. If you make them angry or irritate them, they leave the area at a high speed after making certain you won't be getting up to follow them. *Animals know that emotional displays mean you are frustrated and maybe even dangerous and act accordingly.* It is easy to see that when you become over-emotional, animals get confused. I have had several animals point out to me that, if I am not going to communicate effectively, they will disregard me because they can clearly tell that I am incompetent and incomprehensible. It is difficult to trust incompetence and difficult to make sense of incomprehensible.

The most important lesson I learned from animals in general is that negotiation skills and a knowledge of the species and their native language is important. The most important lesson I learned from dogs in particular is that dominance doesn't really matter. You convey authority to dogs by persistence. *You don't dominate them, you outlast them.*

Since I cannot hand my clients an automatic air of authority, I have devised ways to help them communicate the all important message: "I am making decisions and I am relevant" to their own dogs. The topic of relevance comes up in training programs, but it is not usually discussed as a *specific set of protocols* designed to help a struggling relationship or even minor training problems. To design this set of protocols I used the lessons the animals have taught me by their own examples and feedback. The idea of outlasting the dog is something most people can do if they decide it is important enough to do so, as long as they can see they will get results using outlasting as a strategy. What I

have learned from science and my own personal experience is that Positive Reinforcement works really well, especially under closely controlled circumstances.

That established, the following list contains the items that make up the "glass ceiling" that I have hit when using Positive Reinforcement-based training programs. These are the places where Positive Reinforcement does not easily or consistently allow the trainer to unequivocally establish her relevance. One could argue, I suppose, that I didn't follow the rules of the technique perfectly and so on. From talking to dog trainers all over the United States and Canada I know the bottom line is that many experienced and competent trainers using Positive Reinforcement-based techniques will recognize the following frustrations.

Common Training Frustrations & Irritations Encountered:

The conflict between "Want-To" and "Have-To" is not adequately addressed. A subject that is inadequately addressed within Positive Reinforcement training is what Lisa Lit (clever girl with words) calls "Want-to vs. Have-to." (Lit, 2002) What if your dog understands the behaviour, has performed it on cue under a variety of circumstances, but occasionally decides to go do something else instead? Over-training, a technique used to obtain reliable behaviour, means you train for a level of performance far above what you will "settle for" or "want as the terminal response." For instance, if you want your dog to do a Group Stay at an obedience trial, then you better make certain your dog will remain in place under a variety of circumstances, such as: another dog coming up to him and sniffing; other dogs playing with a ball in the area; people walking around and dropping food nearby; people other than you shouting "Come;" and doors slamming. This technique is crucial to the success of performance dogs.

If you have not addressed over-training, your dog, quite simply, isn't trained, because she will only give you the behaviour under a very narrow band of circumstances (something trainers call "special conditions") and you have not prepared her to work under challenging circumstances. But once you have done your homework, and the dog is still deciding to go do something else, then there is a problem within the Want-to vs. Have-to category. Honestly, when my dogs fail at a

Dogs Need Ways To Learn That Make Sense To Them.

task, nine times out of ten, it is definitely my fault. But there are times when the cue is clear, the dog understands, the over-training has been accomplished, and the dog still occasionally mutinies on me: "I *will* tear off after that other dog's ball..." It is at these times that I must be able to count on my dog understanding the difference between Want-to (chase the ball) and Have-to (continue Heeling or at least stay with me so the other dog does not take offense.). We are back to the Frontbrain vs. Hindbrain states, and how to Switch them about at will - based on your judgment, not the dog's judgment. *So what is at work when you have a trained dog who still doesn't treat you as relevant?* This is a basic short-coming in most training programs: the relationship and level of trust and respect have not been adequately addressed. Oh, everybody talks about it, but it is not sought after in a systematic, deliberate fashion. The "relationship" is talked about in mystical and romantic ways, which makes for excellent reading, but is as helpful as an ancient map with no discernible landmarks in the current landscape. A blueprint is not provided about how to obtain the elusive respect and trust - which was a missing link in my own Positive Reinforcement-based training program. The Get Connected protocol is all about providing you with that blueprint. *The training process should involve always increasing the dog's comfort level with the handler.* More dogs than you would ever suspect are not as comfortable with the owner as the owner thinks the dog is.

Now that I have tossed out those very controversial words, let us define trust and respect, so we are on the same page. Many professionals become upset if we speak of dog training as anything other than "scientific" and "you should never anthropomorphize" (attributing human characteristics and emotions to non-humans). Anthropomorphism is dangerous if humans are using it out of ignorance of the species (My dog got mad at me and when I went to work he pee'd on the floor out of spite). It is recognized by many researchers of animal emotions that commonalities between animals and humans do exist. (McConnell, 2005 and Grandin, 2005.) Some anthropomorphizing occurs simply because humans are trying to express animal emotions and interpret them into our own language. As long as the animal's point of view is what is being considered as opposed to the owner projecting his own behaviour and motives onto the animal, this dialogue is valid. It is not a matter of "believing," I absolutely know that my dogs think (not exactly as I do, but think they do, nonetheless), are

cognitive, problem-solve and clearly they have opinions and emotions.

No one would ever want to admit that their dog doesn't trust them. Trust, in my own dog-training definition and description between you and your dog specifically, means that your dog feels *comfortable* with you and *safe*. If your dog will not allow you to pick up her feet to wipe them off, or clip her nails, she is telling you that she does not feel safe enough to let you "take her feet away." Having their feet taken away is a very significant event for animals and it can really frighten them, as can other forms of restraint. I know that, during the life of my dog, I will be handling her feet, holding her for the veterinarian to do mildly unpleasant husbandry work and restraining her in other ways; with fences, cages and leashes or restraining her so that she does not jump on someone's child. *The dog must be trained to trust you to do husbandry behaviours and to trust your judgment so you can keep your dog safe.* It's bad enough that I have to put in eye drops or ear drops, I do not wish the dog to be *afraid of the procedure as well*. Most dogs do not wish to have eye drops or ear drops, not because the medicines are horribly painful; the more significant reason is because the dog is frightened of being held still and restrained. Over the years, I have had to do a variety of unpleasant or even painful things to my dogs to keep them healthy. Breanna had to have eye drops several times a day for a chronic condition and once, in a miserable dog fight, her front leg was broken and I had to splint it to get her safely to the emergency veterinarian. Because of prior training, she trusted me even though I was restraining her, and allowed me to do both the unpleasant and the painful with no danger to me, other than to lick my face; and causing no further injury to herself. When I work with dogs who have aggression problems, the very first item I address is that the dog must feel that the owner keeps her safe, therefore she will then be free to be relaxed, comfortable and trusting, looking to her owner for help, rather than worrying about defending her personal space by barking and lunging. The training is how we assure the dog that we can be trusted.

Respect is another volatile word amongst some dog trainers. Respect should not involve fear, although the word respect has so often been linked with fear that I think it should certainly be defined clearly for our purposes. Respect and deference are not "bad" words that mean you are placing emphasis on the wrong things in the relationship between you and your dog. Respect is a regard, an admiration that you have for someone you really like and *whose opinion is important to you.* When someone you respect tells you something, you listen, because your past experience has taught you that this person gives you good information, information worth having. Between me and my dog, I want respect to also mean that my dog understands that I have her best interest in mind, even though what I am asking her to do may look a bit unreasonable from her point of view. (Unreasonable to a dog is asking for a Sit Stay when someone is playing with a tennis ball nearby. This kind of behaviour makes no sense at all to a dog, because she does not have human judgment. She does not understand that the other person in the park and their dog might not appreciate her stealing their tennis ball.) The training is important, no doubt. The dog must systematically be taught to sit and to stay on cue. The sit and staying behaviours must be generalized carefully. That the training is properly done is required. Beyond that, the dog must then feel you have enough authority. She must defer to your judgment and allow you to control her when she would rather chase that ball (getting into trouble or even danger if the other dog is possessive about his ball) than sit and stay.

Therefore, training is vital and it must be done properly and in such a way to give the dog clear information about expectations. However, in my book, part of addressing the Want to vs. the Have to involves trust (the dog feels safe and comfortable with you) and respect (the dog will defer to your judgment when requested).

Many trainers are very poor at being clear about setting up adequate boundaries. From my observations, many people interpret Positive Reinforcement techniques as a philosophy to mean that you are passive and allow the dog to lead the way. This is okay if your dog is benign, relatively easy to train, is stable enough to cover your butt for you and you do not have high, or even moderate, expectations. But it is not okay if you have a special needs dog or a dog that is displaying anti-social behaviour or even the average family dog who will do stuff just because he can.

It is also not okay because laxity in this area creates "grey" areas. Dogs are not good at grey areas. They want black and white. They long for clear communication that is easy to understand. This passivity and poor management is NOT the fault of the technique, but comes from the interpretation of the trainers using it. For many, this is their excuse to be passive. *Passive behaviour on the part of the trainer encourages anxiety, frustration and aggression.*

Learning in sterile, micro-controlled environments... does not often imitate the messy and chaotic "real world." There is much to be learned in the laboratory, but the resulting information may require some translation to be useful. If a sterile environment is required to reproduce the results, the method may not work in the real world at all. Most dogs are not able to be trained in the same place where they will compete. If I could have the judges come to my training center, my dogs would get high and winning obedience scores regularly. Out there in the real world, out of our own "tank" my highest score to date is, I believe, a 194 (out of a possible 200). This score is due entirely to the generosity of my Border Collie and reflects my laziness in training competition behaviours.

Even for the training of very basic behaviours, consider the sterility of the environment of an average client. I walk through the door to do an in-home consultation and find a mother who is juggling a child in diapers, a toddler running across the back of the sofa and a six month old puppy in hot pursuit of the toddler. Or, consider my own home. For the first time in 18 years I have fewer than four dogs. When Abbey, my daughter, was at home, the house was often filled with several of my dogs, one or more rescue dogs that I was nursing back to health or rehabilitating and a bevy of her friends, my husband's friends and my friends. (It seems unlikely, but people actually did visit this madhouse and rescued dogs survived to be re-homed.) This is the environment the dog lives in and will be expected to learn in. Is it sterile? No. Is it ideal? No. Is it real? End of discussion.

Positive Reinforcement training encourages dogs to "guess" and experiment. Don't get me wrong, I love watching animals experiment and guess. I have practiced and have gained proficiency in shaping behaviour and in most cases prefer to use this experimentation process. Working in this way is my favorite training activity. The problem is, I am not training all the dogs, my clients are. Some of my clients, even some who are experienced dog trainers, have difficulties using this technique really well. I am simply pointing out that there is no one solution to every problem and sometimes one technique might work better than another when all variables are taken into account. For some situations management and boundaries serve the purpose better than an extensive shaping process.

Before we go any further, let us discuss what "shaping" means. Shaping is a method whereby the handler allows the dog to experiment with behaviour and skillfully Marks behaviours that are "a step in the right direction." The idea is that the learner (the dog) is allowed to *freely choose and extensively experiment with* which behaviour is exhibited and the trainer reinforces ONLY those exhibited behaviours that are a "step in the right direction." Eventually you reach the final goal. As you shape behaviour, it is expected that the trainer will see a various number of incorrect responses during this process and the dog is encouraged to continue trying different behaviours until she "finds" the correct answer. This process is fascinating and you can create behaviours that are limited only by your imagination and by what the dog is capable of offering in the way of naturally-occurring behaviours.

When presented with aggression, this literal use of shaping may not always be a good choice of behaviour modification because behaviours the dog might offer are dangerous and allowing the dog to experiment with aggression is dangerous. (Regardless, any behaviour we wish to teach the dog will be shaped in one sense. That is, any behaviour we wish to teach will always be approximated: broken into easy baby steps to get from unknowing-ness to the end goal.)

Shaping (allowing experimentation) and capturing (Marking offered behaviours) are dependant upon spontaneously offered behaviour. Therefore, in order to shape a behaviour, it must be offered by the dog. What if the dog does not "offer" the behaviour at all? In this case, the trainer must manufacture the behaviour in order to reinforce it. Trainers quickly gain skill in this area if they apply themselves to the process with curiosity and are close observers. Novice trainers with difficult dogs are often too overwhelmed to apply themselves to an extensive shaping process successfully. Mothers and fathers with toddlers may just need the dog to do some very basic behaviours, and they do not wish to have to learn a million new skills to do the job. They are not fascinated by the training process, they just want the dog to be a good companion. I know this client will have to make some compromises, but if I hand this person a clicker and begin to explain shaping, it will merely cause their eyes to glaze over. I know this from personal experience. Even though I am a convincing person who uses the shaping process well, I could not always get clients on board. This was frustrating, because often the client did not return for more "fun" lessons involving shaping. That translates into: maybe the dog got dumped at the pound (not all facilities qualify as "shelters"), maybe the dog ends up tied to a dog house with a chain in the backyard or

maybe the owner takes the dog to a trainer who is willing to use excessive force and/or excessive electricity (inappropriate use of electronic collars) to get the job done.

The use of shaping, where the dog is allowed experimentation, is fun and good if your dog is a sophisticated learner and you are good at capturing (Marking offered behaviours). *Shaping is fantastic for increasing a dog's confidence and gives dogs practice decision-making.* It is good for improving judgment and timing on the part of the handler. The problem is some dogs get really frustrated to the point of shutting down when you are shaping behaviours. This is, of course, because the dog is not a sophisticated learner or has learned from past experiences that learning (experimentation, novel contexts) can be dangerous. This specific frustration also occurs because the trainer is unskilled. Since the majority of clients bring me very unsophisticated learners with problem behaviour, *and* some of those clients also have a poor skill set, I have needed to rely on and develop a vast and varied set of techniques. In the end, the goal must be to help the dog and client to achieve the best possible relationship, not to adhere to a rigid personal philosophy, while still preserving my ethics.

While shaping, some handlers have such poor skills that the dog gives up, which frustrates the handler even more, causing damage to the relationship. When working with problem dogs, particularly in cases of aggression, the technique of shaping will have its uses, but those uses may be limited by the extent of the aggression, how much time I will get to work with the client and the ability of the client to learn shaping skills. I know from experience that to modify certain behaviours (such as aggression) and to be effective and safe, I must PREVENT REHEARSAL of aggression. IF you have lots of time, can manufacture a sterile enough environment with large enough thresholds, *and* the dog's problem is not severe, using only positive reinforcement based shaping is useful for problem dogs. But for many of the dog/handler teams I have worked with, I needed to offer more effective solutions than this, either because of the severity of the aggression OR because I needed a very high skill level in the handler - RIGHT NOW - and didn't have time to develop this before he had to take their dog out for a pee next time. I will certainly add shaping skills to my handler's repertoire, but that takes the luxury of time that is not always available up front.

Dogs Need Ways To Learn That Make Sense To Them. 85

The problem with shaping is, as so often, it is not the dogs, it's the people. Just because a person is not a stellar dog trainer or is not interested in devoting her life to training her dog does not mean that person does not have a dog. I want to find ways that make sense to people and that they can do, even if their skill level is not high. I also want alternative ways to explain things to dogs, because there is no one way to teach dogs tasks. The simple fact is, the more tools you have in your tool box, the more dogs and people you will be able to help and the more you will be able to help your own dog.

Ignoring as a punisher does not always work:
When undesired behaviours are ignored, magic truly can happen. And this is a trainer's dream, a problem so simple and new (unpracticed) that ignoring it (translated into: I don't have to do a thing except pretend it's not happening) will make it disappear. The behaviour temporarily intensifies (the extinction burst) then dwindles away into nothing. When this works, I love it! However, this technique is open to endless misinterpretation. The fact is, the magic will happen with ignoring if:

- the behaviour is not well-ingrained or doesn't have a long history of practice. (Ignoring jumping up with adolescent dogs doesn't work very well as they have a long history of success. It is now a habit and resistant to change.)

- the behaviour is self-reinforcing (spinning, pacing and barking are examples of self-reinforcing behaviours). The behaviours listed are often the spawn of anxiety or frustration and represent a dog's best current coping mechanism for the situation. The behaviour is self-reinforcing in this circumstance because, in the dog's mind, it helps to alleviate his anxiety/excitement. In reality, it is kind of like having a cigarette to relax; this is faulty thinking because nicotine is actually a stimulant. But people have developed the smoking as a way to cope with minor stressors in their life (this is on top of the obvious physical addiction).

- what the animal is openly seeking is your attention. This is the only instance in which ignoring to reduce behaviour works really effectively; in fact, in this case, ignoring works better than any other possible technique.

- the animal is clever enough and sane enough to figure out an alternative behaviour. Therefore animals exhibiting repetitive or stereotypical or anxiety-based behaviours are not good candidates for this technique.

- you can survive the extinction burst. Some behaviours are so annoying or dangerous that surviving the extinction burst is impossible. (Biting is a great example. If you could remain totally neutral through the bite *and* in addition to that, the bite did not gain the dog whatever he wanted (a food resource, more personal space) then ignoring would probably work quite well. But who's going to take that bite?

Dog trainers know that ignoring can be a way of getting rid of unwanted behaviours. *This technique works well if the animal that is being ignored wants your attention.*

One must also take into account that "ignoring" can be understood by the dog as providing a neutral environment. This is because ignoring, in the animal world, can be a form of reinforcement, or, at least of acceptance or neutrality. I know this may be a very different way of thinking for you, but if a group of animals is hanging out together, the simple act of not paying any attention to another's behaviour means that the others in the social group "do not care" about the behaviour that is being exhibited or can mean that the behaviour is approved of.

Therefore, please keep in mind, as you are training, that animals might think of "ignoring" as a different communication than you do. You can easily tell how the animal thinks of your communication by his actions. If ignoring works, then the animal understands your message to be, "I am not condoning that behaviour and you are not going to get reinforced for it." If ignoring does not work, then clearly the animal understands your message to be, "I don't care if you do that and your environment will remain neutral." *In the dog's native language, ignoring or providing a neutral environment may be interpreted as tolerance, acceptance and/or approval.* As always, it is not what you "say," but what the recipient "hears."

Learning Does Not Guarantee Performance.

Dogs are cognitive creatures, that is, they are thinking beings. Cognition is the study of thinking. Thinking includes learning, perception, memory, decision making, concentration and, the all-important item on every dog trainer's mind, motivation. As researcher Lisa Lit says: "...the thing that so many people keep forgetting, is that *learning does not guarantee performance*." (Lit, 2002) Learning a behaviour is requisite for performance, but once the behaviour *has been learned,* prioritization becomes the key: Is "A" more important to me right now than "B"? Sophisticated trainers are consumed with the following questions:

- How an animal assigns priority is determined by motivation: Why is "A" more important than "B"?

- What makes "A" more important than "B," and therefore most likely to occur?

Prioritization

These photographs were taken when I was first teaching Maeve to retrieve. She had the pick up and carry down pat, and here I am adding the Stay: wait for my cue to retrieve.

Even though she understood "Stay," and clearly saw the

cue, she is so sensitized to the motion of the dumbbell that she disregards the Stay and doesn't wait for the Send.

Further training helped her to prioritize and to become desensitized to the motion and more sensitized to my cue. I taught her to override her instinctive reaction to motion and instead respond to a Stay cue and wait for my for my cue to retrieve.

This is a plain old "discrimination" problem - Which cue takes priority: the handlers cue or the motion of the prey object (dumbbell)?

Dogs who are very sensitive to motion find it difficult to stay Frontbrain and thinking when motion enters the picture. Maeve is very predatory and easily excited by motion. She is not trying to irritate me here, she is uneducated.

Dogs Make Decisions

We all intuitively know that dogs make decisions based on more than just the trainer's input. Dogs both respond to and react to the environment, providing us with excellent examples of this on a daily basis: "She said, 'Come.' That means I get a cookie. But, hey, hold the phone, is that a squirrel??!!" The cookie loses.

If you aren't really crafty with your cookie slinging your dog easily figures out that if you don't have cookies, reinforcement isn't available, and therefore her union contract says she doesn't have to perform. I have a good system for this and do happen to be a very crafty cookie slinger, but my first-time dog owners and basic pet owners do not and, realistically, are not going to work hard enough to become truly proficient at this, no matter how carefully the procedure is explained.

My greatest concern is that life with humans is made less confusing for dogs. Improving the animal/human bond between individuals doesn't always resemble the ideal. Both the person and the dog in the relationship may have confines that will have to be dealt with as best as we can, whether my students are good practitioners of training techniques or clumsy ones. The Get Connected protocol gives me more tools to channel students and dogs in the right direction.

Internal vs. External Motivation.

This brings us to the interesting point of internal vs. external motivation. External motivation is what is relied on heavily by the vast majority of trainers. The dog behaves a certain way because of the threat of a punisher (choke collar, pinch collar) or the possibility of the reinforcer (you do it, you get a treat.) Personally, I love Positive Reinforcement training. It is awesome, and I am very skilled in its use. However, I find with many dogs, I hit a sort of a "glass ceiling" when I use exclusively Positive Reinforcement. Even when the behaviour was well-taught and the dog was well managed, when given certain choices, pleasing me first was second on the list. True, I had really creative dogs (a little too creative sometimes), but on occasion what I longed for was a well-mannered dog that wasn't always looking for loopholes. (In which case I should probably give up terriers entirely, but that is a topic for a different book...)

Clients had even more trouble than I did, because they weren't as skilled at management. I wasn't about to go back to the old traditional, tell'em-force'em type of dog training that I learned initially. I would stop training dogs first, as excessive force harms a relationship, as well as being totally unnecessary. I am still on a quest to find out how to strike that delicate balance: how to develop a relationship with a dog that works for both of us, that transcends external motivators, that increases understanding, enhances communication and still gives me the level of performance that I am looking for. And, because I am a teacher, first and foremost: how do I make this balance available to my students?

Relationships Based On Internal Motivation.

I am very interested in what it takes to get a dog to the point that they are internally motivated. Externally motivated dogs are okay, but a dog who is really *in it with you* and not just for what he can get out of you...well there is a dog you can have a relationship with that rises above earthly matters. This is a relationship that is deeply satisfying to both individuals. Many of us have had relationships like this with dogs with whom we never had to make an effort. The dog took care of it all for us, and did it so well we probably didn't even appreciate it at the time. (My dog like this was a little terrier/sheltie cross. Lightnin' was her name. Amazing dog.) So how do you go about developing such a relationship with a dog that doesn't do the work for you? Is is possible for clumsy old humans to create such a thing? I think it is. And even if you don't see heaven with this relationship, you can sure make it lots more satisfying to both parties than it is right now. Helping my students to work toward this type of relationship by teaching them techniques that are practical, effective and humane is my principal focus.

Domestic Animals Live With Us And There Need To Be Rules.

As my friend Beth Duman, who has worked extensively with both captive and wild wolves and has hand-raised wolves, once said to me: "Domestic is a magic word." If you have ever trained or worked with wild or feral animals, you understand her statement with no further explanation. Dogs have been selected for domestic traits, traits that enable them to live with humans: that is friendly and cooperative traits. Research done in Hungary verifies this relative docility that provides the foundation for domesticity. "Our results demonstrate that already at this early age - despite unprecedented intensity of socialization and the comparable social (human) environment during early development - there are specific behavioral differences between wolves and dogs mostly with regard to their interactions with humans." (Gacsi, Topal, Csanyi, Gyori, Miklosi, Viranyi and Kubinyui, 2005) Findings included such tid-bits as "Wolf pups showed more avoidance and aggression toward a familiar human..." and "In addition, the behavior of the dog puppies is characterized by less aggression and avoidance toward humans in parallel with the increase in communicative signals such as vocalization, tail wagging, and gazing, which can provide a basis for positive feedback on interspecific dog-human interaction." Although dogs and wolves are related, make no mistake about it, dogs are not wolves.

Domesticity established, we then need to establish the ground rules of "how we are going to work together." This type of co-habitation requires some sort of tacit agreement on who will make certain decisions and who has the "power to veto." While I humorously tell my clients "this isn't a democracy" when I am discussing my own happy little canine household, neither do I mean to imply that your household must resemble a dictatorship or durance vile (an expression for forced and tortuous imprisonment). For instance, if you have children, you enforce going to school, eating balanced meals and wearing coats in cold weather. You allow the kids to occasionally dictate "McDonalds for lunch," and you allow them to choose to wear a favorite shirt sometimes even when it doesn't match the rest of the outfit. But you do not entrust them with making the mortgage payment on time, or hand your five-year-old the keys to the car. Because you don't allow children to do some things, and you force them to do others doesn't mean you are heartless and coercive: it means you are a person who cares enough to be a good parent, even though the child may not always agree with your assessment of the situation.

Although this picture is adorable and is treasured by me, this wolf kissing me is nothing like a domestic dog kissing me. For one thing, if I want a dog to stop kissing me I can request it and quite likely get my own way even if I do not know the dog. With this alpha bitch I would not even try to request it. Here, with eyes closed and silently praying while she kisses my face ("please, let her like me"), I am on her turf and she calls the shots.

This photograph was taken at Wolf Park in Battleground, Indiana. This is a magical place, where ethology has been studied by incredible and knowledgeable people for many years, particularly the devoted "core" staff. I was fortunate enough to be allowed in the compound with other students and interns. Photograph by Beth Duman.

Domestic Animals Live With Us And There Need To Be Rules.

Promote Thinking, Not Just Tired or Suppressed Dogs

In any training program, physical exercise is really important. If my client has a six month old dalmatian living in an apartment building and is gone to work ten hours a day, we truly have a big problem. The majority of "problem" behaviours this dog is exhibiting are due to lack of environmental enrichment and lack of exercise. Most cases are not this extreme, nonetheless, adequate physical exercise must be addressed before improvement can take place, not just in this instance, but in many other cases, too.

In addition to physical exercise, the owner will have to develop ways to provide the dog with Frontbrain exercise. This promotes calm and "think before you do" behaviours. Environmental enrichment is not just providing the dog with appropriate toys, but involves lots of interaction with your dog: interaction of a type that opens new neural pathways. I can tell you, from personal experience, that I can play ball with my dog for a half an hour and she will come in and lay down for ten minutes and then is charged up and ready to go again. But if I engage my dog in Frontbrain work for a half an hour, she will take a two hour nap.

Suppression Does Not Make For A Thinking Dog

Excessive force will suppress behaviour, but it does nothing to make the relationship better. You can have a well-behaved dog that knows that experimentation is desirable in some situations and not in others. For instance, when I am carrying groceries in from the car, I just want my dogs to do their Down Stay in the dining room, even though I have the door propped open. This is not a time for experimentation, or "guessing" when you are to be released, it is a time for resigning yourself to your fate and enduring a five minute Down Stay. At other times I wish my dogs to experiment and add their own "twist" to a behaviour; for instance, when I am teaching tricks or a Canine Freestyle routine. Dervish, one of my Smooth Fox Terriers, used to fall to the floor with a dramatic thump when I asked him to "play dead," and Punch always added extra "moves" and flair to any Freestyle routine that we did together. Breanna's interpretation of a simple transition from Down to Sit was a show-stopper and much fancier than the version I was attempting to train. She would, from a sphinx-position Down, leap straight into

the air about three feet and land in a Sit, without moving forward at all. It was extremely cute! These expressions the dogs "added in" made training them and working with them quite delightful. Basically, I taught them that experimentation was desired in some instances and not appreciated in others. You do this by setting the stage for experimentation in certain contexts: my dogs know that when the clicker and the treats come out, experimentation is not just okay, it is encouraged. The clicker and the treats place my dogs, through past conditioning, into a more adrenalized and excited emotional state and an "experimenting" state of mind.

When I am nail-clipping, I want to promote a calm, relaxed emotional state. Therefore, I teach the dog how to be restrained, I practice, in tiny approximations, all of the "moves" I will make while nail clipping and discourage experimentation. Experimentation in this instance will take the form of: mouthing at your hands, perhaps even growling or biting to see if that will make you stop; pulling the feet away, repeatedly; trying to leave the area; struggling in an effort to see if you get irritated enough to give up. While I am teaching a restraint, I will certainly do so systematically, bit-by-bit, and at the same time I will discourage any experimentation with struggling by *maintaining my composure and my position* until the dog gives up and lies still and relaxed.

My intent is not to dominate the dog, but to teach her to trust me when I need to clip her nails, which I know is an unpleasant, but necessary task. Once I have out-lasted the dog and she is relatively more relaxed, I can give her a nice massage, talk nicely to her and, *while she is still*, allow her to get up.

Excessive force in this instance, like yelling, hitting, getting emotional or using a choke or pinch collar to force the dog to submit to your ministrations, may suppress the behaviour, but you will only succeed in making future attempts more distressing and frightening. It is possible to win a battle and still lose the war.

Therefore, use contexts to teach the dog whether experimentation is desired or not and understand that excessive force does not teach, it only suppresses.

Frontbrain Activities

The Get Connected protocol, in addition to whatever dog training method you currently employ, will help your dog to become a more "thinking" dog, as well as showing her how to include you in her decision making process. This will improve team work and increase understanding on both of your parts about issues that neither one of you may have considered before. Or maybe one of you is considering those issues but the other isn't even aware of what the issues are.

This work will help you to open neural pathways your dog would never consider or be able to do on her own. Together you become a sum greater than it's individual parts. You are going to create something amazing and wonderful: you are going to cause a paradigm shift in your dog. You are going to teach her how to do a logic override and switch from Hindbrain to Frontbrain on cue. This is no simple task, since I meet many humans who struggle with it. You may go through a paradigm shift yourself as you share this journey with your dog. You are going to increase communication skills. You are both going to get a lot smarter and a lot more aware of each other.

Promote Thinking, Not Just Tired or Suppressed Dogs

The Least You Can Know And Still Get Away With It

To train your dog you must know the very basic scientific principles that govern learning. These items are valuable because if you know about them, you will use them every time you turn around, to teach amazing things to your dog (like how to be civilized). On the other hand, if you are not aware of these items, every time you turn around, one of them will bite you in the bum.

The cat is Arlene, whom I taught to wave. It took me two 3 minute sessions and I didn't use any treats. I used the very basic technique of capturing (reinforcing offered behaviour). Arlene came up to paw my leg for attention and I shaped that into waving on cue. For reinforcement I used exactly what Arlene wanted: me to scratch her chin. I was able to do this because I understand how animals learn and how to identify and manipulate reinforcement and behavioural contingencies.

Photograph by Dave Schrader

This is Zasu, whom I have taught to back in a circle around my legs. Zasu does this with enthusiasm because it is one of her favorite behaviours. During the teaching of this behaviour I had to use tiny approximations, manufacture backing up, touch her body to help her become aware of hip placement and manipulate reinforcement schedules carefully. Then I had to generalize the behaviour so I could wow people with this cuteness any time I like (place the behaviour on cue and increase reliability). We also worked on duration of the behaviour. These learning principles do not just apply to cute tricks, though, they help you live better with your dog every day.

Photographs by Mary Wilmoth

Behaviour Development Periods

We have all heard of social development periods. I want you to think of a behaviour in the same way: a behaviour is a special little entity all its own. Each behaviour an individual: a little being that is born and changes as it matures, just like you or your dog do. Furthermore, because dogs do not generalize behaviour particularly quickly, not only is each behaviour a different entity, each behaviour in each *location* is a different entity. Therefore, the behaviour might be in a different developmental stage at each location.

For example:
- Infants have certain needs that must be met in order for the new baby to thrive. One is constantly maintaining an infant. One end or the other needs attention continuously. If you aren't feeding it, you are making certain it is dry and warm and has environmental stimulation, or it needs help to settle into a nap. If an infant is upset, you check for basic needs and rock it, you don't discipline it.

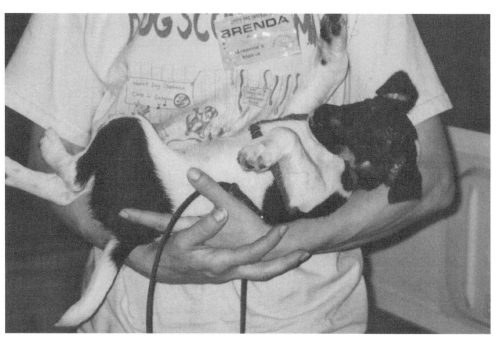

Behaviour Development Periods

Baby Behaviours, like all other babies need constant attention, loving care and a safe place to learn.

Photograph by Joanne Weber

- As a toddler, the first signs of independence mean that the parent must provide management and excellent boundaries. The very first limits are placed on toddlers, "Don't touch; it's too hot, too cold, not yours," to keep them safe and introduce the social boundaries required to get along with others.

- The child needs guidance, and management. The management must be thoughtful: still micro-managed in some areas, but allowed prudent freedom in others. If the process does not move forward in this manner, the child never gets a chance to learn how to make decisions. The child is learning how to make good choices and the consequences of "bad" choices.

Just the right amount of management combined with just enough freedom creates individuals who make good decisions.

Photograph by Joanne Weber

- The adolescent is testing all the boundaries and exerting independence. You can feed it less frequently, but in far greater quantities at each sitting.

Adolescents, whether dogs, humans or behaviours, are constantly searching for boundaries.

Photograph by Joanne Weber

This is an example of an "Adult" behaviour. Zasu maintains and takes responsibility for remaining attentive, even though I am otherwise engaged (teaching a class) and am not monitoring her closely or constantly.

Notice, too, that even though she is near my pant-legs she has not succumbed to the temptation of tugging on them...

Photograph by Dave Schrader

• The adult, if you have done a good job, is a useful member of society, sophisticated and aware. The adult is self-feeding (self-reinforcing) and responsible, understanding and appreciating boundaries.

A Behaviour goes through critical development periods, too. It makes training less overwhelming if you split the process of learning a behaviour into four distinct development periods.

• Acquisition is like the tiny infant. You need to use lots of treats at this stage, and frequently! Maintenance and supervision is constant in this behavioural stage!

• Generalization is like the toddler, child and teen all rolled into one! Here good boundaries and information help keep the behaviour on track, as it is practiced in several different locations and in several different contexts. Information can be given in a much more sophisticated way, because the behaviour is growing in sophistication and precision. You can feed it with less frequency, although more at each sitting, like when you utilize jack potting.

• Fluency occurs after enough repetitions in enough different contexts. Now the behaviour is getting to be really lovely, with automatic responses and is consistent in appearance.

• Maintenance is the adult: the behaviour is in constant and ongoing use, which keeps it looking good.

Just as the child or dog needs different things from care givers during different critical development periods, so a behaviour needs different things from the trainer during its development periods so that it grows up into the kind of behaviour you want to have around!

The dressage master Michel Henriquet characterizes it beautifully, referring to the progressive stages as:
• The time to understand.

• The time to learn.

• The time to do.

• The time to perfect.

To summarize:
• Learning becomes less unwieldy if you understand it occurs in a predictable way.

- Any behaviour will progress in a predictable way through various stages of development.

- Learning is most often split into four manageable, predictable basic stages (development periods).

Progression of a Behaviour

Acquisition - The Time To Understand

The dog needs to complete two basic tasks:

- The connection between the behaviour & the consequence.

- The connection between the cue & the behaviour.

The order listed above is of crucial importance because that is the order in which the dog learns the behaviour. No matter what you think it looks like, the actual order of learning is that: your dog will notice the connection between the behaviour and the consequence first. Second she will notice that "something" preceded the behaviour. It is when the dog notices this entire pattern that the two basic tasks of Acquisition are completed.

When you have established what the behaviour "is" and *the dog can pick out a simple pattern of cause and effect,* then you are through Acquisition, and your baby behaviour is toddling.
As an example:

I see a treat held above my head.

I put my bottom on the ground and hold still.

I get a treat.

Generalization - The Time To Learn

- During Fluency and Generalization is when the famous 6000 Repetitions occur

- Move the behaviour into different contexts. You do this by changing one or both of the following:

Locations

Circumstances

As you take the dog through this process, the dog will have to make choices. As you change locations and/or circumstances, the dog is "challenged" to adapt and make a decision. These "challenges" explain to the dog exactly: What the "window of expectation" is. That is, what will the handler accept as a desired response. What the Cue is. The way the cue is taught to the dog is very important. The most common errors when teaching a cue are: adding the cue too soon, blocking and over-shadowing. (refer to "Selective Attention: Blocking & Over-shadowing" on page 107 for additional information.) At first, in each new location you will "review" each exercise, taking the dog through the original teaching steps. As your dog becomes proficient, you will see her needing less and less of this reviewing process. By the time you get to about 15 or 20 different locations or circumstances, you will see your dog not requiring any review at all! (refer to "Engineering Reinforcement Schedules" on page 99 for additional information.) She is reaching the next stage, listed below: Fluency.

For example, once my dog has learned to assume a sitting position on cue, I will begin to delay the treat for 1 or 2 seconds. This is the first Challenge and begins to teach duration of the behaviour: a sit stay. I will continue to gradually increase the duration until I have a few minutes of sit stay. One way to think about this, is that each time you raise the criteria, you are creating a situation where the dog has to think about the exercise and make a decision. Once the dog is doing at least a 5 second sit stay, I will move the dog to another room. So, if I taught the sit in the kitchen, I will move it into the living room. Then the hall-way, the front yard, the back yard and the sidewalk. These are all locational changes.

Then I might try a circumstantial change. If I taught the exercise when the children were quiet, I might try working the sit when the children are up and moving around. Or, while on the street, teach the dog that she is to sit even if another dog is walking by her on leash. Will she sit when the UPS man comes to the door? Not at first! But she will eventually as you teach her that sit means sit, in several locations and in several different circumstances.

Remember, each time you deviate from an established pattern, the exercise can look "different" to the dog. It is through the process of generalizing that your dog learns that the verbal cue of sit means no matter where you are and what is going on around you, even if it is horribly distracting - plant your bottom on the ground and await further instructions.

Fluency – The Time To Do

- Increased rate of responding.

- More automatic responses.

- More consistent responses.

In the process of generalizing the behaviour, you do a huge number of repetitions. Repetitions increase the reliability of the behaviour. The behaviour also begins to "look" the same every time, it becomes more consistent in its execution.

Maintenance – The Time To Perfect

- Repetition and constant use of the behaviour will maintain the behaviour.

- Constant checking to see that skills remain sharp.

- Habit: The behaviour, through use and prior experiences, becomes self-reinforcing.

- Some behaviours never become self-reinforcing, but they can be maintained through judicious, thoughtful and occasional reinforcement.

- Use it or Lose it!

The more daily use a behaviour gets, the stronger that neural pathway stays. This means the behaviour requires less and less effort on the part of the handler, and the reliability rating is very high. This is the reason you must make sure that your dog develops good habits. It is great when a stay or a come is in the Maintenance stage. The dog is reliable and the handler is pleased with the responsiveness of his dog.

It is just as easy, though, for undesired behaviours, as well as desired behaviours, to reach a Maintenance stage. *Any behaviour that is practiced frequently will become a habit.* If your dog gets in the habit of dashing out the door each time it opens and running through the neighbourhood, it will take a great deal of effort and management on the part of the handler to change this.

Help Your Dog Learn By Understanding Behaviour Development Periods

Once you have a good idea of the sum and substance of behaviour stages, you can apply your training technique to meet the needs of the behaviour as it progresses. To meet the needs of the dog's learning process most effectively is to *change your technique,*

adjusting to each behaviour stage, as you go along. Think of it like this: You have a three-year old child who has learned to pedal her tricycle. As she reaches four, you get her a two-wheeled "big girl" bike, but it has training wheels on it to help her develop her immature sense of balance and to save you the expense and bother of trips to the emergency room. After a few months, you will take the training wheels off her bike. The first time she rides the bike without the training wheels is a tension-filled moment for mom! Mom holds the bike as the child gets on and adjusts her tiny helmet. Then mom says, "Okay, I'm going to help you get started. Just keep pedaling and you will stay upright." The child begins pedaling as mom holds the bike upright and jogs along beside. The child pedals faster and mom keeps up, reminding the child, "Keep pedaling, pedal, pedal, pedal..." Mom's voice rises a bit higher, and she keeps repeating, "pedal, keep going, great job!" as she reluctantly releases the bike, but keeps jogging beside. "Look at you," she exclaims. "Look at you riding that bike!" Mom cheers the child on as she proudly pedals round the drive. This scenario, touching as it is, if repeated when the child is ten and getting ready to ride round the neighborhood with her friends would mortify the child, her friends and any mother with any sense at all. As the child learns and becomes proficient, she and her bike-riding behaviour have different needs.

One of the easiest ways to change your technique and still convey excellent information is to use Reinforcement Schedules. (refer to "Engineering Reinforcement Schedules" on page 99.) As in the example above, at first the mother helps the child, then reinforces the child for a job well done, and eventually pays the child the ultimate compliment of not having to help at all. During this process the child does not merely learn how to ride a two-wheeled bicycle. She also learns how to be competent, take responsibility and feel proud of her accomplishments. In short, her self confidence grows. Dogs grow in self confidence, too, when they are allowed to become proficient at a new task.

Engineering Reinforcement Schedules

Your dog, without the benefit of human (spoken) language, is maneuvering through a predominantly human-oriented environment and trying to figure out which behaviour patterns are most efficient. Dogs learn by many different devices, but, like us, plenty is learned by trial and error, that is, performing some action and seeing what the results are. Mistakes will be made, but this is good information - just as important to the learning process as getting it right. Dogs are perpetually trying to pick out patterns, so that consequences are predictable. This is not so different from how you cope with daily life, except you have the great advantage of living amongst your own species which speaks your own native language.

The information gathered from picking out patterns and making associations between behaviour and consequences enables your dog to make decisions about future behaviour. Strategies that do not work are quickly abandoned and successful strategies are accessed again. Think of behaviour as process of experimentation.

How You Can Help Your Dog Establish The Desired Pattern?

Clever trainers use Reinforcement Schedules to develop baby behaviours into big, strong, righteous behaviours, that are stable and predictable. There are two basic categories:

- Fixed.
- Variable.

Fixed Reinforcement Schedule: What Is It?

A Fixed Reinforcement Schedule is named this because it occurs consistently and predictably: a set pattern that is repeated until the dog can establish the pattern easily. In Learning Theory there are different kinds of Fixed Schedules, but for general dog training purposes, the equation of: 1 Behaviour = 1 Cookie works beautifully.

Fixed Schedule: Why Do It?

- The consequences must be consistent during the Acquisition Stage of learning so the dog can figure out exactly which behaviour it is that you are applying reinforcement to.

- Once the dog has established that there is a behaviour and a consequence, and you have some way that you can "begin" or cue the behaviour, you can move on to a Variable Schedule.

Variable Reinforcement Schedule: What Is It?

A Variable Reinforcement Schedule can be split into four basic categories:

- Variable Interval.
- Variable Ratio.
- Reinforcement Variety.
- Selective Reinforcement. Also called Intermittent Reinforcement or DRE - Differential Reinforcement of Excellent Behaviour.

Variable Interval

- Ask for more than one behaviour before delivering reinforcement.

- Ask for three or four behaviours, then reinforce.

- Instead of always reinforcing a behaviour chain predictably at the end, interrupt a behaviour chain in the middle and R+. (The symbol R+ means Positive Reinforcement.) Used in this way, "reinforcement" usually means a treat, but can be anything that the dog likes that is used deliberately: such as a Marker or playing a game the dog likes, or even cueing the dog to do a different, well-liked behaviour.)

- Reinforce in different time frames. For example, to teach duration of behaviour: R+ the Sit in 1 second, then delay the reinforcer by random time frames: 2 seconds, 3, 5, 7, 4, 2, 8, 3, 10, 5, 7, 10 and so on.

Variable Ratio

Use different quantities or amount of reinforcers to convey more precise information.

- For good responses, feed 1 treat.
- For better responses, feed 2 or 3 treats, one at a time, consecutively.
- For super duper responses or First Correct Efforts feed 5 to 10 treats. This is called "jack potting." Always deliver the treats ONE AT A TIME IN A CONSECUTIVE FASHION. Really make the reinforcement last and draw it out. Feed a treat and offer the next one just as the dog is finished gulping or chewing the previous treat. This helps the dog to remember the behaviour even better.

Reinforcement Variety

Have a variety of treats available:

- Does not have to be food treats, it could be toys or games.
- Can be pleasant touches that the dog likes.
- Have different "values" of food treats, some kibble, some string cheese, some bits of steak left over from dinner - you get the picture.

Intermittent Reinforcement or Selective Reinforcement

My favorite terminology for this is: DRE - Differential Reinforcement of EXCELLENT Behaviour, because it is, for once, a technical term that is an accurate descriptor.

- DRE means that reinforcement is available only when truly top of the line behaviour is exhibited.

Behaviour Is Strengthened, Maintained And Consistent When You:

- Use Variable Ratio, Variable Interval, and Reinforcement Variety.

- When appropriate, take advantage of DRE (Differential Reinforcement of Excellent Behaviour).

What does this mean?

- Ask for two or three or more behaviours before you deliver a treat, although you may choose to use a Marker frequently.
- In short, you are asking for more behaviour from the dog, for less and less primary (food) reinforcement.
- You are teaching the dog to "delay gratification."
- Become unpredictable about when food treats are given.
- Use dog kibble sometimes and pieces of cheese or other special treats sometimes.
- Use one treat sometimes, and for really good efforts or First Correct Efforts, give your dog several treats.
- Use food sometimes, petting sometimes, and games sometimes as reinforcers.
- DRE is how you gain precision and excellence in behaviours. This means you deliver food treats only to "best efforts."
- Improve your reinforcement delivery! Get tricky about where the reinforcers are kept. Work with reinforcers off your body but hidden, then use your Marker and run over to the hidden toy or treat with your dog. Alternatively, work with reinforcers off your body but in clear sight, teaching the dog that YOU will decide when they are available.

Variable Schedule Why Do It?

- Makes Behaviour more resistant to extinction (stronger).
- Makes Behaviour more intense.
- Teaches your dog to overcome adversity and remain involved and on task.

One More Time, In A Nutshell:

A Fixed Schedule Means That Reinforcement Occurs Consistently And Predictably.

- The Fixed Schedule is used when a dog is first learning a behaviour.
- A Fixed Schedule causes a behaviour to be CONSISTENT in presentation.

- The most basic of Fixed Schedules is 1 Behaviour = 1 Treat.

A Variable Schedule Means That Reinforcement Occurs Unpredictably.

- A Variable Schedule is used to strengthen and maintain a behaviour.

- A Variable Schedule teaches your dog to be persistent.

- A Variable Schedule makes a behaviour RESISTANT TO EXTINCTION.

When do I use What?

Use A Fixed Schedule During The Acquisition Stage Of A Behaviour.

Use a Fixed Schedule to avoid confusion when you are first teaching the dog what you want. The basic rule is: remain on a Fixed Schedule until the A-B-C (Antecedent - Behaviour - Consequence) connection is made.

How Do I Know The A-B-C Connection Has Been Made

To clarify this A-B-C thing, the antecedent is something that starts a behaviour; in dog training that would be the cue. This happens to people in daily life, too. When the telephone rings you are prompted or "cued" to drop what you are doing and answer the telephone. The ring of the telephone is the antecedent, answering the telephone is the behaviour and the consequence is that you get to talk to some telephone salesperson. Another possible consequence is that you get to speak to a dear friend and have a few laughs or make fun plans for later. (By the way, this also illustrates a variable schedule: sometimes you get the salesperson, sometimes you get the friend. The possibility that you will get the friend and not the salesperson is what keeps your telephone answering behaviour going.)

Cue Systems And Adding Cues In The Correct Order To Avoid Confusion

Remember at this point, the dog doesn't have a clue about what behaviour you want because he has not "learned" the behaviour yet. Many training errors are made during this stage of training. The biggest error is that people want to add the final cue to the behaviour much too early. The handler is in a rush to add the cue that she wishes to use for the final behaviour. *The problem is, you do not have the final behaviour at this time*. This simple fact makes it difficult to name it.

This causes confusion for the dog and a high rate of mistakes. So the Golden Rule is: get the behaviour first. Then add the final, end goal (usually a verbal) cue, at that point in time when you can predictably elicit the behaviour *and* it is looking pretty good. Another way to think about this is how you would teach a very small child a new word. You do not try to "explain" the word blue, this is too abstract. Instead you find something blue. As you show the child the blue item, you say "blue." This is how you would add a final, verbal cue to a behaviour, by using the same kind of word association game. Once the dog is sitting, then you can say, "sit" while the dog is in the sit position. This "shows" her what the word means.

In the very beginning stages of teaching your dog a specific behaviour, you have some sort of cue you can use (even if it isn't a polished, pretty cue) to start the behaviour. For example: in the beginning stages of a behaviour the cue might be something as simple as a treat held in your hand above the dog's head. Since it is easier to look up at the treat if she is sitting, she will do so. Once this is a predictable occurrence of events, then you know that the dog understands that this behaviour has a consequence.

This is the correct point in time to add your verbal cue of "sit." People tend to add that "final" verbal cue too early and this is confusing for the dog because you are asking her to do too many things at once. Let her learn one small step at a time. Keep in mind that while we depend heavily upon our own spoken language, dogs do not. Motion and the scent of food is most salient (noticeable) to dogs and the verbal cue is the least salient, until the dog has been trained to notice it.

Use Both Schedules During the Generalization and Fluency Stages Of A Behaviour

The Generalization and Fluency stages of a behaviour happen concurrently as you do several repetitions of the behaviour during the process of adding Challenges by changing locations and circumstances. It is during this process of challenging, that you encourage dog to "make a choice" about their behaviour. You are asking the dog a question: "Are you going to hold your sit when a person walks by or are you going to get up?" By the dog's actions in this circumstance you get to see what the dog has understood about your training process. It gives you opportunities to tweak your approximations and to give the dog feedback about her decision. Every time something changes in the envi-

ronment it can look like a whole new ball game to the dog. So, even though you are in a place where you have trained the dog, like at a training class, if a person enters the room after you have gotten there, the dog will be distracted. Until she has been subjected to several such distractions, she may not be able to maintain the behaviour without assistance from the handler. So, let's say you are working on sit stays at your local dog training facility. Your dog is holding her stays. You are feeding her the occasional treat, about every 20 to 60 seconds. This is a Variable Schedule. Then, you hear someone coming up to open the door of the training center. I suggest that you step in and feed the dog a treat every 1 to 2 seconds (going back to a heavier, or Fixed Schedule) until the person is in the room. After this event has occurred a half dozen times, you will no longer need to revert back to the Fixed Schedule because your dog will look at you when someone opens the door. In this example, the person opening the door constitutes a change in the environment representing a Challenge to the dog.

- Fixed Schedule when introducing any new circumstance.

- Fixed Schedule during changes in the environment that are "new."

- After a quick review in each new location or change of circumstance, move back to a Variable Schedule.

When working on repetitions in a location or circumstance that you have previously trained in:

- Variable Schedule.

During Maintenance Use A Variable Schedule.

Behaviour can be maintained through repetition and constant use. It is at this stage that behaviour becomes a habit. Habits can be reinforcing in and of themselves. We all have habits that we do just because that is the way we have always done it. Habits resist change, whether they are good or bad. Once a good habit has been formed, use a Variable Schedule with emphasis on:

- Reinforcement Variety.

- Use of DRE (selective reinforcement).

What If My Dog Gets Stuck? Not To Mention Myself...

- If your dog gets stuck go back to Kindergarten temporarily.

- If you do not know what to ask for next (which approximation to advance to), do something else with your dog until you have had time to think about what your next criterion is. This happens more often than one would think: for example, when the dog gets ahead of you by making a sort of quantum leap in understanding and leaves you standing in the dust unprepared.

- Don't be afraid to do a quick review.

- Part of Maintenance includes reviews. A review consists of a quick run through of the steps you used to originally teach the behaviour, using a "heavy" (generous, plentiful) reinforcement schedule.

Still Confused? A Bit Overwhelmed About When To Reinforce?

Reinforcement Schedules and their manipulation, especially to beginning trainers, feel overwhelming and unwieldy. These are three basic rules that anyone can use effectively. These are the situations in which I would definitely use a reinforcer. If you can follow only these three rules your dog's learning curve will drastically increase and she will acquire behaviours rapidly.

- During Acquisition. Use a Fixed Schedule.

- First Correct Efforts. Utilize jack potting.

- Whenever your dog shows commitment to choosing the correct behaviour when faced with raising criteria (Challenges). Adjust the amount or importance of your reinforcer depending on how difficult the Challenge is. Keep thinking this thought: "What horrid thing could my dog have done in this situation?" Particularly in a situation where she has shown poor judgment in the past and currently displays good decision making, for goodness sake, reinforce her! Let her know you really liked her Frontbrain behaviour.

Reinforcement Guidelines

- Do not leave the dog on a Fixed Schedule for behaviours that are easy for the dog to do. As soon as the dog finds the job easy, it no longer needs constant reinforcement. When you move to a Variable Schedule as quickly as possible, you encourage the dog to try harder. This helps dogs to learn that there is more "value" to a behaviour that has a higher degree of difficulty.

- Some behaviours, once established, will no longer need food reinforcements at all. Just using the behaviour will maintain it. Behaviours that are taught correctly the first time and require no retraining are easy to get into this stage.

- Some behaviours may require a high reinforcement ratio: behaviours that are disliked by the dog or that are not in line with the dog's instincts. For instance, I could probably teach a Basset to retrieve ducks (putting aside the obvious physical challenges involved, such as wet ears that are easily infected), but it might require a lot of effort on my part and the behaviour will tend to fall apart if a very high reinforcement ratio (75% and higher) is not maintained. This is particularly true if the initial teaching of the behaviour was very confusing to the dog and the dog became chronically worried about doing the behaviour.

As an example, one of my client's dogs was confused, and worse yet, corrected, while he was confused, when taught Stays. The dog was brought to me after this had happened, and we started from the beginning. It took a long time, even though the re-training work was done correctly. This dog was not corrected harshly, and he has a pretty resilient temperament, but there was still damage done. This dog still has occasional trouble with Stays, and it took four years to get them anywhere close to reliable. It required an extremely high rate of reinforcement for three of those years - approximately a 90% reinforcement ratio - to maintain the Stay. At this point he is working reliably on 10 minute out of sight Stays, but it sure has been a long haul.

- Use Challenges as a way to continue reinforcing behaviour. This means that you raise the criteria by tiny increments, but frequently. Keep the dog engaged and thinking by giving him solvable problems to solve.

- Once a behaviour is learned, use DRE as your primary venue to "feed" a behaviour. That is, only really excellent behaviours get a food treat: those that are above average.

- Pay very close attention to the developmental stage of the behaviour.

- Use a reinforcer that is appropriate to the behaviour you are teaching. If you want to teach a Stay, for instance, food reinforcers are best, because you wish to surround the behaviour with calm effort. If your dog is doing fantastic Heel work, but it is a little "flat" and you need to bump up the intensity, then get out the tennis ball. You understand that when you get out prey objects, you will sacrifice precision. So you work on intensity, then precision, then intensity, then precision. Reward the intensity with a reinforcer that encourages intensity, like a game of tug or a ball or frisbee. Reward precision with food at first, to "surround" the behaviour with a little more calm; then later in the development period of this behaviour - during Maintenance - you can begin to reinforce precision or intensity with your choice of reinforcers, mixing it up to add interest. Duration behaviours such as stays are best taught when always surrounded by calm events, since relaxation creates the very best stays.

- Catch those First Correct Efforts. A First Correct Effort occurs several times during the teaching of any individual behaviour. Every time you raise criteria there will be a First Correct Effort for that approximation. *The more of the First Correct Efforts that you notice and reinforce, the faster your dog will learn*. Noticing a First Correct Effort can be done with a food jack pot, or it can be noticed by releasing pressure at just the right moment. This encourages your dog to try hard and to develop curiosity about training.

- Above all, have a plan.

What Else You Need To Know

To engineer Reinforcement Schedules effectively, it is necessary to know about the different stages that predictably occur when a dog is learning a task. Those were discussed in *Behaviour Development Periods*.

People are quite flummoxed when, at the point at which they are changing from a Fixed to a Variable Schedule. As this is done, you can be sure you will invariably see variable behaviour! That lovely, consistent looking behaviour that you carefully fed a cookie for each time it appeared becomes inconsistent: sometimes it is quite lovely. Other times it is icky, and, occasionally it is non-existent. This is where people go wrong. They rush for the cookie jar. Expect to see some good stuff and bad stuff as the dog goes through the learning process. This is why it is called "learning." During this stage dogs are asking you constant questions:

- Is this it?

- How narrow or how wide is your window of expectation? That is, will you accept a shoddy job of it and still give me a cookie?

Caution #1: The longer you leave a behaviour on a Fixed Schedule, the more difficult it becomes to get the behaviour onto a Variable Schedule.

Caution #2: If you move to a Variable Schedule too soon, you will lose the behaviour altogether.

Better to err on the second caution rather than the first. If you cause a behaviour to become extinct, that is, it sort of disappears altogether, you can easily go back to Approximation #1 and re-teach the behaviour using the same teaching steps you did the first time. No Big Deal. The struggle will be much greater if you have left the dog on a Fixed Schedule for too long.

Be willing to be flexible. If the dog is having a rough time of it and is confused, be ever ready to go back a few approximations and review what you have taught. This happens even with experienced dogs who are sophisticated learners and have been doing a behaviour for a long time. Making errors and forgetting are normal learning and behaving patterns. Do you know where your cell phone is right this minute? (Mine is at the restaurant I had dinner at last night. The nice manager answered when I called its number as a strategy of searching for it.) These things happen.

Managing Reinforcement Schedules Is One Of The Most Difficult Skills To Master Well.

To plan and use Schedules beautifully you need additional Skill Sets.

- Excellent timing.
- Clear criteria.
- Well planned successive approximations.

Timing Tips

Practice looking for intention behaviours. This might be quite subtle, sort of "micro-behaviors." You know, those little physical movements that tell you the dog is getting ready to do "something." That "something" is either closer or farther from your end goal. The better you are at identifying micro-behaviours and either reinforcing or discouraging them, the more accurate your timing becomes. It is like walking down a path and coming to a fork in the road. The faster you realize you have taken the wrong turn, the quicker you will arrive at your destination.

If your timing is early, you have reinforced something other than what was intended. If your timing is late, ditto.

- Good timing comes with practice. There are no shortcuts.

- Timing problems occur often, not because you have poor timing, but mostly, I find, because students do not have clear criteria.

- Good timing is heavily dependant upon how effectively you are able to concentrate and "stay in the moment." Staying in the moment is a bigger task than you might think. An execellent reference on this ability is the book: *Riding Success Wtihout Stress:Introducing the Alexander Technique* by Joni Bentley.

Clear Criteria

If you do not know what you are looking for, it's unreasonable to expect the dog to know. Therefore, *you must know what you are looking for and have an idea of what it will look like at each approximation.* This sounds scary, but is really not all that difficult, and a little experience goes a long way toward knowing what you are looking for. If you have never taught this behaviour before, ask yourself: Is this a step in the right direction? Is this behaviour closer to or farther from the end goal than a previous behaviour? Just like your dog, you will learn through trial and error which criteria work best with this individual. Teaching each approximation of each behaviour is like a series of experiments conducted to ascertain the best method.

- Work it out on paper first!

- Have the big picture in mind. What is your end goal? (The technical phrase for end goal is: terminal response.)

- Work on details one at a time.

- These "details" or teaching steps are called approximations.

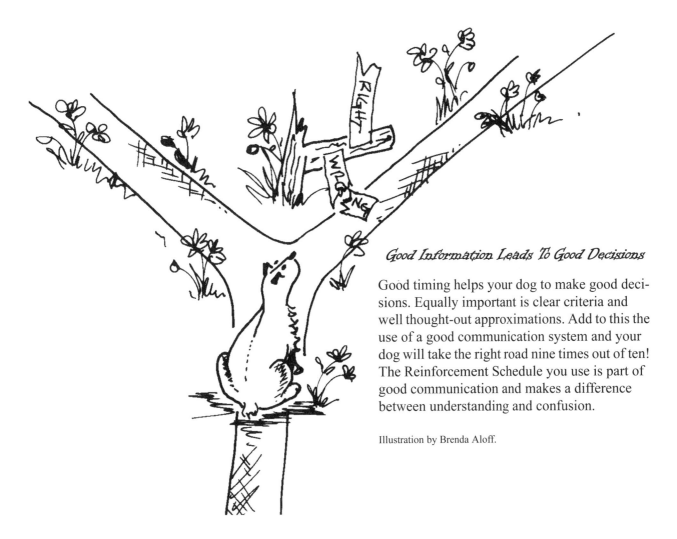

Good Information Leads To Good Decisions

Good timing helps your dog to make good decisions. Equally important is clear criteria and well thought-out approximations. Add to this the use of a good communication system and your dog will take the right road nine times out of ten! The Reinforcement Schedule you use is part of good communication and makes a difference between understanding and confusion.

Illustration by Brenda Aloff.

Successive Approximations

Small teaching steps that are easily accomplished are requisite. You have taken on tasks that are overwhelming (like training this dog...), and you know how frustrating that can be. It is your job to teach the task in small increments, called successive approximations (most often shortened to the word "approximations"), so both of you can succeed!

- Take the end goal and break it down into small increments, little bits of knowledge that the dog can master easily. It is surprising how small you can break a behaviour down. For instance, a five minute Sit Stay, at a distance, and with distractions, begins with one second of Sit with the dog directly in front of you.

There is a hugely long list of reasons why you don't get what you want. This is a list of the most common ones. I include it here only because people just do not seem to take these items into consideration when they run into training problems. Instead they become emotional and ask really irrelevant questions like: "Why won't my dog appreciate all the work I have put into him?" Or they berate themselves, "What have I done wrong?" accompanied by useless hand-wringing. You are best served by taking any feedback from the dog as information about where you went wrong with the training program. Awareness that these technical reasons for screw-ups exist is the first step toward solving the problem!

The Pyramid of Competing Reinforcers

You must control or affect or be at the top of what the dog sees as important and most reinforcing. For instance, if you have allowed your dog off leash, squirrels are present and you have string cheese (a high value treat with you, but your dog prefers squirrels to string cheese), you are going to be standing there impotently watching your dog chase squirrels while yelling and waving string cheese to no avail. People get behind the power curve because they fail to understand that the dog is not gaining reinforcement and information from them only, the environment is always present and always holds potential. In many cases the environment holds more potential for reinforcement than the handler. People get behind the power curve in these ways:

- Failure to use Premack's principle.

- Failure to teach that indirect access means success.

- Failure of management.

Premack's principle applies here – a hierarchy of reinforcers is always present. You must be aware of what is most important to your dog. Preventing direct access by teaching excellent impulse control (Leave It behaviours) is necessary management. Especially if you use Positive Reinforcement-based training techniques, you must be an excellent manager. (The most excellent book on basic management is *Management Magic* by Leslie Nelson, available from Dogwise.) For more information about Premack's principle refer to *Premack's Principle* on page 113.

Teach your dog to use indirect access as a modus operandi and to include you in his decision making process. This process is explained in the *Basic Training Boot Camp* Section of this book, using the *Involvement* and *Think First: Impulse Control* exercises.

Learned Irrelevance

People begin to teach their dogs Learned Irrelevance right away. Every time you tell your dog to do something and then do not make it happen - either by helping or by enforcing - you teach your dog to ignore you. Every time you tell your dog to do something he has not been trained to do and then get frustrated with him you teach your dog that attending to you is an exercise in futility.

- Commands are given that have no meaning. No one has ever bothered to actually teach the dog what is expected and no "word association" to the behaviour has ever been done, so how is the dog to know what the word means?

- Commands are not followed up on by the humans. That is, they give the cue or say the word, but when the dog does not comply, the human is too lazy to get up off the sofa and make it happen.

- We "talk" all the time. How is the dog to know what is relevant and what is not? Use words sparingly during training, confining yourself to cues and words that provide information to the dog. Don't chatter and explain things to the dog using lots of sentences. *Dogs know that actions (body language) speak louder than words*. You want to pour your troubles out to your dog or chat about your day at work to her? Save it for when you are snuggled up on the sofa together in the evening. Shut up (that is meant in the kindest possible way...) when you are training. Your chatter is static on the line.

- Incorrect associations result in watered-down commands. An example is when the animal does not know the command but "sit" is repeated over and over while the dog is standing. The dog associates or "pairs" the word "sit" with a standing position. (For information on this topic refer to *Cue Systems And Adding Cues In The Correct Order To Avoid Confusion* on page 101)

- Diluted cues also occur because of a failure to provide appropriate consequences when the animal did respond correctly.

Selective Attention: Blocking & Over-shadowing

We like to assume that dogs learn by clean and clear-cut associations, and that this association will be predictably made if the dog is presented with whatever items we want them to connect up in a contingent way. That is, if we say "Sit" and lure the dog into a sit and then feed them right away, then surely the dog will learn that a verbal cue of "Sit" means to assume a sitting position. Unfortunately, this is not necessarily so. This simple equation often assumes a complexity that seems ridiculously out of proportion. And over-shadowing and blocking are the culprits. Know thine enemy. Intimately.

Both over-shadowing and blocking have to do with saliency and redundancy.

- Saliency: What is the dog attending to or thinking about right now? That is what is salient to the dog at this moment. Over-shadowing and blocking both have to do with making certain that the dog gets the information you are intending her to have, and not placing her attention on something else.

- Redundancy: What gives the animal "new" or "useful" information? That is what dogs will attend to the most (has the most saliency). Dogs

ignore information that is deemed redundant or those items that do not provide relevant information.

Blocking Definition:

Simultaneous presentation of a new command with a previously learned command means that the new command will be ignored because it provides no "new" information. The dog gets all she needs to know from the previously learned command. In other words, prior learning is blocking new learning from taking place.

Blocking Research

The following research was done by Kamin, 1969. (Flaherty, 1985)

- Rats were given tone-shock pairings.

- The tone quickly produced fear.

- Then a light was presented simultaneously with the tone.

- This light-tone pairing produced a Fear response.

- The big question on everybody's mind now (and the meat of the research) is: Will *only* the light elicit a fear response?

If you think that because of contingency (pairing) the light will take on the same relevance as the tone, then you are mistaken.

- The answer is NO. The light alone did not elicit fear.

Why? The tone already predicted the shock; the light added no new or additional information. The pre-training is what causes the blocking. "...if nothing new is predicted by the *added* stimulus, then it will not acquire an associative strength. In Kamin's experiments the noise already predicted the occurrence of the shock; the added light was thus *redundant* as a predictor of this US." (italics are mine.) (Flaherty, 1985) In the quote, the acronym US refers to an unconditioned stimulus - in this instance the shock.

I see this all the time. My client brings me a dog that is pulling on the leash. The dog is pretty convinced that pulling on the leash works. Most of the time he is right: he drags the owner over to something interesting and sniffs it, or drags the owner to a person who pets him. So as far as the dog can figure, this pulling thing is working out pretty good for him. The client has allowed the dog to pull, and has tried various corrections, like yelling, collar corrections, has changed from a slip collar or flat collar to a pinch collar, and still the dog continues to pull. Some owners have clicker trained the dog and the behaviour is highly dependant upon treats being both available, as well as of a higher value than the interesting smell (for some dogs no treat is better than a great smell!). In fact, the pulling becomes ever stronger because the behaviour has been inadvertently placed on a Variable Reinforcement Schedule. That is, the dog succeeds in dragging the owner to the reinforcement (just one sniff of that enticing mailbox post or one pat from the approaching person constitutes the reinforcement). Pulling, the exact same behaviour, is also randomly - from the dog's point of view - corrected by pops or tugs on the leash or the absence of treats being available. Assuming that the leash corrections are meant to be punishing and are not just random occurrences as the dog makes his way forward, or the handler is intending to punish with leash pops (which may not be entirely correct either because the dog may be desensitized to the leash pops) still means the dog is successful at least 50% of the time. Those dogs fed a treat for desired behaviour and ignored for undesirable pulling devise a strategy in which the dog will take a treat when available and make his own reinforcers when the treat is unavailable. That dog is also successful with pulling at least 50% of the time. Most dogs will take those odds and consider pulling a fine strategy. When I first enter into a training dialogue with this dog about how important it is to keep the leash loose, there will be much resistance and confusion. Pulling has been working, and those neural pathways are well-tended. The previously learned; behaviour - leash pulling - is all the dog thinks he needs to know about getting from point A to point B. Prior learning must be overcome before new learning can take place. It's the old "building new is way easier than remodeling" wisdom.

Over-shadowing (Selective Attention) Definition:

Over-shadowing and Selective Attention are used interchangeably by some scientists and are assigned discrete definitions by others. I am using the words interchangeably here, because for our dog training purposes the particular semantics and pages and pages of dry research I would have to recount seem a bit of overkill. Even when considered discretely, between the two there is a bit of over-lap.

- Simultaneous presentation of two different stimuli will result in selective attention. For instance, if you present a verbal at the same time you present a hand signal whatever is most salient to animal will be noticed and the other ignored.

- Over-shadowing is a form of selective attention. That is: *if compound stimuli are presented, the animals may learn about ONLY ONE of the multiple stimuli present.*

Over-shadowing & Selective Attention Research

The following research was done by Wilcoxin, Dragoin, & Kral, 1971 on selective attention (Flaherty, 1985).

- One group of Quail consumed sour-tasting water, then were injected with a toxin.

- One group of Quail consumed blue-colored water, then were injected with a toxin.

- One group of Quail consumed sour-tasting, blue-colored water, then were injected with a toxin.

- Quail poisoned after drinking sour water avoided sour water.

- Quail poisoned after drinking blue water avoided blue water.

- The third group, who were exposed to the sour, blue water would avoid blue water, but would drink the sour water.

Therefore, the conclusion is "that the quail selectively associated the color of the water with the toxin, and 'ignored' the potential association between the sour water and the toxin." (Flaherty, 1985) (Good Lord, I sometimes dislike reading research...I can logically ascertain the great good to mankind, but mostly I just sympathize with all those poor quail with tummy-aches.)

For us dog trainers, the ramifications are vast. A common occurrence is that the trainer presents the dog with two, three or four cues all at the same time. I see this constantly, such as when I ask a new client if their dog will lie down on cue. "Sure," they state confidently. I ask "What is your cue to get the dog to lie down?" "Down," they reply. I clarify, "You mean you say the word 'Down' and your dog lies down, right?" They usually look at me at this point like I am probably a little slow on the uptake and insist, "Yes, the word 'Down'." I ask for a demonstration. The handler says, "Down," then "Down" again and then bends over and points at the ground while repeating, yet again, "Down." Then the handler looks up at me proudly. I always feel a bit guilty when I continue on, as I figure that for most people I am setting them up for failure with this little exercise, but it is done purposely so I can prove a point. At this juncture I query, "So, I just heard you say the word 'Down' three times, then you leaned over and pointed to the ground. So what was your cue? The word, the bending, the pointing? Because what you just did is not what you told me the cue is." In reality, the vast majority of the time the dog is attending to the motion and unaware of the verbal, whereas the person was convinced that the verbal "Down" was the actual cue. The tragedy is that the handler ends up thinking the cue is one thing and the dog has found something else entirely to be more salient. The problem is, that the dog takes the fall because the cue system stank. The handler misinterprets confusion for disobedience.

I was training Breanna in obedience at the Open level, when I discovered, amazingly that her cue to Finish (return to Heel position from a sitting-in-front-of-you position) was not even close to what I thought it was. I would have bet you a year's worth of baked goods that her cue was a verbal "Swing." After all, this is what I had carefully taught her. I said this word in a bright and cheery voice, and it was accompanied by happy facial movements. One day I discovered that if I said "Swing" in a bright and cheery voice, but not accompanied by happy facial movements, my lovely dog didn't have a clue. She was sitting there in front of me, looking at me adoringly, wagging her little tail 95 miles an hour, and when I said "Swing" nothing changed at all. There wasn't even a flicker of "hey, did you say something to me?" Clearly attention wasn't the problem: she was eager to perform. Puzzled, I began to experiment. Was it my smile? Nope. Was it a small sideways head movement that I had noticed I tossed in there? Nope. It was lifting my eyebrows. My smart dog sprang joyfully into Heel when I raised my eyebrows. Over-shadowing. Tricky stuff.

You risk over-shadowing *every time you open your mouth and say something and move your body at the same time*. I have watched a million people say "Sit," while simultaneously making the motion of holding the treat over a dog's head to teach the dog to sit on cue. Bad, bad trainer. Or the person says something, moves his head as he talks, and motions with his hand, then wonder why the dog doesn't attend to just the verbal cue - the verbal cue always being the item that the person finds the most salient and the dog generally finds the least salient. Present *one item at a time*, so you know what information the dog received. I advise my clients to pretend that they can only do ONE thing

at a time: either move the lips or move the hands or move the feet. Present one item at a time, in the same pattern every time, so that you know for certain what the dog was attending to. This changes the above scenario to: hold very still; say the word "Sit." Pause for 1/2 second. Now use your hand motion or lure. When the dog's bum hits the floor, deliver the treat. This is one of the most difficult things to school my students to do well, as the natural inclination of humans seems to be to unthinkingly present multiple cues simultaneously to the dog.

Dogs *naturally* find most salient:
- motion.
- scent.
- interesting noises (other dogs or possible prey objects).
- food.
- pressure: social pressure, proximity of others.

Dogs *naturally* find the least salient:
- verbal cues.

Let's face it. Talking is all about us. I am not saying your dog cannot learn verbal cues, I am saying that he naturally finds almost everything else in the world more salient.

Syntax of Cue Presentation To Promote Understanding & Prevent Error

There is a syntax to teaching a new cue that will give you predictable results. Do not ignore this syntax as it is just as crucial to teaching the dog as it is if you leave out one of those silly little parentheses when you are doing computer programming. Ignoring the syntax of cue presentation can cause as many "bugs" in your training as it would a computer program. Basically, you split the antecedent or "cue" into two separate phases.
- New cue (this is often a verbal cue that is being added once you can "get" the behaviour by using a lure or hand motion.)
- Pause for 1/2 second, then add: old cues, helper cues, prompts, hand motions, lures, contexts, et al.
- Dog does the behaviour and you...
- Present the dog with the consequence: whatever is most appropriate, meaningful and *provides the*

most information to this dog in this circumstance.

Pop Quiz

You will repeat the above procedure ten or twenty times in a row. You might move a couple of steps in between each repetition to separate one trial from another, but do the repetitions without wasting a lot of time in between each one. Once those ten or twenty repetitions have been done, it is time for a Pop Quiz...

- Use the "new cue"

- Instead of immediately jumping in there and helping, *shut up and stand still!*

- Do nothing and wait for up to a count of ten or so. Literally count this out (to yourself not aloud - the dog has enough without your behaviour adding to the distractions) so you leave the dog enough time to consider the ten or twenty repetitions you just did.

- There is a high probability that the dog will make some sort of connection here and tentatively offer up some version of the behaviour you have just done twenty consecutive times.

- If she offers you the correct behaviour, you make sure you reinforce that generously. Let her know she is super special smart.

- If she stands there looking at you blankly, which is also quite possible, do not despair. She is still trying to figure this out. Once you have counted to ten, repeat the New Cue, and follow it up immediately with the helper cues, just as you did above in *Syntax of Cue Presentation*. You will do another ten to twenty repetitions and then repeat the Pop Quiz.

Continue cycling through the Syntax of Cue Presentation and the Pop Quiz until the Pop Quiz gets a passing grade.

Generalization

This is where we spend most of our training time! Dogs must learn to transfer behaviour and have reliable performance from one context into another. Once taught a behaviour in one location, the dog does not immediately figure out that the behaviour needs to be transferred from one place to another. People do not always generalize well, either. For instance, even though I know how to perform basic mathematical functions, when faced with a real life situation I do not always know how to perform the mathematical functions in the proper order to obtain the answer. Should I divide, then add? Or add the figures, then divide? I always felt a vague sense of confusion when faced with story problems in my high school math classes. The problem is not that I do not know how to do math, it is just not always apparent to me how to apply it. Dogs run into the same sort of dilemma. They know how to sit in the kitchen when told to do so, but when somebody knocks on the door! Well! That is quite a different exercise!

Special Conditions

Therefore, during the process of Generalization, you must reduce special conditions required for the dog to give you the desired behaviour. The list of special conditions is vast: dog performs in specific locations, only on leash, at a close distance, etc. We hear it all the time as instructors. "My dog does this perfectly at home." But when faced with the possibility of social interaction in the classroom, the dog has a difficult time concentrating. He can certainly be taught to concentrate in this situation, he just needs nudges in the right direction to understand that part of understanding the cue means "do this behaviour whenever, wherever." Instructors also hear the opposite, "He does really good in class, but is wild at home." This tells us the handler is either very distracted at home and cannot back up the cue (she is training not just the dog, but three children under the age of 7, with 2 in diapers) or she is not training at home at all or she is very ineffective or she is just plain lazy.

If you do not take your behaviour to at least 20 different locations and 20 different contexts, you cannot count on reliability or predictability of the topography of the behaviour. (Topography, used in this context, means the observable, tangible aspects of a behaviour.)

Assumed Learning

We think the dog has it because the dog performed properly once or half a dozen times in one or two contexts. This is far short of the 6000 PERFECT repetitions required for predictable, reliable, automatic behaviour. I am using the number 6000 because that is one of the agreed-upon numbers of repetitions necessary for learning in humans. If you want a good tennis swing, golf stroke or to be able to do math in your head, it requires lots of *correct repetitions*. Dog trainers, horse trainers and every educator in between, all say it: "Practice doesn't make perfect. Only perfect practice makes perfect."

Spontaneous Recovery

Spontaneous Recovery is a common occurrence in learning. It refers to the reappearance of (recovery) of a behaviour that you thought had disappeared because you haven't seen it exhibited in a while. When the behaviour returns it may appear in the same form or it may be of greater or lesser intensity. As time goes on, in the normal dog, the spontaneous recovery does fade in intensity, duration and frequency. If, over time, spontaneous recovery of undesired behaviours is not fading:

- The behaviour is still getting reinforced somehow. Figure out where, and manage your way out of it.

- You are not being proactive enough to redirect the behaviour cycle *before* it begins. Therefore, the dog keeps "starting down that path."

- Whatever training efforts you are using are sensitizing instead of desensitizing. (Refer to *Sensitizing vs. Desensitizing* on page 183)

- The dog is displaying abnormal learning patterns. In this case you need professional help.

The analogy I use at clinics is that behaviour is like a pair of blue jeans. As you are cleaning out your closet, you find a pair of jeans to which you are particularly attached. You cannot wear them currently, because your butt is much too big, but you think to yourself as you place them in the back of the closet, "I'll lose this three pounds and then I'll wear these trousers again!" Next year, as you are cleaning your closet you think, "I'll lose this five pounds and then I'll wear these trousers again!" You never throw them out. They are still in the back of your closet. You aren't wearing them now, because they don't fit, but if you ever *do* lose that ten pounds, by golly, you'll wear them again! Any behaviour that has ever been exhibited by your dog is like that pair of jeans. They are in the back of the closet, and the dog might periodically get it out and try it on again. This, however, will happen less frequently as time passes, and the pants still don't fit.

Inappropriate Consequences

These are handler issues and involve:

- Poor management. Do you hand the keys to your Jeep to your first-grader? Then why did you let your puppy out the door off leash to go potty? So you could find him squashed in the road? So he can reinforce himself and ignore your pleas of "Come?" Neither is what you intended, but it is what frequently happens. Wake up and smell the coffee. If you are not in control of the consequences by using good management, then you are always behind the power curve, with sometimes disastrous results.

- Poor timing. If you reinforce too early or too late you never did reinforce the behaviour you intended to. Remember: treats, release of pressure and verbal praise are all information. To be clear information, they need to be at the right place at the right time. Droning mindlessly on and on with "good dog, good dog" or doling out treats in a witless (unthinking, unaware) manner doesn't get it.

- Incorrect Reinforcement Schedules. Using food at the wrong time can be confusing and distracting rather than enlightening. Using aversives at the wrong time can be confusing and devastating.

- No consideration of the behaviour's "development period." Is the behaviour in Acquisition or Maintenance? Infancy or Adulthood?

- Inappropriate aversives. You cannot use an aversive if the dog does not understand how to avoid the aversive in the first place. If you need more understanding of this, read *Don't Shoot The Dog* by Karen Pryor. It is a classic.

- Poor boundaries. You cannot be inconsistent. It is confusing, and it does not work.

Inadequate Over-training

Dogs must be Over-trained for the circumstances. That is, you must take the behaviour through the process of Generalization. Over-training refers to a specific part of this process. Let's say I want my dog to do a three minute down stay at a dog show. I will prepare carefully for things that might happen at a dog show. For instance, someone else's ill-trained animal might get up and come over and sniff my dog. Will my dog be prepared for this to happen? People might be coming and going, dogs barking, doors opening and closing, someone playing with a squeaky toy near the ring where my dog is working. All of these distractions must be trained for. In addition, I will try to come up with circumstances that are even more difficult that the dog will have to do at a dog show. I will work on ten, fifteen and thirty minute stays while next to an area where dogs are playing. I will have the dog do a down stay within inches of great smelling treats on the floor. When I take my dog into the Obedience ring at a dog show, I do not wish her to struggle to remain on task and feel stressed. I want her to say to herself, "Jeez, that was easy!"

• Challenging the dog involves setting up little problems for the dog to solve and to practice making the desired decision so you have opportunities to provide information. If your dog is exhibiting good attention skills in the kitchen, try in the living room, then in the front yard, then

stop 20 times on each walk and play an attention game.

• The dog does not have opportunities to practice commitment to doing the behaviour. The trainer does not know how to raise criteria in small, but ever increasing in difficulty, so the dog is stuck at a beginning level and does not progress.

• As soon as your dog has Acquired the behaviour, start in with the over-training. This is how you eliminate special conditions from your work and build dependability and understanding.

Forgetting Is Normal

Remember that! In addition to all the technical reasons...forgetting is normal! Particularly when the environment is chaotic and distracting causing you to think about something else, when you are multi-tasking or when you are worrying about something.

Photograph by Marguerite Schrader

You Don't Always Get What You Want...

What Will Work As A Reinforcer?

Positive Reinforcement is the *only* way to teach many behaviours. In the photographs below, a class of my students and their dogs paint their very first "masterpiece." I learned how to teach this behaviour chain originally from my friend, Lonnie Olson, the founder of Dog Scouts Of America. To teach this behaviour, the students must put a little painting mitten on their dogs, dip it in paint and teach the dogs to target the "canvas." These behaviours are all taught separately and then chained together. This is a good example of a behaviour chain where a clicker is the only way to go. The use of a verbal Marker or a clicker used as a Marker makes precise shaping of behaviour possible. This is a great way to teach many daily living behaviours, as well as obedience, competition-related behaviours and fun, entertaining behaviours (such as painting!).

Determine Positive Reinforcers for Training

Based on material first printed in *Aggression In Dogs*.

Food and games serve as Memory Markers - *information* - in training. This has nothing to do with "good dog" or "bad dog." We are not discussing morality. We are discussing how to best convey information to a species that does not speak your language.

To get started, you will need to make a list of things that your dog likes. The items on this list will be used to *provide information* to your dog about what you want.

What should you use to reinforce desired behaviour? Highly desired items make the best reinforcers. I mean, it is just plain silly to pay someone for a job well done in iceberg lettuce if they like hot fudge sundaes. This means, on familiar territory (such as at home), it may work well to use your dog's regular kibbled dog food

to reinforce behaviour. When in new or more distracting situations, you will need to use hazard pay. Hazard pay consists of super special treats like string cheese, chicken, steak or a brief game with a favored toy.

Premack's Principle

"Give Me Something I Want & I'll Give You Something You Want" is very salient (noticeable and meaningful) to your dog. Trainers who are clever enough to create these opportunities will be extremely successful. An example may be opening a door to let your dog out, but only once she Sits and Looks (eye contact) first. This is using Premack's Principle. Some dog trainers call these "life rewards." You will allow the dog access to something the dog likes to do in return for the dog doing a requested behaviour for you first. It's just like telling your child that she can go to the movies with her friends after she does up the dishes.

Releasing Pressure Can Be A Reinforcer

When you begin the Get Connected Protocol exercises, you will use pressure on vs. pressure off to convey information. The release of pressure serves as the Memory Marker. This sounds simple, but as you will see, it is extremely powerful and meaningful to dogs.

Make a list of things your dog likes. Try to include at least two or three items in each category:

- What are your dog's favorite items to play with?
- What activities would your dog rather do than anything else in the world?
- What kind of physical contact does your dog like the best? (Cuddling? Belly rub? Scratching behind the ears?)
- What are his favorite games or activities?
- How does your dog get your attention when he wants it?
- What are his favorite treats?

All righty then! Now you have a list ready and waiting to choose from when you need a reinforcer. Tag some of the most desired reinforcers to reserve for use as hazard pay.

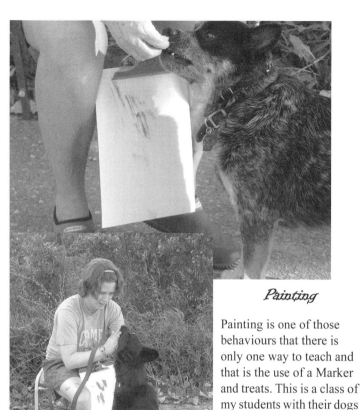

Painting

Painting is one of those behaviours that there is only one way to teach and that is the use of a Marker and treats. This is a class of my students with their dogs doing their very first painting. This is a hoot to teach your dog, but I must admit, as an instructor, I mostly love watching my students teach this to their dogs. The dogs paint the paper, the asphalt driveway and their owners. Although everyone has a good time, there is much learned. The students must use only positives because otherwise this complex behaviour chain is impossible to teach. The student must also be able to touch their dog in a variety of ways. Oh...and wear old clothes!

Photographs by Jim Schutt.

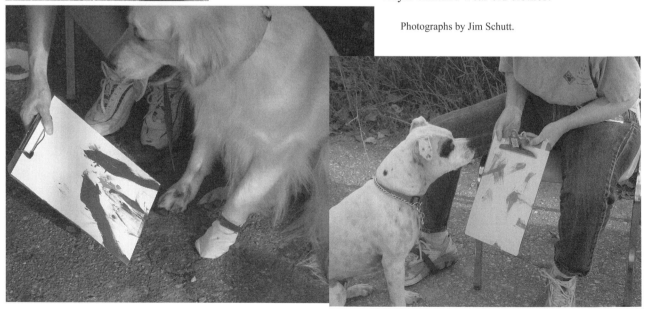

Staying Out Of The Quicksand
Mental Preparation & Equipment

I wish I could just give you a couple of exercises to do and be done with it, but it just don't work that way. For you to get the most out of this technique, you will have to invest. Following is crucial information so that when you get stuck, you'll know how to extract yourself from the quicksand.

Prepare yourself For Training.

Before you begin, be prepared for training:

- Plan ahead. Have a realistic first goal in mind for your first session.

- Be sure you have read this book from the front cover to the back. Then, just prior to training, re-review the exercise you are going to work on.

- Watch the entire DVD to get a feel for the entire protocol, the application of and the release of pressure. Get a feel for the big picture, then work on the details.

- Just before you do an exercise, watch just that one on the DVD.

- Have the right equipment on hand. It is listed below.

- Ready? Read over the first exercise. Watch that corresponding exercise on the DVD. Get a feel for the details of this specific exercise.

- Get your dog and get started.

- Good Luck. Have Fun.

Equipment: Safety first

Use whatever gear you need to be safe. Keep yourself, others and your dog safe. Teaching your dog about touch and pressure may create temporarily scary situations for her. Take your time. Take it slow. Push her *slightly* out of her comfort zone - but do not send her orbiting into space!

For the average dog, a martingale collar or snug fitting flat collar and a six or seven foot leather or cotton leash will be the only equipment required. Round nylon leashes, made from yachting-type ropes are soft, sufficiently weighty and work well. Flat nylon leashes are often thick, too weighty and hurt your hands, or are thin and flimsy and hurt your hands. In addition they have no liveliness, no "feel." Leather leashes are my personal favorites, but leashes made from cotton or yachting or mountain climbing rope are good choices, also.

The Get Connected protocol is not intended to be used with a choke collar or a pinch collar. Nor is an electric collar appropriate for this work. I would think it goes without saying, but if you have an Invisible Fencing system do not do this work with that electric collar on either. These three types of collars are self-limiting and not comfortable for you to hold onto. They also often cause an inappropriate or mis-timed punisher to occur. Remember, I want your dog to get good information, not punishment.

Halti head collars can be used in addition to a martingale collar for resistant or recalcitrant dogs. They are indispensable for handling big, strong dogs that are used to dragging your butt all over town.

Use a muzzle if you are the least unsure about your dog's reaction while doing any kinds of collar and foot holding. If you are worried about the dog becoming defensive or offensive and snapping or biting, unless you are a professional yourself, you need to get help with such dogs.

A very brief discussion in regards to flexi-leashes. The flexi-leash keeps a subtle and constant pressure on the dog's collar. If you want your dog to be sensitive and responsive, a flexi-leash is not a good idea. It encourages a dog to pull.

One particular item that makes training horribly unsafe is trainer reactivity. Stay Fronbrain. Do not push the dog into a defensive state by using too much pressure. Do not lead the dog into a defensive or panicky state by becoming over-emotional, frustrated or angry. Human emotion has a distinct tendency to make a mess of your ability to approximate a behaviour correctly or to time the consequence properly.

Take it slow and easy. Accomplish your goal by using small baby steps spread over as many sessions as you and your dog need. I can easily do each one of these lessons in a few short sessions, but I have been working with it studiously for years. My timing is mostly exquisite, as it should be after all this time, but I too make mistakes in timing, goal setting and approximating. Be patient with yourself. Those who don't make mistakes don't get anything else done either.

Remember: If your dog is especially problematic, reactive or aggressive, or for a dog who is extremely fearful, you need professional help.

Holding Your Leash

When you have sloppy mechanical skills, you get sloppy behaviours and you are ineffective. Holding a leash is one of the most basic behaviours any handler will ever do, and yet, it is so often done in such a way that the dog is encouraged to take advantage of the handler.

There are a few proper places for your leash. One is held at your core, with your hand targeted on a particular part of your body. I tell my handlers to hold their hand next to their belly button, lightly touching their abdomen. Another good target, particularly for walking, is to hold the leash in your left hand (assuming the dog is working on your left side) and hook your thumb

I recommend that you never jerk on a leash. The efficacy of this technique is minimal for the vast majority of dogs being trained. The evidence is clear and all around you: how often do you have to repeat jerking on the leash and how much relief do you get from the pulling dog after a leash jerk or pop?

Leashes, when properly used, are a safety net. Dogs must learn how to walk nicely on a leash because of traffic and a variety of other reasons. However, if you constantly rely on the leash to "cue" the dog (pulling on the leash, jerking on the leash) then it will be difficult to impossible to have reliable off-leash behaviour. Also, because of blocking and over-shadowing, if you constantly use the leash to control and cue your dog, then the other cues do not even "get through."

If your leash is held with your arm loosely at your side when the dog lunges or if he smells something interesting and begins to pull, your arm - and your body - will be hauled along slapdash at your dog's whim. This happens because the leash and your arm feel elastic and make it easy to lunge and pull. The other aspect of this sloppy leash handling is that, as an instructor, I cannot tell if the dog is pulling, the handler is pulling or both are engaged in an inadvertent cycle of tug-of-war.

Leash Held Away From The Body

When the leash is held away from your body, or with your arm hanging loosely at your side, when the dog lunges or pulls you will be put off balance. Here Marylu, a student in one of my reactive dog classes, stages what happens when your leash handling skills are sloppy. When Misty pulls, Marylu could be placed at a disadvantage and is easier to pull off balance.

in your left front pocket. Ah, now we can tell who is doing the pulling.

Who is doing the pulling is very important from an instructor's point of view. I can hardly teach a dog to keep slack in a leash if the handler is constantly taking up any available slack by pulling! I cannot teach a dog to walk properly or keep slack in a leash if the handler is sloppy and unaware of the position of the leash. Also, I tell the handler, "The dog doesn't take the fall for *your* errors. You take the fall for those." If the handler's skills are beautiful and perfect, then maybe we can take a look at correcting the dog. Since the handler's skills are seldom perfect, I guess we know who to correct first, don't we?

For attention and leave-it exercises, just to prevent the dog wandering off at random, you can park the leash under the ball of your foot. Do not place the leash under the arch of your foot, it will just slip through the moment the dog moves. Do not place the leash under the heel of your foot because if the dog moves quickly you will find yourself on your butt.

Leash Properly Held At The Core Of The Body

This is beautiful leash handling. Here Lori works Data with her leash held properly, at the core of her body. We can tell that her hands are stable and still. She is clearly *not* pulling on her dog. If the leash were to be made tight we could tell that it would be Data's doing, not Lori's. In addition, if Data did give a tug on the leash it would feel more like it was attached to a tree or a post - something immovable - rather than a spring with an elastic feel, which feels as if it is easy to pull.

Normal Stuff Happens

Expect the following normal stuff to happen. It is all part of the process, and when handled correctly teaches your dog many coping skills and increases her confidence.

- During this process, if you allow your dog to suck you into her emotional vortex, all will be lost. This means that if your dog gets upset, you remain calm and confident. Stand fast and get her to mirror you, not the other way round. Maybe you are moving too fast and need to slow down your body movements, literally. Maybe your dog is spooky, in which case you need to work carefully in tiny, tiny miniscule approximations.

- Resistance is normal. It is okay. Pouting can be excellent self-therapy. Remain neutral during the exhibition of these behaviours and outlast the dog calmly. This way you are promoting and demonstrating the kind of behaviour that is effec-

tive for training. This way you and your dog will benefit from the new working patterns you develop together. Resistance is a temporary and fleeting part of training, and you should see it disappear after two to three repetitions of each exercise.

- Confusion is normal, too. Consistency with the cue system and reasonable expectations on your part will help your dog through her confusion quickly and with very little stress. Confusion is temporary, too. If it is persisting, you need to stop and re-evaluate. Maybe have someone video tape you working your dog, so you can go over the tape and find your error. If your dog is confused past two or three repetitions, perhaps you are not approximating the behaviour into small enough learning steps. (For examples of approximations refer to the exercises in "Basic Training Boot Camp" on page 120 and *"The Get Connected Protocol: Improve the Relationship by*

using Bodywork & Space; Encouraging Team-
work and Developing Trust & Respect" on
page 196.)

In Regards To Approximations

When we are working any protocol, it helps to know
the meaning of the following words:

- a TRIAL begins with your cue and ends with
  your consequence.

- a SESSION consists of any number of trials that
  have to do with an exercise or a specific approximation of the exercise. A session represents the
  same thing a paragraph should: one topic.

Approximations are tiny, teaching steps that eventually
add up to the finished product.

Each one of us and our dogs may have a different starting point, according to experience levels, and learning
curves differ, too. Be patient with yourself and your
dog. You are both learning new skills. Work until you
get the dog to *try* the new behaviour. Do not expect the
behaviour to look like the finished product you are
longing for the first time! You will use approximations, gradually raising criteria to achieve your goal. In
this Section: *Basic Training Boot Camp* and the Section: *The Get Connected Exercises,* the exercises are
carefully laid out for you.

cific exercises are already approximated for you, so you can follow along step-by-step. Once you have practiced planning and see how effective it is you will never want to work without a plan again!

First, I break each protocol (exercise) down into several approximations (tiny teaching steps). Then, when planning a work session, I might work on two or three different protocols or only one, depending on any time restraints or my current mental or emotional state. As I begin the planned session, my plan might have to change based upon how the dog is assimilating information during our work session.

I keep track of which approximation I am on for each behaviour, from session to session. Working this way makes training easy and provides variety, which is, after all, the spice of life. Variety adds fun and interest for both me and the dog.

Keep a journal, so you know where you are on each exercise. Just as your dog will forget on occasion, so will you. This will help you measure improvement and efficacy, too.

There is a logical progression when teaching exercises, and some exercises are not possible to do unless certain requirements are met. The two tables below give you an idea of which exercises to work on first. For instance, it is of great benefit if, before beginning the work outlined in Table 2: The Get Connected Protocol, your dog has some very basic work in Eye Contact. You need to be able to touch your dog and hold her by the collar. (If you are having trouble with these two most simple of tasks because your dog is getting snappy or is frightening you, you need to seek professional help.) Requisite also is Back Away work. You will progress more quickly if you complete the Get

By far, the biggest problem I see in dog training is that people do not have a plan. Sadly, most do not seem to know they need a plan. (I tell clinic attendees that they should have a plan to walk across the room with their dog, particularly necessary if their dog is reactive.) Others understand the need of a plan but become frustrated because they have no idea about what components the plan should contain. This section will offer you help. First, we will discuss planning. Then, spe-

Between approximation which is included in the *Think First: Impulse Control* exercise.

This preliminary work needn't be a long process, and if your dog has much formal training at all, you have probably worked with attention (eye contact) exercises already. He does not have to be perfect at these, merely have a basic picture of the behaviours. I can ready a dog for the work in Table 2 in about ten to fifteen minutes if the dog has had no prior training at all, other than I my being able to touch him and hold his collar and he can still remain in a relaxed state while I am doing so (he trusts me). It might take you a bit longer as you may not be as familiar with the teaching of the exercises as I am. You are in the situation of learning how as you are teaching. Don't worry about that: it is how I have learned much of what I know, it just takes a little longer the first few times.

If your dog seems particularly resistant to being touched, you might explore TTouch, another great body work technique. Linda Tellington-Jones' TTouch videos show detailed work, and any one of them will do.

If your dog has any physical problems, such as soreness or arthritis, he might not like being touched because it hurts. If your dog has chronic pain, there are exercises that are not suitable for him. Some other diseases, like thyroid problems or Addison's disease, make dogs super sensitive to incoming stimuli, which could include being touched. These two endocrine diseases can also have an influence on how well your dog can concentrate and handle stress. These are obviously matters for a veterinarian to look into. The bottom line is, you must begin with a healthy dog.

The DVD that accompanies this book has valuable information and examples of the exercises.

Table 1: Basic Training Boot Camp

Exercise	Source	Skill Developed
Marker	*Basic Training Boot Camp* on page 120.	Each handler has a word chosen for the Marker cue and one for the Release Cue. The handler understands when to use them. Dog shows understanding of the Marker. (This will take you about 5 minutes.)
Name Recognition	*Name Recognition* on page 129.	Dog turns at the sound of her name and faces her owner. Able to do this in a wide variety of locations and under many distractions.
Release Cues	*Releasing Your Dog: The Stand By Cue & The End Working Cue* on page 130.	Understanding the Stand By Cue & End Working Cue may take up to a week, with you consistently using both of them.
Back Aways	*Back Away* on page 136.	Dog eagerly follows owner's body language and there is no tight leash when doing a Back Away. Must have this behaviour started before beginning the Get Connected Protocol.

Table 1: Basic Training Boot Camp

Exercise	Source	Skill Developed
Eye Contact & Involvement	*Involvement Begins With Eye Contact: Teaching Your Dog Concentration Skills.* on page 148..	Concentration skills are developed. The dog understands that eye contact is "safe." For maximum results, work on Approximation #5 before proceeding with the Get Connected Protocol.
Impulse Control	*Think First: Impulse Control* on page 155.	Impulse control skills are developed. For maximum results, complete Approximation #1, the Get Between, before proceeding with the Get Connected protocol.
Basic Desensitization Bodywork	This may have already occurred through daily living with your dog. If it has not, the Be Still Switch (*The Be Still Switch: Stand Your Feet Still & Be Calm* on page 201.) will be of help. TTouch will help. Pairing touch and touching of the collar with food will help.	The dog can be touched, and the owner can hold the dog's collar. The dog remains relaxed and trusting.
Reading Your Dog	*Canine Body Language* by Brenda Aloff. *For The Love Of A Dog: Understanding Emotion in You and Your Best Friend* by Patricia B. McConnell, Ph.D. *On Talking Terms With Dogs* by Turid Rugaas. *Canine Behaviour: A Photo Illustrated Handbook* by Barbara Handelman. Pay attention to your dog's body language as you are interacting with her. This is the best teacher of all!	The handler's ability to read the dog must be improved, thereby enhancing communication. The Handler should be able to recognize several signals that indicate stress, as well as signals that the dog is using to negotiate and/or calming signals.

Eye Contact and Back Aways

Teach your dog to concentrate and resist distraction.

Multi-tasking: Eye Contact while holding a dumbbell.
Photograph by Amy Morris

Eye Contact with tactile and verbal Distractions
Photograph by Sam Zieggenmeyer

A Back Away, which should be proficient even when distractions are present, helps a dog to prioritize under distraction.

Photograph by Joanne Weber

Eye Contact while moving.
Photograph by Sam Zieggenmeyer

Basic Training Boot Camp

Zasu is attentive and eager to learn a new task. Attention is the first and foremost basic behaviour you must have in order to teach anything to your dog. Impulse control is also crucial, so the dog understands that resisting distraction and remaining on task is how you earn valuable cash & prizes! Translated into your dog's language this means social approval and treats. In this photograph, I am using a clicker and free-shaping Zasu to take a plastic ring and place it in a box. Impulse control is important because I am using treats to train and they are in a bag within easy reach of both of us (right behind me and to the left). Zasu understands that she is to pay attention to me and ignore the bag of treats on the floor. She does this cheerfully and with no resistance. I love that! It makes training fun for both of us!

Photograph by Dave Schrader

The DVD that accompanies this book has valuable information and examples of the exercises.

You cannot wait until January to install your new furnace (at least not in Michigan). You have to have that furnace installed, up, and working long before the snow is piled high, and the icy winds are in full force.

This is true with dog training also: you need to have a basic communication system installed before a working relationship can be established. This consists of:

- A behavioural Memory Marker (also referred to as Marker) to aid in memory and recall.

- Name Recognition.

- Stand By and End Working Cues.

To begin this wonderful new era of communication with your dog, first you must figure out what is appropriate to use as a "paycheck." (Refer to *Determining Positive Reinforcers For Training*.)

There are some behaviours that lend themselves to the use of treats for teaching, such as the behaviours in this section. Since many dogs lose control around food, treats are used to teach the dog impulse control. Treats are also used as a training tool to help the dog remember certain events.

Impulse Control

The puppy chasing the broom thing is cute for about three sweeps. After that it is annoying and might even hurt the puppy if he bites down on the metal parts. Not to mention you wacking him in the head by mistake as you try to get your work done. This is a good situation to use a verbal cue of "leave it."   Photograph by Mary Wilmoth

Name Recognition

When what you see is your dog's tail, disappearing into the distance and you need her to turn and look at you....Name Recognition is just the thing. It is impossible to train your dog without establishing a mutual communication system.

Photographs by Dave Schrader

Installing a Marker, Bridge, Reward Mark, Memory Marker...

"A Rose By Any Other Name..." and all that

No matter what you call it, a Secondary or Conditioned Reinforcer, a Bridge, a Reward Mark, a Memory Marker, an Event Marker, no matter the name the function is the same! Technical literature uses a variety of ordinary terms for this useful and magical word. Reward Mark is the term most commonly used amongst dog trainers, Bridge (the "bridge" representing the time between the occurrence of the Mark and the reinforcer being given to the animal) is the favorite of marine mammal trainers, while behaviorists seem to prefer the rather dry term of Conditioned Reinforcer. My own favorite is Memory Marker because I think that tells the story best. I have shortened this to Mark or Marker, because it is, well, shorter.

One of the most important functions of the Marker is that it serves as a memory aid. What is learning anyway? Remembering to do a certain behaviour at a certain time or on a particular cue. The Marker tells the animal: "Out of the millions of behaviours you do today *remember this*, we'll need it later."

A Marker is used to designate the desired behaviour the instant it occurs, calling the dog's attention to this moment in time, and the behaviour he is in the midst of as you Mark it.

What to use as a Marker

Clickers make an excellent Marker. Because the clicker makes a sound unique in the dog's environment, it is very salient for the dog. The clicker "works on a sub-cortical level,"[2] which is why it is so fast and effective. It reduces processing time.

---

2. I quote Karen Pryor, one of my personal heroes, from a telephone conversation on February 19, 2007, in a discussion of clicker efficacy.

Some ideas for verbal Marker's are, "Yes," "Wow," "Good." Just make it *short* and sweet and keep it *consistent*. That means your tone of voice, as well as the word itself. Do not use a word that you use often in daily language, because every time the dog hears the word casually, it can have the effect of "watering" down the significance of the word as a Marker.

It is entirely possible to use a verbal Marker sometimes and a clicker other times. My own dogs know and understand both a verbal Marker and a clicker used as a Marker. A clicker is extremely handy and installs behaviour more quickly for initially teaching a specific behaviour. A clicker also has the benefit of making you very aware of what specific behaviour you are Marking for the dog. On the other hand, you always have your voice handy, so on those occasions you don't have a clicker with you, or you are past installing the behaviour, your voice will work perfectly as a Marker.

There are times when I use a release of pressure to indicate the desired response, rather than an auditory signal. But, for now, I am going to teach you how to install an auditory Marker.

You may install both a clicker and a verbal Marker if you wish. Just do so during different training sessions.

To Install the Marker:

While installing the Marker do not ask for any particular behaviour.

Choose your Marker. If it is a verbal, have your lips primed. If a clicker, have the clicker handy and know how to make it "click."

Get 30 or 40 tasty treats ready, in a bait bag. My all time favorite bait bag is a two-dollar nail apron from the hardware store. Then:

- 1. Marker (either a "click" or your verbal "Yes").

- 2. Pause approximately ½ second.

- 3. Deliver the food treat.

- Repeat steps 1 through 3 four or five times.

Make sure the Mark itself and the delivery of the treat are 2 separate events. (Refer to *"Selective Attention: Blocking & Over-shadowing" on page 107*)

Now you can raise the criteria slightly to increase the dog's understanding. Next:

- Walk or back up a couple of steps - by now it is usually pretty hard to get rid of the dog! Mark (say "yes" or click with your clicker). Quickly deliver the food treat.

- Repeat the above step fifteen to twenty-five more times.

Reinforcement Delivery

When delivering the reinforcer (giving the treat) *make sure your hand is touching your body.* If your dog is very short, make sure your hand is touching your knee or calf and hold the treat there so she can come up and get it. If your dog is taller, hold your hand on your body at a height that is comfortable for her. It is important that your dog comes *in to you* to get the treat. It is well documented that animals gravitate to the placement of the reinforcement. This means that how you deliver the reinforcer is information. If you hand the treat out to your dog you are telling her to come to within arm's reach, but no further. Since many dogs are made uncomfortable by proximity and people bending over them, this is a great opportunity to send the message that you are safe and want your dog to come in closely to you. Just as sloppy leash handling sends inadvertent messages, so does sloppy reinforcement delivery.

Your Marker Does Not Mean "Good Dog"

A Marker *predicts* a pleasant event for your dog, and becomes *associated* with the pleasant event so it can be used to provide *information.*

A Marker provides the dog with valuable and concise information about his current Behaviour.

While training, when you feed your dog a treat it is of the utmost importance to remember: you are not feeding your dog a treat, YOU ARE FEEDING THE BEHAVIOUR. Always keep this uppermost in your thoughts so you do not stray from your purpose and confuse your dog.

YOUR Marker is NOT an attention-getter

Using your Marker in this way will backfire on you, because then you are technically reinforcing the dog for inattention. Why? *Because once your dog understands the use of the Marker, whatever behaviour he is currently doing when he hears the Marker becomes the reinforced, ultimately the remembered, behaviour.* That means the dog will repeat whatever behaviour was just Marked. If your dog is looking away from you and you use a clicker to get the dog's behaviour back on you, then what you just actually taught your dog was to look away. In this scenario the dog believes her looking away behaviour is what caused you to click and then to treat her.

Practice Using Your Marker

Once installed, immediately begin to use your Marker to provide your dog with pertinent information. Now is a good time to practice using your Marker so you, the handler, become proficient. Use a behaviour your dog already knows. Most dogs know Sit, so, for our example we will use Sit.

- Give your cue for Sit. The moment the dog's bottom hits the ground:

- Mark.

- Deliver the treat immediately following the Marker.

- Now cue for the Sit and wait for a count of 2 until you Mark it and deliver the reinforcer. This is a brief lesson in how you begin to achieve duration with a behaviour.

The Mark As A Continuation Cue

Clicker purists use the "click" to end the behaviour. (For an informative short course about that technique, a good video is *Clicker Magic* by Karen Pryor (1997). A good book is *Click! For Success* by Lana Mitchell (1997). There are more recent materials available, but these are two of my favorites.

Over the years, I have developed a communication system that is wonderfully versatile and creates a very sophisticated training partner. When I use a clicker, which I often use to initially teach a behavior, the "click" ends that specific behaviour, but I have also taught the dog to then come over to me and wait for the next cue. Once I have the Acquisition of the behaviour "jump started," I don't continue to use a clicker indefinitely. At that point, I find that using the *verbal* Marker as a "keep going" cue and having an additional Stand By Cue allows training to be less interrupted and to flow more smoothly than if you allow the Marker itself to "end" the behaviour.

You may use a Marker either way; as the clicker purists choose (the click ends the behaviour) or you can combine techniques as I do (Click ends a behaviour. A verbal Mark, such as "Yes" is used as a continuation cue: Yes, you are headed in the right direction, keep working along that same track.) but you must be consistent. You cannot use a Marker as a continuation cue (meaning: keep going, you are on the right track) one day and an End Behaviour Cue the next. Decide now how you are going to work, and be consistent with how you use it.

Therefore, I use the Marker itself as a continuation cue: not only does the Marker come to mean, "Remember *this specific behaviour*, we will need it later," it also tells the dog, "You are on the right track – keep working!"

Name Recognition

Remember how you installed the Marker? Well, for Name Recognition you are going to do exactly the same thing, with one small variation: Where before you used "Yes" (or whatever verbal you chose) you will use the dog's name, and then deliver a treat.

New rule: in future, do not use your dog's name unless you wish her to look at you!

Get 30 or 40 tasty treats ready. Then:
- 1. Say your dog's name.
- 2. Pause approximately ½ second.
- 3. Deliver the food Treat.
- Repeat steps 1 through 3 four or five times.

Now you can raise the criteria slightly to increase the dog's understanding. Next:
- Walk or back up a couple of steps.

- Say your dog's name.
- As the dog moves toward you, Mark the behaviour.
- Pause very slightly.
- Deliver the food treat.
- Repeat the above step fifteen to twenty-five more times.

Name Recognition & Recalls

Name Recognition is the beginning of your long distance recall and off-leash control. Take it seriously!

Photograph by Dave Schrader.

Releasing Your Dog: The Stand By Cue & The End Working Cue

It is important that your dog understand when she is working and when she is not. Everybody gets all focused on starting the behaviour, but just as much attention should be given to ending the behaviour. If you do not have specific cues set up for this it means you are not being consistent and deliberate in your communication. The consequence is dogs who are constantly guessing about when they get to go do their own doggy thing, like sniff around and eat rabbit poop and pee on bushes, the stuff dogs really like to do when they are not humouring us. Remember this: It is of equal importance to both *begin* AND *end* the behaviour on a cue.

I want to control the end of a behaviour because it makes the dog's behaviour more predictable overall. I can better direct the "flow" of a training session and monitor the emotional state of the dog. In addition, it makes a dog safer. She does not just "assume" that when she is done with an exercise that she can then run off after a squirrel or run over and sniff another dog. For the clicker trained dog, who is encouraged to experiment and offer a variety of behaviours, it gives them a directive about when experimentation is wanted so they are not experimenting when it might not be appropriate or safe to do so.

First let us define the term "release," because it is a word that is interpreted differently by different trainers. In my training sessions "release" does not mean that the dog is then encouraged to jump around and be crazy. Within a training session it merely means, "you are not working right now." As soon as I use an *End Behaviour Cue* my dog waits expectantly for the next cue. To tell her she is on her own time and can follow her agenda instead of mine (so she isn't always guessing and making wrong guesses), I use an *End Working Cue.*

You can think of releasing your dog as a continuum. Once you begin a behaviour, and, when it is complete, you could do one of these things:

- You could cue the dog to do another behaviour. For instance, you could end a Sit behaviour by cuing the dog to "come."

- You could have the dog wait, on Stand By, for the next cue. Your dog is still interacting with you and thinking about you. This prevents the dog from running off and doing what she jolly well pleases when it is not safe or appropriate to do so. The Stand By Cue *ends that behaviour only* and tells your dog, "I still need you to hang around and not run off."

- The other thing you could do is to use an End Working cue to release the dog to explore or interact with the environment, instead of you. Now she is thinking about the environment and you are on the back burner. This is okay, you have given your permission for the dog to direct her attention to the environment if she wishes to do so. You can see how this program prevents the dog from being confused about when she is on your time clock and when she is on her own. Most people do not make this distinction for the dog and then punish the dog when she does not intuitively understand the difference. That is unfair.

Begin Working Cue, Stand By Cue & End Working Cue

- A "begin working" signal is the cue itself, such as "Sit." Or saying the dog's name.

- The Stand By cue places the dog into "stand by" status. That is, the dog waits patiently for her next cue - she is "standing by." This cue ends the behaviour, and allows your dog to relax slightly.

- The End Working Cue is the way you release your dog to play or to tell her she isn't working right now.

Stand By Cue

Zasu "Stands By" as I talk about the next exercise to a class I am teaching. How nice that she can wait attentively for me without getting into trouble every time I take my eyes off her!

Photograph by Dave Schrader

Dogs who are taught this communication system, combined with a Marker (Refer to *Installing a Marker, Bridge, Reward Mark, Memory Marker...* on page 126), become very sophisticated learners. The handler can easily begin a behaviour; keep it going (continuing); ask the dog to pause a moment and wait patiently for the next cue (stand by); or end the work session temporarily and allow the dog to go off and do her own thing (go play). This prevents unwanted guessing and confusion without suppressing curiosity (when appropriate and safe) and experimentation during shaping. (Experimentation is good during shaping. This is when the dog offers up different behaviours in order to say to you: "Is this the behaviour you are looking for right now?" During shaping you want the dog to experiment. During a long down stay you do not.) If you are curious about shaping, I would recommend finding a good video. You really must see it done the first couple of times to understand it well. I think all trainers should be able to shape behaviours as they are a great way to carry on a very free conversation with your dog. Karen Pryor has some excellent videos that demonstrate shaping behaviours.

Owners who do not have this system established get cross at their dogs for guessing, when, in fact, it is their own fault. Teaching your dog to default to you, rather than the environment when you are out and about in public, walking or at classes is the kindest, most wonderful gift you can give to your dog and yourself. Confusion and frustration levels drop dramatically when you are working toward the same goal.

- Good words to use for your Stand By Cue: "All Done" or "That'll do" or "Stand By." or "With Me."

- Good words to use for your End Working Cue: "Go Play" or "Free."

The End Working Cue is necessary for the dog to understand when he is working (on your time) and when he is technically not working (on his own time). This is important because otherwise the dog will constantly "guess" about when he is done working. We see this often exhibited in Stay work. The dog is told to "stay" but if anything distracts him, like a door opening, the dog allows the environment to release him. If taught a clear Stand By Cue and End Working Cue, the dog no longer has to guess. You will tell him when he is "clocked in" and working vs. on "stand by" vs. "clocked out" and on his own time. That means when released from his stay with "That'll do" your dog knows he is in Stand By mode. He waits calmly for the next item on the agenda. If you want to then allow him to go off and sniff or interact with other dogs (when appropriate), you can tell him "Go Play." Once he hears "Go Play" he knows that he is on his own time. No guessing required. No nagging required by you, just clear communication.

To Install the Stand By Cue

Choose your Stand By Cue. Have your dog on leash or in a safe, enclosed area. Also, choose a specific distance that you consider safe. My distance for this exercise is an arm's length. My dog can be sitting, lying down or standing, but she must remain within arm's reach.

- Say "By Me" (or whatever your chosen cue is).

- Pause approximately ½ second.

- Deliver the food treat. Remember to have your hand touching your body.

- Repeat steps 1 through 3 four or five times.

Next, move a few steps. Then repeat the teaching steps above. Move a few more steps, stand there a few sec-

onds then say, "By Me," and give the dog another treat. By now most dogs are getting harder to get rid of. The dog figures that if she hangs around in your vicinity manna from heaven just keeps appearing.

Continue to work on the duration of the behaviour, using your judgment in regards to how many seconds you can have the dog stand there without a treat. *Consciously be aware of how much time passes between each treat.* Have a plan and up the ante in a step-by-step fashion, increasing the time. You can make jumps of 2 to 5 seconds at a time in duration. You can reinforce each increase in duration one or two times, then increase the duration again. If the dog cannot make that large a jump, then obviously you must increase the duration at a rate of 1 second at a time instead of more. This takes longer to put the technique on paper than it does to actually do the work. So go get at it!

Once you have the pump primed, just start using your Stand By Cue on a consistent basis, and reinforce your dog for staying around next to you. Pretty soon your dog gets harder to release to the environment. I'd rather have to tell my dogs, "Go Play," several times than have to beg them to stay next to me.

Common Errors

The Stand By Cue does not mean you release the dog, then play a big game with a bunch of excitement and leaping about. A common misunderstanding is exhibited by people working on a Stay exercise. When they are done with the Stay, they get their dogs up and immediately play a game. What is really being reinforced here? Being released! *If you want to reinforce the stay, the reinforcement must occur DURING the behaviour.* Also, Stays should always be a "calm" behaviour, therefore that is the emotion you wish to promote all "around" the behaviour. The same goes for an End Working Cue. Once you release the dog, that is enough. If you want an eager to please, eager to work dog, make the "work" more fun than the "play." My own dogs don't know the difference between work and play, because work is play. What they have cottoned onto, because of my consistency, is that when they are under orders, so to speak, the chances that reinforcement will occur just went way, way up.

I am not saying "don't play games with your dog," I am saying that you will get superior results if you use games properly – as a consequence. If I am going to use a game as a consequence I start the game right after my Marker. Therefore, if I was working on Heel with the dog and getting great work, I might say, "Yes," then pull out a ball or toy and encourage the dog to begin to interact with me, with a "C'mon and play," or "Get It," cue. In this fashion I use a game as the consequence (positive reinforcement) for good behaviour! BUT I would NOT say, "Yes," then give my End Working Cue, "Go Play," and then start a game. I want to make sure the dog is understanding that the game is a consequence for "good work" if I am using the game as a training tool. The proper syntax is that reinforcement occurs during or immediately after the behaviour. The End Working Cue is used only to signal "clocked-out" to the dog.

- Stand By Cues ("All Done") mean "Stand By" and wait calmly for the next cue.

- End Working Cues ("Go Play") means my dog can go be a dog; pee on bushes, run around mindlessly and sniff. She is "clocked out" then until I give her another "begin working" cue.

Once your dog has the idea (after about 20 repetitions or so), do not feed her if you have to remind her because dogs very quickly back-chain behaviours. For instance, if your dog wanders away and you have to remind her to come back to you, do not give her a treat just for returning. She must show you some duration of the behaviour before she gets a treat. Otherwise, some dogs begin to think in this way: "My handler hasn't fed me a treat recently. But if I wander away, she will "remind" me of what I am supposed to be doing, then she will hand me a treat." This error is very common in all aspects of training. Once through the Acquisition phase of a behaviour, any reminders should mean: "I am giving you an opportunity to return to work. The only way you get reinforcement is while you are working." When the dog understands this is your operating system, she will stop training you to use reminders and then feed her, and prompting you to do so by exhibiting undesired behaviours.

But Really, When Do I Use A Stand By Cue?

All of my dogs that I used extensively as demo dogs in classes or have taken as clinic demo dogs soon learned to ignore everything around them and just follow me around, sometimes for hours at a time. In fact, it was this situation, while I was instructing, that my dogs first taught me how important and how handy a Stand By Cue might be. Of course, at first, I did not teach this formally, but rather out of self-preservation and flying by the seat of my pants (the way that I discover many good protocols). To do this I had to multi-task: the old

"mother has eyes in the back of her head" game. As I would wander around the room talking to the class, I would periodically deliver a treat to my dog. Most of the time I tried to make sure I *was not* looking at her, and would also occasionally deliver a treat while I *was* looking at her. This is because most dogs obviously think that if you are not looking directly at them, they do not need to attend to you either.

Although I was not looking directly at my dog while talking to my class, if my dog wandered off more than a *distance of my arm's length*, I would encourage her back to me. Once she remained near me for whatever duration that was suitable for her training level, I would deliver another treat. In between treats I might glance at my dog and smile, or silently mouth, "good girl," or touch her head or body briefly in a tender way. Maeve was the very best and required the least reinforcement and the least prompting. Zasu is the worst, her ability to concentrate for long periods of time is limited. All of my dogs surprised me pleasantly on many occasions with the strength of their commitment to remain close to me when I thought they would be more tempted by the environment. This shows the power of consistency on the part of the handler. In the end, it is not the treats, but the habit and consistency with which I use the Stand By Cue that maintains the behaviour. After several months (much sooner for the Maeve's and later for the Zasu's...) this behaviour will require little food reinforcement, if any.

A performance event is an excellent place to use a Stand By Cue. This way, in the ring itself, the dog clearly understands: we are done with this specific behaviour, but we are not "done" done.

My students find this cue to be convenient in other public situations, such as Therapy work (visiting Nursing Homes, Hospitals and Schools). It is not always appropriate for the dog to be away from you but it is impossible to keep a dog on high-alert-extreme-concentration mode for lengthy periods of time. The Stand By Cue give us a way to say to the dog: "Stand by, awaiting further orders, but you can relax a little bit. I don't need your complete attention right this minute, but I might need it soon." Used in these situations, the Stand By is also a way of keeping your dog safe and out of trouble, not wandering into IV lines or hospital equipment, or rummaging through a child's desk or pockets because the smell of hidden food is tempting. When I took my two terriers, Breanna and Punch, to Nursing Homes they were well-behaved as a terrier could be. Management on my part is what made those excursions possible, though; and one of the important components was the Stand By Cue. I could put my attention on one of the residents, hold a conversation, and know that Punch, the brilliant opportunist, would not be rifling through her trash can the moment I took my eyes off her.

A Stand By Cue also helps to keep the "flow" going during a training session.

During a walk or off-leash run sometimes it is okay for your dog to be at a distance, but you might want to keep her close when you are approaching a fork in the trail (you cannot see if there are dogs she might run right smack into) or as you approach a road that you do not wish your dog to impetuously run into.

Below, you see the Stand By Cue as a shepherd would. It is used to temporarily pull the dog off the sheep so you can re-group for your next strategy to move those wily creatures where you want them.

Using A Stand By Cue While Working Stock

Rylie is still keen to move the sheep, but I have them where I want them now. It is time to move on to other chores. "That'll do," I say, and encourage her to move towards me. She is inexperienced at working stock in this picture (although she has gained prowess with time while I am at approximately the same skill level), so it takes a little extra body language (an additional, bigger signal using body language, in addition to the verbal cue) to bring her off the sheep. In so many instances for dogs, motion and your body language is much more salient (noticeable) than verbal cues.

Rylie, although she would dearly love to move the sheep around until they all dropped from exhaustion, comes with me willingly, showing no resistance. It is not what she would like to do, but she does not make an issue of it.

Rylie moves ahead with me, glancing back to check in. She is in Stand By mode now, waiting for her next assignment, whether that is moving the sheep some more or moving on to other chores.

Photo essay by Dave Schrader

Back Away

Often, where words do not work, body language will. It is good to have your dog respond to both, so you have one more tool available for use. *The Back Away relies primarily upon body language as the cue for the dog to look at the handler.*

There is no "verbal" cue given, the cue is the body language of the handler.

The Back Away can also be used to teach a dog that if she feels any pressure on the collar, she should orient towards her handler. The Back Away becomes many things to the dog: a cue to look at the handler is the primary item, but when used frequently, it becomes a predictor of reinforcement, as well. Ultimately, *the Back Away becomes an act of faith.* It is how you know your dog trusts you to take care of the situation. You can tell your dog trusts you to keep her safe and "handle it" when she will turn her back, literally, to whatever is worrying to her (or has worried her in the past) and to look at you instead.

In the Back Away, the handler pauses and then backs up a step or two. The dog comes from Heel position to a frontal position, facing you and looking up at you, with her back to the direction you *were* going.

When your dog is aroused or worried about something, she will orient towards it and look at it. If she is aroused, the longer she looks at "it" the more aroused she will become. If she is worried, the longer she looks at "it" the more worried she will become. Most of the time whatever is there is none of her business anyway. When you encourage your dog to look at you instead of what is causing her consternation or arousal, you are teaching her to use you as an emotional anchor.

The Back Away is the backbone of much of my work. It is used to tell a dog a number of things:

- Whatever you are looking at is none of your business.
- I see you are distracted, pay attention to me.
- I see you are a little excited, but we need to go to work now.
- Ignore whatever we are Backing Away from.
- Leave It.
- Use me for an emotional anchor rather than become reactive.
- On a body language note it clearly invites the dog to approach the handler: come in close to me, follow my lead.

When you teach your dog a Back Away you convey the message:

- to the worried dog: "I have this taken care of. You do not have to worry." After this exercise is learned, the Back Away becomes a reassurance that the dog can understand.
- to the reactive dog: "That is none of your business! I have this situation under control." After this exercise is learned, the Back Away becomes a way the reactive dog can focus on you and be in his "Zen Place." This exercise helps the reactive dog to calm down.
- to the pushy, controlling dog: "Leave it alone. It is not for you. I am in charge." After this exercise is learned, the Back Away helps the pushy, controlling dog to prioritize and allows you to direct his behaviour.

I find this aspect of training fascinating: it is possible for the same exercise to convey a desired, albeit different, message to each dog, as each individual dog filters it through their own unique perspective. This eliminates the need to have a million different exercises to fit each type of dog. You can take the same exact exercise and be successful with a wide variety of personality types. The Back Away does not even require much "tweaking" for the individual dog. It is one of those unique recipes that, once taught, invariable works every time; given that the handler has been consistent about using it.

Teaching The Back Away

Begin from a stationary position (a stop).

- With your dog on leash in Heel position...and

- with your *hands anchored on your tummy*, by holding your hands to your midriff (so you do not jerk on the dog)...

- Move backwards from your dog. Physics dictates that when this occurs the dog will come to the end of the leash, and as you continue to back up, the dog will face you. This is not a "jerk" to the dog, but a gentle, firm message: "I am moving and you will be too. "

- When your dog orients toward you (turns to face you): *stop moving*. Mark the behaviour and deliver a treat.

   Use the same pattern of information each time: Marker (either a "click" or your verbal "Yes"). Pause approximately ½ second. Deliver the food treat.

   Always deliver the food treat, itself, in a deliberate manner. (Refer to "Reinforcement Delivery" on page 127.)

- When the dog does particularly well, add to the Mark & Treat: here is a place to be vocal, "Yes! Good Girl!" *Be jolly*. After all, you are going to use this to keep your dog out of all kinds of trouble: approaching dogs; approaching people you don't want her to interact with right now; at the door when people come in; to encourage the dog to come to you when she would rather do something else; as one of the tools for loose leash walking. This is a big deal. Act like it. This doesn't mean you go crazy and encourage your dog to be a Hindbrainer! It means that you let her know you are extra pleased by your demeanor.

When on leash, do *not* jerk your dog toward you as you move away. You want your dog to respond either to a gentle pressure from the collar or merely to the motion of you moving away. There is absolutely no need to

jerk! Your movement will gradually tighten the leash; the dog will notice this and will eventually turn toward you. You do not have to move away with lightening speed, *just at a steady and deliberate pace.* Once you begin backing away from your dog DO NOT STOP backing away until she orients toward you.

The most common error I see here is that people have a tendency to let the leash out longer as they back away. Do not do this. Keep the leash the same length, and your hands anchored on your midriff - your "core" in Pilates work.

To help make this clear to your dog, when you begin walking forward and practicing Back Aways while you are on the move, pause a 1/2 second before you begin your Back Away. This really helps the dog immensely.

As you advance in the Eye Contact work your dog's Back Aways will improve by leaps and bounds.

The Back Away

Theresa walks forward with Zoey. When beginning, I suggest that you walk forward a bit more slowly than normal, and exaggerate your body language slightly.

Theresa pauses briefly and then....

Back Away

...pointedly shifts her weight
backwards, in preparation to....

...step back.

Zoey follows the suggestion of Theresa's body language and comes to a "Front" position: facing Theresa.

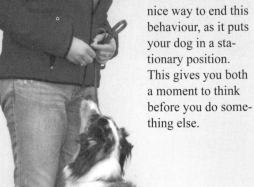

The Sit in front is a nice way to end this behaviour, as it puts your dog in a stationary position. This gives you both a moment to think before you do something else.

Photographs by Dave Schrader

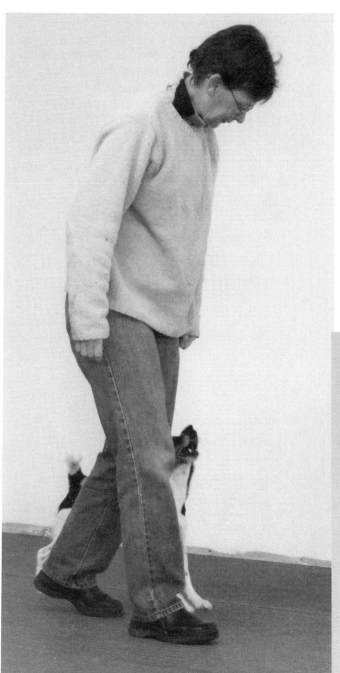

As soon as your dog is doing a stable Back Away, you can begin to test it to see how well your dog has generalized the behaviour. Probably not as good as you think! As soon as you change one small thing, like the location or the distraction level, your dog will probably not notice the cue you provide or she will prioritize the distraction over your cue. Since the Back Away is such a handy, dandy tool, you want your dog to be able to do this really well and have a good automatic response. This translates into: your dog will prioritize the Back Away cue over any distraction.

In the photograph to the left Zasu and I walk forward.

But I mix it up to test her understanding: have I done a good job of teaching her? Instead of just doing a Back Away, I give Zasu a reason to go forward: I toss a treat out in front of us. You can see she knows I have a treat. Even if I didn't have the treat, the motion of my hand alone would be very distracting and interesting to her and could cause her to prioritize the motion over the Back Away. In fact, when you practice, you might want to do several Back Aways without tossing a treat, but just pretending to toss it. Also, when you begin this, the first several repetitions would be ON leash, not off leash, as I am working here. (Zasu is fluent at Back Aways, so I can work her off leash.)

Even though I have paused and started the "rock back" part of the Back Away cue, Zasu is distracted and entranced by the treat. In both of these photographs, her interest in and attention to the treat is evident. Also, very tricky for the dog, is the fact that my eyes are following the treat as I toss it and I am leaning forward - literally my whole body DOES look different than a regular old, garden-variety Back Away. That's okay, this is how Zasu will learn what I want her to prioritize.

In the photograph below you can see that Zasu is beginning to go after the treat.

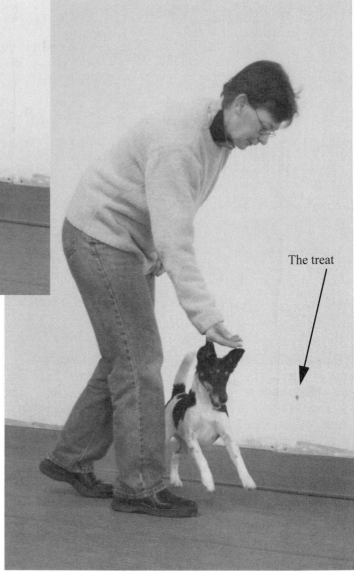

The treat

As I Back Away though, Zasu notices my backward movement and responds by quickly changing her course by coming with me and deserting the tossed treat. A verbal cue was unnecessary, although I could have added it if I absolutely needed it. The danger is then, that the dog continues to ignore your Back Away and waits for you to provide the verbal cue. Wow! This is great! She clearly told me that she has prioritized my cue over the environment. I am so proud of her choice.

The treat is lying on the floor behind her.

I back up another step to keep her coming into me. Do not think that she does not notice that I am getting a treat ready to give to her in the bottom photograph. This anticipation is almost as reinforcing as getting the treat and sort of "drags out" the reinforcement, in a good way, so it makes the event even more memorable.

Zasu literally leaps after me, redirecting all of the energy she would have used to get the treat and, instead, bringing that energy back to me. This always is quite touching to me, because I know this is a very difficult exercise for many dogs and exhibits great impulse control on the part of the dog. On the other hand, if your dog cannot do this, what makes you think that she will be able to ignore anything else that might arouse her, like a squirrel or an approaching dog or person?

Zasu is allowed to get the well-earned treat from me for her good judgment.

This is how dogs learn to make decisions under arousing circumstances. We must practice these exercises with our dogs, because otherwise, when - not if - when, the dog becomes aroused, neither you nor she has any "background" to be able to handle the situation efficiently or calmly.

Again, all Challenges are first practiced on leash!

I jack pot this nice effort, but first ask her to be just a bit calmer in her treat-taking. *I stop and wait* just a second which allows her to calm a bit and also to determine that her over-excited treat-taking behaviour is not earning her more treats, so she sits. Then I deliver to her another treat.

For those behaviours you are using treats for, be very generous with your reinforcer and be very systematic in the delivery of the treats.

Photographs by Dave Schrader

Back Aways

This is part of the correct Back Away: Wilson turns towards me as I Back Away from him and willingly comes into my space. The important parts are that he orients towards me and that he is comfortable to come in close. I have stopped moving my feet and am telling him he is a very good fella.

Interesting note: Wilson was taught the Back Away without the use of any treats at all, but using the Get Connected protocol only. It worked great for him because of the trainer's skill level in communication. I suggest you teach the Back Away as outlined above, using treats, until you are proficient both with teaching the Back Away and using the Get Connected protocol.

Marguerite uses a Back Away to tell Wilson that grabbing an object off the ground is inappropriate. Here we use tempting toys on the floor, but it could just as easily be another dog, a person or rabbit droppings. Wilson is happily compliant, however I wish Marguerite had her hands at her core so as to be most effective. It's okay, she is going to get away with it, because Wilson is handily complying to the request by responding to her body language.

Photographs by Dave Schrader

These photographs were taken in one of my Resocialization classes, a class for dogs who are reactive. Normally, we would be teaching the exercise on a short leash. In this particular lesson, with quite advanced dogs, we were working to see how effective prior training had been. That is, the leash is long on purpose; Marylu is relying heavily upon body language, prior conditioning and training to attract Misty to her. Our goal is to see how much the leash is needed to get the job done.

Here, in the top photograph, Misty is beginning to get "too" focused on the loose dogs playing nearby.

Her handler asks her to turn her back on the distractions and to come in close by using a Back Away. As Marylu backs up, Misty turns around and moves towards her handler.

Because the communication was clear, Misty was able to succeed and gets a tasty treat for her efforts.

The Back Away is great for telling dogs: "What you are currently looking at is none of your business!"

Involvement Begins With Eye Contact: Teaching Your Dog Concentration Skills.

Based on material first printed in *Aggression In Dogs*.

The goal of each session is to add 2 to 5 seconds to the dog's attention span, thereby removing him from the 'attention deficit' crowd and placing him into the whiz-bang class that has 60 to 90 seconds, or longer, of constant attention.

Eye Contact Used As An Emotional Anchor

Jackson remains attentive to Beth even though tempting plates of food are nearby! Jackson is sometimes nervous about activity or chaos around him. He is using Beth as an emotional anchor so he can feel safe and confident, drawing from Beth's strength, instead of becoming spooky. Attention like this is super good for nervous, cautious or reactive dogs, too, because you give them something to focus on besides what is making them so upset.

Photograph by Mary Wilmoth.

148   Involvement Begins With Eye Contact: Teaching Your Dog Concentration Skills.

Acquisition

- Begin in a distraction free environment where your dog feels safe for the very first lesson. After that, you should practice Eye Contact *everywhere, all the time.*

- You need a treat that can be swallowed in 1 gulp: no chewing required by the dog.

- Begin with your dog on leash. Gradually transfer the behaviour of orienting toward you to off-leash when it is reasonable to do so, and only in controlled, appropriate environments. Take into account the dog's safety and how much you can control the environment. Intermediate steps might include you stepping on the leash (Refer to *Holding Your Leash* on page 116) or allowing the dog to drag the leash before working off-leash.

In future I will refer to Marking and the deliberate and conscientious reinforcement delivery as: *Mark & Treat.* This refers to the following pattern:

- Marker (either a "click" or your verbal "Yes").

- Pause approximately ½ second.

- Deliver the food treat.

- Also deliver the food treat in a deliberate manner. (Refer to *Reinforcement Delivery* on page 127.)

If your dog is repeatedly and persistently inattentive, use a Back Away or a Move Into, provided you have taken the time to install one of these. (Refer to *Back Away* on page 136 - an easy exercise - or *Move Into* on page 232 - an advanced exercise.)

Reinforceable Criteria.

Notice and Reinforce, specifically with a Mark & Treat, any or all of these:

- Intention behaviour: as soon as your dog begins to turn his head toward you, Mark & Treat.

- Your dog moves toward you.

- Your dog stays near you.

If you are working outside, or the first several times you are working in any new area: Begin with your dog on a leash or long line. Remember, safety of you and your dog comes first!

Approximation 1: Manufacture Direct Eye Contact

For dogs who are extremely nervous about this whole "eye contact" thing: When your dog is in a relaxed frame of mind, and in a familiar, safe setting, look him directly in the eye just for a split second. Then quickly slide your eyes sideways so you are looking away from or past the dog. Lick your lips (a calming signal). Repeat. Mark & Treat while your dog allows the brief glance of eye contact.

Gradually you will begin to prolong the eye contact before you do the eye-slide. Continue delivering treats for appropriate behaviour. The goal is a dog who begins to meet your gaze with a steady *relaxed* gaze of his own.

Now that you are assured that the dog will ACCEPT eye-contact, you may proceed with safety.

With your dog sitting or standing in front of you:

- Hold a piece of food in your hand (left or right, doesn't matter), with the food held between your finger and thumb and your hands at your sides or held quietly near your chest.

- Show the dog the piece of food by placing it in front of his cute little nose.

- Quite rapidly, but smoothly and calmly, move the piece of food to your nose. As the dog's eyes meet yours...

- Mark & Treat.

- Repeat this sequence four or five times.

- Move a few steps (a new location!) and repeat the above steps. Do this ten or fifteen times. End your session when the dog is doing well. Quit while you are ahead!

Over the next sessions, move to a different room or area and repeat the above steps. Quit each time on a "good" trial.

Approximation 2: Making a Distinct Choice: Voluntary Eye Contact

- Show your dog the food enclosed in your hand – but don't let him have it.

- Move the hand with the treat so you have it held out at shoulder height, with your arm extended and the food visible.

- The instant your dog looks at you and away from the treat, Mark & Treat.

The intention here is to reinforce the dog for making a CONSCIOUS DECISION to look AWAY from the food and look at YOU.

- If your dog tries to leave, make sure you are stepping on the long line or leash and don't allow him to take off into the wild blue yonder. But put up with everything else, ignoring all the other annoying or cute behaviours. This means standing quiet and still and looking at your dog in a friendly, but calm, fashion.
- Suddenly, your dog, probably in frustration, will glance up at your face. (Hey! You! Give me the Food Already!) Immediately Mark & Treat. He must be looking up (at the very least) and preferably at your eyes (Excellent!) to get the treat. Initially, accept even very short glances as successful efforts to Mark & Treat, and be quick with your Marker.

In summary, this particular approximation requires that you play a patience game, with the goal of having your dog voluntarily look at you without you having to open your mouth and intervene. Be quiet and wait for the behaviour to be offered.

Approximation 3: Elaborate on the "Choice" Thing

- Have a leash on your dog with the other end on the floor under your foot.
- Stand still and quiet, with your arms at your sides, your hands easily accessible to the dog, and the food enclosed in your fist or even in both fists.
- Your dog may bark, whine, sneeze, nudge, paw, look at the hand with the food, leap, and try many other cute tricks. Remain neutral and still. Wait.

Approximation 4: Increasing the Threshold

Stop reinforcing swipes (quick glances) and look for that commitment to look into your eyes for longer and longer periods of time. Don't forget to reinforce remaining on task.

At this point you have a dog who is receiving a treat around every 3-5 seconds. Work that threshold up to 20 or more seconds of eye contact between treats.

In summary, you are raising criteria from glances to the dog making a commitment to gaze into your eyes.

Remember, the goal here is to have voluntary involvement.

Approximation 5: Adding the Cue

Don't be in a big hurry to add that cue! The more reliable the behaviour before you add the cue, the more reliable and consistent the ultimate outcome will be. When you have attention that is beyond just a glance and is approaching *5 to 10 seconds of intense eye contact*, you may begin pairing your cue word with the behaviour. That is, as the dog is looking at you, say, "Look," (or whatever your cue word is) and then deliver the treat. I most often feed out of silence. As you increase criteria, you will wait longer and longer before you give the End Working Cue.

- The cue may be verbal, the one you chose in your planning stage.
- The cue may be a certain posture.
- The posture cue may apply most to competition dogs. For instance, when I stand straight and look ahead, with my left hand held in front at my waist, my dogs run over, get into heel position and get "Involved."
- The cue may be contextual. For example, when your dog dashes out the back door, he rushes to the fence to look for squirrels. Or, "Oh, the Obedience Ring – that means pay attention."

I also use an informal "check in" cue with my dogs, which means to orient toward me for a moment. I would use this when we are walking informally. The cue I use is the dog's name, which means: Look at me and see if I need anything further.

Approximation 6: Introduce Premack

If you want to teach your dog that you are relevant, put Eye Contact into every context. This is the key to making every interaction with your dog "count." More effective than drilling your dog on obedience, or working with him formally 30 minutes a day, are the ten second training sessions you do throughout the day.

This technique encourages your dog to notice something in the environment that interests him to look at you for input.

Approximation 7: Multi-tasking 2 Behaviours: Sitting and Looking

- You may have to place your dog into the sit. This is fine. Some dogs just end up sitting in front of you because it is the easiest place to play this game.

- Some dogs are made quite uncomfortable if you are bending over them at all, and shorter dogs will find it easiest to sit back a bit in order to see your face. Again, unless you are working on competition obedience, the exact positioning of the dog is much less crucial than the eye contact itself. If the dog is uncomfortable about personal space, you will have to Shape him into sitting closer to you over a couple of sessions.

- Each time you change position (e.g., Heel to Front) getting Involvement (attentiveness characterized by eye contact) from your dog is a whole new task. A change in position is a change in context, just as surely as a change of location would be, so you may see spontaneous recovery of poor attention.

- Seek to prolong the eye contact and get the dog to commit to paying attention to you. The look you are working to achieve will have the intensity that indicates that your dog is making a conscious decision to make you a target for Involvement.

- If you are training for competition obedience, make sure your dog is in perfect position before you deliver the reinforcer, every single time.

I have taught my Shepherd bitch, who came to me with some rather alarming aggression issues, to default *always* to me. *Anytime* she sees anything in the environment that is interesting to her, her habit now is to glance at it (person, dog, rabbits, deer) and then to immediately look at me for information about what "we" are to do about it.

Approximation 8: Stationary Heel Position – Teaching A Station

Initially you will "step into" or pivot into heel position, because obviously your dog doesn't really know where this Station is yet. That is all teaching a Heel position is. It is just teaching your dog to go to a Station (a specific location) on cue, maintain position with that Station when it moves, and remain in position at/with the Station until released.

The leash is under your foot, or passed behind your body and held in your right hand, with the dog on your left. One treat is enclosed in your left hand, between your finger and thumb. You can "store" the additional treats in your right hand, or in a bait bag.

- Once you have the dog's attention: request a "Sit," then *you* step into Heel position.

- Note: In the following steps I am using the cue "Heel" as a cue that combines a physical location in space AND attention. Thus, the dog comes to associate a specific Station (location and position) with the word "Heel."

- You will introduce the new cue of "Heel." Deliver a treat when your dog is in the appropriate position.

- The treat delivery will have a very specific location, such that the treat is placed where you want your dog's visual reference point for heeling to be. For most dogs this will be somewhere on your pant seam, at a height varying considerably depending on the height of your dog. *Place a piece of tape on your pant seam for a couple of sessions, so you are consistent in the placement of your reinforcement delivery.*

- Begin to wait longer and longer between the "Heel" verbal cue and the Marker. The Marker would be accompanied each and every time with delivery of a training treat at this stage. BUT you will be waiting for ever more duration of the behaviour, by a second or two at a time....

- Now, add a more "formal" posture, making sure you aren't all twisted sideways watching your dog. With your dog sitting in Heel, look out ahead of you, as if you were walking (but don't move yet!), and reinforce your dog for remaining in Heel position. *This is still a stationary exercise at this point.*

Approximation 9: Challenges (Adding Distraction)

Before doing much distraction work I strongly suggest that you have two important exercises installed. These two exercises provide you with a means to communicate clearly to how you feel about distraction as opposed to attention.

The first is a Back Away. As soon as you have a reasonable Back Away, it is used for two different situations:

1. Before the dog is distracted or looks away - sort of as a distraction preventer.

2. If the dog becomes distracted, it is used as damage control and as a strategy to regain the dog's orientation and attention toward you.

(Refer to *Back Away* on page 136)

The second is a Get Connected Protocol exercise, the Move Into. (Refer to *Move Into* on page 232.) It is used in one situation:

1. Any time the dog's attention begins to lag, you can use a Move Into until the dog returns his attention to you, upon which you will immediately step into a Back Away.

The more alert you are to micro-behaviours, such as the dog just beginning to orient his nose away from you, the more successful you will be in getting the idea across.

Strategies for the Inattentive Dog

If your dog looks at the Challenge and does more than glance at it for 1 or 2 seconds, do something to catch his attention.

If your dog glances at the Challenge, then looks back at you:

- Initially accept that glance back at you, Mark & Treat it. However, after one or two trials, do not accept just that quick glance back at you and feed it. Instead, immediately raise criteria so that the dog is remaining on task for a count of 2-3 seconds before you Mark & Treat. Make sure the dog is committed to gazing at you instead of gazing around at the environment before you will hand over a treat.

Other great strategies for the inattentive dog:
- Back Away.

- Move Into.
- Using a VERBAL, like using your dog's name or the word "Look," are my least favorite choice. I discourage (well, actually browbeat) my students from using this strategy, as it is the lease effective.

Select a distraction from the Challenge List below. You may use a treat reinforcer for really excellent behaviour.

Challenge List

Try the following exercises first with your usual bait bag as part of your wardrobe. Then try each Challenge with no food in your hand and no bait bag on your person. You may place the treats in your mouth, on a nearby table, or windowsill. This way you can store food on or near you without being obvious about it.

- At any time during this process, when you get an excellent response or a First Correct Effort, provide hazard pay or a jackpot. Don't be tempted to repeat an exercise until your dog gets it wrong – learn to quit while you are ahead!

- You are to become silent for longer periods of time, giving the dog less frequent verbal feedback. This will harden the dog's resolve to hang in there and continue to pay attention, even though it may be more difficult to do so. This is also a "confidence builder" in that your dog will be reinforced heavily for making correct decisions all by herself without constant prompting, continuous cheer-leading or reminders from you.

- Assume a handler position of Heel or Front. A second person now comes up at a distance of three to four feet. Have this assistant work gradually closer, one step at a time, hardening each response (getting a consistent response over a number of trials: such as three Excellent responses in a row, or 8 out of 10) before you move on to the next approximation. Eventually, this person will be standing next to the dog. It is normal for your dog to glance at the approacher, but it should be a one second glance. The dog's commitment needs to be to you, not the approaching person.

- If you are having lots of inattentiveness, conduct a Review Session. For a Review Session, you will back up to a previous approximation (step)

where the dog was succeeding, and then advance forward again. This means the assistant temporarily increases the distance and gradually re-approaches.

- Toss or drop a piece of food. Pay attention – step on the food or move away from it - if the dog goes for or looks at the food.

- Place food on a chair, allowing your dog to see you doing this. Walk near the chair and ask for Sit and Eye Contact.

- Work backwards from the dog one step at a time, until you are six feet away during the distraction, returning to the Heel position before releasing.

- Have an assistant walk by and toss food.

- Have a person talk while walking at a distance of more than five feet.

- Have a person bounce a ball or gently swing an umbrella at a distance of five or more feet.

- Have a person offer food in a neutral way. If the dog "goes for" the treat, the helper removes the food and turns his back on the dog.

- Have a person approach the dog and stroke it.

  Initially you will want to do this in steps as follows:

  1. Provide a constant feed for the dog as the helper lightly touches dog.

  2. The helper touches the dog, and, if he resists distraction, then provide the Marker and treat.

  3. If the dog loses attention, do not use a Marker to get the dog to look at you. Wait for your dog's attention to come back to you and then begin another trial. I will give the dog this chance ONE TIME. Then if not progressing, use your Back Away or Move Into.

Maintenance of Behaviour

Place Involvement behaviour on a Maintenance, or Variable Reinforcement, Schedule. That is, you will use treats as paychecks on only some occasions. After a while, the response becomes a habit and is integrated into the dog's behavioural repertoire. Each time you introduce a new Challenge, you will have to temporarily go back to the 1 behaviour = 1 cookie strategy (this is a Fixed Reinforcement Schedule). Then you will move the behaviour onto a variable schedule - where you are asking for multiple behaviours or more

duration of behaviour and are not giving so many treats. Instead, you will "hold out" on the dog, and when he has worked hard you will give him three or four or five treats, one at a time in quick succession: say "Yes" - deliver a treat. Just as the dog is finished chewing (that can be really fast - perhaps I should say gulping...), say "Yes" and deliver another treat, and so on.

When your dog has completed this exercise, it is exciting to know that he will voluntarily choose to attend to what is important to the handler instead of what is important to the him. He has good priorities.

When Do I Correct?

After you have presented the dog with many Challenges, and he has proven to you that he understands this concept, only then is it fair to correct. Correction coming at this stage, when the dog has repeatedly done the behaviour under many circumstances, will serve to give the dog information about your window of expectation.

Just so you have a clear picture, a correction might be one of the following:

- A good attention-getter for the distracted dog is a little tap right on the top of his cute little head. This is a tiny tap meaning "Where are you?" – not a hard thump of irritation! You might have to be persistent though, and tap, tap, tap (be that water dripping on stone) several times, being as irritating as you possibly can until the dog looks towards you. If you tap, then stop while the dog is oriented away from you, you "released the pressure" at the wrong time and instead teach the dog to ignore the tapping. The tapping is stopped when the dog orients toward you. As soon as the dog orients toward you in this scenario, do a Back Away and be jolly. The Back Away serves a Memory Marker in this capacity.

- Do a Back Away.

  Now, the part of this correction that will CHANGE THE DOG'S BEHAVIOUR: Continue to move backwards to encourage the dog toward you. When the dog catches up with you, Mark & Treat. In subsequent incidents, begin to wait for 3-5 seconds or more of attention before you Mark & Treat. This maneuver is intended to surprise the dog and therefore encourage her to keep better track of you – not as a means of physical punishment.

- If your dog is boisterous and a leaping maniac and simply WILL NOT attend to you: change to impulse control work. (Refer to *Think First: Impulse Control* on page 155.) This has a very calming "Frontbrain" effect. (Refer to *Brenda's Brain Model* on page 44)

- You can try a Down Stay for a couple of minutes, then resume work on the Involvement.

- Review the "Strategies for Inattention" section in this chapter. The Move Into, once it is taught, can be very effective.

Remember: If you have to prompt for attention more than once or twice, it is time for a review session! Do it right now. Don't wait another minute. This is a temporary process: a quick review for the dog, utilizing the first steps you used to get attention. (Refer to Approximations #1 - #4, this exercise).

IMPORTANT! The biggest mistake you can make is to correct or frown or act irritated when your dog is looking at you. Why? Obviously, this would be applying an aversive to the desired behaviour. Big error. Don't do it.

Eye Contact Challenge

Zoey loves to play, but playing is not always appropriate, especially if around other dogs and it's not your frisbee! At Agility and Obedience trials, or at a public park, Zoey must remain attentive to her handler, and refrain from prioritizing the environment over her handler. Here we are testing Zoey to see if she understands that her handler is calling the shots. She'll get to play with her own frisbee for being such a good girl and resisting temptation! This exercise helps Zoey's handler to keep Zoey safe under a variety of conditions.

Photograph by Dave Schrader.

Think First: Impulse Control

Based on material first printed in *Aggression In Dogs*, with the exception of Approximation 1 - The Get Between.

The environment is very exciting and is always in direct competition with you for your dog's attention. Technically, this is an issue of competing reinforcers. If your dog learns that he can "help himself" to the environment, you will always be on the short end of the stick when you need compliance. Remember the "Pyramid" in the *You Don't Always Get What You Want...?* chapter? (Refer to *The Pyramid of Competing Reinforcers* on page 106.)

"Punishment makes dogs excellent discriminators" translates into real life as: when a dog is punished, she associates any one of a number of environmental factors with the punishment. This could be the location, the punisher (that could be you or a "device"), or the approaching dog or person, either instead of, or in addition to, the behaviour itself. For instance, counter-surfing is SAFE when humans are not around and DANGEROUS when they are. This is how confusion between the species develops. What humans would like to think when we punish the dog for counter-surfing is that the dog will then understand that counter-surfing is BAD. Nonsense! The dog places no moral value on behaviour. The dog learns, with just a couple of trials, the exact circumstances in which a behaviour "works" as opposed to those circumstances in which a behaviour "doesn't work."

Daily life with humans quickly teaches a dog that the handler is powerless under many circumstances and that the dog can take advantage of those situations. Humans inadvertently promote this lesson by lack of management, which is especially detrimental with the young dog or the dog who has behavioural problems. Although dogs do not have morals, you can teach your dog: When I ask you to do something, it is in your own best interest to do so.

Your goal is to get your dog to believe you when you tell him, "It's unavailable, it will never be available, you may as well just quit thinking about it." Do not lie to your dog by allowing him to get an item that you tell him is unavailable. If you are slow (Bad, BAD trainer - and yes, that is a moral judgment) and allow the dog to obtain the food when you have told him "Leave It," you have just told your dog, "This is optional. If you are quicker than I am, then you can have it." Essentially, in this case, you have taught the dog a great game called "If I am Quicker than You and Sneakier, I Can Have It."

Choosing the Handler over the Environment

For best results, work each approximation of this exercise in two different fashions:
1. Use the verbal "Leave It" cue. Then prevent the dog from access to the food by one of the following methods:

 • Use a Back Away.

 • Get Between - that is place your body between your dog and the object of his desire.

 • Cover up the food with your foot or hand.

The reason to do the exercise with a verbal cue is because you want the dog to have a verbal cue in place in case you need to use it. For instance, your dog might have her back to you or be at a distance. In this case a verbal "leave it" will be the most effective.

2. Do NOT use any verbal cue. Then prevent the dog from access to the food by one of the following methods:

 • Say nothing but just do the Back Away.

- Get Between - that is place your body, *without speaking*, between your dog and the object of his desire.

- Cover up the food with your foot or hand without saying a word.

The reason to NOT use a verbal cue is because eventually the ideal response is for the dog to see something in the environment that interests her (anything in the surrounding environment she looks at for more than a count of 2) and see this as an environmental cue to immediately check in with you.

The vast majority of dog handlers, including many who are experienced and should know better, allow their dogs to DEFAULT TO THE ENVIRONMENT. That is, the dog is allowed to learn he can "reinforce himself" at will. The dog responds to, and prioritizes the environment, and it is not until then that the handler tries to step in and become part of the loop. As far as the dog is concerned, by that point the handler is part of the problem and an annoyance.

Your goal is: *the dog defaults to the handler*. The savvy handler has placed herself in the catbird seat by convincing the dog that the handler is The Way and The Light - the liaison by which the dog is allowed to access the environment with permission. If that permission is not granted by the handler, there will still be something "in it" for the dog.

One valid reason I like to train Leave It & check with me as the default, is practicality. After all, when you are out on a walk, who sees the rabbit turds first? If you do not teach your dog to default to you instead of just helping himself, you will always be behind the power curve. It does darn little good to scream "Leave It" in frustration while the dog is consuming the offal.

Magnets

Dog magnets are anything your dog is currently attracted to. For training purposes I often use food as a magnet. Other magnets you encounter out in the real world are other dogs, people, squirrels, candy wrappers, animal excrement (ah, those discerning palates), and other disgusting "delicacies."

Keep In Mind

Dogs need to understand that the presence of children, people, dogs, food, toys, and other desirable items does not mean that these items are automatically available for partaking. You help the dog understand this by teaching him that reinforcement is available from the handler for resisting temptation. This becomes a very powerful exercise and is a strong bonding exercise. The dog learns that the handler is The Way and The Light to reinforcement and to all good things in life, *not* someone who is in the way and preventing access to all the good stuff.

Teaching good impulse control also hammers home the fact that consequences are contingent on behaviour, and that the dog must perform in a certain manner to obtain reinforcement. Life is not a free ride.

The dog's belief system becomes:
- It is reinforcing to substitute my handler's agenda for my own.

- Behaviour that is cued by the handler has the greatest possibility of reinforcement.

- It is in my own best interest to relinquish objects in my possession or objects I wish to possess, when so instructed by my handler.

- My handler, rather than the environment, is the way to the good stuff.

- Direct access is not always the way to reinforcement.

Acquisition

- Begin with your dog on leash. Do not tell the dog to "Sit" or "Down."

- Hold the treat between your finger and thumb at about shoulder height.

- Begin to slowly lower it towards your dog's nose.

- Attend only to her nose. Do not worry about any other part of her body.

- The moment your dog begins to move her nose toward the treat, quickly and smoothly move it straight up.

- Count to 1-2.

- Begin to slowly lower the treat towards your dog's nose.

- The moment your dog begins to move her nose toward the treat, quickly and smoothly move it straight up.

156   Think First: Impulse Control

- Count to 1-2.

- Repeat those last three steps until your dog indicates he is not going to dive for or grab at the food by one or more of these:

  Looking away from the food
  Turning his head slightly
  Backing up
  Looking at the handler
  Looking patient

- Mark & Treat that Behaviour (or combination of Behaviours).

While I will accept any reasonable try during the first five repetitions of teaching this behaviour, my end goal is to have the dog choose "look at the handler." So after the first five or ten repetitions, I will wait until I get "look at the handler" before I would deliver the treat to the dog.

Approximation 1: The Get Between: Using Pressure On/Pressure Off Body Language

Begin impulse control work as a stationary exercise. Later on we will add you and the dog being in motion. In these exercises it is best if your dog is standing. THIS IS NOT A STAY EXERCISE! DO NOT tell your dog to "Stay." Instead be alert and prevent your dog from getting the object you have told him to leave, by using a Get Between (moving between your dog and the object of his desire).

Pay Attention! This Is Important.

The dog is NEVER, EVER allowed to get the "Leave It" item off the floor himself. When you are finished with a trial, *you* will pick it up off the floor. At that point, you put it back in your bait bag to be used as a future treat. Later in the game, when the dog has a much better idea of what is going on, you may occasionally pick the treat up off the floor and feed it to the dog yourself.

When you are teaching impulse control behaviours do not allow *yourself* to be distracted. Concentrate hard and don't worry what the dog's tail or feet are doing; *focus on his cute little nose.* If that nose or the eyes move in the direction of the food "magnet," cover the food quickly with your hand or foot. Do not strike the dog, yell "No," nor prevent the dog from trying for the food treat. "Trying for it" is how you are given the opportunity to provide feedback by covering the food

with your hand to communicate, "This is unavailable." This trial-and-error-learning is how the dog internalizes the lesson. I encourage experimentation, but am always there to make sure that only one thing works: "Look at me."

With your dog on a relatively short, but loose leash, and your leash anchored (on your belly-button at your core):

- Show your dog the treat.

- In a slow and deliberate manner, and within clear view of the dog, drop the treat behind you. You can give it a bit of a toss so it lands a couple of feet behind you if you wish, which will make it easier on the first couple of trials to maintain control.

- Your dog will dive for it.

- Do not say anything. Just keep stepping between him and the treat, specifically by stepping towards his nose. As you step between, also step *toward* the dog, causing him to back up a couple of steps.

- Watch that nose! It tells you where your dog is headed next.

At some point your dog will stop moving and look at you. Be ready, this may be very brief. You are going to ask the dog a question at this juncture: *"What is your decision?"* This question is asked in the following manner:

- When the dog backs up, stops and looks toward you, step laterally away from the treat on the floor, allowing the dog an opportunity to go after it.

- If you see that nose even mildly twitch, step smoothly and quickly in between the dog and the treat and towards the dog, causing the dog to back up a step or two.

- Now you will repeat your question: "What is your decision?" When the dog backs up, stops and looks toward you, step laterally away from the treat on the floor, allowing the dog an opportunity to go after it.

- When the dog indicates he is not going to dive for or grab the food, even though there is a clear opportunity to do so, Mark the behaviour, and then, using a treat in your hand as a lure, turn the dog so his back is to the treat on the floor. Then you may deliver to him the treat from your hand.

Do not stand there the first couple of times for bloody ever. The moment the dog remains in place or glances up at you even though he could try to dive for the food, Mark that hesitation and turn the dog, give him his well earned treat for that one glorious second of impulse control.

Now you are ready to work on duration. Get to the point that the dog will stand and stare at you even though the treat appears to be accessible. I like to work up to several seconds of looking at me and resisting looking at the treat.

Approximation 2: Add A Verbal Cue

I discuss adding a verbal cue here. A verbal cue is occasionally handy and this is a good point at which to teach it. Once learned, occasionally practice the verbal. Keep in mind it is much better for *the distraction itself* to be the cue to look at you.

With your dog on leash:
- Show your dog the treat.
- Say "Leave It."
- Toss the food on the floor.
- If necessary, you will cover the treat with your hand or foot when dog dives for it. Be quick!
- Let your dog bark, fuss, paw, nose, etc. Don't say anything!
- When the dog backs up, puzzled, uncover the treat on the floor and say "leave it."
- When the dog indicates he is not going to dive for or grab the food, even though there is a clear opportunity to do so, Mark the behaviour and then using a treat in your hand as a lure, turn the dog so his back is to the treat on the floor. Deliver the treat from your hand.

Approximation 3: Closer & Closer

- Challenge the dog by placing the food ever closer to him.

Approximation 4: In Motion Leave It: Back Away, Passby or Move Away From It

This exercise teaches: "Orient toward me whenever you see something you are interested in." If your dog will look at you whenever he sees something he wants or is uncertain about, you then have that split second to intervene. The act of looking toward or orienting toward you tells you that your dog is paying attention to your opinion. You are operating as a team and are in concert with each other. The dog, by looking at you, is deliberately telling you, "I am including you in my decision-making process."

Once the stationary "Leave It" behaviour is well established, introduce "Pass-by It." Pass-bys further challenge the dog and establish that "This item is unavailable to you at this time."

Do not under any circumstances take your eyes off the dog! Watch his nose closely, so you do not lie to the dog and tell him that he can play the I-Am-Quicker-Than-You game. Strategically place yourself in a position where you can *always* have control over your dog's ability to get to the doggy magnet by placing yourself between the dog and the treat.

- Begin with the dog on leash.
- Allow the dog to watch food being placed on the floor. You may tie the dog back and have him watch you place the food, or have someone else place the food for you while the dog watches. If you are really clever you can hold the dog back yourself and still place the food, but this is a bit riskier. The food should be placed approximately 8 feet away from you. Or, taking the leash length into consideration, just out of reach of a dog who is at the end of his leash.
- As the dog is focused on this great treat, make sure you do not jerk or pop or correct the dog with the leash, and do not talk to your dog.
- Begin to Back Away from the food treat. CONTINUE TO BACK UP, increasing the distance between your dog and the "magnet." This action will place slight tension on the leash. There will be a distance at which the dog decides: It is too far, I cannot get it. (For some dogs, this may be a considerable distance the first few trials!) At some point, the dog will turn away from the food in some manner, or else orient toward you, or glance toward you, just because of the motion involved in your backing away.
- AT THE MOMENT your dog glances at you, use a Marker, "Yes!" Speed up your backward motion, and as the dog moves toward you Mark & Treat.

158   Think First: Impulse Control

- If your dog just isn't getting it, use a head collar to gain control of where the dog looks – thereby manufacturing reinforceable behaviour.

Repeat the following trial as many times as needed:

- As soon as the previous trial is completed, begin to approach the food treat again.
- As the dog begins to strain and leap for the goodie, back up.
- Mark & Treat orientation away from the goodie.

As you go along, you will discover that each time you turn back to the food treat, the dog is paying less and less attention to "it" (access to "it" is not the sure thing the dog originally thought) and more and more attention to you. You are teaching that pulling toward an enticing object "doesn't work," but orienting toward and including the handler "always works."

Once your dog has mastered looking at you by responding to your Back Away motion, you can begin to do this same exercise by continuing to walk by the magnet, or move laterally away from the magnet.

These In-Motion-Leave-It exercises are going to be used over and over, until it is your dog's HABIT that when he sees something in the environment that interests or arouses him, his *immediate response is to look to you*. It is handy because it is super easy for YOU to do, and it is all you need to remember to do as your FIRST behaviour whenever your dog is distracted or becoming reactive.

Approximation 5: Look-At-Me & Leave It

Raise the above criteria to looking at you before you deliver the food reward with no Back Away required to draw the dog's attention from the food to you. The dog should glance at the treat and look at you within one second, OR pointedly ignore the food or toy on the floor and focus on you like you have information about how dogs acquire opposable thumbs.

- The new rule is: If you have to Back Away or Step Between to get your dog to orient toward you (i.e., you are providing "help"), Marker ONLY (no treat) as the dog orients toward you.
- If the dog voluntarily displays appropriate behaviour, then Mark & Treat, and the occasional Street Party. (Extra social approval, love, kisses, hugs, pats, a quick game. Whatever constitutes a quick little party for your dog that will not cause such great arousal that he loses his head.)

Your goal is to get the dog to the point where he is readily walking PAST this great food treat, and all around it, without even glancing at it. If at any point the dog glances at the goodie, use a deliberate Back Away or move laterally away from it. Any direction is fine, whatever makes the most sense contextually. Most dogs tend to start focusing heavily on the handler by staring at the handler's face, but this is not required, just that the dog orient *away from* the magnet.

After several trials, you will be able to walk toward a magnet, and the item that previously made your dog strain at the leash will become a cue to glance at the magnet and then immediately look to you, the handler.

Remember! Practice both ways: Using a verbal cue so you have a verbal cue waiting in the wings if you need it, and just as often or more often by using the slight pressure on the leash as your cue to "Leave It." If you do enough repetitions, just your body language of pausing or shifting your weight to begin moving backwards will be a cue for the dog.

After several trials (with some dogs, 6 trials, and with other dogs, 200 trials), you will see your dog begin to respond *to your body language* of moving away or backing away from the object of his attraction. I often don't even get a chance to take a step backwards: as soon as my dogs sense my shift of weight and pause to begin backing up, they orient toward me. You know you have achieved your end goal when you see your dog begin to look at the magnet, then quickly glance at you for approval or pointedly ignore the magnet. Obviously reinforce this effort with verbal and social approval and the occasional food treat.

This is the goal of this work. Leash pressure is no longer required. Changes in the environment have become a cue to look to the handler for advice.

Approximation 6: Resisting Moving Objects

Challenge the dog further. Now ask the dog to resist the temptation of a moving object. This is much tougher for the dog because motion naturally attracts his attention.

- As you walk along, toss a piece of food off to the side.

- Expect lunging from the dog, so toss the food well out of reach of the dog. Begin with tossing the food off to the side away from the dog: if your dog is on your left, toss the food off to your right and slightly ahead at about a 45 degree angle.

- Continue walking by the tossed food as if you hadn't tossed it.

- Mark & Feed any indication away from the food, keeping the leash loose.

Approximation 7: Challenges (Change The Distraction)

This will require a list of distracting items for each individual dog, although you may find that many of the same Challenges work for each dog. Depending on the individual dog, objects encountered in his daily work (his "I gotta have thats"), create a list that will challenge the dog. As you progress in this exercise, you will see the dog begin to walk by things that in the past he just couldn't resist!

Consider the following list and screen it with your dog and her particular bugaboos in mind. Only use those Challenges that can be completed safely. Modify this list as required, but a partial list of Challenges might be:

- People
- People with food
- People offering food
- People with dogs
- Loose dogs
- People with toys (squeaky)
- People playing with dogs and toys
- People tossing balls

Ready For Maintenance

Place the behaviour on a Variable Reinforcement Schedule to maintain behaviour. That is, you will use a Marker combined with a food treat on only some occasions. You will find that, after a while, the response is a habit and is integrated into the dog's behavioural repertoire.

Impulse control is an exercise that requires dedicated work and absolute consistency on your part. It requires many contexts and locations for the dog to become fluent with this behaviour. The work is well worth it. Good impulse control behaviours, combined with an excellent Recall, often make the difference between a live dog and a dead dog. When your dog has completed this exercise, it is exciting to know that he will choose, voluntarily, to attend to what is important to the handler as opposed to what is important to him.

Wilson is curious about something on the floor behind Rachel...

Rachel uses a Get Between maneuver to let Wilson know that this item is none of his business. This is the same technique that dogs use with each other.

Do not get distracted - just keep your eye on the dog's cute little nose. This will tell you which direction the dog will move next.

When you Get Between, move as deliberately and as slowly as you can. You will have to concentrate on the dog's intention and be quite lively on occasion to prevent the dog getting the item off the floor, but try not to appear frantic or hectic to the dog as much as possible.

Be persistent - continue to Get Between the dog and the distraction until the dog says to you, "Okay already - I see I cannot get to it, therefore, I will ignore that item."

Rachel stays on task and outlasts the dog.

She concentrates and keeps Getting Between Wilson and the object of desire.

In both photographs, Rachel is quite cleverly stepping toward Wilson, so in addition to blocking him from the object of desire, she is also moving him further away from it, making her job of Getting Between easier. Distance also has a way of making an object of desire less desirable as it looks less attainable.

She does not hurry, she moves deliberately. Use your leash in as limited a manner as possible. Use your body, not your leash to control the dog's movement. Rachel is not "bumping" or bulling him out of her way, she is moving slowly and deliberately, more like an earth mover that is coming through.

Wilson is looking less intense about the toy on the floor now, and is reluctantly beginning to see that Rachel is not about to give up.

Wilson's feet are beginning to move more freely as he makes a choice to relinquish and stop contending about whether the toy is available or not. If you were working him you would "feel" at first as if his feet were "sticky" and resistant. As he changes his thought process, his feet suddenly "feel" as if they were freely moving and lighter. Instead of competing for the toy he is cooperating and negotiating.

There it is! The First Correct Effort. That *moment* that the dog shows the intention we have been looking for: "I am no longer looking at or thinking about the object of desire, but instead am starting to think more about how to deal with my handler."

You could see the seeds of this in the previous photograph, when Wilson's feet began to "free up" instead of "sticking."

Rachel freezes her movement mid stride as soon as she sees the behaviour change in Wilson. This gives Wilson a chance to make a decision and show Rachel his intent: what he is thinking about. Then, as soon as he makes any attempt, the slightest try, to orient his nose towards Rachel...

(Below)
...Rachel backs up one step to release the pressure and Wilson responds by looking up at her, giving Rachel his attention. We have lift off! This means that he has, temporarily, given his allegiance to the handler, not the object of desire. This gives the handler that golden opportunity: the opportunity to reinforce the dog. Rachel praises him warmly, "Good Boy." You could also give him a treat at this moment if you like, as long as the treat promotes calm behaviour in your individual dog.

Wilson's success has much to do with Rachel's body language. While still allowing him to think for himself, she channeled him toward success.

The moment he made a decision in the "right direction," that is the slightest correct try, Rachel stopped moving to allow the puppy to process the information he is receiving. Then, as he "tried" orienting towards her, she immediately stepped back, releasing the pressure and drawing him in towards her. This gives him confidence that he made the right decision and makes the experience "memorable." The Back Away helped to "manufacture" a correct response: looking up at Rachel and being attentive to her.

Now for the most important part of any learning experience: The Re-test. Rachel walks back towards the object of desire and "opens" her body. She does this by placing herself in a position that she could easily step between her dog and the "leave it" object, but turns her body in such a way that the dog thinks he could have access. This gives Wilson an opportunity to show Rachel what he has learned from his recent experience.

Think of your body as a door. You will close the door to show your dog that you do not wish them to go in that direction. Then open the door back up to see if the dog has decided to take your suggestion.

Wilson looks at the object of desire, but stops his forward movement. He is clearly telling Rachel, voluntarily, that he will leave the object. He further shows his intent by orienting his nose slightly towards her. This is like saying, "I prioritize you over the toy." What an excellent boy! This gives Rachel another opportunity to tell Wilson how clever he is. To do this you could use your Memory Marker ("Yes"), or give him a pat or hand him a treat. You can also continue working, which for many dogs, is a treat in and of itself.

Rachel continues to walk around the objects of desire, to further test Wilson's understanding. He obviously "gets it." He is attending to Rachel and ignoring the toys on the floor. This gives the handler many opportunities to deliver praise and, if appropriate, treats. The whole idea of training is to channel behaviour (shape it) in the desired direction and notice when the dog gets it right. *Manufacturing desired behaviour provides an opportunity for reinforcement.*

These impulse control games are fun for both dogs and people when they are approached with a plan for teaching the dog to use their Frontbrain - the executive decision making center.

Photo essay by Dave Schrader.

Think First: Impulse Control

Get Connected - The Mind Set

The relationship that exists between you and your dog is a lovely thing. Enhancing that special connection is what dog lovers everywhere are consumed with.

Photograph by Dave Schrader

Be sure to read this section! It contains important information so you can do the exercises correctly and be effective!

If you wish to refer to an overview of these exercises, refer to *The Get Connected Protocol: Improve the Relationship by using Bodywork & Space; Encouraging Teamwork and Developing Trust & Respect* on page 196.

Keeping your dog Frontbrain is the goal.

We've discussed this! When your dog is Hindbrain, it isn't "bad," but it doesn't often serve your purpose very well. We most often need a dog to be thinking, practicing impulse control, cooperation and being mannerly. It's okay to be Hindbrain, but the dog needs to switch to Frontbrain at a moment's notice when requested to do so. This is much easier on the dog physiologically, too. Dogs whose owners encourage them to be Hindbrain all the time cause their dogs to be under chronic stress, to the point that the dog finds it difficult to return to a calm and relaxed state.

Then there is the small matter of respect. I prefer this old-fashioned word, but if you prefer to substitute the word "relevance," feel free to do so. (a rose by any other name and all that). Provided your training is sound and not confusing, if your dog is still a pushy type, you may have a respect problem: your dog does not think you are relevant. Remember, when I say trained, I do not mean your dog occasionally obeys you. You have to have adequate foundation behaviours installed: Eye Contact, Impulse Control and basic Stays. These behaviours need to have been taught, not haphazardly, but methodically and deliberately. Once you are certain that confusion on the dog's part is not the issue, you may look to a lack of respect (or relevance) as being the next step. If you do not know how to approximate these behaviours, please refer to my DVD, "Foundation Behaviours For Every Dog," or get help from a professional trainer who relies on Positive Reinforcement based methods.

Remember the GaWaNi Pony Boy lesson? (Refer to *The Function of Subordinates on* page 76.) My own little buzz word for the daily interaction that takes place when your dog is testing you for leadership skills is "voting." Your dog does not vote for her leader once every four years. It differs dog to dog, but Breanna voted several times a day. Every interaction with her was important. Maeve still votes about once a month or so. I've had many dogs who voted once or twice during their life span. Once you have forged a relationship with your dog, respect must be maintained. Relationships with dogs are no different than with people in that the relationship is either getting better or getting worse. If you think you are on a plateau, you are probably headed for worse. This is not to ignore the fact that some days are better than others, but over a ninety-day time frame, you should be able to say that your relationship is just getting better and better. If it's not, you are not doing something properly. Most likely it is

correct timing. Perhaps you don't understand what the exercise really "looks like." If you are reading this book and are a kinesthetic learner (like me...), you will have to heave your bum off the sofa periodically, read a paragraph and then try to do the exercise. In that case, be extra patient with yourself. *Do things slowly, one at a time and in a very systematic manner.* Persistence is the key to success, not speed.

Choose Technique Based On Desired Outcome

If I want to encourage offered behaviour or an attitude of experimentation, then I will choose clicker-style techniques. If I want to develop a more specific behaviour for a specific circumstance, such as behaviour at a doorway, I will use techniques that "close doors" on all undesired responses and "open" only one avenue, like using the Get Between exercise in the Get Connected Protocol. This doesn't mean I switch philosophies - using cookies and sunshine one moment and then too much force the next. I can maintain my philosophy and apply common sense (ironically, this is so uncommon...). If dogs are barking maniacally and relentlessly at the window every time someone walks by on the sidewalk, I will use a Get Between, which can become so irritating to the dog that it ruins the fun of crazy window barking.

Some Examples

Stationing behaviours are dependent upon a specific location and the dog's relationship to the location. For example, Heel position is a station. The dog's shoulder is next to your pant seam. If the station is still, the dog should be too. If the station moves or changes pace from Normal to Slow to Fast, the dog should move at a pace to keep his physical position relative to the station.

When *first* training stationing behaviours I will use luring (basically guiding the dog, hands-off with a treat - the old donkey and carrot routine) and modeling (gentle physical guidance, based on "cued touches" to place the dog in a position). My technique will change as the behaviour develops. So at first I might Sit the dog, then step into position myself. I will "name" the station, "Heel," then feed the dog in position. If the dog gets out of position, I might lure him back into position or take his collar and "model" him back into position by using the collar and my hand on his side to reposition him correctly. I won't use the lure or the modeling for 20 sessions, but I will use it for 2 or 3 sessions, until the dog gets the idea, then I can begin to use a mix of techniques to get the Heel work competition ready. This mix will involve some Clicker training; some modeling (a gentle, accepted-by-the-dog physical guidance into position); no luring (or very little); some Move Into (a Get Connected exercise); Backing Up in Heel position (begins as Follow The Feel, a Get Connected exercise, then can be done off leash); Back Aways; Think First! and Eye Contact work, and perhaps other guidance techniques, such as using a dowel to help keep the dog's hindquarters parallel. I will also use cones placed strategically to keep the dog's rear in place and cavaletti as well as metronomes or music to teach me and the dog to move in rhythm with each other. As the behaviour develops, the techniques may change but the philosophy of good communication and a positive approach remains:

- Give the dog good information.

- Be black and white, not gray. (You cannot have it both ways.)

- Be consistent.

- Notice and reinforce what the dog does correctly.

- Undesired behaviours should be looked upon as questions from the dog or further information to aid you in the training processes. These are not a ridiculous excuse for the handler to exhibit emotional behaviour.

- Any corrections to the dog's behaviour need to be informative. Do not look to "punish" the behaviour, instead to channel the dog's behaviour in a direction that is desired.

When teaching an obedience Stay, I use food and keep the emotional state after the Stay calm as well. I would deliver treats during the Stay, quietly release the dog with a Stand By cue, then move on to the next exercise.

If I am working on a Start Line Stay for an Agility dog, I teach the dog to move off the start line toward the jump in a prompt manner, but I do not want hectic or hurried: it is much too easy to knock down that first jump if the dog "explodes" from the start line. Tailor the consequence to the individual: if I wish to speed the dog up, I set the exercise up to get the dog moving quickly, like tossed treats or toys as the dog moves off the start line. If the dog is already squatted on the start line, quivering and whining in anticipation, a tossed toy is over-kill, adding fuel to an already too-hot fire. For this dog, I'd say that allowing the animal to take the first jump is plenty of reinforcement.

When teaching a retrieve, I use a combination of modeling and Clicker training. I start with the clicker, already having established that I can handle the dog around his head and face and open and close his mouth with my hands, with the dog offering no resistance. As soon as the dog is picking the dumbbell up off the ground from ten feet, I don't need the clicker anymore, and can carry on from that point forward without it. Acquisition is over. If the dog is an eager or over-eager retriever, I do not need any treats at all, except for the Stay portion of the retrieve. For the Stay, again depending on the dog, I might use modeling or treats, most likely a combination of the two. I do not use an ear pinch or forced retrieve of any kind. I have never found these methods necessary to obtain a fast and reliable retrieve from a variety of both eager and recalcitrant dogs, whether for obedience or hunting dogs. (Chris Bach has some really lovely retrieving techniques if you care to check them out. Her training program is called "The Third Way" and materials are available on her website.) The first time a trainer convinced me to allow an ear pinch with my Fox Terrier, Breanna, ("it won't hurt her, and you cannot have a reliable retrieve without it," she said...), Breanna avoided the dumbbell entirely and promptly closed her teeth on the trainer's hand without biting down, in a "hold-type" correction bite (she didn't puncture or bruise, merely held the trainers hand in her teeth and dared the trainer to move...). I picked up my dog and my dumbbell and went home, where I proceeded to research and use a clicker trained retrieve. My dog never failed to retrieve when asked, not even the first time I asked her to dive off a dock and retrieve a previously frozen by the dog duck wing. (This is the kind of situation you find yourself in when you have friends with Chesapeake Bay Retrievers.) Without hesitation Breanna did a strong water entry, retrieved promptly and returned the duck wing to hand.

Keeping your dog Frontbrain is the goal.

No matter what technique I am using, either clicker or modeling, it is enhanced by the Get Connected exercises because those protocols provide our working partnership with the most important item: the dog is Ready To Learn. When the dog is no longer nervous or uncertain about personal space or physical handling, you have numerous more ways to get information to the dog, cleanly and precisely.

I work with a lot of therapy dogs and use oodles of clicker training with them, as well as lots of desensitization. We have taught dogs to stack rings on a stick, "play cards" with people, put balls through a hoop, carry baskets with various (feather-weight) objects in them, offer hand shakes, play dead, do skits, or whatever else my imaginative clients come up with. Clicker training techniques are absolutely invaluable for providing precise information to teach these kinds of behaviours, because they encourage experimenting and, when used correctly, produce an amazing persistence. Persistence is required when teaching these kinds of behaviours, because the dog will "get it wrong" a lot. The dog must not be punished for any "wrong" behaviours; if you do the dog will quit working and experimenting entirely. Dogs quit because techniques are too forceful, or because the dog is hopelessly confused. When teaching these kinds of behaviours, one must reinforce experimentation or the dog will never try enough variety of behaviours to find out which is the one you are looking for.

For the Acquisition of many competition behaviours (Obedience, Agility, Freestyle, Tracking, Service Dogs, Search and Rescue dogs, and for Pet Dogs), a clicker is used along with modeling, occasional luring, and the Get Connected Protocol exercises: any technique I think will help that dog to get good information at that moment.

Be Versatile. Be Open Minded. Avoid Rigid Thinking.

My point is, the more tools you have in your toolkit, the better your chances of solving problems. This requires critical thinking on the part of the handler, as well as a willingness to keep an open mind and a spirit of experimentation. This does not mean you change your basic training philosophy every ten minutes. It means that you think about which technique will help you to give the dog the best information. Ask yourself the following questions:

- Do I want the dog to experiment with many behaviours, because that will enhance the end result of this particular behaviour? If the answer is yes, get out your clicker.

- Do I want to get the dog's responses to be more animated? Is the training at a distance or a behaviour that "hands-off" will be best? If the answer is yes, get out the clicker.

- Do I want to increase intensity? Then a clicker, treats and/or use of prey objects (balls, toys) are the ticket.

- Do I want a very narrow set of responses, such as no jumping on people? Then I would suggest anal-retentive management, the Be Still Switch and Move Into. Once the dog has made the desired decision ON HIS OWN with no help from you, then you can calmly, low-key, deliver a treat to the dog, if you like.

When you are problem solving a dog behaviour issue, use critical thinking and take the dog's response to your protocol as feedback. For instance, the very common problem of: do I want to stop maniacal barking at the window? Get Between works great. No treats required. Every time the dogs act like an idiot at the window, go over and spoil the fun. Add a verbal before you initiate the Get Between, and soon you will have distance control. At that point, you could give the dog a treat when you catch her quietly watching someone walking by on the sidewalk instead of doing her usual out-of-control barking. Certainly notice that and give her a big, wonderful treat for her good decision. You could likewise deliver a treat when your dog woofs one time, then runs to find you. I would jackpot that behaviour! What a wonderful solution and good thinking that behaviour represents. What many dogs chain (establish a pattern of) here with treat training that is improperly done is: If I go and bark maniacally at the window, then mom calls me and gives me a treat. I think when trainers give simplistic advice like, "When your dog barks at the window, call her and then give her a treat," they intend to counter-condition, but they end up with the dog misinterpreting the message.

What Does A Belief System Have To Do With Anything?

A belief system is a paradigm (an ideational structure) that one uses for living. Experiences form our belief system and so do our genetics. If a dog has been around kind people and has a curious nature that has not been suppressed, he will feel that people are safe and will be confident around them.

Because a dog's sensory input differs from our own, his belief system may be drastically different than yours. For instance, the average dog thinks that horse manure smells great and is good to eat. This differs from my belief system. While I do not find horse manure to smell particularly bad (which may be different from your belief system), I certainly do not think it would be good to eat and do not think of it as a food source. Another example: I almost never chase wheels. My belief system is that moving wheels might be dangerous (not to mention the fact that I do not find that wheels to inspire me to chase). I have had many dogs, however, whose belief system is that wheels are great fun to chase. I remember one incident in particular involving my Smooth Fox Terrier, Zasu, and a mother innocently pushing her baby in a stroller...Zasu's eyes lit up at the sight of the wheels and she leaped after them with a sudden intensity. My cries of, "It's okay, she's after the wheels," did not seem to comfort the mother. (My dog was on leash at the time, and the mother, child and stroller were attending a dog show.)

Therefore, a belief system is defined by your experiences and also could be affected by instinctive behaviour, as in the illustrations above. It is good to be aware that your dog's belief system could be different from your own. It is also important to realize that belief systems can be adjusted. That is good news. That means that a dog who is afraid of new experiences can change her belief system or shift her paradigm and learn that new experiences are not always bad and can, in fact, be fun!

Communication Is Not What You Say, It Is What Others Hear

One of my favorite concepts from author Wendy Jago[3] is: Communication is not what you say, but what the other hears. This is a terrifying idea, one that could almost convince me never to speak again. But it is one that is of vital importance to dog trainers, especially because of the dog's belief system and species and how they "take in" the information we give.

_____

3. Jago, Wendy. Schooling Problems Solved With NLP (2001). J.A. Allen, London. p. 107. Her words are, specifically, "the meaning of a communication is the message which is actually received."

There can be a gap the size of the Grand Canyon between what we intend the dog to learn and what she actually learns from our teachings. I was discussing this topic with my dear friend Victoria just the other day. She told me, when she came to my clinic her spooky and reactive rescue Border Collie, that she finally had an "ah ha" moment in the midst of the emotional and mental over-load. We had just been working on getting the dog to use his handler as an emotional anchor with Eye Contact, Think First! (impulse control) and Be Still exercises. Through her effort, her dog had improved more than I had expected during the work session. I felt so proud of her! As I released the handlers and dogs off the floor for a much needed rest, Victoria was walking off the floor and allowing her dog to wander over to get pets from people he knew and would allow to touch him. I was watching her and could see that she had not given him specific permission to do so, with a proper End Working or "Friend" cue (the "Friend" cue means the dog can go visit with someone). I walked over and touched her arm and said, "Victoria, you cannot have it both ways." Vic turned and stared at me. I continued, "You can either be black and white or you can be grey. Figure out which you want to be, then base your expectations of your dog on your own consistency or inconsistency." This was not necessarily a kind thing to say to this over-whelmed handler, and I knew it, but it was true and it was good information. I knew I was just as likely to get a black eye as a hug from the handler. Vic looked at me and stood very still for a moment and we held each others eyes. Fortunately for me, she chose to go think about the statement before she reacted. This takes a big person. My students are amazing people, because they are able to go through this process of critical thinking about very emotional topics, which I know is formidable. Two years later as we discussed this, Vic told me that the comment changed the way she handled her dog. She became much more black and white about when her dog could interact with others and when the dog needed to ignore the environment. She no longer let the dog "guess" about this, the most important thing you could ever teach your dog to increase his comfort level.

When trainers discuss consistency, this is exactly what we mean. We are discussing more than the detail: "Be consistent the way you give your cue," or "Always have your dog sit at curbs." We are discussing the larger issue of teaching the dog how to prioritize, as well: let your dog know what is expected of him by

Keeping your dog Frontbrain is the goal.

being consistent in how you live with him, and not forcing him to guess what kind of behaviour you want her to exhibit. Any context you do not train for is left to the dog's judgment. When you allow your dog to guess, and do not provide good structure, you are giving your dog permission to use her own judgment. If you let your dog jump all over you because you do not care or are too lazy to stop it, your dog will jump all over everybody else, too, thinking it is appropriate because you allowed the dog to guess about it. You must see your communications from your dog's point of view and become the solution, not the problem, in the communication between you and your dog.

Think about what you want. Then set about using the most informative and expedient technique. All can be done kindly, with consistency and tempered by critical thinking.

Tapping Into Canine Native Language To Communicate Effectively

All social animals use a very elegant logic with each other. Normal animals who are savvy communicators use a system of warning and increasing discomfort to establish boundaries. Because this kind of communication is easily understood by dogs, is there a humane and sensible way to use this information to establish boundaries for our dogs? First, I do not wish to use violence to communicate to my dog, even though dogs are quite happy to use violence with each other to communicate. I do not wish you to think that "increasing discomfort" means that I would ever condone misusing your dog because he was disobedient, or even willful. Whacking on the dog, jerking on the collar repeatedly, yelling at the dog out of frustration - all these are just emotional and physical abuse which breed fear, contempt and avoidance. Worse yet, from a learning point of view, it is poor communication. *Your emotional output is not clear communication to the dog.*

Establishing boundaries does mean you are going to learn how to be an effective communicator. You will learn how to allow your dog to take responsibility for his actions and make appropriate decisions. How much resistance he wants to use is always the dog's choice. By understanding the dog's body language and using it as feedback the dog becomes more involved in the training process. By learning to release pressure quickly and when and how much to apply makes you a better communicator and more easily understood by your dog. By you learning a little more about your dog's language and him learning more about yours,

you create a special language together - cooperation. That is why you establish boundaries in the first place. Once that item is off the "to-do list" and the rules are established, then the game of training can be engaged in without the distraction of "who gets to do what." Cooperation and trust in the handler are enhanced and both dog and handler feel more connected with each other.

174   Keeping your dog Frontbrain is the goal.

Treats And When To Use Them.

What I can tell you is that, when properly done, there are certain exercises, (specifically the Get Connected protocol), which are not Positive Reinforcement, per se, but do mesh well with a program that is based upon Positive Reinforcement. While relying heavily on treats during Acquisition and Generalization stages of teaching *other* exercises (such as competition Heel work, Eye Contact Work and Think First! exercises), I do not use treats with the Get Connected Protocol exercises; or I do use limited treats only for certain exercises. The techniques work because they follow the rules of learning theory and because you are speaking to the dog using her own language.

When I do not use treats with certain exercises, it is because:

- I want to make the communication very "clean" and broken down to its lowest common denominator. Black and white.

- I want the dog to be able to concentrate fully on what is happening to her body and on making desired decisions by relying on logic override, not blind instinct.

- I want the dog to be able to concentrate fully on the task of responding thoughtfully and not reacting reflexively. I want the dog to respond appropriately by *reading my body language,* which will be presented to her in a consistent manner.

- I want the dog to be able to see treats as the same tool I do, not madly guessing about how to get the treats and therefore not really attending to the task at hand as much as she is trying to figure out how to manipulate me. *I want the treats to provide valuable information, not be the sole focus of the dog's attention.*

- I want to prepare the dog to be Ready To Learn. For the already trained dog, I wish to put treats in a proper perspective - as a paycheck for a job well-done, which increases the impact of the treats. For the unsophisticated or beginning learner I wish to immediately convey the role that treats will play in the learning process.

The Ideal Role Of Treats

I am very excited to see the results of using this technique on dogs, because when the application of the "pressure" and, even more important, the moment of release of "pressure" are executed thoughtfully, the dog's understanding is nearly immediate, within a very few repetitions. The most significant aspects of this work are that it transfers or generalizes to other people and contexts more efficiently and quickly than other techniques I have used, without the fallout. Once a dog has this personal space thing down, he has it down. This makes training more comfortable and meaningful, and *reduces the dog competing for space and treats*, two of the big attention-robbers. By competing, I do not mean the dog is necessarily status-seeking. Most dogs are in your personal space and grabbing at treats because they can. No one has ever bothered to get the message across in a way they understand it that this behaviour is rude and annoying. The dog thinks he can "push" you into giving him treats for a valid reason: you have inadvertently taught him this is so. Once ground rules are established, both dog and handler can relax into learning, which becomes more pleasurable and less frustrating.

Good Boundaries And Consistency Are The Basis Of Good Training

The fact is, good boundaries and consistency are the basis of good training. Dogs get frustrated when they are left out there guessing all the time about what is expected of them. I want my dog to think of me as relevant, as more than just a Pez dispenser. I want him to understand that there are rules that must be abided by, even if it means coming when called instead of chasing that squirrel. And that holds true whether I have cookies with me or not. I particularly like the Get Connected protocol because it provides a great way to show dogs boundaries. It creates awareness and consistency in the handlers.

When Do I Use Treats With The Get Connected Protocol? Timid Dogs May Need Treats.

Now that I have you totally convinced that you don't need treats for this work, I will give you the exception to the rule. If you are working with a timid, insecure or defensive dog, get out the cookies right away for the following circumstance. If the dog begins to get a little "squishy," note that threshold and stop moving ahead. Isolate the specific action you are doing, then pair treats to whatever kind of touch, bending over or other actions on your part that is currently making her uneasy. If the dog gets pushy for the treats, it means you have accomplished your current purpose. Put them away and concentrate again on the physical sensations and messages you want the dog to take away from this session. Once you have addressed the specific movement or item that is scaring her, you can pick up where you left off in the protocol and try again. Do get your timid dog to the point where the treats have been faded out and are completely unnecessary as soon as possible. The treats are used as a temporary distraction.

Be careful you do not teach your dog that if she acts spooky you will get out the treats...You safeguard against this by:

- Isolating the specific action, desensitizing to that, then pick up and continue with the protocol where you left off.

- Anticipating that the dog might be worried about a specific area and breaking the approximations into tiny, micro-approximations. *Slow is fast*, particularly with cautious dogs.

If your timid dog refuses treats, just move ahead in tiny little micro-approximations so you do not overface her. Work in small time frames, stopping immediately on the first sign that your dog is trying or is slightly more relaxed. Give her a rest. This rest may be five seconds. Then you may begin again. The smart thing might be to call it a day and try again tomorrow.

Timid, cautious and shy behaviour is a bit tricky, really, because some dogs have learned that the best way to manipulate the environment is to exhibit spooky behaviour so then the nice, stupid humans will fawn over you feed you nice treats. With this dog, I tend to push a bit and wait for the tantrum. If you are right, immediately after the tantrum, the dog is almost miraculously cured of his shy behaviour because he just found out it isn't working well for him. If you are wrong, the dog will be much worse and you have added significant time to the training process, as well as bearing the guilt of your inept decision.

The tactical dog who is efficiently manipulating his environment through past experience is different than the dog who is holding his fear up as one might a cross to repel a vampire. The fearful dog really is convinced that you are dangerous. They misinterpret any motion or action they have not seen before as dangerous, and this attitude extends to novel ideas or exercises as well. Proceed slowly and thoughtfully with this kind of dog, *ever aware of exactly what you are teaching her*. Err on the side of carefulness with this type of dog, because a mistake made with a cautious dog is a big bad mistake.

The cautious, shy or defensive dog, even though she puts the most road blocks up during the learning is exactly the one who needs the Get Connected protocol the most. Keep repeating the mantra: Slow *is* Fast.

Treats And When To Use Them.

When you wish to change (modify) already learned or instinctive behaviour, what are the first knee-jerk reactions you often get? Resistance. Confusion.

Sure, anything new may feel awkward at first, especially if you already have working patterns developed. Your dog, for instance, already may have developed the working pattern of pulling you down the street on walks. It will take some convincing for her to change her pulling behaviour. If her working pattern consists of mobbing guests at the door, then it will take further convincing for her to greet guests quietly and in a mannerly way.

Belief Systems

Everyone develops a working pattern for the many repetitive tasks that we do. A working pattern has an attitude or emotional state attached to it. Your working pattern is influenced by your belief system. Your belief system is based on context and heredity and shaped by past experience. This belief system is vital, because no matter how poorly it is serving the purpose, it has well-established neural pathways, and it is in use because that individual is convinced that this behaviour keeps her "safe." It is perhaps the best that individual can do with the skill set currently in hand. When you go about changing behaviour, you are really changing neural pathways. This is a physiological process and it will take time.

Resistance Analogy

Therefore, expect resistance. When the office manager comes in and says, "Hey, we are getting a new computer system! It will work better and faster than the one we have now. It will be fantastic and give us more detailed reports." Is this statement met with cries of joy? No sirree. People resist it. They will have to be pushed out of their comfort zones to learn the new software. They will have to burn new neural pathways because the keys used on the keyboard are different. They will be forced to change old habits, and they will have to alter set routines. This makes everyone complain. They groan, they moan, they resist. Three

months from now, new working patterns will be established. Everyone has settled into the new routines and understands the software as well as they did the old software. Now everyone is happy. The new system *is* better and faster. Now, no one wants to switch back to the old system.

Some of this work will feel awkward to you and the dog. Your dog will not always feel comfortable. Remember, you are changing the way he thinks about the world: expect to meet resistance. You will step out of your comfort zone, too. Wrapping your head around some of this will take an open and a learning attitude. The effort is well worth it. *You are rewarded with a dog who is a sophisticated communicator and who makes few Hindbrained, reactive decisions. Instead you have a dog who is wise in the ways of humans and is responsive and in tune with you. A Frontbrained, thinking partner.* Your dog no longer has to be afraid of "silly" things. You will build an amazing amount of trust and respect as you go through these exercises together. Once your dog respects and trusts you and you have a communication system that works, the dog is Ready To Learn. Once the dog is no longer looking for loopholes or competing with you, and knows how to learn, what you teach becomes a detail. Teaching is easy when you have a plan, reasonable mechanical skills and a dog who is Ready To Learn.

What Resistance And Confusion Look Like

So don't expect your dog to chortle with glee when you tell her: "Your old working pattern stinks. I hate it when you lunge at other dogs. Now I want you to give me Two Eyes and use Eye Contact as an emotional anchor when other dogs approach." Or: "I am going to teach you to *give* to pressure instead of bracing or moving into pressure. It will create understanding between us and you will be more mentally and physically comfortable when you learn this." Your dog will resist. Resistance is often shown by looking off into the distance, as if the dog was trying to sight a distant horizon. Resistant dogs often intensify the current undesired behaviour. She may pout and stop working. She may act afraid, because you are not allowing her to stay within the self-proclaimed comfort zone which you have been enabling.

If your dog becomes confused, she may also stop working because she just does not know what to do next. This might show up in the form of avoidance behaviours, such as looking away from the handler and seeking a distraction to latch onto. Many dogs, when confused, will begin displaying displacement behaviours, such as sniffing and scratching. Other confused dogs wander off, in a distracted looking manner. Some dogs become very anxious about being confused and will begin to act in a hectic, frenzied way, running around in circles. Often trainers misdiagnose this heightened activity level as "the dog is having too much fun." Nothing could be further from the truth, the confused dog wishes intensely that she had some clue about what the handler is looking for. The "zooming" and heightened activity level is a displacement behaviour, being used to avoid the confusion.

The good news is: your dog will happily adapt to the new system. Much faster than people accept new computer systems, by the way.

Resistance and confusion are temporary. Within six or seven repetitions and within a session or two the signs of confusion and it's cohort, resistance, will disappear. If they do not, you are doing something to promote them.

When Resistance And Confusion Aren't Temporary And What You Can Do About It

Why Dogs Don't Try - Reducing Resistance

- Some dogs do not try for you because they have learned from past experience that trying doesn't work. They do not trust the trainer because the trainer asks for too much at once - that is, the approximations are too large and expectations are much too high.

- Dogs don't try because the trainer keeps doing the work for the dog. The trainer does not allow the dog the satisfaction of problem-solving. It is not fair to do the home-work for the dog, then toss the dog out in the deep water to take the test. This is not about you! Sure, you can make the dog look good when you do the work for her. Of course, by association, then you look good, too. I think this is one insidious reason that trainers tend to do the work for the dog and do not allow the dog to problem-solve: the trainer doesn't want the dog to "fail." Problem-solving, by definition, means that there will be trial and error involved. Therefore, it is inevitable that the dog will make some "wrong" decisions. This trainer mind-set equates "wrong" decisions with failure, rather than as an integral part of problem-solving. The trainer feels that if the dog fails, then it is her fault. Nobody likes to feel like a failure. People do not even know they are doing this, and they are not doing this to hurt the dog intentionally. But in the long run it is the dog who pays the price - either by being punished for doing poorly on "The Test" or because the owner, when faced with a competition situation where she cannot "help the dog," is disappointed and cross with the dog when the performance reflects the trainer's poor training practices.

- Reward the slightest try at first. That means watching for intention behaviour and any action by the dog that you can interpret as making an effort to comply. This may be as subtle as a shift of weight in the direction you are indicating or a slight glance in the direction of a target. A warm and heartfelt "Good" is okay, as long as your dog understands this as a continuation cue (a "keep working you are on the right track" cue) and doesn't see it as an End Working Cue; that is, the verbal "Good" or "Yes" does not cause your dog to break position.

- First Correct Efforts require extra recognition. That could mean any one of several things: an extra two or three seconds of "rest" between exercises, or stopping the work and playing a game for a few minutes, or stopping the session completely for today, or changing what you are working on. If your dog has really been struggling with a concept, give her a treat IN POSITION, then release her. DO NOT release the dog, then provide the treat.

- Gradually increase the criteria and do not skip any teaching steps.

178   When you wish to change (modify) already learned or instinctive behaviour, what are the first

- Shades of grey do not work in training. Black and white are the name of the game.

- Manufacture, manage, model and shape behaviours with a purpose in mind.

- Some people are too impatient. They do not give the dog time to learn.

- Some people are too patient. They put up with a behaviour that makes them crazy, right up to the point at which it drives them to the brink of sanity; whereupon they explode in an emotional display the dog cannot possibly understand. Because they are so "good" to their dog, they cannot understand why the dog takes advantage of them and constantly pushes at the hazy boundaries.

- Some people are too forceful. They frighten and intimidate the dog needlessly. This does not provide a safe place to learn.

- Some people are too passive. They continue to help the dog, when it would be of greater value to both parties if the dog were encouraged to take responsibility for their "half" of the behaviour. The trainer's half of the responsibility for the behaviour is a clear cue system and a good training plan (approximations and reasonable goals). The dog's half is to try.

When you wish to change (modify) already learned or instinctive behaviour, what are the first knee-

Newton's Physical Laws Of Motion & Their Parallel In The Training Paradigm

These Laws[1] are three rules that are which explain relationships in the physical world and allow you to predict what will happen in a given context, as long as you know some part of the equation. In short, these Laws enable you to predict the future! At least about the direction an object will move and how fast it will move there.

These Laws discuss "Dead" weights and inanimate objects. When we are working with a living, breathing creature it is a bit different, but there are certainly some interesting similarities, too! The biggest difference, of course, is that a living, breathing creature may change her behaviour, therefore altering her course.

The similarities are simple, quite obvious once given a bit of thought, and amazing. For instance, the physical behaviour (remember, we are discussing the physical behaviour of objects for a moment) of all objects can be described by saying: objects tend to keep on doing whatever they are currently doing unless the force changes.

The behaviour of living creatures often parallels this description. Whenever you ask someone to change her behaviour, she wants to keep on doing whatever she has been doing in that context. Even when someone wishes to change a habit, it is difficult! You are fighting those old well-worn neural pathways that feel as comfortable as slipping into your old comfy shoes. In many cases, the circumstances have to be pretty uncomfortable for people or dogs to change their moti-

vation and burn new the neural pathways which must happen in order for the habit to be changed. Even when the change is for the better, the first thing on the agenda is resistance. Stepping out of your comfort zone requires overcoming that resistance, which in turn requires applying a variety of strategies (different kinds of forces) to reach the tipping point. Once past the "tipping point" of resistance, the velocity and volume of understanding increases just as a snowball that is rolling downhill, going ever faster and getting ever larger.

Law Number 1. Every object in a state of uniform motion tends to remain in that state of motion unless an external force is applied to it.

This is Gallileo's "Law of Inertia." It is often stated as: an object at rest tends to stay at rest and an object in motion tends to stay in motion with the same speed and in the same direction UNLESS acted upon by an unbalanced force.

This means that stuff that is still will remain still until something moves it. Stuff that is already moving will continue to move in the same direction and at the same speed will do so until something stops it or shoves it faster or in another direction.

This could be called the Behavioural Law Of Inertia! Unless something significant happens, behavioural changes are not initiated. Something, or in the case of training, *someone*, will have to provide the motivation for change. If you are talking about your dog, that means you. If you are talking about yourself, that means you, too! You are the only one who can be that *driving force*: the motivation that brings about change for the better. Nobody makes changes for no reason, and neither will your dog. Awareness, therefore, is the first step toward change. From there, it really is just a

---

1. I used the Glenbrook South Physics Home Page, csep10.phys.utk.edu/astr161/lect/history/newton3laws.html. Accessed December 2006. From this web page I used the wording of the laws themselves. There were lots of lively descriptions and a great discussion about these laws on this website.

hop, skip and little jump to better quality of life for you and your dog. That hop, skip and jump represent educating yourself about how to best make the changes that are necessary.

Law Number 2. The relationship between an object's mass, its acceleration and the applied force is: The Force is equal to the mass times the acceleration.

This is a fancy-schmancy scientific way to say that when an object moves, that object's speed is dependant upon two variables:

- The net force - how hard is the object being pushed or pulled?

- The mass - how heavy is the object?

The dynamics between these two variables determines how fast the object moves. Remember, an object with a certain velocity maintains that velocity unless a force acts on it to cause a change in that velocity. This Law #2 says: the speed an object moves is directly proportional to the amount of force that is applied to it. Furthermore, any change in the direction of this momentum is determined by the angle from which the Force is applied. Or, to make this even simpler:

- IT accelerates in the direction that you push it.

- If you push twice as hard, IT accelerates twice as much.

- If IT has twice the mass, IT accelerates half as much.

Behaviourally, this Law talks about tipping points. Tipping Points have to do with that exact moment in time when a significant change is made and all resistance falls away. (This concept has been explained very well in a book by Malcolm Gladwell, called *The Tipping Point: How Little Things Can Make A Big Difference*.) For us, as dog trainers, we want to ask specific questions in relationship to this concept of tipping points and acheiving them:

- how you apply pressure (social, moving into body space, specific pressure points)

- when to release pressure

- how much pressure to apply

These questions are deceptively simple, but they do indeed provide the answers to successful interaction with your dog. Each dog will be a little different. Unlike a scientific laboratory, where all the variables are controllable, you are working with a comparatively uncontrolled environment. But that's okay, you live in the real world - you're used to uncontrolled environments! I can tell you when to release pressure. I can give you starting points about how much. You will have to experiment with and learn about how you apply the pressure, and I can give you several kinds of applications to make your learning curve shorter. It may be that the judgment call of which kind of pressure to use for which context will be your biggest challenge. The best advice I can give you here is: when the pressure is being applied because the dog is inattentive or distracted - mix it up. When I say "mix it up," I mean more specifically: do not use the same "correction" all the time. For instance, if your dog forges ahead of you, disregarding the "stay behind my toes" rule, mix it up. One time back the dog[1], another time use a Move Into[2], yet another time use a Yield The Hindquarters[3] to turn into the dog until he gets into the Safe Spot (Heel position). If you started with a cue, follow the teaching steps, which might include the graduated cue system that you used to teach that behaviour. So in the basic Follow The Feel exercise, first is Low Pressure[4], then Medium Pressure and on up the scale.

Law Number 3. For every action there is an equal and opposite reaction.

When put this law into the context of "opposition reflex":

- If you push on IT...

- IT pushes on you.

This one is especially fascinating when you apply it to the living. Animals do have that opposition reflex: when you apply pressure to their body; instead of giving way or moving *with* the pressure, they push against the pressure. Animals also move into pressure when they are anxious and afraid. This includes defensive behaviour: aggression is displayed and the animal moves into what is frightening him, in an effort to get the scary thing to go away. The opposition reflex is also predominantly displayed when a leash or fence

---

1. *Back Up From Heel Position* on page 223.
2. *Move Into* on page 232.
3. *Yielding The Hindquarters From A Front Position* on page 232.
4. Refer to *What is this Pressure Thing?* on page 183 for more information about this training technique. Also refer to *Follow The Feel* on page 222.

frustrates the dog from getting closer to something: a passer-by, a squirrel, a jogger or skate-boarder. The dog wants to give chase to or interact with something that he is prevented from reaching. This is called barrier frustration and is prevalent in dogs. The frustration created by the barrier (fence, tie-out chain or leash) causes the dog to push into, lean against and jump on it (move into pressure). If the dog's frustration becomes great enough, the dog might choose to find an alternative target on which to direct his ire. This is called redirected aggression, because the dog "redirects" the aggression to whatever is handy, available and close: that might be the handler holding the leash, or a dog who is contained inside the fence with the frustrated dog.

However, a living creature, unlike Dead Weight, can CHANGE IT'S STRATEGY! So if you can convince the animal that moving into pressure doesn't work, you cause the animal to re-think behaviours it came hard-wired with. How cool is that?! When you teach an animal to Follow The Feel instead of resisting and pushing against you, magic happens. Once you buy into the concept that *physical resistance is directly connected to mental resistance*, you can see the powerful implications of this. By working with the animals opposition reflex and harnessing the energy that it contains, you can take all the energy that the animal would normally use to be uncooperative and resistant and distracted and turn that same energy into willingness, attentiveness and team work.

From the website, I quote this wonderful paragraph. See any equivalents to dog training?
"The big deal is not the ability to recite the first law nor to use the 2nd law to solve problems; but rather the ability to understand their meaning and to BELIEVE their implications." (Glenbrook South Physics Home Page)

Cognitive Scientists (scientists who study how people learn) have shown that physics students come into physics class with a set of beliefs (a belief system) which they are unwilling (or not easily willing) to discard despite evidence to the contrary. These beliefs about motion (known as misconceptions) hinder further learning. The task of overcoming misconceptions involves becoming aware of the misconceptions, considering alternative conceptions or explanations, making a personal evaluation of the two competing ideas and adopting a new conception as more reasonable than the previously-held misconception. *This is a clas-*

sic case of prior learning interfering with current learning. Both you and your dog will make changes in the way you think by doing the exercises in this book. It has been a fun intellectual and training exercise for me, and has garnered some excellent results. It is my sincere hope that you get the same kind of results that my clients and my own personal dogs have. The relationship is what it is all about.

Be Sure To Understand These Key Concepts

Sensitizing vs. Desensitizing

When you are working with an animal you are doing one or the other.

- You might want your dog *desensitized or habituated* to other dogs approaching, skateboards and bicycles going by or people petting him. When these things happen, you want your dog to ignore them or to at least stand still or, better yet, look to you for advice.

- You want your dog *sensitized* to certain verbal or body language cues, so that when you request it, you get the behaviour you want promptly and with a minimal cue. The dog will also give your cue highest priority even if competing reinforcers are present.

First you must determine *which* you wish to do: sensitize or desensitize. People are pretty clever at creating the opposite of the one they are aiming for.

When you are aware of and teaching your dog to be sensitized or desensitized to specific stimuli, you are also teaching your dog how to prioritize. You are teaching yourself to understand what is important to your dog and her viewpoint of the world. This understanding enhances your relationship.

You must become hyper-aware of:
- *what* you are doing: your body language and movements.

- *how many* pieces of information you are presenting to the dog at a time - the correct answer is ONE. You cannot allow over-shadowing and blocking to occur. For a long and ridiculously involved but fascinating discussion about over-shadowing and blocking, refer to *Selective Attention: Blocking & Over-shadowing* on page 107)

- *when* you are doing things: by releasing "pressure" at the wrong moment, you inadvertently teach the polar opposite of what you intended!

In the Get Connected protocol, the important component of teaching desensitization and sensitization is the intimate understanding of pressure: how the dog perceives it, what causes it, and how to manipulate the use of pressure, just as you would cleverly manipulate a reinforcement schedule. Before I can more fully explain desensitization and sensitization and how to go about it, you must understand what I mean by the term *pressure*.

What is this Pressure Thing?

I am not talking about thug-related force. Pressure can be physical pressure - moving parts of the dog's body first by touch, then by anticipation and finally by subtle suggestion (cue). Pressure can be spatial - by physically moving into the dog's space until she responds; first, by yielding, and eventually by mirroring the handler's actions. Pressure can be social pressure. Pressure can come from a projecting of energy and intent. It can be intuitive or electric - real "The Force Be With You" kind of stuff that science doesn't like to have anything to do with because it is difficult to define. But you have seen it and felt it. Watch a really good Border Collie move sheep. The way the dog projects her energy forward and *takes up the space between* her and the sheep - that's the kind of power I am speaking of. Good orators do this well, galvanizing a crowd. Good teachers do this, by igniting students with knowledge and curiosity. They project their "power" and then draw you along with them. The "power of persuasion," the business types call it. It isn't magic, although it can look like magic. It feels like magic - but you can learn how to do this yourself.

Pressure is also exerted on our dogs by the environment and inanimate objects. For instance, the first time a dog is placed between a wall and your leg, in Heel position, the dog may try to back up or wiggle forwards. He just does not feel comfortable in those close quarters. It is because the wall exerts pressure and so does your proximity. He feels "trapped" between the wall and your body. Most dogs can be accustomed to this situation in about 3 seconds with the use of 1 cookie, but some dogs are much more sensitive to this mildly claustrophobic situation and it takes them longer.

What is most important to be aware of when you are applying different kinds of pressure, whether it is physical or one of the more subtle forms of pressure to move, is: *the dog "remembers" the moment of the release of pressure and will repeat that behaviour.* Another way to think of this is that, *during Acquisition* of the behaviour, when the animal exhibits a behaviour change, so must you: by releasing the pressure on the slightest try by the dog. The timing of the release of pressure is as crucial as the timing of any other Marker.[5]

Mother Nature's "Click"

The release of pressure can serve as a Memory Marker. My own personal way of thinking about the release of pressure is that it is *Mother Nature's "click."* Since the correct response from the dog (behavioural change by the dog) causes a release of pressure by the handler (behavioural change by the handler), the dog can easily see the cause and effect. "Jeez, look at that. My behaviour changed my handler's behaviour. This is interesting and has definite possibilities." For instance, in one Approximation of teaching a dog competition-style Heel-work, I might begin by standing still with the dog on leash beside me. I just stand there and look at the

dog intensely. When the dog finally gets that feeling, "Hey, I think somebody is looking at me," she will glance up at me. I release the pressure of intensely gazing at the dog by moving forward one step and stopping and feeding her a treat *or* by doing a Back Away and delivering a treat. I find the Back Away and treat works best in the beginning, because the Back Away is another, additional, release of pressure. In this case, the dog directing her attention to me by looking at me caused the release of pressure (moving forward instead of standing and gazing intently). She will remember this, and if repeated consistently, soon she will come to believe that she can drive me forward (preferable to standing still and being bored), which is a kind of application of pressure from the dog to the handler, by looking at me. Dogs understand the use of this kind of pressure and they use it all the time, with each other in play, as well as in predatory situations. I am careful with this process and do not move forward if the dog takes her eyes off me. If the dog takes her eyes off me I freeze my feet and gaze at her intensely again. This will be built up into 2, 3 and several steps. I will try to work under the threshold of what I think the dog will give me (if I feel the dog will only give me three steps before looking away, I will stick to one step or two.

That moment of the release of pressure is so very salient to the dogs. I have watched handlers Mark their dog and even give her a treat, but the social pressure (felt by the dog or observed in your body language) simultaneously placed on the dog by the handler is what is remembered in future, similar situations; The Mark & Treat were present, but the pressure was not released at the moment of the Mark. This is rather difficult to explain, but bear with me. If you are training your dog and are frustrated with the process, it can have a big effect on a sensitive dog. You can click and treat if you like, but if you do so with a "Good Lord, it's about darn time you got it" attitude, the dog may still remember the discomfort your attitude provoked over and above the click and treat. In this case you didn't do what you intended to do. You intended to "reinforce" a behaviour and you even went through the motions of properly reinforcing the dog. But if your agitated attitude, for whatever reason, was most salient to the dog then you inadvertently paired an aversive with a behaviour you thought you were pairing with reinforcement. Pressure can be more salient and more remembered by the dog than a treat. When you train, let it be a learning process for both of you. Expect incorrect responses, both on your part and your dog's part. In the following quote you will have to substitute

5.In some exercises, such as Be Still (refer to *The Be Still Switch: Stand Your Feet Still & Be Calm* on page 201 for a detailed description), you will release the pressure later and later into the exercise. This is because Be Still is a duration exercise, therefore, after Acquisition, you are conditioning the behaviour and working on duration and releasing the pressure later works just as delaying the "click" to increase duration works.

"dog" for "horse," but the sentiment applies to all animal trainers: "Listen more. Talk less. Let the horse teach you instead of trying to teach the horse." (GaWaNi Pony Boy, 2005)

Horse trainers are the absolute last word in use of pressure and training domestic species. The use of pressure is reduced to an absolute whisper, almost a thought. For instance, on a "green" horse (not very much training) you might give a light to quite vigorous "bump" with your lower leg (calf muscle - do not "kick" him with your heels) to ask him to move forward. On a intermediate trained horse, you squeeze gently with your calves; the bump is no longer necessary. On a well trained mount, the pressure is reduced to lowering your heel slightly to tense your calf muscle. (To teach this, you always begin with the slight tightening of the calf, followed by a squeeze, followed by the "bump." You would stop "upping the ante" the moment the horse responds. In this way, the horse learns that the lightest "pressure" is the one to respond to.) Because pressure is central to all of our work with horses, and because horsemen and women understand how subtle pressure can be, this release of pressure is paid close attention to; from the groundwork (unmounted exercises) to exacting mounted work. "Lapses of attention or uncoordinated or inappropriate responses interfere with the establishment of conditioned (trained) responses. If we continue pressure when immediate relief from pressure is called for, the lesson is spoiled. Conversely, when pressure is needed, and we relax the pressure, the lesson is again spoiled." (Miller and Lamb, 2005) When riding (or training any animal), you never want to use more pressure than required, always *less is more*. On the other hand, if not enough pressure is used to obtain the desired result, the animal can become dull and unresponsive, or he can simply ignore our "conversation." I will never forget an extremely valuable lesson taught to me by a Morgan gelding I owned, Funquest Bellmore. He was a lovely animal, large and impressive. I was about 16 or 17 at the time, and I couldn't believe I had such a lovely animal to ride. When we went to local shows, Bellmore would always win his first class, but when I would ride additional classes that day, he would slog around the ring, lazy and unimpressive, unresponsive to my cues. Winning was not the only object, but by golly, I knew this horse could do better; he had just shown me that he could! He was like the child who gets remarks on his report card that say, "not working up to potential." I had nagged him and kicked him lightly for months to no avail. So one day, after talking to others (others are

always happy to give advice), I decided to follow their instruction. I got a pair of mild, blunt spurs. I got on Bellmore and started to ride him and I rode him until he was getting just a wee bit tired and starting to get lazy. Then, when he slowed down, I gave it all I had, just as I had been told to do. I gave him a mighty kick with my skinny, little legs (remember, he weighed about 1100 pounds and at the time I weighed about 100 pounds). That horse tossed me so high into the air I can vividly remember it to this day. I counted 3 full somersaults before I hit the ground with a sickening thud, rolling into a ball and trying to take the shock of the fall with my shoulders (as prior mounts had taught me to do. Hopefully, if you fall right, you just crack your collarbone instead of breaking your neck). I heard my neck crack. When I got up, Bellmore was standing about 3 feet away, looking at me calmly; probably wondering if I was bright enough to learn this lesson. Once I recovered my breathing processes I got back on. Bellmore began to shuffle along, lazily, and I asked him, quite gently this time with my newfound knowledge about spurs, and he readily speeded up. I gave him a pat and a kiss, thankful that he hadn't tossed my ass again and called it a day. Good trainers know when to quit. Bellmore was saying, "if you use enough pressure for me to respect it, okay. I'll respect it. But do not walk in here swinging a billy club, 'cuz I just might take you up on it." I couldn't move my head at all for 3 days and to this day, my neck aches in rainy weather, causing me to remember Bellmore and my valuable lesson with a rueful smile. It was okay to use the amount of pressure required, but I'm gonna tell you what, Bellmore let me know that way too much force lacks elegance!

In regards to the "amount" or force of the pressure used, it seems to be human nature to move quickly, grab hard and use way more pressure than is required. This is often due to inexperience, a lack of confidence and lack of thoughtful application. The idea is to behave in an enlightened way, using the least amount of pressure to get the desired result. Depending on the natural tendencies of the dog you are working with more or less pressure may be required. *Be a good listener and allow the dog to determine what amount of pressure makes sense to her.* Listening is an act of love, and animals know this.

Dog trainers use pressure and force inappropriately all the time. Of course there is the obvious example, of the inexperienced trainer using a slip collar (choke chain), pinch collar or electronic collar with the wrong dog (temperament too soft or the dog does not understand what is wanted), using too much force and inappropriately for the situation. Personally, if I thought my skill level was so low as to need a shock collar to teach a dog a Sit Stay, I think perhaps I should be hanging up my leash. There are less obvious examples, as well. I am talking about:

- the average person who becomes frustrated during the training process and takes it out on her dog.

- the trainer who allows the dog to pull on the leash in ten different situations and in the eleventh situation gets angry with the dog and has an emotional fit. Inconsistent expectations place unfair and enormous pressure on dogs.

- the trainer whose dog has told her over and over "I like the work well enough, but I hate going to competition events. There is too much chaos and I just cannot handle it," and the owner, no matter how much over-the-top stress the dog is experiencing, will just not give it up because: "*I* got this dog to be an agility (obedience, hunting) dog. I have a lot of work in this dog."

- the performance trainer whose very nice working dog cannot handle the stress of the precision and pressure involved in training for the upper echelon of the chosen sport (agility or obedience). Instead of appreciating the qualifying ribbons and the lovely work the dog has done for them so far, they are disappointed in their dog for failing to be the equivalent of an Olympic athlete. We are not all made to be able to take the physical and mental pressure of being an Olympic athlete. If you wish to train in the very top levels of your sport, you will have to find, not only a dog who is capable of taking that kind of training pressure, but also a dog who is a perfect fit for your training style.

- the average trainer who places additional pressure on a dog who is confused about what is being asked of her.

This knowledge about release of pressure is intuitive on the part of the dog. He comes with this knowledge, you do not have to install it.

The Sheep press against each other in an instinctive flocking behaviour, while they move away from the pressure of the Border Collie.

Katherine, the lamb, feels threatened by the Border Collie. In response she moves toward the dog. Sometimes animals "move away" from pressure when frightened or threatened and sometimes they "move toward" or "move into" pressure. This is an offensive manuever that occurs because the animal feels defensive. Regardless, when an animal leans into or creates pressure, *which is accompanied by body tension*, it is a reaction to stress and an attempt to cope with the stressor. Katherine is behaving very similarly to the puppy in the photo essay that follows, moving into pressure when stressed. The stressor does not have to be a big, bad stressor, or even something the animal is terrified of, just something that causes minor anxiety.

Photographs by Dave Schrader

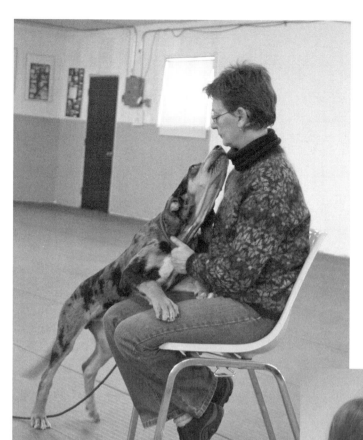

It doesn't matter whether I am sitting or standing, this puppy presses into me. It is not to get my attention, because I am already being attentive and am not ignoring him. When I push at him to move him away from me, he just keeps coming in, pressing into me harder and harder. This is an example of anxiety and the opposition reflex at work in partnership as the best coping skills this puppy has available to him.

In my lingo, this dog is moving into pressure both socially and physically.

The physical pressure we SEE is just a symptom of the anxiety the dog is feeling. This puppy has a combination of genetic traits and learned experience that predispose him to behave in this manner, instead of showing social savvy and calm acceptance.

Many people mistake this sort of anxiety for "friendly" behaviour. This is sad, because then the person doesn't supply what the dog is desperately seeking - a safe, secure boundary and help with coping skills.

Move Into Pressure - Person Approaches Dog

As I approach, this puppy launches himself at me, *moving into pressure*. This is triggered by the anxiety he feels when I approach and come into his personal space. Without me or his handler doing anything, he then turns and launches himself at his handler, crawling up her leg and pushing into *her* personal space.

His anxiety is causing him to behave in socially inappropriate ways, in a hectic and reactive (Hindbrain) manner.

This puppy is using language that is "too big" for the situation. By this I mean that his behaviours could be much more subdued or "smaller" and they would get the job done better. For instance, he could have walked up to me instead of launching himself at me in order to convey friendly, confident behaviour. The fact that he is hectic and contacting me and pushing into me, tells me he is not friendly, but feels very uncomfortable with my approach and does not really know what to do. In fact, he wishes I would move out of his personal space. His coping skills and social manners are totally inadequate. If he used these behaviours with an adult dog, the other dog would be very likely to correct the puppy in a not-very-nice way.

Photographs by Dave Schrader

89

The Back Away

The Back Away, taught in the *Basic Training Boot Camp Section* is an excellent way to "release pressure." From a Move Into (an exercise in this Section) Sharon segues into a Back Away to release the pressure. The release of pressure serves as a Memory Marker.

Photographs by Dave Schrader

Wilson does not like having his feet handled in the least. As I pick up his paw, as one might to wipe off dirty feet or to inspect for injury, he leans into me and tries to bite my hand to show his displeasure. You can see I am not holding his paw tightly, he just does not like it and does not feel safe with having his feet restrained.

The moment the puppy relaxes and allows his paw to rest gently in my hand, I immediately "release the pressure" by letting him place his foot back on the floor.

The release of pressure serves as a Memory Marker. Wilson will "remember" what was happening when the pressure was released: he was cooperative and relaxed, no longer resistant and agitated. The next time I pick up a paw, he will be more likely to relax sooner, if, indeed, he struggles at all.

This is important, that your dog will allow you to do basic husbandry (physical maintenance and care). Many dogs resent having their feet handled to the extent that they will bite if you try to clip nails or wipe dirty paws. I want dogs to be comfortable with all of the touching, bending and restraining that humans must do in order to properly care for the dog. I know that Wilson doesn't like this and it scares him a little, but no one is hurting him and he will soon discover that with firm, sensible, but gentle handling and guidance.

Teaching husbandry behaviours is an area where the concept of "pressure on" vs. "pressure off" is a very valuable technique.

Photo essay by Dave Schrader

Sensitizing: The Concept.

When sensitizing maintain the pressure until the dog yields or moves his feet.

As soon as you get a desired response take the pressure away immediately and reward. The reward is, for the most part, the simple act of removing the pressure. In some cases you can release the pressure and then deliver a treat. After extensive experimentation with this technique, I find this work much more effective and clear to the dog if no treats are used. In fact, the less you chatter and the more you allow you and your dog to concentrate on just the touch and the Pressure On vs. Pressure Off, the smoother and faster the work goes. Understanding comes more quickly to the dog because you are allowing her to think about one thing at a time. Also, you are communicating a a dog's most basic language. Human language is not instinctive to a

dog. Patricia McConnell discusses this fact in a truly moving way in her books: *The Other End Of The Leash* and *For The Love Of A Dog*. If you have not read these two books, you must. They are published by Ballantine Books, New York.

One of the most splendiferous things about sensitizing work is the way it builds a willing partner. This occurs primarily because of the specific way the material is presented. You will use a very elegant and systematic presentation: something I think about as a Graduated Cue System. When you use this properly and consistently the dog can most efficiently discern a pattern, because you present the cue to the dog in *exactly* the same pattern each time. As you do this, you are naturally building a humane correction or penalty into the behaviour as the dog is learning it. The dog gets lots of practice making decisions and controlling what happens. The human learns much about interacting while

192

using this technique. You can come to see how subtle the dog's own language is and how *little*, not how much, pressure is required to obtain optimum results. This old and amazing technique is little discussed in dog training; or at best is used in a clumsy manner, with corrections that are too big and "out of the blue."

It is of the utmost importance that the person doing the sensitizing be extremely aware of the dog's feedback. When the handler is sensitive and willing to release the pressure in response to the slightest try by the dog, this technique creates a wonderful communication loop; one that is sensitive and very much a conversation between the dog and the handler.

Desensitizing: The Concept

When Desensitizing you will apply pressure in a consistent, rhythmic way, and you will maintain this, no matter what, until the dog stops moving his feet and orients his nose toward you.

Desensitizing is what I think of as preparation for the real world. Desensitizing helps to teach your dog to accept weird behaviours and approaches. The dog comes to understand that touch is okay, and even that odd behaviour and a variety of touches are safe. It teaches the dog to remain calm and to override that panic button. It teaches your dog to stand still, stay there until cued to move, to relax and to not move into pressure. It teaches over-excited dogs to accept petting and greetings calmly, and timid dogs to gain confidence. The whole idea of desensitization is that you make the dog comfortable and relaxed.

Touch is one thing a dog is expected to take a lot of. Unfortunately, many dogs are afraid of touch or are nervous when any "new" kind of touch is introduced. Dogs, rightfully so in many cases, are suspicious of people grabbing, touching and reaching toward them. Many times when people grab it is followed up by something else unpleasant. Touch is crucial to proper development. "Touch does more than help the brain manage the body; it is critical to the development of a healthy emotional system later in life." (McConnell, 2005) I want my dog to be educated about all kinds of bizarre and, from the dog's point of view, inappropriate human touching. Then she never has to be scared or worried, instead she can be, at least neutral and confident. At best, she will be social and friendly, understanding that being around humans can be odd, but non-threatening.

Touch is just one item that dogs might need help learning about in a safe and educational way. There is a variety of things that happen around humans that dogs find scary. Large crowds, parades, halloween (and other holidays), other people's children; the list of "novel stimuli" is endless. Many of our own children view their very first halloween with suspicion, it is not unusual that many dogs do so as well!

Every time you do work with sensitizing, you must follow it with desensitizing. Desensitizing emphasizes that while we do want the dog's respect, we do not want him to be afraid of us and all the weird things that domestic dogs are exposed to because they live with us bizarre humans.

Whatever you do on the left side, always repeat the exercise on the right side. This works both hemispheres of the pre-frontal cortex and will prepare your dog for tasks like Agility and Freestyle where the dog is expected to be ambidextrous.

Approach & Retreat

This is a technique that animals themselves use when they are unsure or cautious about a novel object or circumstance. They might walk toward an object, then move away from it, then approach it again; on each re-approach coming a little closer to the object. The animal is experimenting to see if the object in question is "safe." As long as each approach and retreat is completed safely, the curious animal (be it dog, horse or sheep) will re-approach. In essence, the animal is devising her own program of desensitization and habituation. An over-cautious animal (excessive caution is smart in the wild, sometimes dysfunctional in domesticity) may be so afraid that she will never develop this program for herself.

While Desensitizing, you might come across an area on your dog's body that is a No Go area. This is discerned by the dog's response or reaction when you reach this area. The dog might become violently opposed to you touching his body there, or you might see something such as his feet were still but he begins fidgeting his feet each time you hit the No Go area. This response also can be as subtle as his turning to look at the hand that is causing him the bother.

When you reach an area like this, you will use Approach & Retreat. Rub the dog's body in a Go area,

193

and then approach the No Go area casually and at the same speed and pressure. However, you are not going to stay there, you will get in and out, moving your hand into the area and rubbing out of the area before he even gets a chance to fuss about it. Stay in the Go area for a bit, then venture into the No Go area for one rub and then back out.

This little Corgi jauntily sports a muzzle and Halti head collar. We had to desensitize her to these pieces of equipment so she would wear them without fear and to quit fussing over the loss of control they represent. Since this little cutie had both dog and human aggression problems, it was necessary to use these training aids to keep handlers, helpers and dogs safe while we desensitized her to being around other dogs and to human approaches. When done properly, the muzzle becomes a "safety cue" and makes the dog much more comfortable.

I use squeeze cheese and peanut butter on a wooden spoon to help make this process fun for the dog.

Photograph by Sam Zieggenmeyer.

Examples of Desensitization

If you have ever been around sheep, you will know how unusual this sheep's behaviour is (especially for a sheep who was not bottle fed as a lamb). Boris has been desensitized to a few humans. This allows my friend Katie to give him a big hug! In addition to the hug, he is wearing a jolly Christmas hat. It took Katie and I about 10 minutes to get Boris desensitized to wearing the cap.

Some of his natural reactions to the cap were to attempt to run away from it (flight & avoidance), shake it off his head and posture as if to butt at it when the hat was held out to him (fight & aggression). Eventually, he just ignored the hat and wore it, as he ascertained through experimentation that there was a recurring pattern: the hat didn't go away; the hat did not cause any harm; the hat was not good to eat; the hat did not fight back. Boris became "desensitized" to the hat; that is, he learned that tolerating the hat did not threaten his safety, therefore, he could ignore its presence.

Photograph by Brenda Aloff.

194

Become Water On Stone

Dogs count on humans giving up in frustration or despair. You must become water on stone when you are training. Keep "holding" your cue until you get the response you want, then release the pressure. You will indeed have to prove your resolution by outlasting the dog. However, once you have outlasted the dog on a couple different occasions, the dog will offer less future resistance, no matter what the context. Because physical tension and resistance are just a facet of mental resistance, as you rid your dog of body tension you rid him of anxiety. The more you emphasize "no resistance" as a way of life, the more cooperative your dog will become.

When with my dog, no matter what behaviour has just been requested, what I pay close attention to is the amount of resistance with which any request is met. It is not the behaviour I emphasize as much as the attitude that accompanies it. If I notice any resistance, hesitation or mutiny, I address that each and every time and immediately. If you are consistent with this expectation, it becomes an integral part of the relationship with your dog.

Therefore, when I ask for a learned behaviour, I seek balance and fluidity in the execution. Do I and my dog have less than perfect moments? Of course we do, but the connection is never far from my mind. This means we have less than perfect moments, but those moments do not turn into days, or episode upon episode of irritation between us.

In these exercises, your technique must include persistence. Persistence is more important than treats or force or amount of pressure. The persistence must be applied with clarity, you cannot just bang your head against a wall without giving any thought to what you are being persistent about. But when thoughtful persistence and good mechanical skills are applied in unison, you will be mightily effective.

Before beginning the exercises contained in this table: The Get Connected Protocol, the following behaviours are prerequisite. These prerequisite behaviours are listed in the Table in *Basic Training Boot Camp* on page 120.

- Eye Contact. For maximum results, work on Approximation #5 before proceeding with the Get Connected exercises.

- Get Between. (refer to *Think First: Impulse Control* on page 155.) For maximum results, complete Approximation #1, the Get Between, before proceeding with the Get Connected exercises.

- Back Away. (refer to *Back Away* on page 136.)

Handlers should have trained at least one dog with the training exercises in the Basic Training Boot Camp so they understand how dogs learn and how a behaviour develops.

Table 1: The Get Connected Protocol: Improve the Relationship by using Bodywork & Space; Encouraging Teamwork and Developing Trust & Respect

Exercise	Skills Developed	What Your Dog Learns & Other Benefits
Be Still on page 201. Using Be Still to improve Approaches & greeting behaviour on page 206.	The quickest way to teach a totally untrained dog how to Switch from Hindbrain to Frontbrain.	Desensitization: that his body has no NO GO areas. This is a basic husbandry exercise. As a bonus: your veterinarian and veterinary technicians will love you. Your dog learns to be less fearful on veterinarian visits, where, inevitably, he must be restrained for routine health care.
	Gives the handler a way to get the dog to stand still and be calm.	Plant your feet when the Be Still cue is presented. This can help a fearful dog to feel safer, and it also allows you to put a collar on your dog without getting a bloody nose!
	Your dog deserves to be comfortable in a variety of situations involving touch, leaning over her and basic husbandry behaviours.	Great for teaching a Stand For Exam for competition work. People can approach without being mobbed and jumped on, there are better ways to greet. You do not have to be anxious when people approach. This is also a trust exercise: "my handler would not let anyone approach me who is not safe."
	To teach the dog that the world is not a frightening place and that he can trust you.	The dog relies on the handler and if the handler does not appear to be alarmed then the dog follows this lead.

Table 1: The Get Connected Protocol: Improve the Relationship by using Bodywork & Space; Encouraging Teamwork and Developing Trust & Respect

Exercise	Skills Developed	What Your Dog Learns & Other Benefits
Follow The Feel (following the guidance or "feel" of the pressure) on page 222.	Teaches dog to change how she sees the world. Teaches dog to use logic overrides to overcome instinctive, reflexive behaviours. Teaches the dog the concept of "no resistance." Fosters a relationship of cooperation and communication. You can take hold of the dog's collar from any position, even the front, or from over his head and he is comfortable.	Sensitization: Yield to collar pressure. Use pressure on the collar as a guide to "Follow" the direction of the pressure with no resistance or fear. The handler can influence the dog to step backwards by slight pressure on the chest using the fingers, or a slight pressure on the collar. Collars are used in very confusing ways for dogs. Sometimes they are used to guide and sometimes they are used to jerk and correct. Or people yell and jerk, frightening the dog into defensive behaviour. To be safe and for good communication to develop, use of the collar, like Eye Contact, must have a predictable outcome. The collar should be used in a consistent way, teaching the dog that guidance by the collar is information, not a punishment.
Move Into (Do not be worried about personal space.) on page 232.	Teaches dog about personal space; yours and his. Increases owner awareness of how dogs perceive space: who moves whose feet *is* a big deal. The handler is able to use her body language consistently and clearly. The dog offers no resistance but willingly and cheerfully moves out of handler's space and looks into the handler's eyes (and soul), meaningfully.	Dog immediately allows you to displace his body (move him) and turns to look at you. Dog understands that a shift in the handler's position, body weight or intent is information. At the very least, the dog immediately orients toward the handler when the handler moves toward or into the dog. The handler becomes relevant to the dog, therefore the dog will more likely prioritize the cues given by the handler.
Walk Nice (loose leash walking) on page 265.	The dog understands to keep his toes behind your toes. If you wish him to be able to go do "doggy" stuff out ahead of you, you will cue him to do so.	Your dog learns to "keep his toes behind your toes" when walking. You can walk your dog without requiring rotator cuff surgery. You will not be knocked down by your dog and you will not have to be dragged anywhere ever again. Your dog and you will both enjoy the walk.

Table 1: The Get Connected Protocol: Improve the Relationship by using Bodywork & Space; Encouraging Teamwork and Developing Trust & Respect

Exercise	Skills Developed	What Your Dog Learns & Other Benefits
Mirror & Switch Games on page 284.	The dog will follow your body language suggestions fluidly. Increasing awareness of each other's body language. This is an excellent means to learn to control your dog when she is aroused. This is a Switching game as well, including prey-type games and how quickly the dog can Switch from activity to calm stillness.	The dog will mirror your body, following the suggestion and direction you indicate with your body. This exercise promotes a really wonderful feeling of togetherness. It takes the meaning of no resistance to a new level. This work is very fun (for both of you!) and your communication loop improves in leaps and bounds. Arousal does not mean that you do not have to pay attention to your handler. Aroused dogs may be a danger to themselves (because they are not thinking before they act) or to others. The dog will go from an active, aroused or predatory state to a state of calm focus. (Or at least under some control...)

Get Connected: The Exercises

Photograph by Dave Schrader.

At last, with much anticipation, it is time to get to the core of this work. This is the stuff that I got you all excited about at the beginning, but you had to do all the preliminary *Basic Boot Camp* exercises first. Training is not for sissies! It is time to stand up and be counted. Don't be intimidated by the foreign concepts and the new behaviours you will have to learn. You can do this. C'mon guys, if I can get my horse to do this stuff (he is a lot bigger than your dog), and have taught some of my sheep to Move Away From Pressure, backing up on a slight touch of my fingers, (sheep are much spookier, hind-brain animals than your dog), surely you can teach these valuable, oft-neglected-but-absolutely-necessary behaviours to your domestic dog. My own dogs and my client's dogs have sold me on these techniques. The changed attitude of both dog and handler, the dog's responsiveness to the handler and the increased understanding are indeed jewels in the crown of the relationship.

The Get Connected Protocol perfectly embodies "actions speak louder than words," and "a picture is worth a thousand words." The following exercises will best be learned by watching the DVD. These are definitely not exercises you can read about, then go do successfully. You must see them done, in real time, and then go practice in order to become proficient. The protocols are briefly outlined below, and in greater detail on the DVD portion of this material.

The DVD that accompanies this book has valuable information and examples of the exercises.

The Be Still Switch: Stand Your Feet Still & Be Calm

This is the first *desensitizing* exercise in this protocol. This is the exercise you will revert to again and again as you do the other exercises. In addition to the many other benefits of this exercise (refer to the table in *The Get Connected Protocol: Improve the Relationship by using Bodywork & Space; Encouraging Teamwork and Developing Trust & Respect* on page 196.), it is also used as a way to signal that an approximation has ended and this is the "rest period" before we begin another approximation.

• Hold your dog's collar with one hand.

• With your other hand rub your dog all over.

• Use a FLAT HAND and a FIRM Touch.

• Begin with a benign area, easily accepted by most dogs, such as the rib cage and back.

• DO NOT stop the "rubbing the dog all over thing" until TWO things happen:

> 1. The dog's feet STOP MOVING.
> 2. In addition, *once the feet are still*, at least ONE of the following must ALSO be present:
> > the dog licks his lips
> > blinks his eyes
> > takes a deeper breath
> > or his feet are still for a count of five.

• A short and quiet Marker such as "Yes" is okay at this point if you like, but the more silent you are the better it is. Certainly do not indulge yourself in a lot of chatter. Really, all the chit chat is all about you. Shut up! Another valid reason for silence is that the majority of handlers do not Mark the behaviour at the right moment, or drag the Marker out too long by saying, "Yes, good girl," or something similar. A "click" at this point makes many dogs look for a treat, which can really disrupt the flow of this work. Many dogs have been taught that "good" or "yes" is an End Working Cue. If this is the case with your

dog it will really interrupt the flow of the behaviour.

• Stand up, as you have been bending over the dog to rub his body. Count to 2.

• Begin another trial (repetition of the exercise) using well-tolerated areas of the dog's body.

• Eventually you should be able to rub the dog's legs, face, pick up the feet, etc. There should be no No Go areas.

• With a highly aroused or dog who dislikes being controlled in any way, at first the still feet may be fleeting, and you need ask only for a couple of seconds as long as you see one of the other observable signals, such as lip licking. These indicate that the dog is "trying" to come from Hindbrain to Frontbrain. Once the dog's feet are still and a Frontbrain signal criterion has been exhibited: STOP rubbing the dog IMMEDIATELY, by lifting your hand off the dog.

As a goal, I want you to be able to begin rubbing the dog's body and have the dog immediately stand still. Wiggling, movement, trying to pull away from you, etc. are signs of anxiety and sycophancy, or sometimes of resistance or frustration over not being able to control the situation, and do not necessarily indicate friendliness.

The way you touch with your "flat hand and a firm touch" is important. Touch the dog like you wish them to notice that an event is happening. I have found that dogs much prefer a firm, deliberate touch than a light, "spidery" touch. Experiment a bit with the amount of firmness until you find one that works well for you. I think about exerting about as much pressure as if I were rubbing the dog's body while holding a two pound weight and allowing that to rest on the dog's body.

If the dog is particularly hectic when you begin, allow him to move, but not forward. Keep your feet within a small, imaginary circle about the size of a turkey platter. To do this, you will be allowing the dog to move if he wishes to do so, but you will be turning in a circle so as to remain with your feet on your platter. This will allow the restive dog to move, but will restrict the movement enough so that he will slow down. It is okay to encourage the dog to stop, but do your darndest to allow the dog to make this decision on his own. He will eventually drift to a stop when he realizes that you are both turning in small, tight circles. Dogs are quick to recognize a lack of progress!

With the hectic dog, begin with a quicker, firmer touch and after about 5 or 10 seconds, slow the motion down. See if you can bring the dog with you to a less hectic state.

Any No Go areas will be catalogued by you, and you will begin to systematically desensitize each of these with an Approach & Retreat technique (refer to *Approach & Retreat* on page 193).

- Repeat this exercise ten or fifteen times, consecutively. In future sessions, use your judgment. As soon as the dog has done two or three really nice repetitions, move on to another exercise or quit for that session. If the dog is really struggling with this exercise and you get a couple of good moments, end the session calmly and you may work on this exercise again later today or tomorrow.

Now raise criteria to gain duration of the behaviour:

- Begin again, still using well-tolerated areas of his body.

- After the dog's feet are still and one or more Frontbrain, "I am with you" signals are evident, you will not stop rubbing immediately, but you will continue the rubbing for an additional few seconds. You are conditioning the dog to *stop moving his feet* when he feels you rub his body and then working on duration of the behaviour.

- Now you can move on to less-tolerated areas of the dog's body, working on this systematically until the dog has no No Go areas, and will remain still for longer and longer periods of time. Work up to at least a two minute time frame.

You will know the dog is "getting it" when he stops moving his feet almost as soon as you begin rubbing his body. Now the behaviour is at last useful! You can get your dog to be still and relax whenever you need to. Better yet, you have conditioned your dog to stop moving his feet when people lean over to touch him.

Other ways to use the Be Still Switch:

- Useful for teaching greeting behaviours, as discussed later in this chapter.

- Teaches a wonderful Stand For Exam exercise for competition dogs.

- Gives you a way to calm a distraught or frustrated dog. I started using this exercise years ago for dogs with aggression problems, as a way to work effectively with dogs who had serious personal space issues.

- Teaches basic husbandry behaviours. Domestic dogs need to accept a variety of touches.

- Helps fearful dogs to learn that different touches or being touched in sensitive body areas is okay, humans can be trusted.

- Builds trust and respect between dog and handler.

- The handler learns much about pressure and it's application and release. The handler also learns how to recognize signals from the dog as valuable feedback. In fact, it is the dog who is controlling this exercise to a very great degree. So both handler and dog learn a bit more about cause and effect.

The Be Still Switch

The puppy begins by squirming, moving his feet and constantly bumping into and leaning on my body.

As I continue, he finally stands still and relaxes; he stops displaying anxiety and constantly trying to control my movements. In the third photograph, I am just about to release the pressure and stand up to let him think about what just happened. This allows him to process and learn the maximum amount from this experience.

Leash Too Long

Rachel holds onto the puppy with her leash too long. She begins to rub the puppy all over, and the long leash places the puppy in the circumstance of having way too many decisions to make. This means he will make lots of wrong decisions, prolonging the time it takes to do the work properly.

The Be Still Switch: Stand Your Feet Still & Be Calm

Much better! Rachel holds the puppy by the martingale collar in such a way that it is not tight, but the puppy won't be able to slip away, either. This channels the puppy into making the desired choices quicker. It also helps the puppy by introducing a "boundary" gently and helpfully.

Using The Be Still Switch To Improve Approaches & Greeting Behaviour

How Do Approaches Get To Be Such A Mess?

When a dog invades personal space, people talk to the dog or push at the dog, and most inadvertently step back to avoid the onslaught. When the approaching person pets the wiggling puppy, he usually pets a moment, then stops, while the dog is still wiggling in excitement. If you think of this in the context of pressure on/pressure off, you can see that in those situations, the pressure is "released" at exactly the wrong time. Instead of *desensitizing* the dog to wiggling and frantic behaviour you actually *sensitize* the dog to being wiggly and hectic.

In addition, many owners allow approachers to train the dog, which is naive in the extreme. The handler is the one who should insist upon polite greeting rituals, and during early training it is the handler who must control the action. Do not allow the approaching person to train your dog, because she will only ruin your training efforts.

This puppy used in the photo essays that follow, is a particularly persistent jumper. In this photo essay, I am doing a little experimentation to how much progress we can make with this problem in one session, and therefore, do a great deal of good in a very short time. Because I am an experienced approacher and I have a plan, I can enhance the training process. In later photo essays you will see the responsibility placed more on the handler, where it should be for the majority of training situations.

Look at Wilson's body language, he is alert and judging at what moment he should spring into action.

This puppy is a rescue and, as far as we can figure, he left his mother much too early. His real problem is not just the jumping, but is a personal space issue. He exhibits a lot of anxiety about approaches, and at the same time, he is very pushy and ready to become inappropriately assertive. You can read Wilson's entire case history in the *Case History* section of this book.

Using The Be Still Switch to Teach Approaches: Approach Number 1

Rachel has her leash neatly bundled and her hands firmly anchored at her "core." I begin to approach the puppy. The puppy is in "preparing to launch" mode.

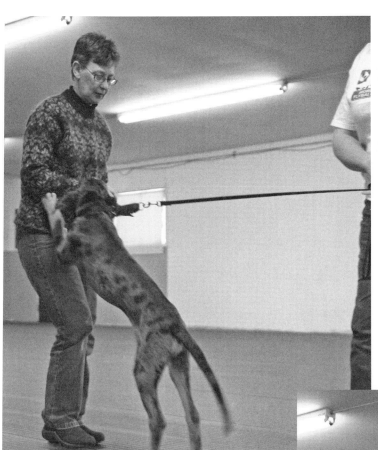

And sure enough, he launches toward me, contacting my body. I get closer, I do not rush in, but instead move slowly and deliberately, in a calm way. Think of a large bulldozer moving sand, or oxen pulling a heavy load. You just slowly, deliberately and steadily move forward.

Wilson keeps jumping, but my calm forward movement is causing him a problem. Instead of him causing me to lose my balance, he is beginning to lose his balance. In the past, if you jump on people it often has the effect of the approacher stepping back, therefore gaining the puppy personal space. I calmly continue to step forward into the puppy's space...I want him to find that a great way to regain your balance is with four feet on the ground. Like other lessons, those answers you discover with your own brainpower seem to be the quickest and best learned.

You must be careful! Do NOT step on the dog's feet or get pushy or rough with the dog in any way. You are merely a venue for the dog to obtain the information: jumping does not work as planned.

I continue moving neutrally and slowly into the space between Wilson and I until he finds it easier to keep his balance by putting four feet on the ground. This Moving Into the dog must be done calmly, slowly and deliberately. Do not talk to the dog. Do not "bull" into the dog, do not move quickly. This just encourages the dog to misinterpret your actions as rough play or intimidation.

At last Wilson tries a little Negotiation Signal with me, a Lip Lick.

Rachel gets hold of his collar and we both begin rubbing his body, using the Be Still Switch that we have already worked on.

We will continue to do this until we get the result we wish to see: still feet, calm body. These observable physical signals indicate a calmer mind, too.

The Be Still Switch: Stand Your Feet Still & Be Calm

Wilson, in his mad squirming, loses his own balance and topples over, in protest, wiggling and mouthing at our hands. We ease him down so he doesn't just fall over, softening his topple. In addition, through all that, we just continue "holding our cue," rubbing his body, being a "presence," no matter what he does.

Think of asking a recalcitrant child to do the dishes. She protests. "Please do the dishes," you repeat. "But moooo-oomm." "Please do the dishes," you repeat again, in the same calm tone. Soon the child stops protesting, seeing that her protests are getting her nowhere and the quickest way to "win" is to just go do the dishes.

In this photograph, Wilson is biting at my hands and Rachel's. He is not fearful, exactly, but he is certainly not comfortable either. He is biting because he wants to have his own way and is "trying on" biting to see how successful a strategy it will be. Notice how neutral and relaxed both Rachel and I remain. We do not become angry at his resistance and protests, we do not have "to tell him off" about it. We just remain calm and neutral until he follows our body language instead of allowing him to pull us into the vortex of his agitated emotional state.

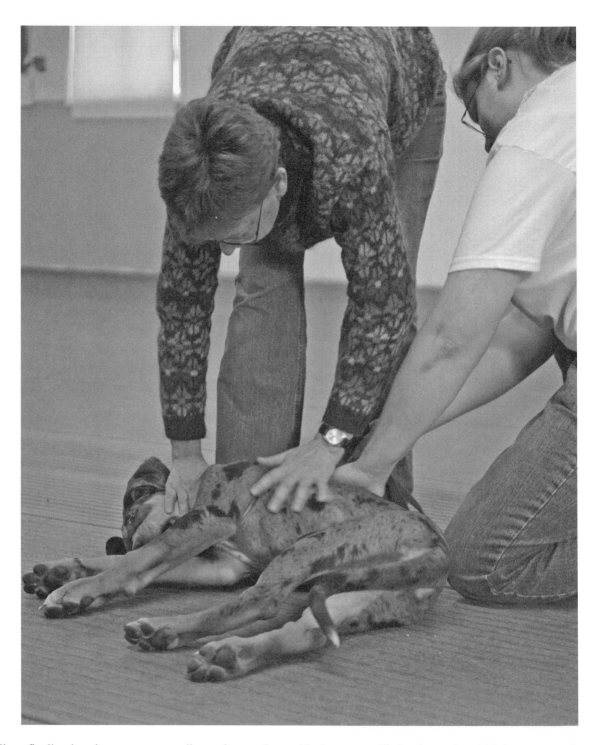

Wilson finally gives it up, stops struggling and protesting and he becomes still. See how relaxed his legs are now? He is still making his decision, though. We leave our hands on him, gently pressing downward (think of holding a one or two pound weight: about that much pressure) on his body for just another second or two, waiting for the moment that his feet are still and he gives us one further indication that he is relaxing. My left hand on his flank will help me be aware if he takes a deeper breath, one signal of relaxation. You can literally feel him becoming more and more relaxed underneath our hands and then...there it is: a deeper breath.

Some dogs will still their feet and movement, but still be very tense, just waiting for the moment that you release her so she can leap to her feet.

The Be Still Switch: Stand Your Feet Still & Be Calm

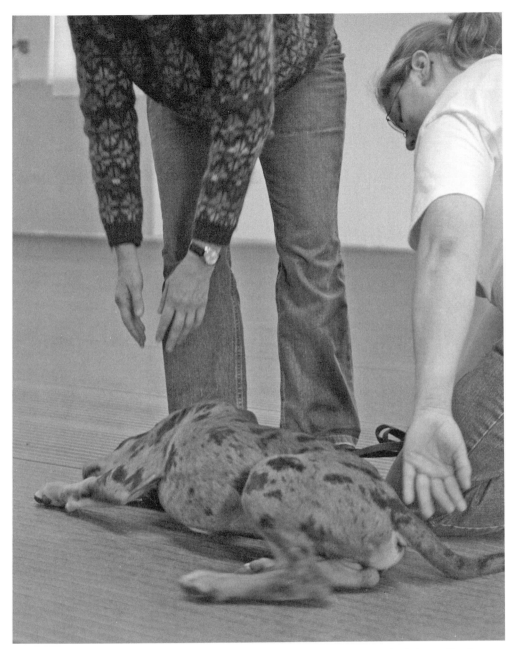

When Wilson takes a nice deep breath, signalling further relaxation, we both immediately "release the pressure" by lifting our hands off his body.

In this photograph he has chosen to lie quietly near us for a second. This is an excellent sign because it means he is beginning to feel comfortable enough to really relax around us, even though we are close and I am still bending over him. I want this dog to feel so comfortable that he never has to feel uneasy or worried about human proximity or our body language. You can see he is just beginning to move his left rear leg prior to getting back on his feet.

Okay, Trial #1 completed.

Do I need to reiterate this is NOT an alpha roll? We are not disciplining the dog. We are calmly waiting for calm behaviour. There IS a difference!

Say, this is a less intense launch. I like that response. He's still getting it wrong, but he is starting to think, not just react.

You must notice these efforts, while not the "end goal," are still a step in the right direction.

He gets off my body much more quickly.

Wilson is still mouthing my arm, as a warning: "Get your hands off." I ignore this (if he was going to bite me really hard, he would already have done so). This is a great chance for using ignoring to my advantage. It will work here because the biting is being used as a way to see if he can "change the subject." If biting doesn't make me go away and doesn't "change the subject" or allow him to control my movement, the biting will be discarded as a strategy.

Ignoring biting, of course, will not always work this way, but with a young puppy who has not gotten a lot of "good" results with biting, a puppy who has reasonably good bite inhibition (is aware of how much pressure is being exerted by biting down) or a dog who is not terrified, I will garner good results. If a dog is extremely frightened (not just a little nervous or irritated), you cannot count on bite inhibition. I am making a judgment call based on years of experience: a judgment call I might not always get away with. Here, I am counting on this puppy's past behaviour and young age to prevent a really hard bite.

You must understand I am ignoring the immediate biting, but not ignoring that there is a problem that must be dealt with. I am working on the bigger issue of personal space. I know that, often, if I can take care of the root of the problem, the "symptom": that is, the biting, will take care of itself.

Photograph to the right:
Within a few seconds, he offers up a "Sit of Peace." He is using an upturned face, long lips and is in a "puppy licking" posture. This body language indicates that now he is actively trying to negotiate with me instead of immediately seeking to keep me off balance.

Rachel and I release the pressure. We do this by lifting our hands calmly off his body and standing up.

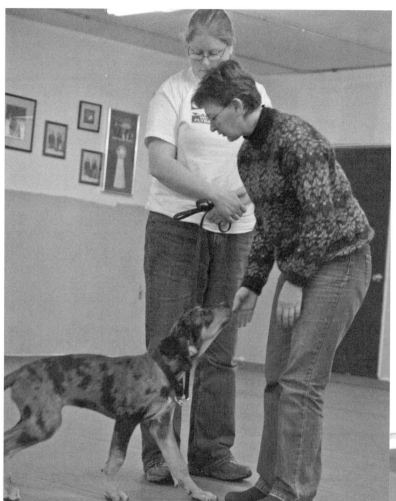

A few more approaches later and look at this! This is more like it. As I come into the puppy's space, instead of behaving in an anxious, hectic and defensive manner, he comes up to see what I am about. He looks more submissive and is on his way to confidence.

Do not mistake hectic, frantic greeting for confidence: it is false bravado covering anxiety. In this photograph we see what his hectic greeting behaviour has been about all this time: he is a bit confused and nervous about human approaches. At least a part of this dog's anxiety is his inability to "control" humans and anxiety about what people are going to do as they get closer. In short, he does not trust people.

Wilson's body is relaxing more quickly now, and he is interacting with me without Rachel's support. We have worked up to a more normal state of affairs: someone approaches and you just go up to politely meet them.

I am still placing my hand on his collar, not to "hold him down" in any way, but because we have established that as cue of reassurance, helping to remind him to be calm.

The Be Still Switch: Stand Your Feet Still & Be Calm

He finally sits and then has enough confidence to look at me softly. What a treat for me! He is not totally confident yet, but he is improving quickly. When you present material to dogs in a way that is easily understood by them and makes sense to them, they learn very rapidly.

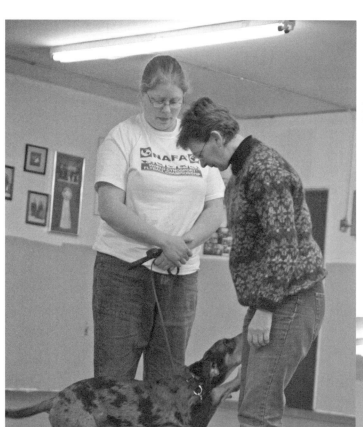

As I approach once again, Wilson puts his foot on me.

Then, because of old habits and a little frustration at change, he makes a little leap, which he directs toward Rachel. He is re-directing the anxiety and frustration about approaches towards her. When she does not respond by yelling or moving in any way, or doing anything to make him feel threatened or defensive, he...

The Be Still Switch: Stand Your Feet Still & Be Calm

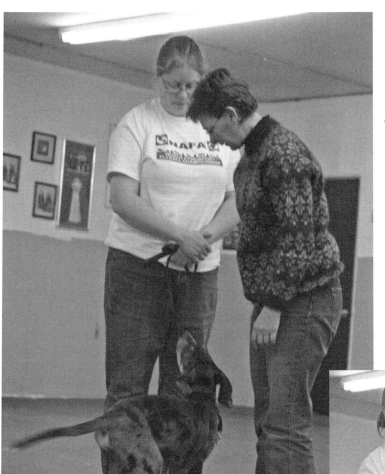

...quickly remembers his recent lessons.

Then he offers a sit. I rub his body a few times, then stop. You can stop at any point at which the dog's feet are still.

If you are rubbing his body and his feet stop, but before you release the pressure by stopping the rubbing, the dog suddenly starts moving his feet again: no problem. Begin rubbing his body and keep rubbing his body until his feet stop again.

Wilson hasn't been worked with this exercise since last week. Rachel has been able to do daily body work, though it has been limited due to her work schedule. Today we will continue to generalize desired greeting behaviour to new approachers.

(Top photograph) Wilson is able to relax now when he sees people approaching. That is definitely better than last week: remember the "preparing to launch" behaviour on approach? This is super fine behaviour because he was not "cued" in any way to lie down, he came up with this as an alternative behaviour all by himself. Good thinking on his part and a sign that he is starting to understand that thinking can make him feel more comfortable; by extension all of the people around him are more comfortable, too!

(Left photograph) Of course, as the person gets closer, he still gets excited and is still feeling a little anxious. Old habits and all that. But he is no longer launching himself towards people. He is still pushy, but improving. His changing behaviour shows us how he is changing his thinking.

Rachel still steps in on this first approach by a new person, to help Wilson feel supported, and also to control Wilson should he become hectic again. No matter when the approacher stops petting, Rachel will continue to rub Wilson's body until his feet are still and his body is more relaxed. We want him to be comfortable with approachers.

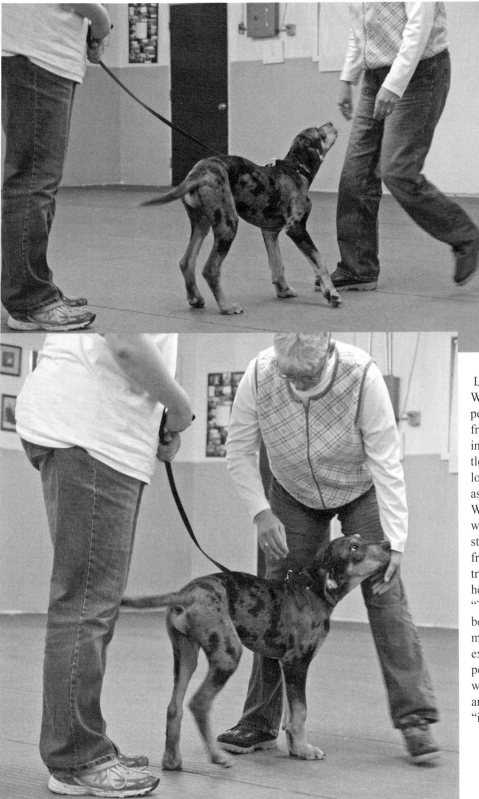

Even without Rachel micro-managing, Wilson is keeping himself calmer. This trial is being used as a Pop Quiz, so Rachel is standing back and observing what happens. This way we can determine how much Wilson has learned. (For information refer to *You will repeat the above procedure ten or*

Look at how much "softer" Wilson is upon approaching people. This softness comes from confidence and a feeling of safety. He is still a little wide-eyed, but he is no longer trying to repel people as his first line of defense. Wilson is trying out different ways of behaving, no longer stuck in a rut of anxiety and frustration. He is learning to trust Rachel so much, that if her body language says: "This approacher is safe," he believes her. This, in turn, makes Wilson start to explore new ways to greet people. His new strategies will be based on feeling safe and trusting rather than "invaded."

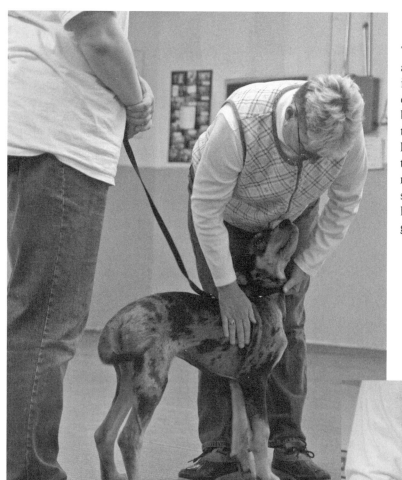

This is beginning to look like a real interaction, with an exchange taking place, instead of Wilson alternating between excitement, anxiety and defensive behaviour. Wilson is moving closer to the approaching person in response to her hands on his body. This is a sign of trust on his part. Wilson becomes more relaxed as the approacher remains in his space rather than increasing his activity level and hectic behaviour as the person gets closer.

Wilson sits and continues to get ever more relaxed. He didn't need help from Rachel. His confidence grows as he begins to trust Rachel as well as feeling more comfortable with the approaching person.

We aren't done. He will need help again in the future. He is not over the life-long attitude of feeling uncomfortable and not trusting (a habit of twelve weeks duration is a life-time habit if you are twelve weeks old).

This kind of spontaneous recovery is normal, but with consistent handling and expectations, the behaviour will fade, until those neural pathways are seldom, if ever, accessed. (For information refer to *Spontaneous Recovery* on page 111.)

The Be Still Switch: Stand Your Feet Still & Be Calm

The Be Still Switch creates a lot of trust between the handler and the dog. In addition to the other things that have been taught, you are also teaching:

- the dog that the world is not a frightening place and that he can trust you.

- that you can take hold of the dog's collar from any position, even the front, or from over his head and he can be comfortable.

- the dog to rely on the handler and if the handler does not appear to be alarmed then the dog follows this lead.

Remember, collars are used in very confusing ways from the dog's point of view. Sometimes the collar is used to guide and sometimes it is used to jerk and correct. Or people yell and jerk, frightening the dog into defensive behaviour. To be safe and for good communication to develop, use of the collar, like Eye Contact, must have a predictable outcome. The collar should be used in a consistent way, teaching the dog that guidance by the collar is information, not a punishment. One of the important lessons I hope you learn from this exercise is how to use the collar consistently and thoughtfully.

This is the first *sensitizing* exercise in this protocol. Moving Away From Pressure exercises cause the dog to think very differently. Your dog's natural reflex is to move *into* pressure, rather than to move away from it. This is because of that opposition reflex, so handy if the dog were living a very natural life as a social predator or a scavenger, and so unhandy in so many situations when domestication enters the picture. These exercises will help with problems like lunging and pulling on the leash. They also help reactive and aggressive dogs to learn that you can move out of social pressure and remain calm instead of charging into it.

This exercise will cause one of the first big paradigm shifts for your dog. (For a review refer to *Why Do I Want My Dog To Have A Paradigm Shift?* on page 73.) It is pretty obvious that most dogs think that collar pressure means, "Move into it and pull even harder!" The goal of this exercise is to teach an incompatible behaviour: pressure on the collar means Follow the Feel and go with the flow instead of pull or push harder. Once this lesson is learned, life is much easier for dog and human. Basically, you will change the cue of pressure on the collar to mean, "Back your feet up" instead of, "Charge forward disregarding any humans who are with you." Dogs who pull on the leash and ignore the handler, are ditching the handler. Obviously, the dog feels that the handler is in the dog's way: a part of the problem and not the solution. After all, he could proceed much faster and do more interesting things if he did not have to drag the handler along. The walk serves a different purpose for the dog than for the handler. The dog is hunting, checking pee-mail, answering pee-mail messages and increasing his neck strength by dragging a 100 pound plus weight behind him. The handler is walking through obligation of "exercising" the dog, and is also walking to relax and exercise herself and spend pleasant time with her pet. The handler

did not plan for her exercise to include falls on the ice or slippery ground because the dog suddenly lunges, or to require rotator cuff surgery because of the chronic stress placed on joints when the dog drags his human around.

When teaching Move Away From Pressure exercises you will apply pressure in four distinct levels. You will begin with light pressure and increase it systematically. Soon the dog will respond to the lightest pressure, in anticipation of the increasing levels. Obviously, if the dog responds to the lightest pressure, he will never have to undergo the increasing pressure and resulting minor discomfort.

- Low Pressure: Touch the animal with enough pressure to depress the hair. Count to 3 and increase to Medium Pressure OR if the animal moves, *release immediately.*

- Medium Pressure: Touch the animal with enough pressure to depress the skin. Count to 3 and increase to High Pressure OR if the animal moves, release immediately.

- High Pressure: Increase the pressure until you can feel the muscle tissue. Count to 3 and increase to Maximum Pressure OR if the animal moves, release immediately.

- Maximum Pressure: Press as hard as you need to get a result and hold it there until the animal moves or shifts her weight or shows some intention of moving. The idea is that this is enough pressure so the animal cannot ignore you and is just mildly uncomfortable enough for her to want to move away from it. This has less to do with the amount of pressure and more to do with you *outlasting* her, keeping in mind it must be at least enough pressure that she cannot just ignore it. *Hold this pressure until the animal moves. The instant the animal shifts weight or feet:* release immediately.

Yield To Collar Pressure – Never Have To Have A Tight Leash Again.

- Stand by the dog's side, both of you facing the same direction.

- Using the dog's collar, apply pressure, firm but light, in a motion straight back toward the dog's tail. If you keep your hand low and close to the dog's shoulder and back for the first repetitions, the dog will understand more quickly.

- While maintaining the slight but firm collar pressure, begin to apply pressure to the dog's chest. Begin with Low Pressure and move up the levels of pressure as required, using your Cat-woman fingers (refer to the photograph on page 224.)

- As soon as you get any foot movement backwards, immediately release.

- If your dog keeps sitting every time you apply the collar pressure, make sure you aren't lifting the collar straight up, as this seems to cause most dogs to sit. Also, if the dog keeps sitting, just carefully and slowly shuffle your toes under his tummy and touch his back toes with your toes until he stands up.

Remember, do not begin the presentation of a cue with 2 things at a time. This is like one of those recipes that require that each ingredient be added one at a time. It is crucial with this exercise that you put light pressure on the collar, and, before adding the pressure on the dog's chest, count to 1. This slight pause gives the dog time to notice that there is pressure on the collar. So the pattern is:

- pressure on the collar. Count to 1.

- pressure on the chest. Count to 3 before increasing any pressure.

- move up the levels of pressure as required.

- as soon as the dog moves, or, in the very first few repetitions, shifts his weight; release the pressure immediately.

Continue this work until you feel the dog shift his weight backwards and then begin to move his feet backwards as soon as you put slight pressure on the collar and do not need to use the pressure on the chest.

Once the dog is moving promptly and freely off a light pressure on the collar alone, you can begin to cue him for more than one step at a time. Do this initially by Approximating: first you will cue for 1 step with a slight pressure on the collar. Release the pressure just for a count of 1, then reapply the slight collar pressure to ask for another step. For several repetitions, cue for the step with the collar pressure and release for each step you get. So you are applying pressure, getting 1 step, releasing the pressure for a count of 1, reapplying the pressure, getting 1 step, releasing the pressure for a count of 1, and so on; repeating this pattern until you have gotten 2 steps and a longer rest (of 3 to 5 seconds) before asking again. When 2 steps at a time is pretty easy for the dog, you can ask for 4 or 5. Once you get up to 5 steps, you can just apply a light, but steady pressure to the dog's collar and hold that until you are ready to stop the backing up behaviour.

The Only Time To Break The Pattern Of The Graduated Cue System Of Pressure

Sometimes a dog has the idea very well because you have done several repetitions. You know that your dog understands the cue, because she has responded to this cue in 20 different locations and contexts (that is, she has generalized the behaviour). When you request (cue for) a known behaviour in a context where your dog has repeatedly done the behaviour correctly, and your dog pointedly ignores you or is downright disobedient, it may be time for a lesson that addresses the "want to vs. the have to." You must be fair! The proof for her understanding must be a palpable truth, something you have evidence of. *This is not an emotional decision: it must absolutely be based on fact.* Once are certain (and have proof) that your dog understands and is being willfully disobedient: for a *very well-known behaviour*, and when you feel your dog is making a conscious decision to ignore your request because he doesn't feel you are relevant, you might choose to use the cue (Low Pressure, the very lightest pressure) to request the behaviour, then jump to Maximum Pressure right off the bat; just to let the dog know that your request is not to be ignored.

Back Up From Heel Position

Next, see if you can get your dog to back up from Heel position, just by beginning to back up yourself. Begin by standing with your dog in Heel position, by your side. It might help to begin with your dog next to a wall to prevent her swinging her hips to the side, thus backing up crookedly.

- Move your left leg back. I do this in a slow, slightly exaggerated manner at first, so that this action is readily noticed by the dog.

- Keep slowly backing up, and, if your dog does not understand to back up also, put a slight pressure on the dog's collar to encourage her to back up with you.

In this Approximation we are introducing another new pattern: handler's left leg moves back, pressure on the collar, stop your movement and release the pressure on the collar the moment the dog moves backwards.

Refine this until you can back around the work area, changing directions, circling, etc. and the dog stays in Heel position and mirrors you with no resistance. Once the dog is doing this handily you can remove the leash. You are now doing some pretty fun and fancy stuff. Better yet, you and your dog are learning how to move together and you are teaching your dog the skills he will need to be off-leash.

Each dog will differ in the amount of pressure and persistence it takes to get that first backward step. This puppy is particularly resistant. It takes twice the effort and about ten times the time frame that I would consider average.

First, put slight pressure on the collar, with a direction that is more toward the tail than up towards the ceiling. I put more pressure in an upward direction on this puppy than I normally would because he keeps diving towards the ground with his head, neck and shoulders every time the collar is even slightly touched.

The order is important and you must not risk over-shadowing. Therefore, put slight pressure on the collar, count to 1, then apply pressure to the chest with your fingers.

Please keep in mind as you watch the DVD and look at these photographs that Wilson, the puppy I used to demonstrate this technique, was extremely resistant. The average dog will not be so difficult.

C-Shaped Fingers

Use C-shaped, Catwoman fingers for getting a dog to move away from pressure.

All photographs in this chapter by Dave Schrader.

I have placed pressure on the collar and have just added pressure to his chest with my Cat-woman fingers. Then we go up through the levels, Low Pressure, count to 3; increase the pressure, count to 3; increase the pressure, count to 3 and then hold the pressure until I get a shift in weight or backward movement of any foot. I am not horribly strong, so I cannot bring a lot of strength to bear, but I count on persistence to get the message across.

You can see that Wilson has finally lifted his hind foot and is doing his first tentative "Follow The Feel" instead of using his opposition reflex.

As soon as I feel Wilson make that effort to follow my suggestion instead of pushing back as hard as he can, I immediately release the pressure and rub the area of his chest and neck. I tell him he is a good boy. He acknowledges this with a Lip Lick and less body tension.

In fact, that Lip Lick is beginning to look like Puppy Licking, specifically; a signal a dog would use with an adult dog he liked and wanted to please. Could it be the beginnings of respect and trust? Yes, indeed. We will see more resistance because that is the working pattern this dog already has established. However, we are definitely making headway.

#1: As soon as I touch Wilson's chest, with the slight application of Low Pressure, he shoves into *me* with all his might. This is the root of all of Wilson's undesirable behaviour - he never even considers thinking or cooperation as a possible strategy. He is reacting not responding.

He pushes both forward and down and is attempting to bite my hand.

Persistence will carry the message. I maintain a steady pressure and keep a calm, neutral manner. I do not wish to punish him or tell him he is "wrong" in any way. I am merely the venue through which he can gain information to behave in a different way.

When he realizes that his current modus operandi is not going to work, he adapts. He is not stupid, he has just never developed any Frontbrain skills.

When force, frantic behaviour and intimidation, all directed toward me, fail to work, Wilson begins to think about how to get himself out of this fix...and shifts his weight backwards. Hindbrain behaviour is not working, so he will try a Frontbrain tactic. Yes! This is very good news.

Good Boy! I immediately release all the pressure and will rub his chest and neck, where I was applying the pressure. Try this on yourself. It feels funny if you put pressure on a small area, such as we are covering with our fingers, and then just stop. It feels much more "complete" or "finished" if the poky feeling is rubbed away. Massage therapists use this technique all the time. They will perform a release on a trigger point by holding the tense spot with a thumb, for instance. Once the tension is released the therapist will remove her thumb and then rub the area with her whole hand.

I apply pressure to the collar, count 1, apply pressure to the chest, and he pushes into my fingers and pulls down on the collar. To see if I can show him how to take pressure off the collar, I sort of "break a rule" and take the pressure off his chest, even though he hasn't moved backwards yet, and...

...lift his chin with my hand. This technique is very effective. If a dog is pulling on the collar, once you lift his chin, you take away all his physical power. It would be ideal if I had three or perhaps four hands, I could have kept the pressure on his chest and, with my third hand, lifted his chin. Working with my physical limitation of two hands, I lift his chin to help him understand how to overcome a piece of his opposition reflex.

When you do this, really think of "cradling" the dog's chin in your hand. Let your hand, arm and fingers feel relaxed, so your hand is something that "feels good" and welcoming to the dog. Remember, you are going to succeed by outlasting the dog, not by forcing him.

Good. It did help. When I reapply pressure to Wilson's chest, he keeps his chin up and the weight shift happens.

As soon as I get those sticky feet to move a little bit, he gives me a nice big step backwards.

In addition, he gives me a lovely signal of negotiation: he licks his lips as he lifts his chin, feeling comfortable enough to look right up at me.

Then it is like a flood of understanding. Wilson literally flows backwards another whole step. Oh, baby, baby! This is the breakthrough I have been seeking. Wilson is really concentrating in this picture and watching me closely for more clues. You can see how lightly my fingers are touching him.

I rub Wilson's body where I have been concentrating the pressure, then rub his whole body. Time to rest so he can think about what has happened.

You have just seen a paradigm shift happen before your eyes. It has never occurred to this young dog that cooperation and thinking get you good results. This is the only message I need to convey to the dog: negotiation and cooperation work.

To break through his built-up defenses, I had to make him feel a bit vulnerable first: I put him in a fix where he had to think his way through and take me into account too, as I was just not going to go away. Then, as soon as he "asks for help," I am right there 110% to work with him and tell him how very clever he is. He thinks he is clever, too. Look at his relaxed face and soft eyes. I always get the feeling that the dog is proud of his accomplishments, just as I am, when I learn something new and realize that a door has just been opened for me. Wilson and I have turned a page and are on our way to a much better relationship for both of us.

Move Into

This is the second *sensitizing* exercise in this protocol. Always follow an exercise in which you sensitize with a session of Be Still Switch (a desensitizing exercise). This helps keep your training in balance, so your dog does not become dull and unresponsive or hectic and over-sensitized. You would also use the Be Still as an exercise to toss in the middle somewhere, between any two approximations; using it as a "break" and a way to calm a dog who is becoming hectic or uneasy.

In this exercise, your dog will learn to move out of your space when you move into hers, *keeping two eyes on you.* She will do this calmly, and will end up facing you, with her nose and eyes oriented toward you, waiting for her next instructions.

This exercise is fantastic for inattentive dogs who do not seem to be responding to any other cue. Soon your dog will give you her attention if you look towards her and even suggest with your body language that you are going to move towards her. This works well for dogs who are constantly distracted and will not respond to a Back Away or who are constantly sniffing the ground. Keep in mind, the sniffing may be a Calming Signal or a displacement behaviour. Sniffing may be a signal by the dog that says, "I am feeling overwhelmed or nervous right now." Just because sniffing may be an indicator that the dog is stressed does not mean that you have to allow the dog to sniff and sniff. Sometimes sniffing occurs because the dog is distracted, or may find the scent much more interesting than you. Regardless of the reason, it is okay to interrupt the sniffing. It is good, however, to know what you are interrupting. If the dog is distracted, that is one thing. If the dog is nervous or stressed, it is notable, because you can then begin to work on that particular "trigger." This ensures that your dog will be more comfortable in similar situations in the future.

Yielding The Hindquarters From A Front Position

This exercise will help every performance dog to be more aware of the "engine," the hind-quarters and rear legs.

- As you begin this exercise, if your dog is standing, rather than sitting or lying down, the work will be easier for her.

- You will need a flat or martingale collar and a leash (and any other safety gear required for this individual).

- Your hold on you dog's leash will be quite short for the initial approximations of this exercise. The leash is held short to help you control the movement of the dog's forequarters: his head and shoulders.

- Later, when your dog is proficient and has a good understanding you will use a longer leash and eventually, the exercises are easily done off leash.

    The length at which you will hold the leash depends on your height and the dog's height. Basically you want the leash short enough so that you can control the dog's forequarters (his head and shoulders). It will be mildly difficult for the dog to move out of your way, but not impossible. So for the average-sized Golden Retriever, your leash length might be 9 to 18 inches.

- With the leash held very short, but not placing any tension on the dog while you are both stationary, place yourself in position to begin the exercise.

- Stand in front of your dog. (Front position: you are in front of your dog and she is looking up at you, facing you.)

- Look pointedly at one hip.
- Lean over, towards her hip as you look pointedly at it.
- Step towards the dogs hip until he yields his hip, by stepping his hip sideways, away from you.
- Release the pressure, by stepping back.

I wish your dog to move calmly and serenely, but promptly out of your way. Further, as soon as you pause in your forward motion and still your feet, your dog should stop his feet moving, too. He should now look calm, relaxed and waiting for your next cue.

Work this exercise until your dog can do this easily and off-leash. His feet should feel "free" and not "sticky."

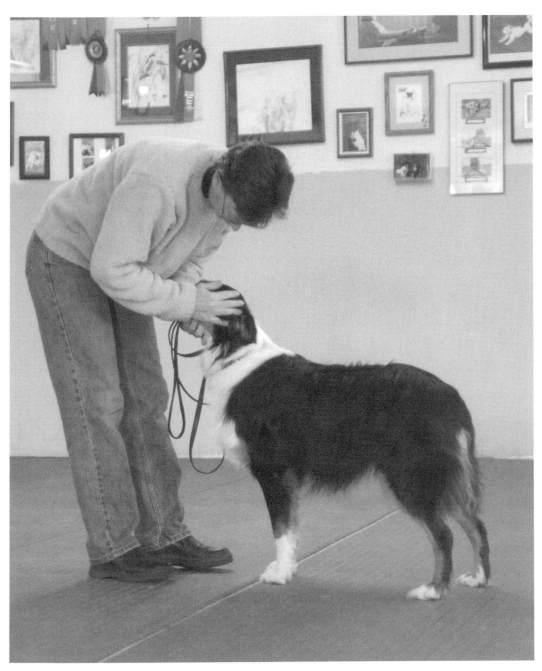

Check The Comfort Level

Before I begin moving Wyndsor's feet around, I want to make certain that he feels comfortable with me standing in front of him, bending over him, looking at him intently as I bend over him, and will allow me to cradle his head in my hands and rub his face and jaws.

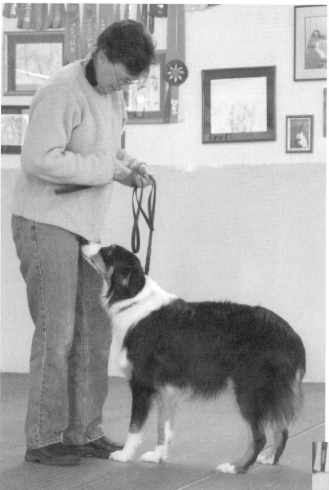

Furthermore, if I stand in front of him and step towards him, what does he do? Does he jump at me? This means he is uncomfortable and trying to get me out of his space, or he thinks that I wish to play.

Below:
If I do step towards him and then reach towards him, does he become nervous, frightened or resentful? In the photograph below, he is mildly worried, but not so much that I do not feel I can continue. If he increases in worry, I will back up several steps, find his comfort zone, do one small approximation within his comfort zone and then let him rest. Then I can begin again tomorrow, once he has had a bit of time to think about it.

These little pieces of information about the dog's comfort zone must be determined before you begin the actual Yielding The Hindquarters exercise. This preliminary work is part of determining thresholds before I begin to teach. I will not ask Wyndsor to do long division until he can add and subtract. Making sure he is comfortable with the basic body movements I will be using, and breaking them down into separate parts is smart training and good communication.

Wyndsor is very sensitive about personal space, as many dogs are. Inherited "herding" behaviours also influence how he reacts to motion and invasion of personal space. I can make him much more comfortable and teach him better judgment about when to exhibit herding behaviours by entering into a conversation with him about personal space: his and mine and how it intersects.

As we progress, if you watch Wyndsor's body language closely, you will see he is sometimes mildly uncomfortable, but certainly gains in comfort and confidence as his understanding grows over a few repetitions.

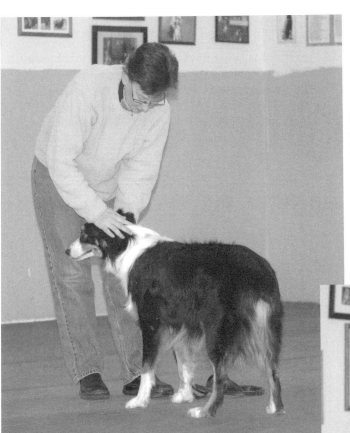

Yield The Hindquraters: Trial No. 1

Since I have ascertained that Wyndsor is comfortable enough with basic handling I can begin. I rub the top of his skull and touch his ears and then pick up the leash and park my hands at my core in preparation to begin.

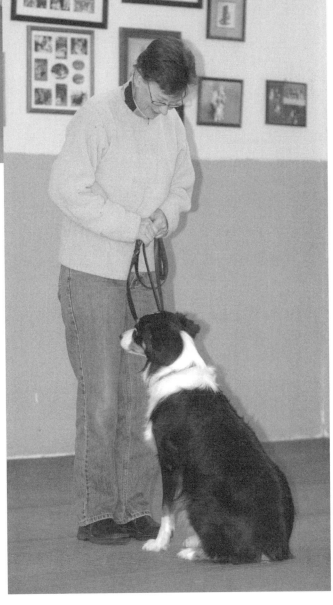

Wyndsor, confused about me standing in front of him and looking at him without any other movements, wonders what I am up to. He sits: a safe, previously learned behaviour. This is a very nice offering, but not what I want. That's okay, I am going to continue explaining exactly what I want, step by deliberate step, until Wyndsor gets the "Ah ha!" moment. We have a good start because even though he is not sure where this conversation might be going, he is curious about my body language and is noticing it rather than trying to leave the area.

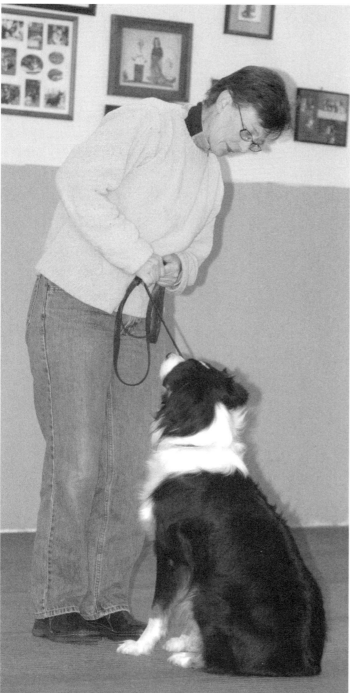

I look pointedly at the hip I plan to move. I pause there about a 1/2 a second or a second. Wyndsor looks at me, probably wondering what the heck I am doing now. He does not yet see this as valid information, but is watching me closely for clues.

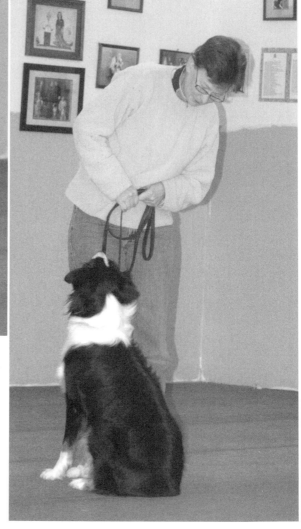

I exaggerate my body language and lean over as if to get an even better view. Wyndsor watches me, matching my intensity, trying to figure out what this all means.

I hold this position, also, for about 1 second.

Move Into

Then, I step towards the hip I am still pointedly looking at. Sometimes people do best when I tell them, "Step towards your dog's tail." Wyndsor sees that I am stepping towards him, so he gets up and moves out of my way. I really like it that his mouth is open and he looks comfortable and relaxed, not nervous or skittering out of my way frantically.

If he did get panicky or scared, I would very calmly step one more time towards him and then do a Back Away. This is the most graceful exit I can make, because at this point, I am already in a bit of trouble. You see, if the dog gets panicky and I stop altogehter, the dog will rightfully figure that panic got him out of a situation he saw as stretching his comfort zone. That means, the next time the dog is mildly uncomfortable or even a bit confused or does not know what you want, he may use spooky or panicky behaviour as the coping mechanism. Since I wish to promote interacting with me and thinking, I want to make certain that I am careful to convey that by my actions. By taking one more step and then doing the already learned Back Away, I am saying, "See, I am not trying to scare you, I planned to release the pressure on you all along." With the skittery dog, you must proceed slowly - not just in the breaking down of the teaching steps or approximations, but also literally: make all your movements in slow motion, so the dog has lots of time to assimilate the incoming information.

As soon as Wyndsor makes one small movement in the direction my body language suggests, I segue into a Back Away, to release the pressure. Because Wyndsor likes to play, I contact him with my hand and smile as I Back Away, in a playful manner. This brings him towards me and makes him feel bolder and confident. This is a judgment call on my part. Because I know Wyn and understand he can get a little squishy, I wish to do things that I think will make him feel braver. The Back Away and allowing him to move forward freely will increase his confidence.

This was an extremely successful first trial. If Wyn had continued to hold his sit as I approached, I would have taken tiny baby steps until my toes were barely touching his hind toes and then encouraged him with my voice to move as I step in place. I could make a kissy noise with my lips, or in a happy tone of voice used any phrase that might help that individual dog to move his feet. These verbals are only "helper cues" and would not continue to be used past the acquisition of the behaviour.

Immediately following the Back Away, I reposition and place myself in Front position with Wyn again, and let him know we are going back to work by cradling his head in my hands, stilling my body and engaging in eye contact with him. Look at how lovely he is mirroring my message back to me. This shows that he is sensitive and involved with the process. This photograph is taken roughly 5 or 6 seconds after the photograph on the previous page.

Of course, even a dog involved in the process gets distracted! The clicking of the cameras and the movement of the photographers causes Wyndsor to disengage with me and to check out the environment.

I do not do what 99% of handlers would do, which is turn and look where the dog is looking. This is a very instinctive and reflexive thing to do. For instance, imagine yourself standing amongst a group of people, and one of them turns toward the door. Almost without fail, all the other people in the group will turn and look at whatever the first person is looking at. People and their dogs will do exactly the same thing. If I turn and look at what Wyn is indicating, I validate his distraction, and, in fact, may be cueing him to continue to look at the distraction. How puzzled dogs must be when they indicate like this, the handler mirrors the dog, and then a second later, the distracted handler remembers what he was supposed to be doing, notices the dog is not looking at him and then punishes the dog for inattention. Instead of "following" Wyn I "hold my cue" behaving as if Wyn were still engaged with me.

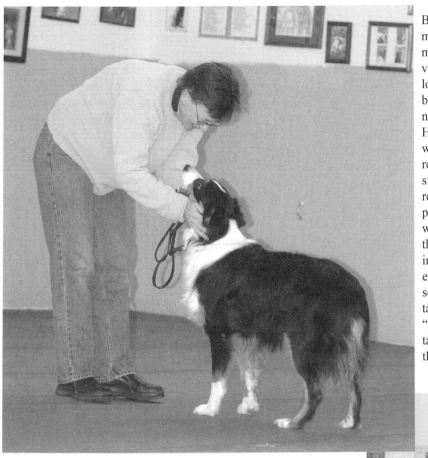

Because I hold the cue and maintain my stillness and encourage him (by my body language example only, no verbal) Wyn notices that I am not "following" him. This causes him to turn back to me. When he does so, he does not see a nagging, displeased handler. He sees me waiting patiently for him with a pleasant look on my face and a relaxed demeanor. I love his expression here, he smiles back at me, relaxes his body again (compare with previous photograph) and re-engages with me. Because of the way I handled this, the flow of the session is barely interrupted. If you want your dog to engage with you, you must make yourself available for that involvement to take place. I often tell my students, "Make yourself available for eye contact to occur." By this, I mean to stand there and look inviting and relaxed.

Now that I have Wyn's attention again, we are prepared for me to introduce the new material that we are learning, the actual yielding of the hindquarters. Just as before, I shift my weight and peer intently at Wyn's right hip.

A fascinating note: look how Wyndsor is mirroring my position, lifting his left front foot almost exactly the same amount I am lifting my right foot. Wyndsor is really trying hard and is being very cooperative. *You absolutely must notice these efforts your dog makes to get it right.* People tend to get bothered and frustrated because the dog does not attain the end goal in the first couple of trials. They become so focused on the end goal that they forget to notice or are unaware of, the tiny movements the dog is making which show how very hard he is trying to follow along and cooperate with you. To note some of these movements, you may have to have someone film or photograph you as you work, as dog training involves prodigious amounts of multi-tasking. Once you have watched the film a few times, you will be more aware of those times the dog was making efforts that you failed to notice during the training session. (Such as: this lifting of the foot I missed until I saw this photograph. I knew Wyn was engaged with me by his eye contact, but it was amazing to see the extent to which he was trying to engage with and cooperate with me.) This will help you know better what to look for during training, as well as pointing out your training errors to you!

Move Into 239

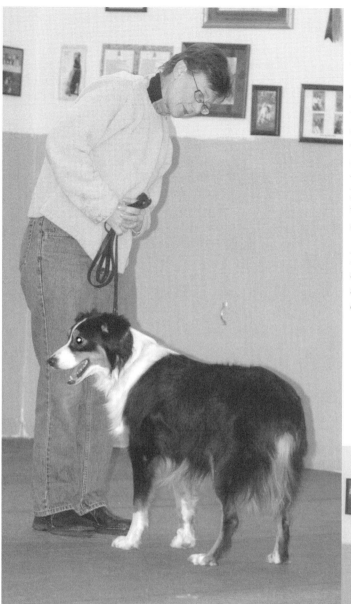

Once again, Wyn glances toward the previous distraction (his owner, taking photographs), and we temporarily "lose our connection." And again, I calmly "hold the cue." I maintain my position and just give him a second to process. He is being very Frontbrain about the distraction. I know his natural inclination would be to move towards what interests him (he is not frightened of the distraction, but curious about it. You can tell this by his body language.) If he moved toward the distraction any more, I would interrupt him with a touch on his head or body, and perhaps re-cradle his head in my hands and begin over. But nine times out of ten, if you just hold the cue and refuse to "follow" the dog, he will come back to "follow" you.

If I become emotional or start talking and moving around, the connection I am trying to foster will suffer and this lesson will be even more confusing for the dog.

Indeed, when I do not succomb to the distraction, Wyn looks back at me and sees me still standing there "lasering in" on his hip.

Our connection has been re-established!

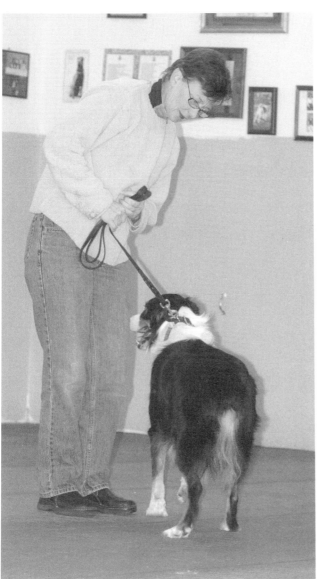

The connection is only the first part of learning, though. Wyn is not quite sure what I want, and as I move my feet, and lean over a bit more, he moves his front feet. He has been taught to go to a Heel position from a Front position, so he might be trying to go to Heel, as his best current "guess" about what I want.

Because of the way I am holding my leash, it prevents him from making, in this particular case, the error of going into Heel position. In other words, the leash controls or restricts the movement of his forequarters. This is good, because he will learn that this body language is not a cue for "Heel," but instead means, "Yield Your Hindquarters." Another way to express this concept is that I "closed a door" with the leash, thus encouraging him to find a different, "open" door.

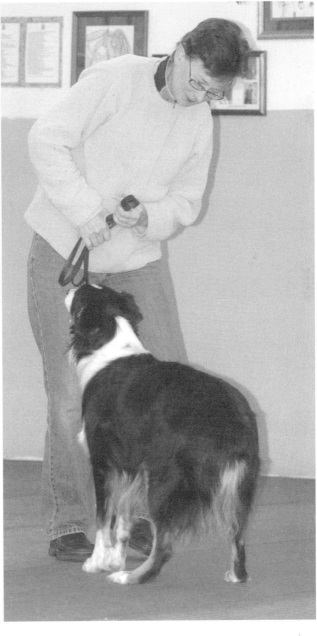

To give him more information, I lean over more and begin to step towards his tail, while looking at the hip I wish to move.

Wyndsor shifts his weight onto his hindquarters, and begins to yield, stepping his hindquarters around and pivoting on his front feet.

I pause for about 1/2 of a second and then...

...Yes! Those "sticky" feet start to move freely as I take another step towards his tail. His mouth is open, his facial features are relaxed and his tail is coming up. He is beginning to gain understanding and along with the understanding comes confidence.

As you can see in this photograph, Wyndsor is now moving very freely and comfortably yielding space to me with no resistance.

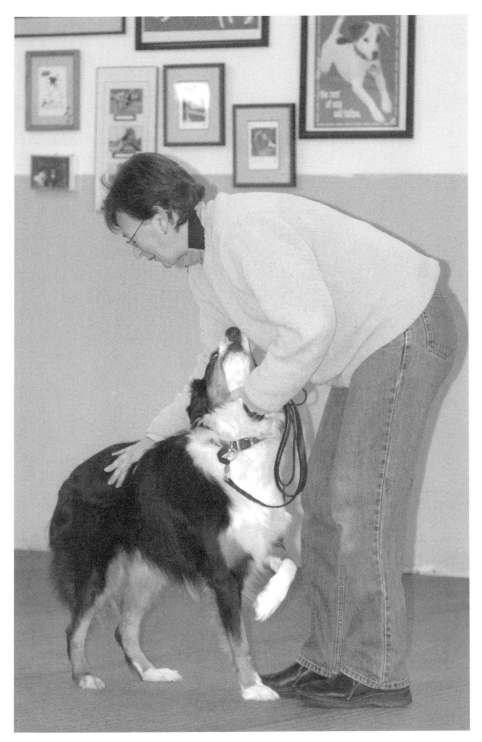

What a good fella! I tell him, verbally, that he is a good boy. These are the first words I have spoken to Wyndsor since beginning this trial. This allows him to really focus and concentrate on what is going on and reduces multi-tasking for him. Speaking less and only in an informative way makes it easier for Wyndsor to learn.

I really like how he is unafraid of the "shelf" my upper body makes as I lean over him. He is also allowing me to cradle his chin and is involved and interactive.

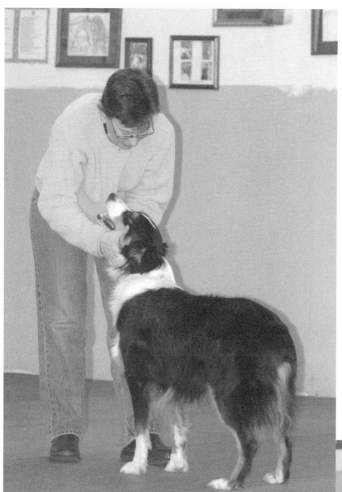

I take off the leash and then begin just as I did at the very beginning. The leash is off, which means, for the dog, the situation is vastly different. Therefore, I will start with a review of the "Comfort Level Check." I will make sure that I can do all of the same things with the leash off.

I cradle Wyndsor's head in my hands. He is very accepting and is enjoying the contact. You can tell because he is not moving away from me, is allowing me to cradle his head in my hands and has his mouth open in a relaxed way.

Wyndsor looks right up into my eyes. His lips are long and relaxed and his body does not feel tense. We are ready to begin.

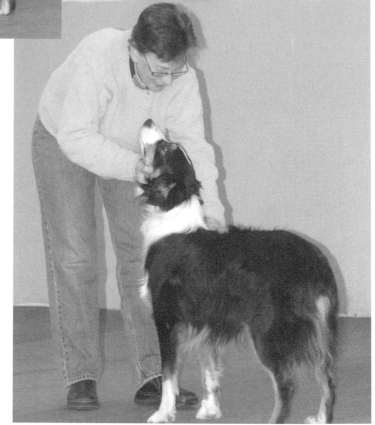

Move Into

I stand up straight and pause for a second and then lean to my left and look at Wyndsor's right hip: the one I am going to move.

Wyndsor has learned fast! As I step towards his hip, he intently watches my face and body and begins to shift his weight. His feet are not going to be sticky at all. There is no resistance, only cooperation. Practicing cooperating in this way prepares Wyndsor to be cooperative in many other ways. The best part is that these exercises are so easy to do. The other benefit is that the dog learns them very quickly. Actually, the learning curve is so quick with these exercises because the dog already "knows" them, and it is us, the human partner, who takes longer to learn these exercises. I can work through the Yield The Hindquarters exercise with even a quite difficult dog in fifteen to twenty minutes on average. It will take more sessions and longer if your dog is fearful or gets really nervous about you "sharing" personal space.

Wyn yields his hindquarters, pivoting around his forequarters. The best part is how relaxed he is. See his open mouth and relaxed ear carraige? Another great clue about how stressed or tense the dog is, is how freely he moves his feet. Sticky feet mean resistance, which can be interpreted as tension, stress, confusion, or, on the rare occasion, "No, you are not going to tell me what to do."

Wyndsor, though, does not have sticky feet and is having a good time with this. I think that dogs look very relieved that we are finally communicating to them in a way that is natural to them.

I continue looking at Wyn's hip and stepping toward his hip, pausing ever so slightly at each step to subtly "release pressure" before asking for the next step.

Wyndsor has done a lovely job. I give him a big release of pressure in the form of a Back Away. You can see he is moving towards me readily as I shift my feet to take another step backwards.

I still my feet, pause for a second and smile at Wyndsor. He mirrors my still feet, my emotion and even my facial expression. Isn't he too cute?

With about a count of 2 or 3 of stillness, I lean over and look at Wyndsor's left hip. I want to make sure he will yield both ways. Most dogs will have an "easy" way and a way that is more difficult for them to do. This is normal, just as you find it easier to brush your teeth with your right hand (provided you are right handed) or find it easier to write with one hand or the other.

Sure enough, Wyndsor looks confused and tried to step forward, past my leg. No problem, I just cradle his chin in my hand to discourage his movement in that direction and turn his head. This will cause his balance to shift the direction I wish it to and will encourage him to take a step "in the right direction" in order to keep his balance.

I continue stepping towards his hip, looking at his hip and keep my hand under his chin to give him the information he needs from me to complete the task. He feels awkward, but he is very cooperative and is trying really hard to get it right.

I reward his shift in balance and the single step he takes by doing a Back Away and totally releasing the pressure. This is the "click" or Marker for his effort.

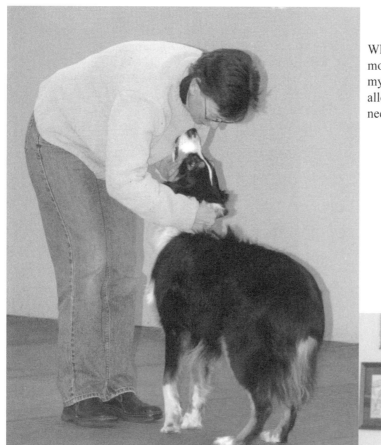

When I stop, so does Wyndsor. I take this moment to look into his eyes and to make myself available and inviting to him. This allows us to share a moment of closeness: a connection.

Whew! That was hard work and a lot of concentration. I cue Wyndsor to come up and do a bit of playing with me by giving him a little push and then stepping away from him (a pre-established play cue). I know he likes this, and I am not allowing a free-for-all rough-housing, I am just going to play "his way" for a moment as a special reward to him. Plus, it will be easy to put Wyndsor in neutral if he gets too rough or too aroused, I can just step towards him or take his collar and use the Be Still Switch, or I could use our new behaviour, Yield The Hindquarters, to get his feet back on the ground and his brain back in Frontbrain mode.

Photo essay by Dave Schrader

Move Into The Shoulder To Yield The Hindquarters

Do not begin this exercise until your dog and you have really got the *Yielding The Hindquarters From A Front Position*. You should be able to look pointedly at your dog's hindquarters, from a Front position, and have the dog shift easily, either on the glance or as soon as you show some intent that you are moving into her space by leaning your body forward a bit, or taking a small step towards the hindquarter you wish to move over. The dog's feet should feel "free" and not "sticky."

Before you begin this approximation, watch the DVD and read the approximations very carefully. Read the cautions and the suggestions for working with individual traits below, also before beginning. Of all the exercises in this protocol, this one will show you what the dog thinks of your relationship or if your dog is frightened by certain body movements. You may find your dog scoots out of your way, nervous that you are coming in so close, feeling mildly threatened. This is common, particularly for the tiny toy dogs, who probably have been stepped on a time or two because they tend to be easy to trip on when they are darting about directly underneath your feet. You see, your dog probably thinks that you have the same kind of timing and vision that she does! Another dog, especially one of her size, would easily be able to keep track of her and not bump into her unless as an intended message. However, we slow humans most certainly do not have that sort of reaction time.

This exercise is intended to clarify personal space. When used correctly the Move Into does that very well, providing excellent opportunities for you and your dog to discuss a topic that is seldom approached logically and systematically. I do not care if you prefer off-hands training or not, this discussion about personal space is of an all-consuming importance to your dog. She is longing for you to have this discussion with her so that fewer misunderstandings occur. It is like having that "birds and bees" talk with your kids. It really is of that much importance and must be handled just as thoughtfully. *If you do not have this discussion, then your dog will get her information however she can and this might mean she gets misinformation instead of good information.*

Caution:

If your dog has ever shown any aggression toward you (snapped or growled at you), this is a risky exercise for you to use. In your case, it is inappropriate unless your dog is muzzled and you can ensure that you are safe and will not be bitten. Think, too, about the lesson that will be taught. Unless you have the ability to neutrally outlast any behaviour your dog will toss at you, don't use this exercise until you have worked out the other "bugs" in the relationship. If your dog has shown any aggression, you need to get help from a professional dog trainer (not your neighbor, who once had a "mean dog" and "cured" him of the aggression), a veterinary behaviorist or pet behaviour counselor.

Move Into The Shoulder

- As you begin this exercise, if your dog is standing, rather than sitting or lying down, the work will be easier for her.

- You will need a flat or martingale collar and a leash (and any other safety gear required for this individual).

- Your hold on you dog's leash will be quite short for the initial approximations of this exercise. The leash is held short to help you control the movement of the dog's forequarters: his head and shoulders.

- Later, when your dog is proficient and has a good understanding you will use a longer leash and eventually, the exercises are easily done off leash.

  The length at which you will hold the leash depends on your height and the dog's height. Basically you want the leash short enough so that you can control the dog's forequarters. It will be mildly difficult for the dog to move out of your way, but not impossible. So for the average-sized Golden Retriever, your leash length might be 9 to 18 inches.

- With the leash held very short, but not placing any tension on the dog while you are both stationary, place yourself in position to begin the exercise by standing facing your dog's right side, with your knees near to your dog's shoulder.

- Shuffling your feet, *keeping them close to the ground* so you do not step on your dog and hurt her, step towards her shoulder. Take small steps and do not rush into your dog's space! Move with a slow, steady and deliberate pace. When I

first begin teaching this exercise I will take a small step and then hesitate a second or so, to see if the dog shifts her weight or makes any effort at all to move out of your way. Continue stepping into her shoulder with a steady, slow pace, keeping your leash up short to keep control of the forequarters of the dog, until she figures out that if she orients her nose toward you, it will cause you to IMMEDIATELY STOP. As you stop, allow the leash to slide through your fingers and loosen a few inches so you can BACK UP a step. This back up step is familiar: you have already done Back Aways to prepare for this exercise. Also, as you back up that step, it makes it very easy for your dog to be facing you and be able to find your eyes with hers. I do this to make the exercise easier for the dog and to get it right sooner.

- As soon as your feet stop moving, your dog's feet should stop moving, too. If you back up a step and your dog steps forward, step into her space, pause, then back up and stop your feet.

- Reward. You can use a Click & Treat if you absolutely must. You may use a calm "Yes," with no treat. Personally, I prefer to keep it very simple: shut my mouth, stop my feet and just stand there, facing my attentive dog with a relaxed posture and pleasant look on my face - *making myself available for eye contact to occur.* The very best reinforcement for you and your dog is to not break this spell. *Once you and the dog have made the connection of eye contact, still your body and your mind. Savor the moment, look at your dog with love and allow her to return that look to you.* Remain there for at least a few seconds, both of you just enjoying the wonderful connection you have just found. When you are ready you can continue your session, by backing up and inviting the dog to come with you by the motion of your Back Away, adding verbal encouragement if absolutely necessary.

- If your dog breaks the eye contact first, you will step toward her, in such a way that she might actually back up a step, or you could look as if you are going to yield her hindquarters. If this does not gain you immediate eye contact, escalate into a Move Into until the dog is paying attention to you again.

If your dog does not begin to yield, or if you do not see *considerably less resistance within 5 or 6 repetitions* of this exercise, you are not releasing the pressure soon enough or are releasing the pressure too soon. The dog is confused and does not understand what you want.

Another reason a dog will not yield to you is if you are timorous or have an uncertain attitude when you move towards the dog: from her point of view you really do not look like you are coming through and your wishy-washy body language confuses the dog. Sometimes (and this is quite common in people who are trying these exercises for the first time), people step towards the dog fast and in a hectic manner and push the dog out of the way. This can cause a dog to feel defensive and squishy and make the dog want to avoid you, not work with you. *Step in calmly, firmly and slowly with a deliberateness to your movements.* You do not wish to confuse the dog or make the dog defensive. You do wish to make it known that you will be calm and persistent.

Fearful Dogs Need Extra Consideration And Help

Dogs who are fearful are convinced that *the fearful behaviour is the only thing that is keeping them safe.* The fear is held up like a talisman against evil, like using garlic to repel a vampire. Until you can break through this habit and teach the dog to trust you, that you will keep him safe, and that other behaviours "work better," the fearful behaviour will continue to be the default. Proceed very slowly and calmly with this dog. You will need to teach without terrifying, but at the same time you will need to ask the dog to step *slightly* out of his comfort zone in order to progress. This takes careful planning on the part of the trainer, as well as a willingness to relax and increase criteria in a very fluid way.

With fearful dogs, take this exercise very slowly. Desensitize the dog in very small approximations, first by just allowing you to stand by her shoulder quietly and reinforce (the reinforcement can be releasing the pressure. You may also add a treat if it will help your dog to relax.) Then move toward your dog, one slow step at a time, until she moves slightly out of your way or indicates less body tension. Once you see her shift her weight or observe that her body is less tense, encourage her to face you by backing out of her space and releasing the pressure on her. Basically, you do more of the work for this dog, really making the way easy. Work up to the exercise above.

The Confused Dog

For the dog who is moving out of your way, but reluctantly due to confusion, a well-timed treat or two usually overcomes any resistance she might have about cooperating. This dog can be distinguished from the resistant dog by his manner. Instead of having a grouchy, "I cannot believe you are asking this of me, I do not have time for this," the confused dog will vary in his responses. He may give you a slow, hesitant movement one time and a hectic movement the next. This dog will also try avoidance, looking away from you, but may constantly look back at you in between, searching your face and body language for a clue of what behaviour to try next. This dog may feel sticky, just as the resistant dog does, but he will probably have more body tension and may even look a bit fearful. A confused dog often becomes fearful when he cannot figure out what you want him to do. Take it slow and easy, make your body language slow, clear and deliberate; this is how you help the confused dog. Make certain you are releasing pressure for the slightest try: this could be as small as a shift of weight. Then each time you ask again, ask for just a wee bit more movement on the part of the dog.

The Resistant Dog

You may come across a dog who has never been told he is wrong, and the first time you do so, he is not pleased about it. He may show his displeasure by being resistant and grouchy, moving out of your way, but slowly and in a reticent manner, similar to the attitude exhibited by a snooty adolescent who says: "Okay, Okay, I'm doing the dishes!" and then stomps off in a temper to obey. As you repeat the exercise and he learns you are not going to "just go away," he will begin to obey more cheerfully. This dog can sometimes be won over with the timely application of a treat for a successful repetition. Do not continue the treat-giving after two or three repetitions, though, because with this dog you might find it actually encourages resistance. This type of dog usually has his owner trained very well already, and this is the basic cause of his resistance. If you place him on a Fixed Schedule of reinforcement using a treat, he may continue to be resistant unless he knows you already have a cookie in your hand...This is likely a game he has already perfected.

This dog will often move slowly and feel very "sticky." When he does move, he will drag his feet and try to see just how little effort he can put into this.

The princess cannot believe you are finally telling her that you own the space your body occupies. She always thought that all she sees belonged to her, and that includes your personal space also, thank you very much. She will protest in a variety of ways. She will fling herself about, striking your body with hers. She will aim for high drama. She will probably try to climb up your body. She may be vocal, barking at you in frustration that she is not getting her own way. Calmly outlast her. When she finds out that high drama is not working, she will try negotiating and you two will be on your way to an entirely different way of understanding each other.

If your dog does not become cooperative to your requests within five to ten trials, perhaps you have neglected a part of your dog's education. You must be certain that the dog has the necessary prerequisites: the Be Still Switch a Back Away and Eye Contact.

Do Not Continue With Dogs Exhibiting These Behaviours

While the Move Into exercise has the most potential for versatility of use and improving understanding between dogs and humans, there are some dog/handler teams who should not proceed.

For dogs who allow you to do a Move Into two or three times, then become increasingly volatile as you approach for the next trial, STOP. I am talking about the dog who starts "gunning" for you by staring and warning and then progressing to freezing, growling or getting nasty with you. You need professional help. These exercises are designed to help relationships improve between normal dogs and normal people. If your dog is abnormal or is aggressive with you, this exercise may not be appropriate.

If your dog is extremely resistant, tense and gets very, very still, you need professional help. Abort the exercise and get it. If your dog growls and tantrums, you need help also. If the dog is just pushy and really mouthy, but is merely displaying frustration and not being aggressive (freezing, growling, getting progressively worse instead of better), you should work with the dog muzzled; proceed slowly, rewarding frequently for any sign the dog is *less* tense or less hectic. You reward by releasing pressure, and, if it helps your dog to relax instead of making her more hectic, you can deliver a treat to her.

The Get Connected protocol does have a way of pointing out the kind of relationship your DOG thinks you have, and this exercise in particular can easily be made into one of conflict. You must be slow, calm and deliberate and clear with your body language. This exercise also quickly points out a dog who is convinced that you do not have the authority to tell him what to do. In this case you discover a problem that you may not have been aware of. This is not a pleasant discovery. Dogs who are super bossy and arrogant can become very nasty when you attempt to change their paradigm. The bossy dog likes the current one: where he is boss and you are not. Since no one has ever outlasted him, he has never considered negotiation as a strategy and his current modus operandi is to use reactivity and force instead.

The second approximation, the Move Into from the shoulder position exercise, may also not be appropriate for humans who do not have good balance or who lose their temper easily. You must be honest, at least with yourself, in your judgement of your own abilities.

Position yourself such that you can easily step towards the dog's shoulder.

The idea is that the dog will yield and allow you to move his body, first because you touch him, then later requiring only the suggestion of you moving towards him.

I step slowly and deliberately into Wilson's shoulder, careful to keep my hands still and held close to my body. Wilson pushes into me and Looks Away. This Look Away is not one of negotiation, and I know this because of the physical resistance. Besides, looking away is not what I want, I wish to see him step out of my way, face me and give me eye contact. The only way to convey this clearly is to "hold my cue," that is keep the pressure up until Wilson orients his nose towards me.

While I fully understand that a Look Away may also be a Calming Signal, in this instance, I do not wish the dog to Look Away in any capacity: I want him to orient to me. Also, a Look Away used as a Calming Signal is often quicker, not this prolonged looking away in a determined manner accompanied by body tension (This dog's behaviour indicates avoidance and resistance, "If I ignore her long enough she will go away.").

There it is! Since resisting by pushing into me and looking away from me ("if I ignore it maybe it will go away") didn't work, he will, in a split second, change his behaviour and see if something else will work.

As soon as Wilson turns his nose toward me I immediately stop my forward movement.

You can see that I am now backing up a step, giving Wilson the "release" of pressure.

I continue to back another step, which further releases the pressure I have exerted on Wilson. This also helps to pull him right into a position of facing me, just what I wanted. Once I "maneuver" him into position a couple of times, I will let him "find" this front position more on his own.

Now you can see he is getting engaged, interested in what I am doing, and attracted to me. This is indicated by him looking at me and following the suggestion of my body language.

I am getting ready to still my own feet and see if Wilson will follow suit, that is, when my feet stop moving, so should his - like a game of Follow The Leader that children play.

When I stop my feet, he stopped his. I only ask for a second of stillness at first, then I invite him in for a rub and approval. He is touching me and leaning on me, but this is okay, as I have encouraged him to come into my personal space. This is all I ask of the dog, that he stay out of my personal space until I invite him in. He can certainly "ask permission" to enter my space also, but not by obnoxious attention-seeking behaviours like pawing at me or slamming into my legs.

Photo essay by Dave Schrader

I set the Boxer up for the Move Into by standing facing his shoulder. He responds to this by jamming his nose into my crotch. It is exactly this sort of rudeness that will be addressed with this exercise.

I slowly and carefully begin to step into him.

Note:

This is a 12 month old, intact, male Boxer who was just rescued from the pound. I am using this exercise as one technique to evaluate the dog's temperament and safety levels. He is anxious and pushy at the same time, a common combination observed in dogs have not had good education about social skills. He is not convinced that people are all that relevant and quite likely has valid reasons for thinking that.

You will like to know that he is placed in a loving, forever home. I love happy endings!

I stop, to give him a chance to turn towards me, but he does not. Instead, he continues with some minor resistance, walking forward as if I am not even there.

I step towards him again, the entire time keeping my hands anchored near my body. Keeping my hands thus insures that, in that moment when he moves towards me, I do not inadvertently "take up the slack," by moving my hands backwards. Therefore, he will feel an immediate cessation of the pressure.

There it is! His nose is turning towards me, and I begin to Back Away instead of Move Into.

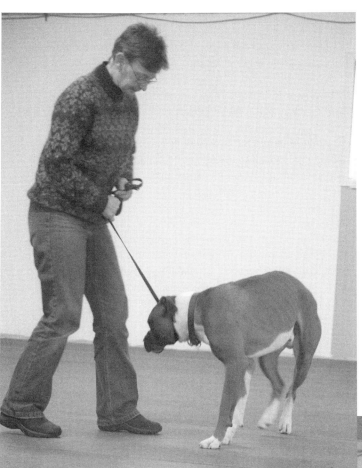

This creates exactly what I wanted, the dog orienting towards me.

Here I have just stilled my feet and am waiting to see if he will copy me. He doesn't so...

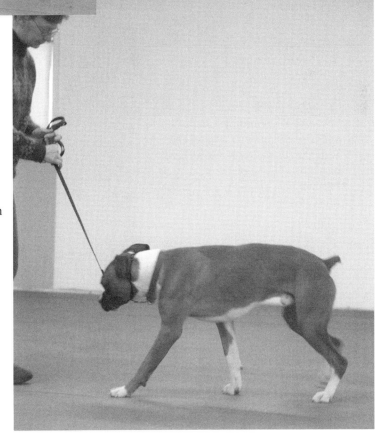

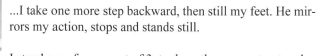

...I take one more step backward, then still my feet. He mirrors my action, stops and stands still.

I stand now for a count of 3, to draw the moment out and make it more memorable. I make myself available for eye contact, by looking at him with a pleasant expression on my face and blinking. Sure enough, he takes me up on my invitation and begins to look at me. Perhaps he thinks: "If this person won't go away, maybe I should try to communicate with her. Maybe a human can be relevant after all!"

Take this pause and connection VERY SERIOUSLY! This is the moment in which the dog and you come to an understanding and the dog becomes comfortable with the exercise. This might be a dog you have lived with for years or a dog you just met: this pause and connection are the reason you are doing the exercise!

Instead of pushing rudely into my space, he waits calmly. I show him social approval, with a warm and welcoming touch and rub his head and body. We are on the right track. He clearly is liking the attention and thinks my approval is worth having.

Photo essay by Dave Schrader

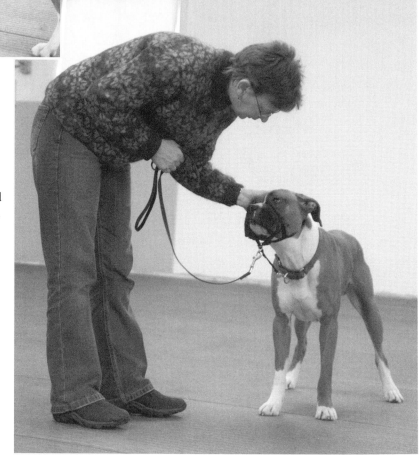

Move Into

Move Into Off Leash

Soon it is a fun game. Zasu sees me looking at her and moving toward her.

She quickly moves sideways, backs up a step and swings around to face me all in one smooth motion.

As I still my feet, she stills hers.

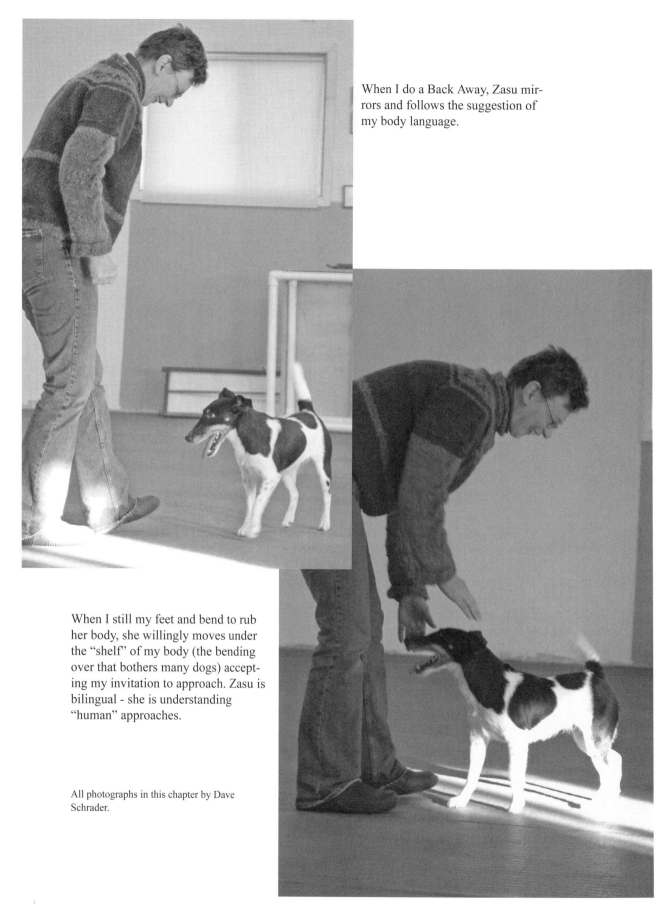

When I do a Back Away, Zasu mirrors and follows the suggestion of my body language.

When I still my feet and bend to rub her body, she willingly moves under the "shelf" of my body (the bending over that bothers many dogs) accepting my invitation to approach. Zasu is bilingual - she is understanding "human" approaches.

All photographs in this chapter by Dave Schrader.

Walk Nicely With Me

Pre-requisite: Be Still;Back Away; Follow The Feel; Move Into.

When we say we want to the dog to walk nicely, or "loose leash walking" as dog instructors call it, what is discussed and emphasized is that the dog will eventually get the concept of keeping the leash loose.

The first thing I think about when I think about walking a dog is: what is important to you is not always important to your dog. When you dream of walking with your dog, you probably visualize an idyllic scene in which you and your dog stroll along in perfect harmony. The weather is balmy, the birds are singing, indeed they will even light merrily on your hand if you hold it out, just like Snow White in a Walt Disney movie, as your dog looks on with love and approval. (With most of the terriers I have owned, this story would now take a very tragic twist, because birds are prey objects...)

For many of us, the wish to get mild exercise and to relax after a harrowing day with work and/or child and family duties sounds like a good thing to do. Walking with your dog is the perfect excuse to get away from people who are talking to you and "needing" stuff. Not that we do not love the people in our lives, it is just that we sometimes need a few minutes break from them! When your dog goes for a walk, depending upon his temperament, he might be happy to mosey along with you, mirroring your mood and getting some mild exercise himself, enjoying your company as much as you are enjoying his.

What most often happens, though, is a walk that does not resemble the idyllic dream walk whatsoever. The dog drags the owner down the street, eager to move at a much much faster clip than the person wishes to go. (While you feel exhausted after your demanding day, your dog is not. He has been resting up all day and may have limited access to exercise while you have been at work.) The dog is in hyper-drive. It is difficult to get

the dog's attention, because he is too busy peeing on every post, bush and blade of grass, although when he pauses to do so, it at least gives your rotator cuffs a brief respite. When he is not engaged in dragging you from pillar to post, he is busily sniffing and scanning for another hapless dog attached to a person, or perhaps a rabbit that will provide an excuse to give chase. This really ramps up the excitement, and dogs react to this in different ways. Some pull even harder (ha! you thought that wasn't possible, didn't you!?, while others begin to bark and lunge in frustration: "If only I wasn't attached to this slowpoke!" every time they see another dog and/or person.

Other dogs pay lip service to you, keeping the leash relatively loose (or at least not pulling too terribly hard) until they see something interesting, whereupon they lunge forward, dislocating the shoulders of the handler - provided the handler is fortunate enough to stay upright at all.

Because of the opposition reflex, and because people do not use their body as an effective, consistent means of communication, the vast majority of owners quickly teach their dog to pull, then complain bitterly when the dog does so. How does this terrible miscommunication begin? Many owners have rewarded their dog endlessly for a tight leash. How? Easy: the dog pulls and you pull back and follow (This would be the dog's interpretation. Most people would say the dog drags them). Repeat this twice, and it is now a habit that will take lots of time and effort to re-shape into something more appropriate.

The other thing that people do on a regular basis is they do not have any idea of the criteria that might be important to the dog. Therefore, instead of teaching the dog to keep the leash loose in a consistent and systematic way, the handler assumes, hopefully, that the dog will just "get it." This usually doesn't happen, or at least not until the dog is getting old and feeble and isn't in such a rush anymore. Instead of the dog "getting it," what happens is that the dog is allowed to have a tight leash and pull sometimes, while other times the dog is punished for a tight leash. This inconsistency sets the dog up for a lot of grief.

The majority of handlers allow the length of the leash to be variable during the teaching stage as well. Please be aware of the length of the leash. If it is constantly variable, then the dog must range out to the end of it to discover what the limits are for the walk each time. During the Acquisition of a behaviour, consistency is vital (a consistent presentation of events is how the dog establishes a pattern). One way to help your dog to understand that pulling is frowned upon, is not by using punishment, but instead, by using a consistent length of leash. I encourage the handler to tie a knot in the leash so she can put her hand on the knot, place her hand on the core of her body and then she is ready to walk her dog. When safe or appropriate, you can cue your dog that he will be allowed to have a bit more line to travel on, such as when you are allowing him to relieve himself.

Some of the problem is a mechanical one: the handler has the leash wrapped around her hand, (never, ever do this - it is quite unsafe and can result in injury) with her arm stretched out away from her body, or her arm held loosely at her side with her hand hanging out in space. When I see a handler that is presenting this way, and the dog is pulling, it is quite impossible for me, as an instructor, to know if the dog is pulling, if the person is pulling or if both are engaged in a perverse and unhappy tug of war. If a handler continues to pull back when the dog pulls forward, the dog is forced to continue pulling, bracing against the handler in order to keep his balance. However, if I have my handler anchor her hand by holding it close to the core of her body (held over the hip bone or over the abdomen) and the leash is tight, then I know it is indeed the dog who is doing the pulling. If the handler's hand is anchored and is not moving around, she cannot be the one who is originating the pulling. Another handy way to modify the person's bad habit is to have her bundle the leash into a figure 8 shape and then, holding the leash, hook her thumb into her front jeans pocket. This anchors the hand, keeping it close to the body, and gives the handler a "target" to remind her when she is getting sloppy. This practice also places the hand in a consis-

tent position which serves as a cue to the dog, in addition to any verbal cues the handler wishes to install.

You must be black and white: you cannot be grey - especially about walking on a leash. For many dogs, this is one of the most difficult lessons. This Walking Nice needs to be a Zero Tolerance area. Make up your mind. Either you commit here and now to your dog never having a tight leash again, ever; or you do not. If you make the commitment, it means that if your dog makes the leash tight, you are bound to do something about it. Chiseled in stone bound. Knights of the Round Table bound. Whatever your mind trip, make it now and be done with it.

I think it is also important to remember that, during this process, *I am not trying to teach the dog to keep a loose leash, per se, but to target my body, notice my body language and mirror it.* Teaching a dog a fairly abstract concept such as "loose leash" is very difficult and time consuming. But teaching a dog to target a part of your body and to Station there is easily and relatively quickly accomplished. If you think of this during your teaching phase, you will find that your dog soon understands that *keeping his toes behind your toes* is the key to success.

If you have to get from Point A to Point B, and you know you will not have the time and/or the patience to enforce the Zero Tolerance of the tight leash, put a Halti or some other kind of head-collar on your dog. Use a harness or, if the dog is small, carry him. *Just do not allow, ever again, the dog to have pressure on the collar with you following her mindlessly.* When you do this, from the dog's perspective, you are "agreeing" with her that a tight leash is okay.

Be Proactive!

You can either be proactive and teach; or you can constantly practice damage control after the error (or disaster) has already occurred. If all you do is practice damage control (which is the "plan" for the vast majority of dog owners), you will never teach your dog anything except to point out the obvious: that you really do not have a plan at all. My garden variety advice for students is this: For the next two weeks, no matter where you are walking, at a random number between every 2 to 7 steps, you will conduct a proactive maneuver. This way your dog will learn! A proactive maneuver might be a Back Away or it might be this exercise, Backing Up In Heel Position, or it might be to Yield The Hindquarters. It might be to stop and have your dog Sit or

Lie Down. After 2 weeks of being this proactive, your dog will be much improved. In the subsequent 2 weeks, you can perform a proactive maneuver every 2 to 12 steps. In the next 2 week time frame, criteria can be raised again, with the top limit being 15 steps. By the end of 8 weeks, you will be amazed. That is, you will be amazed at the astoundingly wonderful results, IF you were consistent in your execution and didn't get in a big rush to get round the block.

The message is this: do not wait for the disaster or error to occur, then try to fix it. *This does not work in animal training for the same reason that punishment is so ineffective in the teaching process: it occurs after the fact.* Typically, a student will tell me that his dog lunges at other dogs on the street and will ask for advice: "What should I do when my dog lunges at other dogs?" What this person really means is, "How do I stop my dog from exhibiting this annoying, embarrassing (perhaps dangerous) behaviour?" The way the question is framed tells me clearly that this person does not understand a crucial point: you must get in ahead of the undesired behaviour and redirect it if you want to both prevent it from occurring and to change the dog's response to the cue of approaching dogs.

When queried further, inevitably the student will express puzzlement because the dog does not always lunge at other dogs, only sometimes. The student wants to know, "How can I 'predict' this?" My answer to this conundrum is this: act as if your dog is going to lunge at another dog every time you see another dog approach, do not wait for the disaster to occur. In addition, act as if your dog is going to lunge every 2 to 7 steps for the next 2 weeks, whether there is another dog approaching or not. If the student does this, the message to the dog is this: pay attention, because my handler feels compelled to change the equilibrium of things frequently. Because a high rate of reinforcement is available when we "do things" it is best to pay close attention. You are also instilling in the dog a habit: check in with my handler frequently. The behaviour modification occurs when the dog realizes that a pattern is 100% consistent: "whenever I see anything of any interest, or there is any change whatsoever in the environment around me (particularly approaching dogs) it is a CUE to CHECK IN WITH MY HANDLER. This eventually translates to including the handler in the dog's decision-making process. When I can get this simple concept across to students and they take it seriously, many reactive dog problems are solved or

drastically improved. *By using the same philosophy, endless dog problems are prevented.*

Loose Leash Walking And The Efficacy Of Various Techniques.

One difficult behaviour to teach well, and the one that takes a lot of time for most dogs to master, is reliable loose leash walking regardless of context. For a four year time frame, I demonstrated and offered to the students in the beginner level and puppy classes four techniques to choose from to teach loose leash walking:

- Clicker training. Using a clicker, you click and feed the dog for keeping the leash loose.

- Red Light-Green Light (Stop if the dog pulls the slightest bit, only go forward when the leash is loose).

- Back Aways, which are detailed in the DVD, *Foundation Behaviours For Every Dog* and the book, *Aggression In Dogs*, consists of taking two or three steps forward, then backing up until the dog comes in front of you, stopping and rewarding. Step forward again and take two or three steps. Do this over a few days and soon once you take two or three steps the dog looks at you: "Are you gonna back up yet?" At this point you can feed the head turn and do not have to do the entire Back Away unless the dog gets aroused and begins to be unruly.

- Get Connected Walk Nicely, an exercise detailed in this book. Efficacy is increased when Back Aways are used in conjunction with it.

More than half of students chose the fourth technique right away and used it successfully. By mid-session, the majority of the remaining half switched over to it because they see their classmates making faster progress. This technique gives students a way to teach the dog what is expected and gives them ways to humanely channel the dog into desirable behaviour.

Clicker trained loose leash walking works well if the student is obsessive about the Clicker training and no other family members are "helping," particularly very young children under nine or ten, surly adolescents or husbands who already "know it all." (Obviously not all children are too young, not all adolescents are surly and sometimes it is the wife who is uncooperative.) Add to that list elderly people in the household who use a walker or cane, those who have arthritis, and are overwhelmed by extra equipment.

With the skill and timing my students have, Red Light-Green Light is the least effective (working on the fewest number of dogs), as it teaches most dogs to stop, then lunge ahead, when the leash tightens return and grab for the cookie, then lunge again as soon as the handler takes a step. This doesn't happen because my students are stupid. Nor does it occur because I am a bad teacher that does not present the material well. This is just one of those techniques that most students find ineffective and which easily breaks down under the slightest arousal on the part of the dog. The reward of the loose leash vs. the pull of the tight leash are too lacking in contrast to motivate most dogs to work for one and avoid the other. This technique failed miserably with my own terriers. Let's face it folks, not everyone is going to devote their life to dog training. The training process needs to be effective and meet the needs of a wide variety of client/dog teams. For pet dog trainers all family members need ways to control and live with the dog.

Back Aways work well and require less skill on the part of the handler. Back Aways are also an excellent way to get the dog diverted away from distractions. Only a few physically handicapped students are unable to perform Back Aways. The clients understand the technique quickly, which works well for a six week class.

Exercise 1: Backing Up In Heel Position

From moment to moment, the dog is either pulling on the leash or he is not. This is not difficult to determine as long as your hand is anchored close to your body. Pulling is a Pass/Fail test.

Because of prior learning and the naturally occurring opposition reflex, and because handlers move much too slowly to suit most dogs, pulling is the default for the vast majority of dogs. With this very simple exercise we will teach the dog to think about the pressure of the collar differently. If the pressure on the collar is a cue to back up instead of surge forward, then you are using a very clever behavioural technique: teaching an incompatible behaviour. During the process of teaching an incompatible behaviour, your dog will also have a paradigm shift about his opposition reflex.

This exercise, Backing Up In Heel Position, is part of a program to teach your dog how to be pleasant on a walk. This same exercise can be used as part of damage control. Therefore, you can utilize this exercise any time when the dog's toes pass your toes...or, the dog begins to blast by and is pulling on the leash, as well as using it as one approximation of a behaviour chain.

Approximation 1:

Your dog should be wearing a martingale or flat collar. You might want to begin next to a wall or a sofa, something to keep your dog's body parallel with yours.

- Begin from a stationary position. It is easiest if your dog is standing, not sitting.

- With your right hand anchored, your left hand on the leash near the dog's collar (your left hand may also be on the dog's collar, as mine is in some of the photographs) and your leash neatly coiled, lift up your left leg and slowly move it backwards. The first few approximations I wish to exaggerate the leg movement by moving slowly. This helps the dog to notice your leg movement as an important cue about direction of travel. (These instructions assume your dog is on your left side. You can do these exercises from the right side as well, modifying the instructions accordingly.)

- . Put a slight, steady pressure on the dog's leash until she backs into the specific location you want: her toes are behind your toes, and she mimics your still feet.

- As soon as she is in position, *immediately* release the pressure on the leash. Do not release the pressure hesitantly. I literally almost toss the leash toward the dog, by letting go of the leash with my left hand entirely. Make this a big, noticeable release.

    As you release, or even if the dog feels some cessation of the pressure, some dogs will step forward, or even leap forward, again. Be ready and at all costs (well, within reason): keep your feet still.

    If the dog moves forward slowly, takes a step forward or only leans forward, repeat the steady pressure on her collar until she is backed into a proper position: her toes are behind your toes. Once her toes are behind your toes: immediate release.

If you see your dog begin to move quickly, or you are pretty sure your dog will lunge forward the second you release the pressure on the collar, be ready: pivot around so you are standing directly in front of her to stop her forward progress. Now take a step toward her and have her back her feet up a step or two. This is to help her think "back up" instead of "surge forward." Now you are in a position to pivot back into Heel position and try again.

- Repeat this, "pressure on with an immediate release of pressure when you get the desired response" information sequence, until the dog ceases moving her feet.

- Once her feet are "following" your lead, that is when your feet become still and so do hers, just stand there a moment and enjoy each other's company. You can hold her collar and rub her body if you like, as in the Be Still exercise.

- Note: If your dog gets wary about being between you and a wall and tries to scoot away, slow down and take your time. Stand three feet from the wall and encourage her to come into Heel position. Mark & Treat her as soon as she comes into Heel position. Repeat this 2 or 3 times, then move six inches closer to the wall and repeat. Do this, raising criteria by moving six inches closer each time until your dog feels comfortable. Then walk forward along the wall a few steps, stop and Mark & Treat. Only once your dog is comfortable with the proximity of both you and the wall, can you proceed.

If you have to haul backwards on your dog's collar rather than getting the desired response by using a light, steady pressure, you have not done your homework! You need to practice the Follow The Feel exercise until your dog understands that exercise well. And never, ever, ever do you use a jerking motion. That is verboten (forbidden).

Approximation 2:
Still near your wall or sofa or a fence to keep your dog's body parallel:

- Be aware of where your hands are and that they are properly placed and anchored so you can tell if your dog is the one pulling or you are.

- Begin to walk. Take one or maybe two steps forward. No more! If your dog lunges before you even get one step forward, take one half of a step.

  Do not wait! Particularly while in the Acquisition phase (teaching steps) of a behaviour, be proactive and remember: the most effective way to teach the dog is to *stop moving your feet BEFORE* the dog lunges by you. This is called being proactive.

  Important! Take these steps in slow motion. I use a visual aid to help me with this: I think of myself walking along the bottom of a pool, moving underwater. This helps me to avoid quick or abrupt movements that may startle a timid dog. Quick or even normal-speed movements may it more difficult for your dog to learn this new "dance." If I were teaching you a dance step, I would move slowly so you could imitate me more easily. After a few repetitions, you would be able to do the dance step at a faster speed.

- Stop moving your feet.

- . Put a slight, steady pressure on the dog's leash until she backs into the specific location you want: her toes are behind your toes, and she mimics your still feet.

- As soon as she is in position, *immediately* release the pressure on the leash. Do not release the pressure hesitantly. Make this a big, noticeable release.

- Some dogs will step forward, or even leap forward, again. Be ready and at all costs (well, within reason): keep your feet still.

- If the dog moves forward at all, repeat the steady pressure on her collar until she is backed into a proper position: her toes are behind your toes.

- Repeat this, "pressure on with an immediate release of pressure when you get the desired response" information sequence, until the dog ceases moving her feet.

- Once her feet are "following" your lead, that is your feet are still and so are hers, just stand there a moment and enjoy each other's company. You can hold her collar and rub her body if you like, as in the Be Still exercise.

Exercise 1: Backing Up In Heel Position   269

Follow The Feel Review

These two pictures are a quick review of the Follow The Feel Exercise., which teaches your dog to back up in response to a slight pressure on the collar.

Refer to the *Follow The Feel* chapter for specifics.

In the top photograph, I am applying slight pressure to Wilson's collar and assisting his understanding to move backwards - Following The Feel that the pressure indicates - by applying a slight pressure to his chest as well. He has already moved his right front foot backwards and is just picking up his left front foot to move it backwards in this photograph. Look at the interest and concentration on his little face.

In the photograph to the right, I have released the pressure on the collar and am rubbing his chest: once you have taught the Be Still Switch, this now tells him to keep his feet still and that he has done a good job.

Photo essay by Dave Schrader

Exercise 1: Backing Up In Heel Position

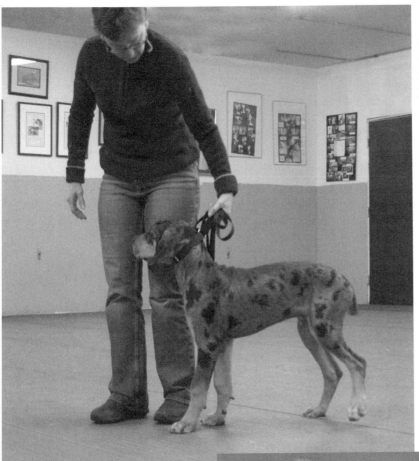

Once the dog is responding readily and easily to the pressure on the collar with the assist of the pressure on the chest, you can advance to using just the pressure of the collar to back the dog up, as illustrated in these two photographs.

Wilson is attending to me and responding to slight pressure on the collar by moving his feet backwards. I am moving my feet backwards also, which, later on in your practices, will become a cue in and of itself. That is, the dog will mirror your feet - if you move your feet backwards so will he.

The photograph to the right shows the next approximation: I am using a longer leash and backing up with Wilson. You can see that the leash has very little pressure on it - the snap is almost slack. He is watching me closely and is beginning to mirror my body language.

I know that my arm is away from my body. I have taught myself to be very aware of how much pressure is being used even when my arm is away from my body. When you first begin to do these exercises, you might want to start with your arm touching your body. In this instance, I am holding my hand directly above Wilson's collar to direct him gently backwards.

Photo essay by Dave Schrader

Exercise 2: Teaching Your Dog a Stop Cue

I see it all the time, everywhere. People cease to move forward and slam to a stop, and they have given the dog no clue whatsoever it was coming up. Then the dog is disciplined for not noticing the non-existent cue. If you want your dog to be well-trained, polite and mannerly, you must be so, too, and set a good example. Good manners for dog trainers and teachers requires that we prepare our dogs for the task we wish them to do, no matter how small and obvious that task might seem to us.

We are going to present the Stop cue to the dog in a consistent manner using our best tool of communication: our body.

- Walk along.

- Turn toward your dog and face her shoulder while stopping your feet.

- If she does not immediately stop, you will step into her space and keep it up until the dog gets her feet behind your feet. Turn in small circles to the left, continuously stepping toward her tail to encourage her to get her body into the safe spot, which is in Heel position. This is a Move Into, as practiced in a prior exercise.

The Stop Cue

My friend Wilson is pulling on the leash. My hand was positioned close to my body and resting on my thigh; and Wilson is pulling so single-mindedly that he has moved my hand from it's original position against my leg. I could have been wiser and prevented him pulling my hand so far from my body by hooking my thumb in my front pocket! (Bad handler!) I can already hear the remonstrances from my students, as I have corrected them about this small item on plenty of occasions!

I begin to turn my body sideways,

Wilson looks at me (well, at least at my feet), but doesn't have a clue what this change in my position could mean. At least is is looking at me; attentiveness to changes in my position are the first key to learning what they signal!

I add slight pressure to the leash to help slow his feet down and to guide him into a better position. That gives me an opening to tell him how very clever he is for noticing the guidance. I manufactured the correct behaviour and that creates an opportunity to reinforce the behaviour.

Do not think that one correct repetition means Wilson understands what is going on! Au contraire.

This is the next repetition. I begin to turn my body towards him, but he has already charged past me, finding the environment much more interesting than I am. In his search for fun smells and maybe even dropped food, he has ditched me.

I step in front of Wilson, putting my toes underneath his cute little nose, which at least has the effect of him looking up at me because I am very difficult to ignore there. I look at Wilson's left hip and begin to step towards his rear flank. This will turn him and eventually place him in heel position. (This is one reason why you practiced Yielding The Hindquarters.)

left hip

I continue to step towards Wilson's hip, to keep turning him. I am "chasing" him into position - but remember, it's not a real chase, because I am moving quite slowly. I want Wilson to have a lot of time to look at my body language and interpret it, so in the end he will require a very small gesture on my part. With a trained dog, if out of position, I might be able to move them into place by just "looking like" I was going to step towards the him. This is why you look at the hip first, very deliberately, then you begin to step towards that hip. By continuing to present the cue in a proper, predictable sequence, eventually you will be able to fade the initial "big" compound cue into a single, very subtle cue.

Exercise 2: Teaching Your Dog a Stop Cue 275

Here Wilson, remaining attentive, is getting his body turned around 180 degrees, so that in a moment, he will be in Heel position. Then I can pivot back into place, and we will both be facing the same direction, ready to try again.

Wilson will have learned a valuable lesson: when his toes pass my toes, I get in his way!

Once set up again with Wilson in Heel position, I step forward. Wilson is staying behind my toes for a bit longer period of time - that is, he has taken a couple of steps and hasn't passed by me yet!

I turn my body sideways, facing Wilson's shoulder and stop my feet moving. Look at that! Wilson stops his feet moving and just stands quietly and waits for my next signal. Yes! He is beginning to understand that my body and its position may be important. *Now it is my job to be very consistent, so he can pick out a discernible pattern.* Then I can reinforce correct responses. The best reinforcement in this situation is to move forward again and continue our walk.

I will take just one, two or three steps forward, before I will repeat the Stop cue. I will repeat the Stop cue every few steps for a few to several days, depending on the dog and how "charge-y" (how inclined the dog is to blow by or ignore your signals and cues) the individual is. Then you can begin taking more steps, but adding the Stop cue frequently, just to make certain the dog is paying as much attention as you think he is!

Photo essay by Dave Schrader

A super Move Into and the understanding to yield space is one pre-requisite for teaching Walk Nicely.

As I wait for the go ahead from the photographer, Rylie waits cheerfully with me, watching for my body language to tell her what we are going to do next. I know she is cheerful and expectant because her body feels relaxed, but you can see it, too. Her mouth is open wide in a doggy smile and she is looking at me attentively. Her paw is raised in a friendly, curious "What are we doing next?" manner.

I use a Move Into. Rylie stays visually connected with me and begins to swing her body to face me.

Rylie opens her mouth in a friendly, relaxed manner as I continue to step calmly and quietly toward her. She is not afraid or nervous of me coming into her space: she understands it is information.

She turns her body until she is facing me. With a dog who is in the Acquisition stage of this exercise, now is the moment you would release the pressure and still your feet or, preferably, use a Back Away.

Since Rylie is experienced, I can continue to stop toward her and she will back up as long as I do so. I do not need to release the pressure immediately anymore, I can segue right into another cue or signal, in a seamless manner. She remains confident and is concentrating. Her rounded back is not because she is afraid, but because she is transferring her weight onto her hindquarters.

Notice the intense look of concentration in Rylie's countenance. She is backing up and watching me closely to see what cues will be given next. If I jumped backwards and began to run, she would give chase. If I moved sideways, so would she.

However, I still my feet and she "mirrors" this by stilling her feet. As she does so, she gives me a little bit of moving room, which is polite and a correct response. When I stop, I do not wish the dog to be crowding me and pressing into me. This is an indication of anxiety, insecurity or it could even be a signal of bossiness or aggression.

I will end this with a Back Away - always ending exercises, whenever possible, with a release of pressure.

What I like about this sequence is that Rylie, although she is concentrating and intense, is also comfortable with everything I am doing. You can tell that she is relaxed by her open mouth, even though her tail is held down, which is typical of dogs who are concentrating hard. Her hind legs are nicely underneath her in preparation for our next move.

Rylie is concentrating hard and has her tail in more of a "working" position, rather than up over her back. Some people would mistake her dropped tail for a dog who is nervous and feeling afraid. Dogs will also drop their tail when they are not afraid, but are concentrating or working. I say this because many Border Collies, when herding, drop their tail quite low.

Photo essay by Dave Schrader

Exercise 2: Teaching Your Dog a Stop Cue

Merlin Walks Nicely Even Though He Gets Distracted

Merlin gets distracted and heads off in his own direction.

Rachel is smart, though, and has her hand nestled against her body - where the core of her strength is. Because Merlin has been trained to Follow The Feel instead of to resist and to employ his opposition reflex, as soon as he feels a slight pressure on his collar, he "self-corrects" and turns back towards Rachel. No begging, no bribing, no jerking, no anything. Merlin understands what he ought to do and does it.

Your dog will always make mistakes. This discussion is not about whether a dog is perfect, but rather about how willing he is to substitute your agenda for his own and how cooperative he is when you remind him of a task. It is also about how sensitive you are to the dog's feedback to improve his learning curve.

This means that Merlin comes in closer to Rachel and does not continue to resist. The walk can continue unhindered.

When Merlin steps past Rachel's leg, intending to walk ahead of her (if that is allowed, the chances that Merlin will keep going faster and begin to pull on the leash are high), Rachel turns her body sideways. As she turns her shoulders towards Merlin and steps toward him with her foot, his attention is pulled to Rachel immediately and the enticing distraction he was heading towards (the photographer) becomes secondary. Rachel becomes more important.

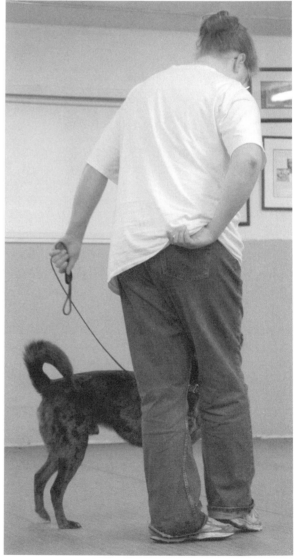

Rachel continues to have Merlin move his feet backwards until his toes are behind her toes. She doesn't have to step into his space anymore; she can give him a reminder by pointing to his toes with hers, calling his attention to their position relative to Rachel.

My favorite part is that Merlin is really paying attention to Rachel and is happy and relaxed. They look like they are walking together instead of held together only by the leash.

Rachel doesn't even have to turn sideways all the time anymore, just if Merlin gets distracted. Here, as soon as she pauses and long before she turns sideways, Merlin brings his feet to a halt and checks in with Rachel, smiling, to see what will be the next move.

Photo essay by Dave Schrader

Mirror & Switch Games

Mirror & Switch games are the absolute ultimate. For all of us who love animals, the real thrill is that feeling that you and this creature, even if for only a few seconds at a time, are of one mind. This is like dancing with a fine partner, whose moves are anticipated as soon as they are thought of, and transferred to the other partner, effortlessly mirroring each other's behaviour.

Before you begin these games you must have a Leave It and a Lie Down to die for. Some dogs get quite fired up and will exhibit predatory behaviours, up to and including using their teeth, inappropriately. Therefore, it is imperative that you have a couple of behaviours already on cue that will take your dog out of drive and place her into neutral.

I begin this game with puppies, especially puppies from "working" lines who display high activity levels and predatory behaviours. A large percentage of these personality-type puppies will be easily aroused and I want those puppies to get practice allowing me to intervene in and control their arousal levels as early as possible. This exercise is also very good for timid puppies, or for dogs who you want to increase their "drive" for dogsports. As always, the exercise will need to be tweaked to suit the individual. For the pushy, drive-y dog I will begin with very short periods of "revved up" and longer periods of "be calm." When a dog is driving towards me hard and pushing into me, contacting my body a lot and maybe even getting mouthy, I will keep the game more sedate. Only over time, and as the dog can manage more arousal without getting out of control, will I promote more arousal. For the timid puppy it will be the opposite. With the timid or cautious puppy, who does not have as much self confidence, you must be very careful to encourage moving forward and have a low-key, playful attitude.

To play this game, I begin by getting the dog just a little revved up. After 2 or 3 seconds (more duration as the dog shows me she is capable of handling more arousal without losing it entirely) I then calm her down using an already installed Be Still. I rev her up (switch her into her Hindbrain), by running around with her and shoving at her playfully and lightly, engaging her in slightly rough play, then requesting a Sit or a Down. I generously reinforce the Sit or Down. Most often, in the beginning you can request all you like and not get the behaviour! For that reason, do begin this game on leash and allow the dog to drag the leash about. Then when you request a Sit or a Down, you can easily pick up the leash to contain the dog and lure her into a Sit or Down. After I have lured the dog into the Sit or Down a dozen times, I will request the behaviour and then use a slight pressure on the collar to enforce the Sit or Down; I then feed the behaviour only after it has been manufactured. For the Sit, the pressure is slight but steady and upward; for the Down, the pressure is slight but steady and straight towards the ground. If you practice this enough, you will be amazed at the way you can turn your dog off and on, using conditioned responses to your body language and learned cues.

This game is important because dogs are super easy to control when they are in a safe, familiar environment and that environment is not arousing. But as soon as a dog becomes aroused, all our lovely training flies out the window. But it doesn't have to be that way! This game will help you and your dog develop a relationship such that arousing circumstances actually increase the dog's attention on you.

This "Switch" part of this game is all about getting really good control of that Reticular Activating Switch that we discussed early on in this book.

This game gives your dog practice following YOUR lead, and it gives you practice maintaining your composure even when the dog is aroused. If your dog becomes aroused or reactive, and so do you, then you have effectively told your dog who is leading the game! You must be calm and deliberate in your movement, even if you are moving a bit quickly. There is a difference between moving quickly and efficiently and being frantic and hectic. I was trying to describe this to a client the other day, and she said to me, "Think of the queen. If the queen comes through you happily give way to her. AND the queen never, ever hurries. She might occasionally hasten, but she never hurries." We had a fine giggle over this, but she was exactly right! How you comport yourself matters.

How you carry yourself has as much to do with your mind and attitude as it does with your body. Your body is just the vehicle for your mind in matters of intentional or subconscious movement. Again, I will pull on my dressage education from the famous writer Sally Swift, who has helped literally generations of riders with her mental exercises. Sally Swift's words are just as relevant to any kind of animal training as they are to the dressage riders that she is directly addressing: "If the desired movement is to be performed efficiently you must allow your center to direct the coordination with what I call clear intent, a precise, positive understanding, and picture of what you want." (Swift, 2002) Her point should be well taken: you must have a calm and resolute manner, and you must have a mental picture of what you wish to accomplish. (The "center" she is discussing is what Pilates would term your "core." This is a circular area in your body bounded by your belly button and the top of your pubic bone.)

In further discussing clear intent, she describes how in the practice of martial arts strength can become effortless: think of standing with your arm outstretched and having someone press down on your arm to bend it. If you think of resisting this effort, you will tighten all your muscles and grind your teeth: your body will be tense and your mind will feel anxiety. "What would happen if you replaced your stiff resistance with a clear intent that your arm will not bend? Try standing calmly centered...Decide absolutely that your arm will not bend." (Swift, 2002) Being good with clear intent is not magic and takes a tremendous amount of discipline and concentration on your part, along with being able to maintain a relaxed composure.

Clear intent means that if you do not allow the dog to distract you with her reactivity, but instead remain calm and resolute about your goal, the dog will follow (mirror) you. If you allow yourself to be distracted by whatever the dog is distracted by and you mirror her behaviour, you have told her that she is making the decisions and you are following. If you ask for a Down, do not allow the dog to distract you from your goal. If you ask for attention, do not allow the dog to change the subject.

Exercise 1: Drop Out Of Motion

- Begin with your dog on leash.

- For best results, your initial goal is to teach the dog how to stop and do something else which is:

  1. Out of motion and
  2. Requires the dog to change his train of thought abruptly.
  When you are playing with the dog, and then you suddenly ask for a Down or something similar, it is non sequitur to him.
- Do not begin by getting the dog super excited.

- Therefore, you will just begin by moving around at a jog and changing directions, encouraging the dog in a happy tone of voice.

- Stop quickly, and change your body language. Stand still and relaxed and straight. Take a deep breath and ask the dog to Sit or Down. I prefer using a Down.

- If the dog complies immediately (rare) you should Mark and feed the behaviour. Be generous with the food treat, give the dog 2 or 3 yummies one after the next. Draw out the reinforcement by spending some time with the dog in the Down. Let him enjoy his treats and the social approval.

- Then you can begin a new trial. First release the dog from his Down, then start up with your jolly game again, keeping it rather low-key at this learning stage.

If the dog does not comply when you request the Down (quite likely) shorten the leash to curb his exuberance, but do not jerk, pull or yell at the dog and...
- You might need to lure the dog into the Down with a treat the first few times. If you have done your Follow the Feel work correctly, you will also be able to give your dog additional help in the form of slight pressure downwards on his

collar or on his shoulders with your hand. DO NOT PUSH the dog into the Down. The physical sensations should be more like a guide downwards, not a correction downwards.

- Once the dog is in the Down, Mark and feed the behaviour.

- Begin a new trial, keeping the activity level rather low-key these first trials. Once your dog and you are active, perhaps running and jumping around a bit, give your Down cue and immediately lure the dog into the Down again. Repeat this "cue and immediate luring the dog into the Down" pattern, ten times in a row.

Pop Quiz

Now it is time for a pop quiz! This is not to fool the dog or "get" him, but rather to see if or what he has learned from the previous ten trials.

- Begin another trial by moving around joyfully with your dog.

- Request the Down. You do so not just with your voice, but by stopping, standing still, taking a breath and then saying the cue. Your body language is as important as the spoken cue, more so at this point in time.

- Wait 5 seconds or even 10 - standing perfectly still, only saying the cue ONE TIME. You could repeat the cue if the dog stopped moving and then looked at you quizzically like, "What? Did you say something?" You could also repeat the cue if the dog looks as if he is thinking about going into the Down. Otherwise, shut up. (I say this with the kindest possible intent...) During this 5 or 10 second time frame we are hoping that the dog notices that you have stopped moving. Remember, he cannot notice that you have stopped moving unless you continue to stand still, even if he himself does not. Once he notices that you have stopped moving and are just standing there, we are desperately hoping that it will have occurred to him that the last 10 repetitions we just did you stopped, stood still, said "Down," he dropped and then you gave him a treat.

- If it does occur to him to Down, for goodness sakes, jackpot it.

- If it does not occur to him to Down, that's okay. You don't learn everything in a few repetitions either. I still cannot school myself to keep my cell phone in one location so I do not lose it 58 times a day, which forces me to find another

phone and then traipse all over the farm calling the cell phone to find it. So, in the case that your dog has not shown you a Down, you will immediately repeat the cue and lure or use the slight collar pressure down as a helper cue. You will now do another ten repetitions as before, saying the cue one time, then immediately luring and/or helping the dog into the Down position. Do not test this behaviour during these ten repetitions, just do them.

- Then try another pop quiz to see if the repetitions have "stuck" yet. Keep repeating the ten repetitions followed by the pop quiz, until you have a successful pop quiz.

- If the dog has an unsuccessful trial at any point you can resort back to this ten reps, then a pop quiz sequence until the behaviour is slick.

You will know when the dog is getting it, because at some point the dog might anticipate your Down cue and start to drop. If you see this during the repetitions, you could try a pop quiz the next trial, just to see if the dog has gotten it.

Once your dog can do this game at a low level of activity, start getting him more excited during the activity segment of the trial.

Later, as you progress, see how excited you can get your dog and still get the Down. I look for a Down that is slick and smoothly executed, fast and shows absolutely no hesitation or resistance on the dog's part. I will work very hard to make this happen. This behaviour has saved my dog's lives a time or two, and I have used this Drop Out Of Motion behaviour to call dogs off game, such as when they jump a bunny out in the field. If I can call my Smooth Fox Terrier off game, you can teach your dog to come off squirrels, skateboarders and cars on request. This behaviour may take you some time to perfect.

Once the dog is paying close attention to my body language, and I have a Drop to Die For, I can begin to really mix it up. I try to get my dogs revved up pretty good, very Hindbrain, and then see how fast I can switch them to their frontbrain. This is one way to see how much control you have taught your dog in regards to the Reticular Activating Switch.

Once your dog has that lovely Down, you can intersperse activity with stillness, sometimes requesting the Down, sometimes not. At this point you will really start to play Mirror & Switch games with your dog, with your body language expressing direction and speed and your dog will begin to mirror your direction and speed. Dogs love this game because it resembles hunting and pack running, and, therefore, speaks to every canine, whether that animal has ever had a chance to be an avid hunter or has ever run with a pack.

I use this game frequently as part of teaching competition Heel work, as well as Agility work. I can begin by Heeling or playing and segue from one to the next seamlessly. This way, your dog believes that Heeling and playing or paying attention during Agility runs is all one and the same thing. I find, when correctly done, this game can build drive into timid dogs and can make bold, charge-y dogs stop and think.

Caution

Have fun with it, but stay safe! When a dog gets fired up, especially if you do not have a relationship of respect and trust well established, she very well might reach out and snap or take a bite of you, either because of arousal or because she feels defensive. This game is not to be done if your dog has EVER shown any aggression toward you. If your dog has aggressive or reactive tendencies, you need to have professional help, and this game is not appropriate for you and your dog.

Further Thoughts To Help You Understand

When I was discussing this chapter with my friend, Priscilla, she talked to me about how foreign this concept might be to many people. She mentioned that, in this exercise, I am really talking about making minute adjustments to my body language to "talk" to the dog. This is an excellent point, and because I am so accustomed to using my body as language, I do not even think about the specific movements I make. I also depend heavily upon kinesthetic learning when mastering a new task. (I absolutely have to do it and experiment with how it emotionally and physically "feels.")

Mirroring is so very important to animals, and to people, too! This is because the ability to mimic or copy another is a very natural way of learning. In fact, amongst conspecifics (same species), it is one of the most basic and primary learning tools. Mirroring is also a very special way to convey information.

Neuro-Linguistic Programming (NLP) studies how people (specifically people who are excellent at communication and therapy) think and communicate and describes the processes. Understanding what effective communication is comprised of is tremendously useful information and can help you to become a more effective communicator yourself. In the field of Neuro-Linguistic Programming, mirroring another's body language is considered to be one thing that a really effective communicator uses in a natural, instinctive and intuitive way. As an example, if you are sitting across someone at a cafe table having a drink and that person leans forward, elbows on the table and looks intently at you, you might find yourself "mirroring" her body language because you are interested in the topic she is speaking of. You find yourself drawn into her personal space, both because of the enthusiasm she is projecting and the "invitation" created by her leaning towards you in this intimate manner. Anyone walking by could see that the two of you are in concert with each other and engaged with each other, simply by observing the similarity (the mirroring) of the body language you are both displaying. A person approaching you, if he is polite and observant, might hesitate to interrupt at all; if he chooses to interrupt your tete-a-tete he might try to insert himself into the picture by first clearing his throat or saying your name to get your attention in a subtle way as opposed to barging in without warning.

Animals take mirroring very seriously. When Pat Parelli works a horse, he speaks to the horse so clearly that the horse quickly understands the concept he is presenting. One of my very favorite things I have seen him do is actually an extremely simple exercise, but it is earth-shaking in its implications. Mr. Parelli will stand beside a horse that he has worked for a limited time. Then he will stand at the horse's left shoulder in order to lead the horse forward. If Pat steps off on his left foot, so will the horse. If Pat steps off on his right foot, so will the horse. Pat Parelli is not "training" the horse to do anything, the horse naturally does this because she has accepted Pat, on this level, at least, as being trustworthy enough to follow. In watching his training techniques on several films, I have seen him be able to predict the moment that this "mirroring" will begin to occur. Once he has this respect and trust on one level, it becomes ever easier to transfer the state to another level and into other situations. The horse clearly indicates, by mirroring, that he is feeling cooperative and safe.

This feeling of being cooperative and safe is the foundation that you need to build future training on, but an

even bigger thrill is the effect that this attitude has on the relationship. It is this aura of connection, of bonding and being so close that feels so very wonderful to those involved in the relationship. Even if you are not directly involved in the relationship, the idea of it is so appealing, that simply being able to observe it happening is a thrill. You feel enlightened in some spiritual way by being even on the peripheral edge.

The most difficult thing about these Mirror & Switch games (exercises), is that I can give you a list of ingredients and a very general recipe. However, you will have to experiment extensively to master this exercise. There is a PBS radio show called The Splendid Table. I do not cook, but this show has one fascinating aspect for me and it catches my attention every time. It does indeed speak to the expertise of the hostess of the show! Listeners can call in with a random list of ingredients ("I have tomatoes, broccoli, and cheese lying around...") and the hostess will, on the spot, make up a tasty recipe for the caller to "whip up." This exercise is a bit like this, you have the list of ingredients:

- your body

- your dog's body

- the "space" that exists between the two of you

- the "energy" that can be conveyed with movement

- the stillness of your body when you stand your feet still

- the "intent" that you bring with you (a frame of curiosity and wonder is a nice intent to bring.)

- A Lie Down cue (see the *Drop Out Of Motion* exercise above.)

- when advanced, you might add toys to your game

- how relaxed or tense you are

Now you can make up a recipe. I hope the following photographs and the film on the DVD help you to create your own wonderful recipe for Mirror & Switch games. The only real goal is to get to know your dog better. The better you can read your dog and anticipate his emotional state, the more you increase your awareness. Increased awareness can help you to teach your dog how to "switch" from an aroused emotional state to a calmer, or to a waiting (anticipatory) emotional state. Practice will help you and your dog learn to "switch" from movement to stillness, from active and aroused to calm.

Learning the mechanical skills may feel awkward at first. Expect to experiment. Begin slowly. I mean this literally, move slowly then move quickly, then Down your dog on cue. This is enough for one trial! Give yourselves a count of 5 to "think" about and assimilate what just happened. Then begin another trial. Really observe your dog and be aware of your own body movements. You might even have someone film you and your dog, this will be very illuminating!

I walk forward and look where I am going. My body language says: "We are going this direction." Rylie happily follows - why wouldn't she?

When I turn around and direct my motion and energy towards her, she stops, then backs up as I keep coming into her space. Notice that she mirrors my energy level, as well as my body language.

As I shift my weight backwards, she moves towards me. She does this because this particular movement (the weight shift) is more salient (gives her more information) than my upper body leaning towards her.

As I turn my body and indicate I am going in a different direction, she mirrors that motion and turns to move in the same direction I am indicating.

I walk in a peppy manner and so does Rylie.

When I stop and face her and lean towards her, she stills her feet and leans towards me. This is her style: some dogs would still their feet and lean slightly away from me. There is not necessarily a right or wrong response - there will be individual responses. What is quite apparent is that we are "in it together," and she is willing to follow my foot movement and body orientation.

Here you can see the action is beginning to get her fired up. Look at the hard, intense eye and note how close she is. She is not quite giving me a muzzle punch (an intention behaviour that can be preliminary to a correction bite), but it is getting darned close. See the tongue flick towards me, combined with a shortened commisure (her lips are short)? That shows intent to move me or control me, to the extent of biting. The shortened commisure indicates that she has confidence in her ability. For a working stock dog, this is appropriate and indicates a dog who is showing herding behaviour. A younger, less educated Rylie would show much less impulse control, and I would have had to stop her and put her in a Lie Down, right here (at the latest, but a few seconds sooner would have been better). Because Rylie and I have already had this conversation many times, I can press her very hard and she will not cross the line and become over-emotional and lacking in impulse control. She takes it seriously, but knows this is a game and what the rules of the game are. Rylie is a credit to her breeder because she shows high intensity; feels light and controllable; and has excellent herding instinct.

Rylie shows me her self-control as I step towards her again, continuing to pressure her. Notice the tongue flick towards me again and the whale eye (whites showing). She is wound up all right! Her instincts tell her I am a very pushy sheep and need to be muzzle punched and moved out of her way. But her training reminds her that this is a game, a Hindbrain/Frontbrain game. She will give way to me instead of following her instincts, without ever threatening me or biting me, not even in play. This is a courtesy that she would not grant to a sticky sheep.

The idea is not to get the dog fired up so you can "take her down" and engage in conflict. The idea is: how close to the edge can you get the dog to dance without falling off? Work this exercise carefully and in tiny baby steps, and over time you will be rewarded with a dog who shows lovely Hindbrain intensity and emotion paired with glorious frontbrain control and thoughtful action.

Having put on plenty of pressure, I remove it, by stepping slightly away from her. This slight release of pressure causes so much less intensity that Rylie opens her mouth in a big smile, "That is such good sport! I love it when you will be a pretend sheep!" She *remembers* that we are "pretending," respects the space I made between us and waits at the ready to see what fun thing we will do next!

As I turn to move in a different direction, Rylie approves of the continuation of the game with an exuberant movement in the direction my body indicates. I could have her Lie Down and Stay at any time, but I am having lots of fun "dancing" with her, playing a game that dogs love and understand intrinsically. I love it, too: it is so apparent that this is a very interesting and bonding game for dogs.

With bold dogs, you must play this game very carefully, keeping the intensity within a range the dog can easily control, or you will be bitten and thus only teach the dog more inappropriate arousal behaviours. Increase the intensity levels slowly over time, using the game as a tool to teach and to inspire your confidence that you can handle all the drive your dog can give you.

This game is not designed to create arousal, but to teach your dog how to cope effectively and safely with the arousal levels that she will experience. You are teaching your high arousal dog how to do a logic over-ride.

With timid dogs, you must play this game very carefully, with lots more releases as opposed to "pressure on," and in short time frames, until the dog feels "brave" enough to experiment and participate. This is a great game for building confidence and drive in dogs who are not bold by nature.

I have taught Rylie that this body language means Heel position. This is a non-native piece of body language, one that she has learned. So, as soon as I "look" like Heel position and give her a verbal cue of "Heel" she immediately Switches gears and complies.

We continue our game with a little spot of Heel work. If your dog thinks that work and play are the same thing, then it is easy to get passionate work from your dog. This is the tricky part, admittedly, because the dog must also learn to commit to whichever behaviour the handler is currently requesting. This level of commitment and balancing the want-to with the have-to is where the top echelon of trainers excel. This cannot be learned by the dog unless the handler is consistent. The more consistent you are with body language, cues and expectations, the more committed your dog will become. Remember, that expectations must be tempered by the stage of learning the dog is in. For instance, during Acquisition, the expectations will be different than for a dog who is fluent with a behaviour that is well understood in several contexts.

Photo essay by Dave Schrader

Mirror & Switch Game With Zasu

Zasu has a very different style than Rylie. She responds to pressure very quickly by getting her teeth out, and without the preliminary "warning" and pressing back into me that is evident with Rylie. Zasu's tendency is to treat all "pressure on" as if the pressure were being exerted by conflict with a prey animal.

Here you can see, as we begin the game, Zasu is already lunging for my hands (the part of my body that is showing the most motion), with her mouth open.

As she comes in closer to my body, I look in the direction I am going to go next. This also provides a subtle "release of pressure," as well as showing my intent. This gives her an opportunity to "mirror" my body language.

Zoomer (aka Zasu) mirrors the turn of my body. I keep my shoulders turned towards her slightly and look at her. You can see this sends her out a little wider on the turn. This is not happenstance: she is responding instinctively to my body language messages. My "stalky" crouch can be interpreted to mean that I could change direction and move towards her, so she leaves a bit more room to maneuver.

See how clever she was! Indeed, I do change direction suddenly. Because she was out away from my body, she can easily change direction also, right with me, not falling behind. She has placed herself in a strategic predatory position to maintain control of the prey.

As I straighten my body and begin to shift my weight backwards, she moves towards me.

As she comes in close, I look at her and reach towards her. This type of motion, when the dog is aroused, really turns the heat up!

Here my body invites Zasu towards me. Instead of facing her directly, I look at her while turning my body slightly away from her.

Think of opening a door to encourage the dog to pass through it. You "open" your body, just like you would a door to channel the dog in that direction. If you open a door, you don't pass through closest to the hinged side, you head for the doorknob side, where the opening is widest.

Once I indicate the direction with my body, I can slow down Zasu's movement. Here I have begun to turn away. She is moving fast, as you can see in the photo above, and I want to "warn" her that I am going to change direction again. I encourage her forward but close the "door" halfway (see my right shoulder moving towards the dog?) Zasu is moving so quickly she must send her motion "vertical" to slow down.

When she lands, she is ready for the change of direction she predicted from my prior position.

I contact Zasu as we both turn, which will "heat" up the activity and increase her arousal level. Terriers love conflict!

In both of these photographs I continue to "pressure" Zasu, by contacting her (by pushing gently on her with my hands) and leaning over her and moving into her. I am not "hitting" her hard with my hands at all. You must keep your body relaxed and have "give" in your arms, so when you contact the dog by pushing, it is a gentle, elastic shove: indeed, done properly and with good timing, it can invite the dog back towards you. Yep, she is aroused now! She is maintaining bite inhibition at this point only because of prior training.

I started these games with this dog as a tiny puppy, as she did not have good bite inhibition and she was also a virulent resource guarder. I took a couple of good hard bites from her as a puppy while she was learning. In the end, though, I have much more control over her arousal levels. By turning her up on "high" and then putting her into "neutral" I have taught her how to Switch from Hindbrain to Frontbrain and am able to control her arousal levels handily.

I am not saying that the intensity demonstrated here with my dogs is appropriate for every dog/handler combination. But a watered down, gentle version of this game is useful for every dog and handler team. Agility teams really benefit from this game and become much more aware, through experimentation, of each other's body language and therefore can predict intent of the partner more rapidly. You can rev up the Heel-work of your competition obedience dog. And you can make your pet more attentive as well as learn more about alternative ways to communicate with every dog. Dogs love it when you "speak" their language, even if your attempts are clumsy.

I begin to straighten my body to slow the action down. This serves as a release of pressure and shows my intent is to "calm" down the situation. Zasu gives a last exuberant leap - she wishes we were going to continue playing hard...

...but as I continue to release the pressure by beginning a Back Away, she responds by coming quietly and with control into a Front position.

This game, with the handler carefully judging the intensity level the dog is capable of handling, can help a timid dog to get braver and more confident about the handler's - and his own - body language. Bold dogs learn how to channel their drive appropriately. The handler now has more precision because she can make decisions about when it is applicable for the dog to be in drive or when to Switch the dog into Stand By or neutral.

Zasu follows me, mirroring my body language, but even more important to me, she is mirroring my lowered energy level.

This is how you find out how "together" you are with your dog.

My body language indicates that I wish Zasu to stay on my right hand side: my hand is out (a learned cue from teaching her to target my hands) and my body language also encourages her to come forward. I have opened my body to invite her in closer to me and channel her direction. She does not just "mirror" by following the directional intent of my body, she is also mirroring the less active emotional state I am exhibiting with the slower body movements.

Zasu remains on my right, and I keep her there initially by closing the door to prevent her from running around in front of me, which would be her natural tendency. I close the door, as you can see in this photograph, by tilting my left shoulder slightly towards her. This "intention behaviour" that I am deliberately manipulating, closes the door by "looking like" I might be changing direction and moving towards her. Her movement across my body is "blocked" by this maneuver.

As she settles into a position by my right leg I can straighten my body more and point it straight forward, so Zasu knows the direction we are going to go. For competition Heel-work, I would also have my eyes straight forward, but for this work, I want to watch her until I think she is committed and quiet where I "put" her.

Since I know that Zasu is still excited from the adrenaline rush of just a few seconds ago (I am speaking of personal experience with this dog. She does not "come down" off that rush as easily as some others do), I am going to give her a pop quiz, to see how much Frontbrain response I really have. So I request a very well known behaviour, "Sit." She hears me, (after all, she is standing just about 12 inches from me), but her little brain is still racing from the earlier fast-paced action. It must seem so non sequitur to her! She is at least mirroring my body language and standing still, but the addition of a verbal cue is just too much to process at this moment.

Because Sit is a well known behaviour (I am not asking her to do something she is incapable of because she has not "learned" the cue), I must explain to her that it is important that she respond. I do this by gently touching her and lifting her chin (another previously taught behaviour). This gives Zasu the *information she needs from me right at this moment to complete the task*. I ask myself that question frequently: "What does the dog need from me right now to understand?"

Note: I do not have a collar on her for a few reasons: 1. she is reliably trained; 2. this is a safe area. She will have a ways to go before she gets to a road. 3. I have had terriers get stuck on underbrush by their collars. Remember also, if a terrier gets away from you in this type of environment, it is possible she will go to ground. An out-hanging root in a woodchuck den could prove deadly if the dog became entangled.

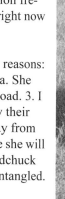

Once "helped" Zasu is happy to comply while I exchange comments with Dave and Marguerite, who are doing the filming. She wasn't trying to be "bad" or to ignore me, she was still in a mental state not conducive to Sitting. The Switch needed a little more assistance. Physical touch can serve to ground the dog and reconnect with you in times of excitement. This must be taught in a systematic manner if it is to be useful in circumstances of high arousal, or otherwise you may find yourself the victim of re-directed aggression.

Photo essay by Dave Schrader

Let's Do It!

Photograph by Mary Wilmoth

It is mandatory that all exercises are regularly practiced in all rooms of the house, in the yard and especially during walks, mostly before you need them, but also as damage control if your dog becomes aroused and over-excited. You might also review the section *Get Connected - The Mind Set*. Before attempting any new exercise, read the applicable chapter and watch that exercise on the DVD as well, so you are prepared and make the fewest errors as you proceed.

A 10 Session Work Plan

The following tables provide you with an example work plan to teach both the Boot Camp and Get Connected exercises. The times listed to complete an exercise are approximate. For instance, with some dogs I will get through a particular approximation in ten minutes and other dogs will take only two minutes. Or what I thought I could teach a dog in one minute turns into twenty. *Be ready to be flexible and take the time it needs to take.*

When training you do not have to do formal one hour long work sessions. You can choose any five or ten minutes and work on an exercise. The very best training is when you are training as a way of life, where every interaction with your dog is one of training and communication. Indeed, if you are to succeed and have the best possible relationship, this is the only way to live with your dog, as it is the only way you can bring the sort of consistency that is necessary. Keep in mind, too, that you are constantly communicating with your dog, whether you intend to or not. The more aware you are of what you are communicating the less difficulty your dog (and by extension, you), will have to endure. After a couple of weeks of living this way with your dog, in fact, it becomes your habit, too, and is effortless - you won't even have to think about it for the next several years that you and your dog live in blissful harmony. Well, as blissful as any relationship can be...

Table 2: Let's Do It! Session #1

Exercise	Source	Notes
Install a Marker 5 minutes	*Installing a Marker, Bridge, Reward Mark, Memory Marker...* on page 126.	
Install a Stand By and a End Working Cue	*Releasing Your Dog: The Stand By Cue & The End Working Cue* on page 130.	Use this cue consistently now, every time you are working with your dog.
Name Recognition 5 minutes.	*Name Recognition* on page 129.	
Eye Contact Approximation1 Approximation 2 Approximation 3 5 to 10 minutes	*Involvement Begins With Eye Contact: Teaching Your Dog Concentration Skills.* on page 148.	Practice Eye Contact constantly, all day. You do not need to work for extended periods, a minute at a time will do. It is the number of repetitions in different locations and under distracting circumstances that will gain you ground.
Back Away 5 to 10 minutes	*Back Away* on page 136.	Practice this everywhere. On your daily walks you should do a Back Away every 2 to 7 steps for at least two weeks.

In addition to the exercises listed in the *Let's Do It! Session #1* table, make certain your dog is very comfortable with you holding onto his collar before you proceed to Session #2.

Collar Holds: •

- Take your dog by the collar and feed him a treat. Repeat this five or ten times.

Do this periodically in all contexts. You want your dog to feel safe when you hold his collar, not threatened. This is a trust exercise.

- Hold your dog by the collar and pet him. Can you hold your dog's collar for 15 or 20 seconds and he remains relaxed the entire time?

Make certain that collar holding is a safe thing to do, and he doesn't feel threatened. It's okay if he is not happy about it, but he shouldn't feel frightened or defensive. If this is the case, stop and get professional help.

If you are doing other training with your dog, work on that for a few minutes, ending on an easy and successful approximation, or end by doing a familiar exercise that your dog does well.

Table 3: Let's Do It! Session #2

Exercise	Source	Notes
Review Name Recognition. Do ten repetitions, moving around the work area. 2 minutes	*Name Recognition* on page 129.	
Practice ten to fifteen Back Aways. 5 minutes	*Back Away* on page 136.	
Eye Contact Review Approximation 2 & Approximation 3 Begin Approximation 4 5 to 10 minutes	*Involvement Begins With Eye Contact: Teaching Your Dog Concentration Skills.* on page 148.	Move around the work area as you do this. Set up and do some eye contact work, switch to Impulse Control (Acquisition approximation), then go back to eye contact work. Also occasionally do a Back Away.
Begin Impulse Control Work. Work on the Approximation labeled: Acquisition. 5 to 10 minutes.	*Think First: Impulse Control* on page 155.	Work until your dog is calm about this exercise.
Begin Be Still Switch 5 to 10 minutes.	*The Be Still Switch: Stand Your Feet Still & Be Calm* on page 201.	Once the dog is doing well in one location, under one context, move the dog to another room or another familiar area, like the yard or the car and practice. Periodically during your walks, stop and use the Be Still Switch. Use your Be Still Switch for all approaches, from now on. Soon your dog will be handling the approaches from others appropriately and without your help.
Stand By Cue 3 to 5 minutes	*Releasing Your Dog: The Stand By Cue & The End Working Cue* on page 130.	Begin to use this constantly in every context. The dog is either on Stand By or released with an End Working Cue.

Collar Holds, Grabs and Confined Spaces.

- Make sure you can reach over your dog's head from the front, or be at the dog's shoulder and take hold of the collar.

- Can you stand by a wall or piece of furniture with your dog, so he is "hemmed in" by objects and still take him by the collar without him being spooky about the claustrophobic area?

Table 4: Let's Do It! Session #3

Exercise	Source	Notes
Begin with Eye Contact work, starting on the last approximation your dog did well, then progressing to the next approximation. Work on this for about 5 minutes.	*Involvement Begins With Eye Contact: Teaching Your Dog Concentration Skills.* on page 148.	Every so often, stop the eye contact work, take your dog by the collar and work on the Be Still Switch.
Impulse Control: Acquisition; Approximation #1: Get Between. 5 to 10 minutes.	*Think First: Impulse Control* on page 155.	Every so often, stop the current work, take your dog by the collar and work on the Be Still Switch.
Begin Follow the Feel protocol. 10 minutes.	*Follow The Feel* on page 222.	Every so often, stop the current work, take your dog by the collar and work on the Be Still Switch.
Back Aways ten to fifteen repetitions	*Back Away* on page 136.	As you are working Back Aways, segue into working on Eye Contact.

As always, end your session with an easy and successful approximation of any exercise you are working on or a familiar exercise your dog does well.

Table 5: Let's Do It! Session #4

Exercise	Source	Notes
Begin with Eye Contact work, starting on the last approximation your dog did well, then progressing to the next approximation. Work on this for about 5 minutes.	*Involvement Begins With Eye Contact: Teaching Your Dog Concentration Skills.* on page 148.	Every so often, stop the eye contact work, take your dog by the collar and work on the Be Still Switch. Mix up the Eye Contact and Impulse Control work, by doing a couple of trials of Eye Contact, then a couple of trials of any Impulse Control approximation your dog already knows.
Impulse Control, starting on Approximation #1, then progressing to the next approximation. 5 to 10 minutes.	*Think First: Impulse Control* on page 155.	Every so often, stop the current work, take your dog by the collar and work on the Be Still Switch.
Follow the Feel	*Follow The Feel* on page 222.	Every so often, stop the current work, take your dog by the collar and work on the Be Still Switch.

As always, end your session with an easy and successful approximation of any exercise you are working on or a familiar exercise your dog does well.

Table 6: Let's Do It! Session #5

Exercise	Source	Notes
Work on Eye Contact & Impulse Control, whichever approximations are appropriate. Mix up the exercises as you have done on previous sessions, smoothly segueing one into the next.	*Involvement Begins With Eye Contact: Teaching Your Dog Concentration Skills.* on page 148. *Think First: Impulse Control* on page 155.	Every so often, stop the current work, take your dog by the collar and work on the Be Still Switch or the Yield To Collar Pressure.
Back Aways several repetitions	*Back Away* on page 136.	Every so often, stop the current work, take your dog by the collar and work on the Be Still Switch or the Yield To Collar Pressure.
Begin Move Into. Work until you have two or three successes.	*Move Into* on page 232.	Begin with Yielding the Hindquarters. Work this approximation only, until you have really smooth responses.

As always, end your session with an easy and successful approximation of any exercise you are working on or a familiar exercise your dog does well.

Table 7: Let's Do It! Session #6

Exercise	Source	Notes
Warm up with a variety of exercises, mixing them up for interest. Spend 5 to 10 minutes on this.		Every so often, stop the current work, take your dog by the collar and work on the Be Still Switch or the Yield To Collar Pressure.
Move Into	*Move Into* on page 232.	
Begin loose leash walking with the Walk Nicely exercise. Work until you can turn your body sideways and the dog will stop. Once you have a couple of successful repetitions, you can stop and move on to something else.	*Walk Nicely With Me* on page 265.	Every so often, stop the current work, take your dog by the collar and work on the Be Still Switch or the Yield To Collar Pressure, Eye Contact and Impulse Control.

As always, end your session with an easy and successful approximation of any exercise you are working on or a familiar exercise your dog does well.

Table 8: Let's Do It! Session #7

Exercise	Source	Notes
Warm up with a variety of exercises, mixing them up for interest. Spend 5 to 10 minutes on this.		Every so often, stop the current work, take your dog by the collar and work on the Be Still Switch or the Yield To Collar Pressure.
Move Into. A few repetitions until the dog is working smoothly.	*Move Into* on page 232.	Practice this randomly throughout the day. Just do one or two repetitions out of the clear blue sky.
Walk Nicely.	*Walk Nicely With Me* on page 265.	Every so often, stop the current work, take your dog by the collar and work on the Be Still Switch or the Yield To Collar Pressure, Eye Contact and Impulse Control.

As always, end your session with an easy and successful approximation of any exercise you are working on or a familiar exercise your dog does well.

Table 9: Let's Do It! Session #8

Exercise	Source	Notes
Warm up with a variety of exercises, mixing them up for interest. Spend 5 to 10 minutes on this.		Every so often, stop the current work, take your dog by the collar and work on the Be Still Switch or the Yield To Collar Pressure.
Walk Nicely.	*Walk Nicely With Me* on page 265.	Every so often, stop the current work, take your dog by the collar and work on the Be Still Switch or the Yield To Collar Pressure, Eye Contact and Impulse Control.

As always, end your session with an easy and successful approximation of any exercise you are working on or a familiar exercise your dog does well.

Table 10: Let's Do It! Session #9

Exercise	Source	Notes
Warm up with a variety of exercises, mixing them up for interest. Spend 5 to 10 minutes on this.		Every so often, stop the current work, take your dog by the collar and work on the Be Still Switch or the Yield To Collar Pressure.
Begin Mirror & Switch Games.	*Mirror & Switch Games* on page 284.	Once you have done some Mirror & Switch games you can work on other tasks, intermittently tossing in some Mirror & Switch.

As always, end your session with an easy and successful approximation of any exercise you are working on or a familiar exercise your dog does well.

Table 11: Let's Do It! Session #10

Exercise	Source	Notes
Warm up with a variety of exercises, mixing them up for interest. Spend 5 to 10 minutes on Easy Stuff.		Every so often, stop the current work, take your dog by the collar and work on the Be Still Switch or the Yield To Collar Pressure.
Work on new approximations of exercises or do some review work on "sticky" spots of other exercises.		Every so often, stop the current work, take your dog by the collar and work on the Be Still Switch or the Yield To Collar Pressure, Eye Contact and Impulse Control.
Mirror & Switch Games.	*Mirror & Switch Games* on page 284.	Mix this work into your daily walks and Walk Nicely exercises. Also, remember, this is one of the ways you now "play" with your dog.

As always, end your session with an easy and successful approximation of any exercise you are working on or a familiar exercise your dog does well.

After you have completed ten work sessions, as outlined above, you will have a good jump-start. Even after ten short sessions, you and your dog have a much better understanding of personal space and how you interact together. Now you understand how to plan work sessions and how important it is to *integrate these behaviours into the daily life* of you and your dog. Use these ten sessions as examples for your plans for future work sessions for you and your dog so you can continue to improve. Once taught, you will be using these exercises constantly, as a way of living with your dog, so that the repetition keeps the exercises fresh and useful. You also will have these behaviours ready to use to prevent future problems and solve current problems.

For instance, the Move Into stops jumping problems cold. Once a Move Into has been established, dogs just don't keep jumping, because you are using clear language to them about how you feel about that. The Move Into is also valuable for dogs who are constantly inattentive or distracted. Now you have a method hammered out ahead of time to use when you need it. Frightened or spooky dogs will have made vast progress towards being more confident after the desensitizing exercises, and will be more trusting. Mirror & Switch games are the icing on the cake, where you get excellent control over easily frustrated, aroused and predatory dogs. You can use Move Into-type pressure to teach your dog to stand back from doorways and allow you to go through first, then call the dog through the doorway to you. There are endless opportunities for teamwork once the team has been established.

You Go, Girl. (or Boy, as the case may be.)

Once you master these basic exercises, your dog will be amazingly more calm, cool and collected. You will be too, because your confidence level will be high when you have worked with your dog under a variety of circumstances, including controlling her when she is aroused. Here are some of the biggest changes you should see from these exercises:

• Fearful and problematic dogs have built skill sets that were undreamed of before starting this work. Your dog will begin to understand that fearful behaviour and defensive behaviour are not the best working patterns anymore.

• Your dog's confidence levels will soar. You now have many cues to keep your dog Frontbrain when she starts to go Hindbrain on you.

• You have built respect, because you have taught your dog boundaries that make sense to her.

• You have built trust, because you have taught your dog extreme coping skills. Now you are both ready for anything the environment can dish up!

I have loved discovering these techniques. I find different ways to use them every day, because, if you listen, your dog is generously willing to teach you. Enjoy this work and let me know how it goes! You and your dog deserve a happy, respectful and fulfilling relationship. True love!

Case Histories

Included in this chapter are a few case histories which provide examples of behaviour problems and the protocol used to modify the behaviours. These case histories were filled out by the clients themselves. They used a format that I provided so comparisons can be made easily, but I encouraged them to put down their thoughts freely, to write down things that they thought might help others, and to include any criticisms. Since my clients tend to voice their opinions freely to my face I figured that honesty would not be an issue. My own input is also included: how I interpreted the interactions between the dog and handler, my impressions of what the major problems were (in the "Presenting Issues" section), the protocol recommended; and my findings on a recheck at 30 days.

As a result, each case history is presented partially by me and partially by the client. The client's input has the potential to give you a lot more information than my listing, in clinical language, what occurred, so I include the client's own words. As a counselor, I look for hard evidence that the protocol is working, and I get my information from the dog's and the client's level of relaxation, confidence and how satisfied the client feels with the result. Another crucial measuring device is the dog's level of contentment and comfort. Hearing what the client has to say is valid for you, dear reader, because their experience and their emotions as a pet owner is different from my point of view and has the potential to give you information from a different viewpoint.

These case histories represent just a very few of the dogs and clients with whom I have used the Get Connected protocol. Many of these clients have been working with me for months or years and have obviously done extensive work, the extent of which is not evident in these short versions. Some of the case histories come from dogs I have not worked with beyond a session or two. I thank the people who allowed me to use case histories particularly, because some of these clients and their dogs are the ones who cooperated in the early development of good recipes for exercises that work and are repeatable. We did a fair amount of experimentation both with individual exercises and the order in which they were taught. These people hung in there, giving me invaluable feedback. Even though I told them the protocol was not necessarily well-proven or endorsed by university-based research, these people trusted me and had faith. Some of the training requests I had surely must have looked pretty "out there" on occasion, especially when I would preface the exercise with, "I don't know if this will work" or "I don't know what I'm doing, I'm just doing stuff until something works." I owe even more to the dogs themselves. They gave me the most valuable feedback and the cleanest information and met me more than half-way. Some dogs were generous and kindly showed me the way. Others were intolerant and resistant which taught me how to communicate better and perfect my mechanical skills.

One of my concerns is to address the emotional state of my clients and their dogs, and to give them both tools to communicate better so they can live together in the very most satisfying way, as good companions. The people in these case histories have generously fessed up to problems, the handling of the problems and are very frank about their emotions. This takes a tremendous amount of courage. They all have my respect and gratitude for their bravery. All of them sincerely hope this information can be of help to you, too.

My clients are dear to me every one. I hesitated to print some of their comments because the praise is sometimes so effusive it is embarrassing to me. The important item to remember as you read these case histories is: no matter how much credit the owners give to me, it is the technique used, mechanical skills perfected and the devotion, persistence, consistence and investment in the dog that the owners put forth that makes the real difference. I was merely a compass to point owners in the right direction. Once pointed, the work is out of my hands and it is up to the dog and owner to forge a relationship that works for them.

As you read the case histories, do remember each case history is different and the dynamics in each situation are each unique. Therefore, while these case histories provide a general example which will help point you in the right direction from which to begin your work, keep in mind that each dog is different and the level of response to stimuli is different.

Without exception, each of these dogs came to me with a clear physical by a veterinarian. In addition, dogs with problematic behaviours or exceptionally hyperactive behaviour or any aggression were screened for thyroid levels and Addisons disease.

Also, the protocol listed for each case history may not be complete. The protocol shows a part of the dog's history or training: the part that was helped specifically by the Get Connected protocol.

In the Case Histories below, the clients words are in the regular body type and my words are in another font.
So my words will look like this.

This is done so it is easy for readers to distinguish whose voice is currently speaking.

Zoey

Owners: Marguerite and Theresa
Australian Shepherd, female, spayed
DOB: 3/8/2003

Photograph by Marguerite Schrader

Social & Environmental History

- Acquired at 8 weeks of age, from a reputable breeder. Both the mother and father had good temperaments and were being shown.

- Rural neighborhood, wooded.

- Several on-leash walks per day. Obedience and agility training daily, loves to retrieve a tennis ball. Zoey was an only dog for 2 years, but then we got another Aussie, a male, Wyndsor. Zoey goes to group classes regularly, both agility and obedience.

How would you describe your pet's personality? Friendly, cuddly, loves to work, non-fearful, inquisitive, problem-solving, very easily excited and slow to calm down once excited.

Medical History

Normal Medical History in general, with the exception listed below.
Spayed at age 2 1/2 years. Late spay due to being shown in the breed ring and by the daughter, Theresa, in Junior Handling. Zoey was having hormonal problems, low blood counts, etc. so she was spayed.

Education History

How many dogs have you trained? 3, Zoey is the 2nd one.

What is your training experience? I still consider myself a novice to intermediate trainer. I have been showing Zoey in Obedience and Rally for two years, but she is the first dog I have shown.

Do you have any competition titles? Theresa has put many agility titles on Zoey.
AKC: NA, NAJ - UKC AgI - CPE Level 1 Handler
Zoey & I have done obedience: AKC: RN and an ASCA (Australian Shepherd Club) CD.

Age when you started lessons/training with this dog: 8 weeks, in puppy class. Have continued with both group and private lessons for performance events.

How was daily living with this dog? In the house she was fine, easy to housebreak and fun to have around. In basic puppy class obedience she was really good. Learned fast, but was a little over-excited coming into class. Also when coming into the training building, she would get so wound up that she would wiggle and sort of squeal in a high-pitched voice because she was so excited. While glad to see her so happy, it was very irritating. She would do the same kind of thing at home when we started our walks. When we started taking her to shows, she was always a real "hind-brainer," difficult to settle down and get her to concentrate. We spend plenty of time on her training, but she was still over-excited in lots of regular situations where she should have been calm because she was used to them.

How did obedience training go? Zoey is a fast learner, but is easily bored. Also, coming into class it would sometimes take 15 minutes or more for her to settle down enough to work, which causes a great deal of frustration. We reached a training plateau where she was doing okay, but we all felt she could do a lot better, like she wasn't working up to her full potential.

What kind of technique was used? Positive Reinforcement

Anything else you would like to tell me about your dog's training? Zoey is a challenge for a relatively inexperienced trainers, because she pays a lot of "lip service" but then as soon as you are not intensely engaged in getting her to behave she just goes right back to doing whatever she wants to do and being impulsive.

Behavioural History

Can you take food or toys from your dog?. Yes This has never been an issue.

Have you ever been uncomfortable because you thought that your dog might bite you or someone else? Zoey is such a super-friendly dog that we have the opposite problem - she is too friendly and wants to run up and socialize with every person and dog she meets. This is good, sure, but not always appropriate.

List any behaviours that were of concern to you: Zoey is a very hind-brained, too easily excited and too slow to settle down. She is not abnormal in any way, she is just a real handful sometimes. We wish she would be a little easier to control sometimes. We don't mind that she gets excited, but wish she would calm down quicker.
How long had this behaviour been occurring or at what age first observed:
Since late puppyhood.

Has the frequency or the intensity of the occurrence of the behaviour changed since the problem started? We started using the Get Connected protocol seriously and consistently about a year ago, on Brenda's advice. Zoey is getting so she can get control of herself and calms down more quickly. She is also getting older, so maturity is helping, but we noticed a definite "spike" in improvement once we got consistent in applying the Get Connected protocol to daily life.

Presenting Issues (from Brenda's point of view)
Zoey was easily aroused and difficult to calm down once aroused. The clients had been doing Reinforcement training since Zoey was a puppy.

Protocols & Management (Brenda's instructions to the client)
No more barking at the door and barking at the window. When this occurs the clients are to interrupt the behaviour immediately. They may call the dogs, place the dogs on leash and put them in a Down or crate the dogs for a few minutes until they are more easily controlled. An additional strategy is to use the Be Still Switch. These techniques may be used together, alternatively, whatever works for the individual. I do not want the dogs practicing arousal behaviours. Zoey is already easily aroused, she does not need practice. When aroused it is important the clients practice Switching her to a calm emotional state right away.

- Since cookies and Click & Treat were not working and had been used long enough to get whatever results we were going to, the Get Connected protocol will be added to daily training.

- The Get Connected protocol exercises will help to make the handler more aware of treat-giving behaviour and will help the dog to have less dependence on the treats. Zoey is difficult to "fade" off treats and because she is so excitable it is easy for the handler to depend on treats in spite of the handler knowing and using a Reinforcement Schedules reasonably well. This will prepare the dog for times when treats are unavailable or inappropriate.

- Use the Be Still Switch on the Agility Start Line, before Rally and Obedience classes in addition to techniques already in use instead

of relying on treats or physical "holding" of the excited dog.

- Move Into will be used for inattentive behaviour that is difficult to interrupt.

- To gain control when Zoey gets excited and pulls while on leash use Follow The Feel (loose leash walking) technique.

Recheck & Brenda's Conclusions at 30 days

- The owners have been working hard at reducing arousal in the home. They report it is better, but will need continuing work. After teaching the Be Still Switch, clients report Zoey is better on the Agility Start Line (she was breaking the start line) and much calmer while running.

- As an update, the clients are also using some nutritional supplementation of Vitamins C, E and B vitamins. They see a change that this is also helping Zoey cope with stress more appropriately.

- The client is obviously more aware of her own treat-giving behaviour in class, has much better control of Zoey and has the dog under control within seconds using the Be Still Switch. This is in contrast to the five to fifteen minutes of inattentive and over-excited behaviour upon entering class that she had previously.

- The Move Into has given the handler another tool for inattentive behaviour. When inattention is interrupted quickly, before the arousal cycle gets into full swing, Zoey can calm down immediately and go back to work. This exercise gives the handler an additional tool to use with the Back Away, Impulse Control work and Eye Contact work that is already in place.

- I am most pleased with the increased awareness on the handler's part and how much more quickly she reads the dog. Also improved is the owner's proactive behaviour in noticing and gaining control of arousal in the dog.

Owner's Input After Using Protocol

The specific or precipitating reason for using the Get Connected protocol: Positive Reinforcement and frustration reached a plateau. We were doing okay, but well short of performing at a competition.

This added work is simple to do, so you tend to sort of think, well, how will just rubbing my dog's body or displacing her by Moving Into her make any difference? But after we added the Get Connected protocol there was a marked increase in our obedience and agility performance. We also made some changes at home, like not letting her be hyper at the door, which was a big change for us in our way of thinking, but you can really see that the protocol makes a difference, changing our behavior and being more aware of how the dog sees things, and helping Zoey and us to have more fun together.

What Exercises did you use?

- Be Still Switch: I use this one at competitions to get connected with her. She gets very excited at competitions. She used to never look at me when in the ring at an obedience trial. At an agility trial, as soon as she missed a jump, she would start circling the jumps (herding? anxiety?) Since using the body rubs, she works with me at obedience trials, and she hasn't shut down in the agility ring with Theresa. I have used this tool when the dog before us in Rally had a melt down and ran around the ring after grabbing the distraction toy. Zoey got pretty wired and wanted to herd that dog. I was pretty nervous at how wired Zoey was, we had to go in the ring soon. I used the Be Still Cue to get her back into working mode. We went in the ring about 30 seconds after the other dog left and although she was still pretty aroused, Zoey maintained enough to work for me and got a Q. I was pretty proud of her. Before we learned this technique, I wouldn't have had a tool to help me out in that type of situation - food wasn't working.

- Move Into - as long as I persist this helps get Zoey's attention when trying to get her to Heel. Even though she has been carefully and properly trained, she has the habit of looking at me, and then going back to whatever she was doing as soon as I release the pressure. I have had to learn to persist past her "lip service" (or perhaps I should say I am still learning to do this), but when I do persist this technique has really improved her Heeling. As I mentioned above, I really feel the Get Connected protocol has improved the ability for Zoey to perform even when she is in distracting and arousing environments, and is getting excited. Even though she is clearly excited we can get her Front Brain and thinking and performing. We are more aware of where her attention is. we are more aware of her state of arousal, and feel there is something we can now do to affect it. I feel she is maturing, and I think the Get Connected protocol has as much to do with that maturation as her increasing age, because we saw a big improvement spike as soon as we got consistent about using the Get Connected protocol.

- Follow The Feel (Pressure on the collar causes the dog's feet to back up) - helps with walking.

- Walking on a loose leash by teaching "Keep Your Toes Behind My Toes." - helps get her under control at a trial or in public without making a big fuss, or if I do not have cookies readily available.

Which exercises did you feel helped your dog the most? Desensitizing, Move Into

Changes observed after the Connected protocol work: The Get Connected protocol worked when other training did not give us a very big improvement. Zoey would be so hyper, and she would take the treats, she would even hold the Stay we put her in to calm her, but she would lie there whining in frustration and look like she might get up any minute. Sometimes she would lie there for a minute, then just leap up and go after whatever had interested her. She understood the behavior we were asking for, she just would lose control of herself.

The Get Connected protocol gives us tools to use to "get her mind back." She still gets excited, but we can calm her down in a quarter of the time it used to take. This means that we get much less frustrated with her, and so all of us are more comfortable. It feels good to know what to do and to have behaviors installed ahead so they are there when we need them.

She works much better and stays on track better even when she is aroused. There was a big change directly after starting to use the Get Connected protocol.

Changes in General Activity Levels?

Before the Get Connected protocol: Zoey was usually relaxed and normal around home, but would switch to being over-active and hyper fast, like if somebody came to the door. Then it would be hard to control her and get her to calm down.

After the Get Connected protocol: We are more aware of her arousal levels and using the tools of Getting Between or Be Still, or using a Move Into to get her attention on us. Now she calms faster and will stay better when we put her in a down.

Changes In Your Dog & You Interaction?

Was your relationship with your dog ever nervous, tense or did you feel the relationship was under strain? Yes, we loved her, but were puzzled and frustrated with her sometimes. She would train well for a while, then not perform in class or at shows the way she did when at home and relaxed. It's not like we didn't take her out and train her in other areas! We knew she needed to generalize behaviors, but we felt like we were doing everything possible, and it still wasn't always working. The more hyper she got the less attentive she got and the more frustrated I got, which was causing a downward spiral in our training and some tension in the relationship.

After the Get Connected protocol: This protocol gave us many extra tools to get Zoey's attention and get her calm. When she becomes erratic and food isn't working or I am getting "lip service" I can use body work (rubbing her body) like the Be Still Cue, Getting Between her and the distraction, or a Move Into.

Did you ever feel that you were indifferent to your dog or (s)he to you? Yes, Zoey is great with selective hearing and attention! So she would ignore me at trials and at class. When I wanted her to pay attention the most, she was the worst!

After the Get Connected protocol: Now we have lots of tools to help both of us stay in the moment. Because Zoey is easier to control, I get less frustrated. Also having something effective I can use makes me feel less helpless.

Animal reaction to strangers entering the room, noises in the room, being left alone in the room, other pets in the room, etc.: Zoey is still slightly stressed and over-excited when strangers come into the house.

After the Get Connected protocol: This still needs work, but it is improving. Because we have taught Zoey to back off from a dowel, (This is advanced work that is not covered in this volume, but will be in Volume 2) we can now keep one at the door

to help control her if we don't have a leash. We often use a livestock mover, which looks like a plastic oar. These are used to herd livestock through a chute. The "pig paddle" as we jokingly call it, is also often used in herding, to teach the dogs to keep a little more distance between them and the sheep and to direct the dog's movements. You don't hit the dog with it, but tap it on the floor towards them until they back up, then you can praise them and/or toss them a treat. Because she has been practicing over-reactivity at the door for a couple of years, just using a treat and hanging on her collar for dear life was not working. Once we added a second dog it was chaos. She might grab the treat, then still mob the guest, or duck away from us. We know we should get a leash on her, but not everybody was consistent with this and we were just restraining her with the leash anyway, she wasn't learning to control herself like we wanted. We sometimes put her in her crate, and while that protects our guests, the dog doesn't learn anything. Now, with all the understanding of the

"space" stuff it has really helped, because Zoey understands she is not supposed to go by the "pig paddle." Soon we know we will be able to fade the pig paddle and just use our obedience cues to get her to control herself.

Did you notice any adverse changes in your dog's behaviour After the Get Connected protocol? No.

Did you feel your dog was placed under excess stress during this protocol? No

Do you think that this protocol changed any ways that you think and interact with your dog? . We are much more aware of when she is attentive and when she is not, and more pro-active about intervening before she gets too wound up.

Wyndsor

Owner: Dave
Australian Shepherd,
male, castrated
DOB: 2005

Photograph by Marguerite Schrader

Social & Environmental History

- Acquired at 8 weeks of age, from a reputable breeder. Both the mother and father had good temperaments and were being shown.

- Rural neighborhood, wooded.

Several on-leash walks per day. Obedience and agility training daily. Likes to play with a tennis ball and the other family dog, Zoey. Attends group classes regu-

larly, both agility and obedience. (Brenda's note: See Case History for "Zoey," who is the other dog in the household. Dave's wife and daughter were having so much fun with the dogs, so got Wyndsor so he could participate with his own dog.)

How would you describe your pet's personality? Friendly, intelligent, inquisitive but cautious, somewhat fearful sometimes, loves to work, fairly

calm and calms down easily even when excited, very playful and sometimes plays really rough.

Medical History

Normal Medical History in general. He had lived on a farm and had gotten into giardia and coccidia and so we had trouble with loose stools and the parasite infection for a brief time. We castrated him at 9 months old, we were planning to show him in the breed ring, but after a lot of discussion decided performance events were more important to us and his hormonal influences were interfering with training and intellectual activity. We decided we didn't want to deal with having an intact male, so we castrated him.

Education History

How many dogs have you trained? 3, Wyndsor is the 3rd one. Our family participated in the training of all 3 dogs. Theresa, my daughter, and Marguerite, my wife, train Zoey.

What is your training experience? Novice to intermediate trainer. As a family we have learned quite a bit and have been showing.

Do you have any competition titles? Yes, CPE Level 1 Handler

Age when you started lessons/training with this dog: 8 weeks, in puppy class.

How was daily living with this dog? Wyndsor is very different from Zoey, maybe because he is a male. There were plenty of issues with who was in control (typical adolescent behavior) and he was physically more rough in many ways. My wife, Marguerite, who doesn't like to rough-house with the dogs, found this mildly alarming. He would jump on all of us, and did a lot of herding behavior using us as substitute sheep. He was skittish about being touched and goofy about stepping on moving boards or high things, a bit of a problem because I got him so I could run agility. He was fearful of new situations and objects. This bothered our instructor a lot, I know.

How did obedience training go? He learned basic obedience well. Marguerite, my wife does his obedience training and I do the agility training. He is attentive in obedience and what our instructor calls a "plodding" learner - slow but steady. It takes a few more repetitions than our other dog, Zoey, but once he has it he retains it well and is very reliable.

What kind of technique was used? Positive Reinforcement

Anything else you would like to tell me about your dog's training? Because of Wyndsor's spooky behavior we started using the Get Connected protocol early in his life: Rubbing his body, desensitizing him to all kinds of touch, and using Move Into to control his pushy behavior.

Behavioural History

Can you take food or toys from your dog?. Yes This has never been an issue.

Have you ever been uncomfortable because you thought that your dog might bite you or someone else? No, he does some grabbing at us when we run agility sometimes when he gets excited and starts with herding stuff, but we can easily distract him by Moving Into him or having him lie down. This has improved a lot since we started with him.

List any behaviours that were of concern to you. How long had this behaviour been occurring or at what age first observed:
Fear of new objects, which we noticed to be very prominent at about 12 weeks of age.
Over-sensitivity to being touched, leaned over, moved toward, which was observable right from the start.
He wanted to be in charge and was very pushy, and this started at 5 to 6 months old, adolescence.

Has the frequency or the intensity of the occurrence of the behaviour changed since the problem started? Fear of new objects: got worse around 6 to 8 months, and has improved steadily ever since.
Over-sensitivity to being touched, leaned over, moved toward. Improved a little after the parasite problem was solved. He wanted to be in charge and was very pushy. This is very infrequent now.

Presenting Issues (from Brenda's point of view)

This dog was quite a cautious puppy and very spooky. This worried me much more than it did the clients. I knew Dave wanted to do agility and this puppy was sometimes very cautious about approaching objects and footing. Also, as an adolescent (herding dog) he was displaying a lot of leaping,

body slamming and open mouth punches when Dave was working him in agility.

Protocols & Management (Brenda's instructions to the client)

- While Dave doesn't mind giving treats and does use treats more appropriately than most of my clients (he doesn't give too many), like many men, I felt the Get Connected protocol exercises would fit his training style well.

- Be Still Cue, as well as further desensitization using similar technique. This will build trust between the dog and handler, necessary in a dog of this temperament if he is to be able to do performance events. This will also alleviate his extreme body sensitivity.

- This dog is much calmer than Zoey, their other dog. Honestly I was quite intrigued to see how these two dogs of very different temperaments would respond to the Get Connected exercises.

- Because Wyndsor is so spooky, I wanted to make sure Dave was very aware of this dog's body language. When you teach the Be Still Switch and the Move Into exercises you must be very sensitive to the "feel" of the dog and to reading body language. I knew by teaching these exercises Dave would learn a lot about reading his dog.

- The Move Into exercise for teaching the dog about personal space. For the jumping and inappropriate mouthing when playing, Dave could use Move Into. Merely having the dog Down, which does work with some dogs, was not working well with this dog.

- Gaining control when Wyndsor gets excited and pulls while on leash will be accomplished by using the loose leash walking techniques: Follow The Feel and Move Into.

Recheck & Brenda's Conclusions at 30 days

- Much improved with the body sensitivity.

- Approaching the teeter totter better.

- Handler has improved control when the dog is body slamming during agility.

- Wife also likes the Move Into because when she walks him she has a tool to calm him down

quickly (Be Still Switch) and when he gets playing too rough on walks she can use a Move Into.

- Improved handler awareness.

- I am glad we started with the Be Still exercises and Move Into exercises very early with this puppy. It really helped get us all through the fear periods that occur developmentally.

Owner's Input After Using Protocol

Was there a specific or precipitating reason for using the Get Connected protocol? We wanted more control and were worried that he would have hyper behavior and be easily distracted like our other dog. When Brenda told us her worry about his cautious behavior we started this work within a few weeks of getting Wyndsor.

What Exercises did you use?

- Be Still Cue

- Further desensitization with other objects

- Move Into

- Follow The Feel (Pressure on the collar causes the dog's feet to back up)

- Walking on a loose leash by teaching "Keep Your Toes Behind My Toes."

- Desensitization to footing and new objects - we would rub the new objects on his body, using the same technique as using our hand. Lots of Approach & Retreat towards agility equipment, poles on the ground, etc.

Which exercises did you feel helped your dog the most?

- Desensitizing - Wyndsor was sensitive to touch, especially in the hindquarters. Just touching him and using treats, or the regular grooming wasn't making a huge difference, he kind of tolerated it, but was still not great. Using the Be Still Cue and Rubbing his body all over, using Approach & Retreat technique, has gotten him over this sensitivity. This technique has also helped us get him over some of the skittishness he had about new objects.

- Move Into - This really helped him start respecting our movement and the need to pay attention to us when walking.

- Follow The Feel - Again, this really helped him pay more attention to us. We can move him anywhere with the slightest pressure now, and he never flinches or worries about it.

All of these exercises have helped with training him for the Stand For Exam in Obedience, as well as for interacting with him in daily life. We have better control of him on walks. He is doing better in performance sports (Rally and Agility so far). We are using these techniques at home to get better control over him when people come to the house. He stands calmly when being examined by the veterinarian. He accepts grooming without difficulty.

These are now the tools we use first to get control over him. Rather than try to beg him to behave or bribe him with treats, we use the Be Still Cue and Move Into until he pays attention to us. Wyndsor can calm himself down quickly once we get his attention.

All of these exercises helped immensely with a lively adolescent dog during icy, potentially dangerous winter walks!

Changes observed after Get Connected protocol work: This protocol improved Wyndsor's fearful, spooky behavior almost immediately. We were glad we already started this work before that 2nd fear period set in, because we feel it lessened the impact considerably. He is much better with touch, and we use the Be Still cue frequently, both to calm him and to maintain the desensitization. He is much more respectful now, the castration helped on that too. The protocol though, gave us tools to control him well when he was pushy so we got the full behavioral benefit from castration and didn't have a lot of old habits to break, once he was castrated we could just move ahead a lot faster. The protocol helped a lot with the footing issues, like the teeter totter. We used plenty of Positive Reinforcement, but the Get Connected protocol helped Wyndsor understand that he might as well get the job done, because we weren't going to let his spooky behavior run the show. When he would get fearful, we could use rubbing his body to calm him down (Brenda's note: the Be Still Cue), and we could check stress levels by gauging how much he was moving into pressure. It gave us tools to know when to insist and when to give him a break. With a fearful dog you don't want to let them think that their fear means they get to run away from everything, we would have never gotten him on the equipment. And when he is super stressed, he

wouldn't take food, he just wanted to back away from everything, so wouldn't go close enough to the equipment to even learn about it. If we have to go really slow, fine, but I also didn't think he needed to be so scared that he wouldn't even try and he needed to trust me. The Get Connected protocol helped establish good boundaries and trust.

More respect at home. More trust, so he counts on me and doesn't have to be scared of silly things. Better control and enhanced performance in sports.

Changes In General Activity Levels?

Before the Get Connected protocol: When Wyndsor was in familiar surroundings he was okay, but even then if new things happened he was slightly apprehensive, and cautious.

After the Get Connected protocol. He is more confident. Sure some of it is the exposure to the big wide world, but HOW you expose the dog has a big effect. The protocol helped us to handle new situations so Wyndsor learned what we wanted him to.

Changes In Your Dog & You Interaction?

Was your relationship with your dog ever nervous, tense or did you feel the relationship was under strain? Not really, I was more concerned about him being too rough and pushy with Marguerite.

After the Get Connected protocol: Teaching him to respect personal space helps him deal with everybody, not just our family. He greets politely now.

Animal reaction to strangers entering the room, noises in the room, being left alone in the room, other pets in the room, etc.: At home when people come to the door or there is a lot of noise and people, he is a little tense. He barks and is aroused until he knows the intruder.

After the Get Connected protocol: We have not worked as hard at this as we should

Did you notice any adverse changes in your dog's behaviour After the Get Connected protocol? No

Did you feel your dog was placed under excess stress during this protocol? No

Ben

Owner: Sharon
Golden Retriever
male, castrated
DOB: 2003

Photograph by David L. Whitfield Photography

Social & Environmental History

- I bred Ben and have had him since birth. I worked with the parents and grandparents. No other puppies from these lines have not had Ben's personality quirks.

- Suburban neighborhood, wooded.

- Ben gets plenty of exercise and he also runs on the treadmill and plays ball. I own a boarding kennel and training center and Ben goes to work with me almost every day. He spends the day in my office, as he has since puppyhood. He has had more than usual socialization with people and with dogs.

How would you describe your pet's personality? Friendly, cautious, fearful and reactive.

Medical History

Normal Medical History. I kept him intact until age 2 for health benefits. Then I had him castrated because of his reactivity. I knew at this point that he would not ever be used for breeding. After careful consideration and on Brenda's recommendation, and involvement of my veterinarian, Ben takes Fluexotine to reduce his anxiety.

Education History

How many dogs have you trained? 10 of my own.

What is your training experience? I am an experienced trainer. I have instructed and helped clients with behavior problems with their dogs for many years, now. As mentioned, I own two boarding kennels and a training center. At our training facility we have board and train options, grooming and do over thirty group classes every week, from puppy to advanced obedience and agility.

Do you have any competition titles? I have placed many competition titles on dogs, including UDX (AKC Utility Dog Excellent) and OTCH (AKC Obedience Trial Champion).

Age when you started lessons/training with this dog: 7 weeks, in puppy class. Plus all the training and handling and socializing I have done with him since he was born.

How was daily living with this dog? Hectic. He was an over-active puppy, who was constantly looking for something to fixate on. He was obsessive - just taking him out to potty was work, as he would grab rocks and sticks and leaves frantically. When you tried to take things away he would swallow them or try to. It was a never-ending battle.

How did obedience training go? I was not horribly pleased with Ben's progress. He did not generalize behaviors well. He was reactive in busy environments even though he had been around different environments plenty.

What kind of technique was used? Positive Reinforcement, lots of shaping work as a puppy.

Anything else you would like to tell me about your dog's training? Ben remembers things that happen outside of training and carries it into training. For instance, if you stepped on his paw or tail accidentally at home he would not want to get into heel position at all, and it would take additional work to get back to square one. He has always been super body sensitive, especially his ears and his rear or around his tail. Even though I did lots of handling him and grooming and know what I am doing, he still would be agitated easily when handled.

Behavioural History

Can you take food or toys from your dog?. Yes. We worked on lots of trades and he has never been aggressive towards me.

Have you ever been uncomfortable because you thought that your dog might bite you or someone else? I worried that when Ben was in his reactive outer-space state that he would bite just because he was so aroused and didn't seem aware of what was going on. He just couldn't think.

List any behaviours that were of concern to you. How long had this behaviour been occurring or at what age first observed:
The biggest concern, especially since I wanted to do competition obedience with Ben, was his reactivity and growling at other dogs. He would do this if other

dogs in the area looked out of control or startled him by running up on him from the rear. He didn't like other dogs running up into his face either. This started at a very young age, about four weeks old I noticed it even at home with dogs he knew well.

One of the reasons that I had contacted Brenda for help was because we had an "incident." I had Ben in the training area and one of the people did not have her dog under control. I was standing there feeding Ben a treat. The dog was loose and broad sided Ben, which really startled Ben. It also hurt him. Ben whirled around and snapped at this dog. After this incident it seemed like all my previous hard work was gone. He became very fearful of all other dogs. He would growl and was becoming ever more reactive around other dogs. He couldn't even see this dog that had run into him, his hackles would go up and he would carry his tail high and stiff.

Presenting Issues (from Brenda's point of view)

Ben was displaying panic attacks and defensive behaviour after a trauma-related incident. This is an extremely well-socialized and well-trained dog. Sharon's dogs are, in fact, better trained than my own. Because I know how dogs respond normally to the Get Connected protocol, I can use the teaching of the exercises as part of an evaluation as well as a protocol to modify behaviour. This dog had a very extreme reaction to one trauma. We had determined he would likely need medication, but as I tell clients, behavioural medication will not train your dog, it will just make behaviour modification possible. Ben was extremely body sensitive, to a degree that is abnormal. He displayed inappropriate anxiety, particularly for his degree of training. The experience level of his handler makes a difference, too. This is a very experienced and savvy dog handler, and Ben was still sometimes difficult to handle. Ben was hyper-aware of personal space. Ben has displayed abnormal behaviours, pica specifically, since puppyhood. He also displays possessive aggression (resource guarding).

Protocols & Management (Brenda's instructions to the client)
- We did five consecutive days of work because Sharon lives 13 hours away.
- Sharon is a very ethical person, and it was interesting to note that other puppies from

the same bloodlines did not have the issues Ben does. Sharon, in fact, kept Ben out of the litter because she had concerns about his behaviour from the very beginning and took responsibility for him by keeping him.

- Ben is very spooky in some situations. Sharon is to make sure that Ben felt safe and like she was "taking care of the environment" so he will not have to. When people approach, particularly with dogs, Sharon could use a Back Away to gain more space or she could Get Between Ben and the approacher.

- Ben was extremely body sensitive, to an abnormal degree. We did a lot of desensitization and body work, including the Be Still Switch. When handlers learn about when to apply and release different kinds of pressure, they can begin to influence the dogs reactivity more effectively. Some of the body work was done with hands and some was done with a dowel. Ben was, at first, terrified of the dowel and extremely reactive in regards to it. After one thirty minute session, he was much improved and after that got much less reactive about other kinds of touch as well.

- Working on the Follow The Feel will help Ben think instead of react when he feels panicky. This will prevent a tight leash causing further frustration and arousal.

- Move Into will help teach Ben about personal space, alleviating anxiety.

- Walking properly on a loose leash will promote impulse control and also help Ben feel safer because he knows Sharon is controlling the environment for him.

- Ben should not be allowed to reactive and bark in the office, or rush to the door.

- Incidents of resource guarding will be carefully monitored and interrupted. A Get Between and other Impulse Control type exercises will be used. Toys that are "too valuable" and likely to cause reactivity will be picked up, at least temporarily. As the dog feels the handler is more relevant and is more relaxed about personal space I expect this to become improved and easily manageable.

- Ben displays extreme anxiety and through previous consultations and working through a veterinarian, had been placed on medication.

The medication had been started (just over 30 days) when we began the Get Connected protocol. The client had already seen some improvement in behaviour with the medication.

Recheck & Brenda's Conclusions at 30 days

- After 5 days of concentrated sessions, Ben had made vast improvements.

- A couple of the sessions were intense when working on body sensitivity. Ben would begin to get panicky and Sharon was amazing and level-headed through this process. With quiet persistence from the handler he would calm down. By the end of two thirty minute sessions he was improved beyond my expectations. This could not have been accomplished without the handler maintaining calmness when the dog became agitated.

- The Be Still Switch changed Ben's paradigm about touch and personal space, making him much more comfortable. He was able to maintain a Front Brain, thinking state in situations where he was displaying panic. I am most pleased with the effect of this exercise as it started the snowball rolling and all subsequent exercises went smoothly.

- Once the panic attacks are under control with behaviour modification and with management he will do just fine at performance events.

- The relationship between Sharon and Ben was good to begin with, but I was pleased to see improvements. Ben relaxed more when Sharon made it clear that she was taking care of him in a way that he understood.

- Not allowing Ben to get in front of Sharon and pull made observable differences in how attentive Ben was, therefore he was encouraged to use Sharon as an emotional anchor to a greater degree. Increased handler awareness of how crucial this was for Ben made the dog more trusting and the handler more relevant.

- Once Sharon got home, she reported that she made the changes we discussed about Ben's daily arousal levels (they were to be interrupted and minimized). This meant changes in the office where Ben spent a good deal of his time. He was vastly improved.

- Use of Negotiation and Calming Signals increased immediately upon beginning the Get Connected exercises. This is always an excellent sign - it means the dog is responding instead of reacting. Use of signals such as Shake Offs and increased use of Lip Licking is an indication the dog is working hard to maintain Front Brain state. This means, by extension, he is burning the neural pathways and opening learning channels.

- Update: Approximately three weeks after Sharon went home she called me with some excellent news: Ben had entered his first Obedience Trial and got his first legs towards his CD (AKC Companion Dog title). At the Golden Retriever Specialty he got a 195 and a 198.5 which garnered her a 1st place. Sharon had been concerned about other handlers at the show getting their dogs too close to Ben and causing him to be reactive. She was pleased to report that with the exercises we had done he was much calmer than she had expected him to be. She was able to use all of the exercises at the show at one time or another to make Ben feel safe and to maintain a Front Brain, thinking state. I was so thrilled to hear this news, as it exceeded my expectations. In October he got his Rally Novice title and completed his AKC CD. Sharon and Ben got a WC (Water Certificate) from the Golden Retriever Club for water and land retrieves. Ben got his AKC Jr. Hunter title, too. Sharon plans on beginning Tracking with Ben, next.

Owner's Input After Using Protocol

Was there a specific or precipitating reason for using the Get Connected protocol? Brenda's methods have worked in the past. I felt stuck in a rut and wanted help to get me and my dog back into a good working relationship. I love my dog and it was hard to see him distressed about everyday things. I know the meds help too, but there was a marked difference after the protocol even though he had already been started on the fluexotine.

What Exercises did you use?
- Be Still Cue
- Further desensitization with other objects
- Move Into

- Follow The Feel (Pressure on the collar causes the dog's feet to back up)
- Walking on a loose leash by teaching "Keep Your Toes Behind My Toes."

Which exercises did you feel helped your dog the most?.
- Be Still Cue

- Desensitizing - This helped Ben immensely. He was so odd about things touching him. After we could rub his body all over we got out the dowel. Ben got really upset, but we kept working with him until he got over his fear. Even though we were approximating slowly, he would get to a certain point and want to panic. We would keep using the Be Still cue to calm him and after about 20 minutes of Approach And Retreat we could rub his body all over with the dowel. It was amazing how fast he got calm once he understood that we were not going to give up and that nothing was hurting him. He was less worried about approaches from the rear after this and was using a Shake Off much more frequently, which you could see helped him get rid of his stress. I praised him every time he used a calming signal.

- Move Into - This helped Ben with his worry about being bumped. Once he understood more about personal space, he relaxed more even around me and looked more comfortable, like he actually had more control of what was going on.

- Follow The Feel - This was another really difficult exercise for Ben. His opposition reflex is so bizarre and strong that the slightest touch or pressure would make him push into the feel of the pressure or pull on the collar in a really extreme way and he would get more agitated. Now he knows how to "follow the feel." This does take sensitivity on the trainer's part, to learn when to apply and when to release pressure to help the dog understand.

Ben was one of those dogs that did beautiful competition Heel work, but when you walked him on a leash he had a tendency to lunge sometimes or pull really hard on you suddenly. Once we worked him with a dowel for walking, teaching him to keep his toes behind mine, he got a lot more aware of where I was in relationship to where he was. He stopped being so reactive about the environment and paid a lot more attention to me, which is nice and more comfortable for both of us.

We also changed some of the things that I do at the office, like when he runs up to the half door, barking wildly and excited to see people who visit. I had tried already to just call him back and give him a treat, but if I wasn't prompt about calling him or I wasn't there, he was still aroused and hard to calm down. I did a Get Between (getting between Ben & the door) for a couple of weeks and now he is calmer. I was kind of surprised after that when people came up to the door, he would actually remain playing with some of his toys and not even bark when people came up to the door. He approached visitors more calmly too.

Changes observed after Get Connected protocol work: After a week of intensive work with Brenda, we returned home. Once we were home I continued the protocol with Ben, we really kept at it. After a couple more weeks of work other people that have been around Ben a lot started making comments like, "What is going on with Ben? He just seems like a different dog." I was so happy about this. Ben was already trained through Utility when the incident above happened, which was in October of 2006. Ben & I went to see Brenda in January of 2007. In February Ben was doing so well and he had even been around the dog he was particularly defensive with that I took him to a Rally trial, figuring if he got reactive I would just leave. He did super! Not one reactive move, he was calmer than I thought he would be and worked really well. A couple of weeks later, I took him to an obedience trial. Again, he did not display his prior nervousness or reactivity. We got a 198 1/2 on one day and a 2nd place. The following day he got another good score and another leg on his AKC CD. I am so happy, I really thought at one point that after all the hard work Ben & I had done that it would not be possible to even show him at all. I know that Ben will always be extra work and that he is not a "normal" dog. But we have certainly done a lot with what we have!

Changes In General Activity Levels?

Before the Get Connected protocol: Overactive.

After the Get Connected protocol: Quieter, more attentive to me. Accepts and copes with stressful situations much more easily.

Changes In Your Dog & You Interaction?

Was your relationship with your dog ever nervous, tense or did you feel the relationship was under strain? Yes. Ben was extremely frustrating and the reactivity was alarming. I was afraid he would hurt another dog when they bumped him. Other dogs shouldn't be out of control, but it does happen, so your dog has to be prepared to deal with it if you are going to have them out in public and at shows.

After the Get Connected protocol: I feel like I have things I can do now to keep Ben safe and happy. I can control him and he trusts me to do that. Ben has better boundaries which make him feel stable, there is more consistency.

Animal reaction to strangers entering the room, noises in the room, being left alone in the room, other pets in the room, etc.: This was a problem with dogs, but not so much with people. He was nervous, tense and stress was evident.

After the Get Connected protocol: He is now relaxed and looks normal, even in high stress situations like a show.

Did you notice any adverse changes in your dog's behaviour After the Get Connected protocol? No

Did you feel your dog was placed under excess stress during this protocol? No. It's not that Ben didn't get stressed, but he was anyway. There were times when he looked more stressed, but it was short-lived, usually within 15 to 30 seconds of increased stress. The only thing that was longer than that was when we started work with the dowel, (note: this is an advanced desensitization exercise, which will be covered in Volume 2) and interestingly, that was the work that helped him the most in the end, and at the end of that session he gained a lot of confidence. Even starting the protocol during the first session, you could see that the work was relieving Ben's stress.

Do you think that this protocol changed any ways that you think and interact with your dog? Increased awareness of space and how dogs see it helped me to be aware of how important it is for Ben to feel safe and for me to take the steps to make him feel safe. I am very good at being precise about compe-

Ben

tition behaviours and now I am much more clear and precise about the boundaries for everyday living, too.

Duffy

Owner: Lesley
Belgian Sheepdog (Groenendael)
male, castrated
DOB: 2004

Photograph by Lesley Ashworth

Social & Environmental History

- I got Duffy from a reputable breeder when he was 9 weeks old.

- Training and socialization started immediately. I had planned to show Duffy in the breed ring, so left him intact until he was about 18 mo. old. At that point I changed my mind and castrated him, figuring that he would be easier to handle, for one thing, as he wanted to guard me from approaching people and was becoming ever more reactive. Duffy is a very environmentally aware dog, in general.

- Duffy's socialization includes parks, stores, dog camp (at age 12 weeks and 14 months) as well as individual and group classes. Duffy has an excellent understanding of dog language and interacts well with other dogs, and did so when he was intact.

How would you describe your pet's personality? .Reactive at times. Anxious at times. Can be pushy. Very smart and learns quickly. Very loving.

Medical History

Normal Medical History. Fed raw diet.

Education History

How many dogs have you trained? Four of my own dogs. A Border Collie mix and two Belgian Sheepdogs. I also assist and teach group obedience classes.

What is your training experience? I have a good working knowledge of routine and competition dog training.

Do you have any competition titles? My dogs have earned novice companion dog obedience titles in UKC and AKC. Also the AKC CGC (Canine Good Citizenship) and Dog Scouts Of America certifications and badges. Agility titles in UKC and CPE groups. Pack Dog titles. I have also competed in Open Competition obedience as well as drafting and weight pulling competitions.

Age when you started lessons/training with this dog: His training started one hour after I picked him up from the breeder.

How was daily living with this dog? Very good. But demanding of attention at times. Disliked being home alone. Psycho barking at the front window at foot traffic on the sidewalk. At first hated being crated,

Duffy 333

but was good with training and once I fed all his meals in his crate.

How did obedience training go? Very well. Great attention. Loves to work. I was so happy with his progress and he was very smart.

What kind of technique was used? Positive Reinforcement, Clicker training. We added the Get Connected protocol work.

Anything else you would like to tell me about your dog's training? Duffy still did not like to be held down or restrained in any way. Plus my other dog and he would bark at the window with any type of movement outside. Duffy was constantly trying to protect me from approaching people.

Behavioural History

Can you take food or toys from your dog?. Yes he does guard food and toys. With early training and management I can take anything away from him under all circumstances now.

Have you ever been uncomfortable because you thought that your dog might bite you or someone else? Yes, because of his reactivity and lunging I was very concerned. He would lunge at people approaching us or if we were already in a building and someone entered the area.

List any behaviours that were of concern to you. How long had this behaviour been occurring or at what age first observed: Lunging toward people when he was on leash. It started around 6 months of age. And even though I worked with handling him, he still hated any kind of restraint, and wasn't all that fond of being touched unless it was under certain circumstances that he made the decision.

Has the frequency or the intensity of the occurrence of the behaviour changed since the problem started? As he got older, the problem increased as he moved through adolescence. It was more intense and he seemed to be ever more anxious.

Presenting Issues (from Brenda's point of view)

Duffy was becoming ever more reactive, even though Lesley had been training him using Positive Reinforcement techniques from day one. This was alarm-ing to the client and to me. Even though Lesley lives approximately 2 hours away, I had been working with them since Duffy was a puppy. As the dog entered that 12 month to 18 month developmental period, he became ever more reactive. Because he is from a breed that displays guarding behaviour, one would expect to see it, but it was his lack of respect for his owner that concerned me. He was also body sensitive to an extreme degree, even though he had been handled extensively since puppyhood. Through additional questioning I discovered that he had become impossible to control at the door and he was manic about any people or dogs passing by on the street outside. This is problematic for me because he is constantly practicing arousal and inappropriate guarding behaviour.

Protocols & Management (Brenda's instructions to the client)

- The first thing to change is the reactivity at the door. The protocol for "Wait At The Door" and "Territory Entry and Appropriate Greeting Behaviours" from *Aggression In Dogs* will be followed. Basically, the dog will be worked on endless Down Stays in the area around the door, where people enter "territory." The client is to knock on the door from the inside. This will elicit the reactivity so Lesley can practice getting Duffy calm. The client is to begin this work on leash and knock on the door, then have Duffy lie down and Stay. After this is accomplished helpers can knock on the door from the outside, until Duffy can remain calm through the entire procedure: one or two alarm barks might be allowed initially, but he must quiet down immediately upon request from the handler. Getting this behavior under control is crucial to improving the overall behaviour of this dog. She will eventually use a Get Between instead of the leash to control the dog if required.

- Get Between to teach Duffy that approachers are under Lesley's control and none of his business.

- The dog must not be allowed to be reactive in regards to passers-by on the street. Duffy is constantly practicing being aroused at the visual cue of people and dogs. When away, cut down on the visual stimulation by blocking windows with blinds or curtains or taping cardboard up temporarily until the owner has

better control. If the dog tears at the curtains or blinds prevent access to the area with baby gates or other appropriate barriers. The dog may be crated in another area if that works out better. When the owner is home, training can occur. The dog should be allowed access both physically and visually to the window. Whenever Duffy goes to the window the owner will use a Get Between. If Duffy refuses to pay attention to her and she cannot catch him to put him on leash, she will use an animal mover, such as we use in herding to teach the dogs to stay off the sheep. This is shaped like an oar and has a long handle. The dog is first desensitized to the animal mover so he is not afraid of it. This animal mover will give Lesley a 'longer arm' when needed. The dog is never to be hit or frightened with the animal mover, but it is to be placed between Duffy and the window, by tapping it on the floor. She must be persistent and consistent. Duffy may be given a treat if he comes away from the window when called or stops barking and follows the owner away from the area of arousal. A leash may be required to get the dog to come away from the area initially. We did additional work with Duffy to teach him to back up on cue from a dowel. (This is advanced work that is not covered in this volume, but will be in Volume 2.)

- Duffy was body sensitive, to an extreme degree. We did a lot of desensitization and body work, including the Be Still Switch. Body work included desensitization with a dowel and other objects, such as bags, toys - anything that could be held against his body. This dog needs to have his confidence built up so he is not so inclined to be defensive (the lunging behaviour is defensive and fear-based, not confident behaviour).

- Working on the Follow The Feel will help Duffy by preventing a tight leash, which is causing further frustration and arousal.

- Move Into will help teach Duffy about personal space, alleviating his reactivity about having his personal space invaded.

- Walking properly on a loose leash will promote impulse control. It will increase his respect for Lesley and make her more relevant. If required, we will add directing the dog's movement with a dowel and using the dowel as a Get Between if

Lesley cannot get there efficiently. (This kind of dowel work is advanced and will be covered in Volume 2.)

- Lesley will have to change the way she lives with this dog on a daily basis if she wishes to gain control over him. She should be particularly aware of personal space and never allow this dog to violate her personal space by jumping up (unless he is cued to do so) or to come up and solicit attention by poking his nose at her or by coming over and laying his head on her and demanding attention. He may come near her and if she invites him into her space with a specific cue (it may be body language or verbal) he may lay his head on her and get attention and petting. Lesley must determine when she is done petting and not just mindlessly pet Duffy just because he is near her. If Duffy puts a foot on her during "loving" sessions Lesley should stand up and use a Move Into to remind him that she occupies and is controlling space.

Recheck & Brenda's Conclusions at 30 days

- After two weeks of work on all the exercises at home and preventing arousal in the house at all costs, Lesley reports that Duffy is like a different dog. I encouraged Lesley to get him back out on the street and visiting pet stores and taking him back into group classes, activities which she had been curtailing until she had better control of Duffy.

- After 30 days Lesley says that Duffy is so much improved her confidence in handling him has returned. She feels that she has several tools that are effective. His body sensitivity is much reduced. When she brought him to the training center I was pleased to note that his reactivity if someone walked into the room had changed drastically - now Duffy turns to Lesley immediately. If there is a reaction, it is more of a glance at the door, and Duffy is easily interrupted. Duffy is more attentive to Lesley, and she reports that during the day (Lesley is a nurse and works swing shift and sleeps during the day) she is able to sleep uninterrupted now. The first couple of weeks Duffy would still erupt at the window. After the first week she could quiet and calm him by getting up and using a Get Between and the animal mover was required. By week two she could interrupt Duffy with a verbal call off. By week 3 he would bark once, then stop himself. By week four he was remaining non-reactive. I am very pleased with this, and Lesley is getting caught up on her sleep.

- Lesley has improved vastly in a couple of areas. One is she verbalizes much less, allowing Duffy to read her body language better. She is "helping" less, allowing Duffy to figure things out for himself. Lesley has much more confidence and smoothness in her handling. She looks in charge now, making Duffy feel safer in any environment. She has also taught Duffy that she will stand in and take control.

- Duffy's walking on a loose leash is lovely. Lesley reports it took about two weeks of Follow The Feel and we also did dowel work to get this jump started. (loose leash walking using a dowel is covered in Volume 2).

Owner's Input After Using Protocol

Was there a specific or precipitating reason for using the Get Connected protocol? Severe reactivity to novel situations. We had been doing beginning competition level training. Due to the distance I live, I was bringing Kozmo, my other Belgian, and Duffy to Brenda at least a couple of times a month, as well as taking other group classes locally. As Duffy was getting older, he was getting increasingly reactive. In general, I was pleased, Duffy had pretty good attention and freely offers up behaviors which is the fun part of training.

We went to a clinic at Brenda's facility. Duffy seemed very agitated at all the other dogs in "his" place, and was barking when people came in. He and I were sitting in an area common to this kind of clinic, where we were sort of hemmed in by other chairs and crates. He was reactive and hard to get control of, and actually lunged at a lady walking by. Luckily she had a problem dog herself and was so understanding, but this terrified me. He had been a little reactive, but my hopes of ever showing him were looking like they would never come true. I talked to Brenda and we worked out a management plan to keep in place while we were training. This long heart-to-heart talk was extremely difficult for both Brenda and myself. During this "come to Jesus" meeting, Brenda pointed out that Duffy had plenty of training, in fact a lot more than most dogs get. He had been socialized constantly and his compe-

tition training was coming along nicely. The one element that seemed to be left out was that Duffy chose to go his own way or got reactive whenever he got a little frustrated. Brenda said there was either something horribly wrong with the dog or with the relationship between us. Okay, I will say it - there was a lack of respect for the handler.

What Exercises did you use?
- Be Still Cue
- Additional desensitization
- Move Into
- Follow The Feel (Pressure on the collar causes the dog's feet to back up)
- Walking on a loose leash by teaching "Keep Your Toes Behind My Toes."

Which exercises did you feel helped your dog the most?.
All of the exercises were helpful. The body work and yielding to pressure were the best. Duffy did not like to be touched at all. After using the exercises using pressure, others as well as myself can handle any part of Duffy's body. Duffy was walking on a loose leash within a week and half - and I don't have to remember to always carry treats with me to get good behavior. He now responds to any light pressure on his collar, following the direction of the pressure instead of becoming ever more frustrated and reactive. The body work is very effective in potentially stressful situations. It keeps Duffy in the mind set to work and to look to me for guidance and leadership decisions.

- Desensitizing - The first exercise was body work. We started with long relaxing strokes along his body. Duffy responded by being stiff. This continued until he started to show signs of relaxing. Previously, as a puppy, Duffy did not like to be touched or held/restrained. We started with the shoulder area and hip area on both sides of his body.

- Next we used the Follow The Feel exercise. Pressure was applied with the finger tips in stages from light to firm to Duffy's chest. When he moved away from pressure, it was immediately released. At first he would just push back, but within three repetitions he was "following the feel" and moving off the pressure on the second level, another couple of repetitions and when you touched his chest lightly, he would back

right up. Just a couple of steps at first, then several. Soon Duffy would respond calmly to a light touch on his fur. This sensitizing and desensitizing to touch and pressure did amazing things. It seems like such a simple and obvious exercise, but you could see some changes in Duffy right away. He started to think when we touched him instead of reacting with opposition. Now he was trying to figure out what the touch meant instead of arguing before he even knew what he was arguing about.

• Then we added pressure to the collar, pressure to the chest, so Duffy would learn that any pressure on his collar means: Back away from the pressure, or follow the feel of the pressure, don't just pull harder. This ended up helping Duffy and me with two problems: frustration whenever the leash got tight and making him more reactive and walking on a loose leash.

• Loose leash walking was a problem. Even though I had tried to gradually fade Duffy off the treats for loose leash walking, we still had problems with this. There were times when it didn't matter if I had treats, anyway. When Duffy was reactive he would ignore the treats, not wanting them. If Duffy got stressed or even a little nervous, he didn't want treats and was not interested in working for them at all.

• We started with Duffy on the leash and teaching him to move when I moved and stop when I stopped, and also giving him a definite "target" on my body. So he could understand what we wanted. If his toes passed my toes there was a "penalty." This never, ever included any collar pops, raised voices or even expressing any kind of disapproval. The penalty is carried out with an attitude of, "Here, let me help you get into position." It worked like this: If Duffy moved ahead of my feet, I would shorten the leash, smoothly without jerking at all, and turn and step directly toward his head until he backed up a couple of steps. Then I would stop my feet and see if he stopped his feet. Then I would turn my body back in the direction we were originally going. If Duffy still kept his feet still, I would tell him he was a good boy. When I moved my feet to go forward, he could move his feet. If he moved his feet before I was ready, I would repeat the whole procedure again. In a private lesson, he caught on to this very quickly, and soon I didn't even have

to wiggle my leash, he just stopped his feet when I stopped mine.

• (Note: the work described in this paragraph is advanced work and is covered in Volume 2 in detail.) Next we used a dowel. I held the dowel in my right hand. We would walk forward and before I wanted to stop, I would turn my body toward Duffy, then stop. If Duffy's toes passed my toes, I would tap the dowel on the floor. First tap at my right side, second tap in front of me, third tap in front of Duffy. Of course he tried to bite the dowel. But I just kept tapping, now towards his toes. I touched his toes lightly with the dowel and just kept on, lightly but relentlessly tapping no matter what Duffy did. It seemed like forever the first time, but probably lasted about 15 seconds, and then he moved his toe slightly back. I immediately "holstered" the dowel, that is put it back by my right side and used my verbal Marker. Duffy learned within two repetitions that the best place for his toes was behind my toes. Within two weeks of doing this exercise, no matter where we were or what was going on, Duffy was walking beautifully on a loose lead. I no longer needed the dowel at all, a wiggle reminded him. When ever he goes ahead of my toes, the leash wiggles. He quickly backs into position. It is important to understand the dowel work. You never, ever hit the dog or act angry with him. You do not want the dog afraid of anything in your hands, you want the dog to understand the behavior and to also understand that once a behavior is learned there will be consequences for not minding.

At home Duffy would still lunge and bark at things in the neighborhood (cars, joggers, people walking by the house, etc.). The plan was to stop him practicing this reactive behavior so I could have more control of Duffy out on the street. It starts at home and how you live with your dog every day. Every time Duffy barked, I would enter the room and get between him and the window and with a pig paddle tap the floor. *Again, never hit your dog!* The pig paddle is a big object that you can use to get the dog's attention, more by distracting them and interfering with them being totally immersed in whatever they are barking at. It is not a tool to abuse your dog! Before I would enter the room I would say "Quit it!" Then I would come into the room, tapping the pig paddle on the floor and getting between Duffy and the window. I just concentrated on being a pain in his butt, getting in his way so he couldn't bark and jump at the window undisturbed. I never touched Duffy at all. This out of his head barking at the window had been going on forever. Nothing had worked, and I had tried teaching the word "quiet" and distracting him with treats, crating him (rather dragging him to his crate because he would act like such a goofball). Within a couple of weeks Duffy was not screaming at the window anymore. As well as "sensitizing" him to the pig paddle, I made it a point to desensitize Duffy to the pig paddle being rubbed on his body, just like it was my hand. I did not want him afraid of the pig paddle. I wanted him to understand that his behaviour caused the pig paddle - and me! - to act differently. He understood that his barking would make me act unpredictable and weird to stop his fun.

I worked night shift at the time, and when I was trying to sleep, now if I heard Duffy start I could just yell "Quit it" from the bedroom and he would just stop. This was awesome. I was getting uninterrupted sleep. The ultimate test was when the UPS man came to the door, knocked and rang the door bell. Duffy did not bark. I was floored. This was great. Duffy came over and sat next to me. This gave me a chance to jack pot him with praise and treats for his excellent response. He stayed in place while *I* handled the transaction instead of mobbing the door.

We still practice a lot of self control and attention work. He is working under a fair amount of distraction now and maintaining good attention, such as on the street in the neighborhood, at the pet store and in group classes and walks in the park with our friends and their dogs.

Changes observed after Get Connected protocol work: Duffy doesn't lunge anymore when people approach. He looks at me now and has more self control. Over time his anxiety about people approaching me when he is on leash is diminished. He feels confident and looks to me for guidance.

The use of his understanding of my body language and understanding more about space and how we are going to both use it has given him the relief of no longer having to "take charge" of any situation. He no longer lunges when out of the house. He now often voluntarily looks at the handler when he is starting to feel agitated, and before he gets reactive. He is confident (and me too) that I am in charge and will take care of the situation.

Changes In General Activity Levels?

Before the Get Connected protocol: Overactive and particularly the psycho, uncontrollable barking at the window.

After the Get Connected protocol: Much more relaxed and calm. Decreased episodes of anxiety. No barking at the window. If he hears noise or car outside he runs to me and sits. Front Brain 80 percent of the time. Finally.

Changes In Your Dog & You Interaction?

Was your relationship with your dog ever nervous, tense or did you feel the relationship was under strain? Yes, I was always on edge that he would act out of control in public. It was embarrassing and upsetting.

After the Get Connected protocol: Now I have a working partner, a joy to have around. I can control his reactivity if it occurs.

Did you notice any adverse changes in your dog's behaviour after the Get Connected protocol? I have not observed any adverse changes.

Did you feel your dog was placed under excess stress during this protocol? No. In fact, he is more engaged. He starts working with me much faster, and doesn't have to scan the environment and get agitated, then I have to calm him down to work. Now he just starts working right away.

Do you think that this protocol changed any ways that you think and interact with your dog? Yes!!! In many ways. I no longer feel that I cannot handle my dog in stressful situations. I have the skills to handle my dog in ANY situation and am able to remain calm. When I get upset Duffy becomes very anxious and wants to take over. This is potentially dangerous. He now looks to me for security.

Duffy is still very aware of the environment and always will be. But now he no longer has to worry about being in charge and making the wrong choices. His frustration and mine is much lower. I now have the training and the techniques to remain calm and maintain control of whatever comes up.

I now have a working partner and a wonderful pet. A major change in my feelings toward him. Though I loved him, I had thought of returning him to his breeder. Now he and I have great interactions.

The use of his understanding of my body language, use of space, and how I use all this has given him the relief of no longer having to "take charge" of any situation.

He no longer lunges at approachers. He often voluntarily looks at me when he is starting to feel anxious /agitated, and before he gets reactive. He is more confident (and me too) that I am in charge and will take care of the situation and him. He has passed his Canine Good Citizenship test and is preparing for Rally and Novice competition obedience. Yeah!

Beacon

Owner: Jean
Golden Retriever
female, spayed
DOB: 2000

Photograph by Jean Colby

Social & Environmental History

- I got Beacon from a breeder when she was 6 1/2 weeks old.

- Beacon lives in a suburban neighborhood.

- I do therapy work at hospitals and schools with my dogs. Beacon lives with 2 other dogs, both very friendly.

Medical History

The breeder game me some meds for loose stools when I picked her up. Over the next months of her first year, my veterinarian worked with me to control her diarrhea and now, occasional vomiting. I had contacted my breeder about Beacon's condition. I was advised that her litter mates did not have a problem. I was offered a new puppy. I loved Beacon so much, in spite of her tummy troubles, she was a sweet and loving dog. I kept her. Numerous tests were run and rerun with no real questions answered. Various medications, supplements and diet changes were made. We also took Beacon to veterinary specialists, but no one could find anything physically wrong that was causing all of these symptoms. She was put on a venison and potato diet that seemed to work controlling the diarrhea. Beacon had slow weight gain. She also developed pica, eating anything she could, including the other dog's stools. This had to be watched carefully as she would cycle back through her digestive problems.

Education History

How many dogs have you trained? 5 with formal training. Have had dogs my whole life.

What is your training experience? I do therapy work with my dogs. I have trained dogs for several years and consider myself an experienced handler.

Do you have any competition titles? No

Age when you started lessons/training with this dog: 8 weeks old, as soon as we got her.

How was daily living with this dog? tough, she had health problems and behaviour issues, nervousness.

How did obedience training go? Slow.

What kind of technique was used? At first "traditional" methods, using a choke collar. This worked poorly, so I switched to Positive Reinforcement.

Anything else you would like to tell me about your dog's training? Positive Reinforcement worked much better. Beacon is a very "soft" dog and gets upset easily.

Behavioural History

Can you take food or toys from your dog?. Yes. This has never been a problem.

Have you ever been uncomfortable because you thought that your dog might bite you or someone else? No, Beacon is the sweetest dog alive!

List any behaviours that were of concern to you. How long had this behaviour been occurring or at what age first observed: Beacon would get stressed and then not be able to stop being stressed. It mostly showed up with when you tried to teach her things, she would just shut down, even though I was teaching her things very kindly. Also, whenever she got stressed she would have tummy troubles that day to go with it. Very frustrating for both of us.

Has the frequency or the intensity of the occurrence of the behaviour changed since the problem started? We no longer have a problem now. But before, it had sort of reached a plateau.

Presenting Issues (from Brenda's point of view)

Beacon had a history of being anxious, constantly. She fit a diagnosis of Generalized Anxiety. Although she presented as a friendly dog, Jean said that at home she rarely joined in games with her other two Goldens and often went off by herself. This didn't seem to match up with Beacon's friendliness. Jean's other dogs are not rough in play, nor are they impolite or pushy with other dogs, so this seemed odd to me. Beacon also had a history of physical (health-related) problems, all related to her GI tract. Beacon's hair coat was thin and dull. I thought this could be related to the chronic stress symptoms that Beacon exhibited. Beacon would shut down every time you tried to teach any new behaviours. Some of this was caused by the owner: the dog had been sick ever since Jean got her and so whenever Beacon didn't want to do something, Jean paved the way for her. I did have to try to figure out how much of the anxiety was learned and how much was "there" that Beacon could not control, if any. We worked with Beacon for a few months, teaching her the Basic Boot Camp behaviours (refer to *Basic Training Boot Camp* on page 120). I wanted to go super slow because of Beacon's anxiety issues. From this process, it became ever clearer that Beacon had abnormal learning patterns: even though the teaching was positive and Beacon was friendly, she still would melt down (become so anxious she couldn't work at all) any time she didn't know exactly what was expected of her. Because Jean is such a softie with her dogs and tends to "overhelp" I ascertained this behaviour was not coming from prior force or corrective type training techniques. I wanted to improve Beacon's confidence and reduce her anxiety levels. Jean and I talked to her veterinarian, and he prescribed fluexotine for Beacon to see if her anxiety would be reduced.

Medication helped Beacon immensely. Her physical health had also improved and her coat was thick and shiny. Beacon's chronic stress levels had affected her physical health. Her veterinarian was as pleased with her progress as Jean and I were. Beacon was no longer a nervous wreck all of the time, but there was plenty of residual habits - a lifetime of them - to deal with. I had started developing the Get Connected protocol after Beacon went on her medication. Jean and I added the Get Connected work to Beacon's regular obedience training.

Protocols & Management (Brenda's instructions to the client)

- Beacon was quite body sensitive if you were facing her or from other positions in front of her. We did a lot of desensitization and body work, including the Be Still Switch. Body work included desensitization with a dowel and other objects, such as bags, toys - anything that could be held against her body. One of Beacon's residual habits was to shove her head between Jean's knees to get Jean's

attention and to "hide." This is okay to do, but Beacon felt it was one of the only "safe" ways to have people pet. It was Beacon's preferred method of getting petted and attention, particularly if she was a little stressed. I would like to see Beacon come up to people and be comfortable and confident while in a "facing the person" position. I encouraged Jean not to allow Beacon to put her head between Jean's legs and have Jean give Beacon scratches on the top of her back.

- Working on the Follow The Feel will both help Beacon's owner walk her and teach Beacon to stop pulling. Beacon gets anxious and then begins "moving into pressure" to the point she is choking. She will pull hard and in a panicky fashion. Once Follow The Feel has been taught, Jean will be able to use the tight leash to gauge Beacon's stress levels. If the leash gets tight Jean can check and make sure Beacon is not getting frightened or trying to leave an area quickly out of avoidance.

- Move Into will help teach Beacon about personal space, and because I know this exercise will stress her a little bit it will be valuable for learning how to cope with stress. The Move Into is versatile in this respect, because you can be very slow and careful, thus controlling the amount of stress the dog feels and will have to deal with. Once learned, the Move Into will also give Jean a way to get Beacon's attention when she is inattentive in a way that the dog understands already, thus reducing further stress on the dog.

- Walking properly on a loose leash will promote impulse control. It will make walks more pleasant, too. Jean will be able to "correct" Beacon with information that Beacon understands. Avoiding confusion, especially for this dog, will really reduce her anxiety levels.

- Jean is encouraged to let Beacon "figure it out" even if Beacon gets a little bit stressed. All exercises will be broken down into VERY small approximations so Beacon gets a lot of reinforcement and treats for her efforts.

- Negotiation Signals and Calming Signals, such as Shaking Off are to be reinforced. These are Signals dogs use when they are thinking, or coming from a tense state to a relatively more relaxed state. We want to notice and reinforce any states that are relatively more relaxed.

Recheck & Brenda's Conclusions at 30 days

- Jean now does therapy work at schools with physically handicapped and other special needs children. All of the desensitization work really helped Beacon with her body sensitivity. We taught her several tricks that Jean could use to draw the children out and to entertain and stimulate the children. Beacon is still a very "soft" dog, but she is able to handle stress much more effectively. The medication made a huge difference, but the Move Into and other desensitization work increased Beacon's confidence and taught her better ways to cope with her stress.

- What makes me even happier is that Beacon is participating fully in all family activities now. She does not go off and want to be by herself because daily living is no longer so stressful. I very much credit the medication with this change. Also, Beacon is learning more functional ways to deal with being around her people; this is the help the Get Connected work offers her.

Owner's Input After Using protocol

Was there a specific or precipitating reason for using the Get Connected protocol? To help Beacon learn to cope with stress. She was stressed a lot, and had a hard time learning new things.

What Exercises did you use?

- Be Still Cue: Rub the Dog's Body all over to Switch them to Front Brain

- Move Into

- Follow The Feel (Pressure on the collar causes the dog's feet to back up)

Work with a dowel to walk on a loose leash (This is advanced work that is not covered in this volume, but will be in Volume 2.)

- Walking on a loose leash by teaching "Keep Your Toes Behind My Toes."

- Desensitization to footing and new objects - we would rub the new objects on his body, using the same technique as using our hand. Lots of

Approach and Retreat towards agility equipment, poles on the ground, etc.

Which exercises did you feel helped your dog the most?.

- Be Still Cue - The first thing Brenda and I talked about was Beacon's inability to deal with stress. She said that Beacon was stressed, but never would shake off her stress. So we started with body work. We worked on touching Beacon all over both with our hands and a dowel. The we did further desensitization with other things, like plastic bags, sheets of paper, etc. Finally Beacon started to Shake Off. She was praised lavishly and once she started Shaking Off her stress, it was amazing, because she would use this all the time and be calmer afterward.

- Follow The Feel - this was super hard for Beacon, because she would push back hard at first, pulling on the collar, pushing on your hand when you touched her in a way that was almost like fearfully, definitely not in a thinking way. But soon, Beacon learned that she could follow the feel of the pressure and move away from it instead of frantically pushing into it. This really changed the way Beacon handled herself. Her confidence level went up.

- Move Into - helped with walking and Impulse Control exercises.

- Walking on a loose leash - we used turning toward Beacon to teach her to keep her toes behind my toes. This changed lots of things. Beacon is now much easier to handle on a walk.

Changes observed after Get Connected protocol work: I brought Beacon to Brenda on the recommendation of a friend of mine who had worked with her. Beacon was about 3 1/2 years old. We started with body work first, then added other exercises. I was noticing some great changes in Beacon, she was more confident and was able to recover from stress more quickly. She was walking on a leash much better, and I could now walk more than one dog at a time easily (we have 3 dogs at home). After much discussion, Brenda urged me to discuss putting Beacon on some anti-anxiety medication in addition to the protocol. I was pleased with the progress, Beacon was finally realizing some of her potential, but Brenda was still concerned with Beacon's stress levels and thought that Beacon had some problems that required medication. She said that she had done the Get Connected protocol with a lot of dogs and although I was happy, she thought Beacon should be responding even better than she was. We worked with my wonderful veterinarian and put Beacon on fluexotine. This helped with Beacon's stress, but it had an added bonus: Beacon's tummy troubles went away. Adding the medication relieved her anxiety that had showed up as irritable bowel syndrome. Beacon is now six years old, her weight is good, she is eating regular (not special) dog food and several kinds of treats for training. Beacon is now doing therapy work with disabled and mentally ill children. She has learned all kinds of tricks that get the children involved. She can stack rings on a stick and "plays cards," "goes night-night", retrieves different colored items and so many more that are too numerous to list. The meds helped, but the Get Connected protocol taught Beacon how to deal with her stress and cope with all the things that she runs into living her daily life. It also helped prepare Beacon to learn and gave me ways to help Beacon deal with her stress so she wouldn't shut down when she was learning something new.

Changes In Your Dog & You Interaction?

Was your relationship with your dog ever nervous, tense or did you feel the relationship was under strain? No. I was frustrated because I wanted to help her and didn't know how, but the relationship was not strained.

After the Get Connected protocol: .Beacon is happier now that she is more comfortable about personal space and understands my body language better. I feel closer to her because she looks more relaxed.

Animal reaction to strangers entering the room, noises in the room, being left alone in the room, other pets in the room, etc. Beacon was always friendly with both dogs and people.

After the Get Connected protocol: I did notice that Beacon wants to participate more. Even when it is just us at home, sometimes she would go off by herself, but now she wants to be in with the rest of the group more. (Me and my husband have 2 other dogs.)

Did you notice any adverse changes in your dog's behaviour After the Get Connected protocol? Nothing adverse. There is a good change though, Beacon is much more confident and comfortable.

Did you feel your dog was placed under excess stress during this protocol? Beacon was stressed a lot anyway. She certainly showed stress during the beginning of some of the exercises, or when learning new things, but by the end of the session she was always more comfortable. This is a key part of the exercises, stopping once the dog IS more relaxed so the right message is sent and the dog is habituating to each exercise and the handling.

Do you think that this protocol changed any ways that you think and interact with your dog? Yes. More awareness of how the dog learns and Beacon is much more comfortable in general. I am more observant of her body language and so get better feedback. This helps me train effectively.

Yuki

Owner: Andi
Wirehaired Pointing Griffon
male, castrated
DOB: 2000

Photograph by Cheryl Ertelt

Social & Environmental History

• I got Yuki from a reputable breeder when he was 9 weeks old.

• Yuki lives in a suburban neighborhood.

• I am very physically active and take the dogs for several walks and off-leash runs. I have two dogs, Yuki was the first dog obtained. My other dog is a rescue Border Collie, and the dogs get along very well together. Both dogs attend group classes and private lessons on a weekly basis.

How would you describe your pet's personality? exuberant, outgoing and super friendly with people and dogs, nervous about new objects.

Medical History

Low thyroid problem discovered in 2006. He now takes daily thyroid supplement, otherwise a normal physical history. Castrated at 6 months of age.

Education History

How many dogs have you trained? Have always had dogs, this is the first one that I have trained for competition.

What is your training experience? I'm working on it!

Do you have any competition titles? Yuki has a CD and a RN. We are just beginning to show in Open. We are training Utility behaviours.

Age when you started lessons/training with this dog: as soon as I got him home. We started group lessons when he was a puppy.

How was daily living with this dog? Always an adventure, but a pleasant one! Yuki is a very sweet dog, but with a lot of energy and a very active mind. I make sure he gets a lot of exercise, walks and runs in the woods. We also attend training classes on an ongoing basis to keep his mind busy.

How did obedience training go? Yuki takes a lot of repetitions to learn new things, but once he has learned it he doesn't forget it.

What kind of technique was used? We started out with traditional slip (choke) collar training, but switched over to Positive Reinforcement.

Anything else you would like to tell me about your dog's training? Numerous repetitions are required to acquire desired behavior. Your cues must be really consistent. I cannot be sloppy.

Behavioural History

Can you take food or toys from your dog? Yes. This has never been a problem.

Have you ever been uncomfortable because you thought that your dog might bite you or someone else? No.

List any behaviours that were of concern to you. How long had this behaviour been occurring or at what age first observed: Attention deficit. Very short attention span. From puppyhood.

Has the frequency or the intensity of the occurrence of the behaviour changed since the problem started? Situation dependent. Like at shows or when he gets stressed. Stays have always been very difficult for him.

Presenting Issues (from Brenda's point of view)

Yuki is a wonderful and fun-loving dog, although he exhibited sporadic and inappropriate anxiety. Andi had enrolled him in puppy classes locally and had continued on to their beginner classes. They had recommended using a chain slip collar and a pinch collar to help Andi control him. She is a very petite person, and Yuki is a vigorous and active dog. She was not making the progress that she wished to, and the first time I saw Yuki he was approximately 12-18 months old. He had worn most of the hair off of his neck where the slip collar fit. Andi was distressed about this and frustrated about the fact that he still pulled on the leash constantly. He was pulling like a freight train and sometimes anxious in learning situations. I recommended a martingale collar and a Halti™ head collar so he could be walked more easily. We worked on his recall and basic skill set (refer to *Basic Training Boot Camp* on page 120). Soon Andi, a very determined person, was soon showing him in Novice (AKC Obedience classes), and she continued on in my advanced competition classes. Yuki did not always cope with stress as well as I thought he should. I know that sounds very nebulous and not very "formal," but with the amount of time Andi spends with him, and the now very positive training, Yuki was still very stressed sometimes, mostly over Stays and, rather surprisingly, new objects and footing. Teaching him the broad jump was a nightmare, not because he didn't like to jump, but because he was so spooky about the jump itself. This felt "off" to me, and, coupled with his hair coat, which was thin and sometimes patchy, I recommended having her veterinarian do a thyroid and an addisons panel. Yuki did have hypothyroid disease. The medication did help a bit with the stress-related behaviour, and his hair coat improved. He was still anxious on Stays, although better. About this time I was beginning to develop the Get Connected protocol and was looking for people who would be willing to try some new techniques.

Yuki had a few specific problems that I wished to correct: he still pulled on the leash when he got anxious and would snatch the cookies then race back out to the end of his leash, even when Andi was using the food properly and using Reinforcement Schedules properly. He was having a terrible time with the Stand For Exam and the Long Sit and Down exercises for Novice Obedience. He still did not always habituate as quickly as I would like to see.

Protocols & Management (Brenda's instructions to the client)

- The Be Still Switch to keep Yuki calm before classes and at shows. The Be Still Switch will also be used to settle him and keep those feet still for the Stand. Use the Be Still Switch before leaving on the Sit & Down and when Andi returns instead of using food treats. On the Stand, the "Judge" comes up and uses the Be Still exercise as does the handler, who has pivoted directly in front of the dog. Once this is going well, the handler will stand one step back from the dog, while the Judge does the Be Still exercise. Any foot movement or fidgeting on the dog's part causes the handler to walk directly towards the dog and have him back up a couple of steps, then the handler repeats "Stand" and moves carefully back into position a step away. As the handler moves back into position she must be careful that the maneuver does not look like a Back Away or the dog will surely follow. This can be accomplished by having the handler turn their body slightly laterally to the dog as they move back into position. Approximate this exercise at the dog's rate of understanding, until the handler is at the requisite six feet distance away and the "Judge" has faded the Be Still Switch to a stroke from head to tail or the three touches that Judges often use: one on the head, one on the back and one near the tail. Habituation and work with a dowel to direct the dog's movement will be added, if required, to help stabilize the Stand. (Directing the dogs movement with a dowel is an advanced exercise and will be covered in Volume 2.)

- Working on the Follow The Feel will help both with loose leash walking and his competition style Heeling.

- Move Into for inattentive behaviour while doing competition style Heeling and for loose leash walking.

Recheck & Brenda's Conclusions at 30 days

- The Be Still Switch along with extensive Challenges is improving the Stand For Exam. The Sits and Downs are improving slowly.

- Yuki is better when presented with new exercises. The Be Still and additional desensitization done using body work instead of treats when he is introduced to the new objects is working better than I expected. Once he has approached new things and has begun to relax, THEN Andi Marks the behaviour and will use a treat. Basically, I wanted to allow Yuki to think and help him stay "grounded" and in touch with the handler, then once he is relatively a bit more emotionally stable and less spooky is when the treat is delivered, if needed at all.

- The Move Into did give Andi better control while Heeling and avoids using verbal cues, which I find that some dogs desensitize very quickly. This also corrects sniffing in a really gentle and effective way. Yes, we want address any stress, but dogs do not sniff just because of stress, sometimes they are avoiding work or distracted.

- Yuki's loose leash walking has improved. This is a great relief to me on many levels, one of which is handler safety. In addition, it is good practice for impulse control and makes the handler and dog more aware of each other's movements.

- Update: Several weeks after we started the Get Connected protocol Andi started Yuki on some supplements. Andi and I had discussed supplements. She did her research and found a product called Stress Free Calmplex.[6] She reports that Yuki is handling stress better. It is mostly observable in class on the stationary exercises such as Sit and Down. Vitamin B complexes are also excellent choices for stress and helpful for animals with thyroid disease. (Note to readers: of course you should ALWAYS check with your veterinarian for nutrition and nutraceutical and supplement related advice. Over supplementation can be unhealthy.)

Owner's Input After Using Protocol

Was there a specific or precipitating reason for using the Get Connected protocol? Yuki is a high energy dog and could easily be totally out of control without training. In addition, I wanted to show him in Rally and Obedience so he needed to learn appropriate

---

6. by Spring Time Nutraceuticals. The web site is: www.springtimeinc.com.

responses beyond being a pet dog. His breed requires "a job" and since I am not a hunter, I knew I had to provide him with a job. Obedience training is a challenge, but gives a great feeling of accomplishment when it is achieved.

What Exercises did you use?

- Be Still Switch

- Move Into.

- Follow The Feel (Pressure on the collar causes the dog's feet to back up).

- Walking on a loose leash by teaching "Keep Your Toes Behind My Toes."

Which exercises did you feel helped your dog the most?.

- The leash walking exercises were of the most help.

- Move Into also helped to get his attention and keep it on me.

- Yuki responds most dependably to nonverbal (i.e. body language) cues. I need to exactly reproduce a cue to get the desired result. He notices slight differences in my body language, so me being aware of his body language and learning to control my own body language has been of great benefit to both of us. When I get it correct, his behavior is automatic and immediate. He has taught me to be very aware of how I use my hands, body, shoulders, and feet, as well as my tone of voice.

Changes observed after Get Connected protocol work. He is much less stressed when he clearly understands what is expected of him. The way he responded to stress during training was one of the ways that we decided he might have some physiological problem, so Brenda suggested that my veterinarian do a thyroid panel. His stress level has decreased significantly with the addition of the thyroid hormones. Yuki has always gotten stressed when learning new behaviors even though it is presented to him in a positive way, and is reticent to do a behavior until he clearly understands exactly what he should be doing. At that point, the behavior he was reluctant to do becomes his new favorite behavior, and is very enthusiastic about repeating it. Learning more about how our personal space affects each other helped us to communicate better, reducing Yuki's stress level, both learning new behaviors and to keep him attentive to me. These exer-

cises gave me another way to relate to Yuki, and the Be Still cue and awareness of personal space really helped reduce stress levels significantly and very quickly: you could see changes within one training session.

Changes In General Activity Levels?
No, Yuki is active, but not hyper-active. This has not been a problem.

Changes In Your Dog & You Interaction?

Was your relationship with your dog ever nervous, tense or did you feel the relationship was under strain? Only when I was showing him and he would be really inattentive and difficult to get him to focus. Teaching attention work is good, but it is also nice to have some tools, like the Move Into and all of the Backing Up exercises, that do not require treats to use when I cannot have treats available.

Did you notice any adverse changes in your dog's behaviour After the Get Connected protocol? No.

Did you feel your dog was placed under excess stress during this protocol? At times we deliberately placed stress on Yuki. This sounds odd, but we did this with a purpose and controlled the amount of stress. We did this so we could teach him to look to me for support and also to raise his ability to cope with some stress, like that we would find at a dog show.

Do you think that this protocol changed any ways that you think and interact with your dog?. Yes, I am more aware of his body language and he is more aware of mine. I am now able to be more consistent with my body language as a result of this awareness.

Kip

Owner: Andi
Border Collie
male, castrated
DOB: 2004

Photograph by Cheryl Ertelt

Social & Environmental History

• I got Kip from Heather, who has done Rescue and fostering of dogs for many years. She is very experienced at handling dogs and problem dogs. Heather got Kip from the Animal Shelter and kept him until she could find a good home for him. Brenda had talked to Heather and thought that Kip would be a good fit in our home. I got Kip when he was 18 months old.

• While Heather did not do much formal training, neither did Kip develop any bad habits under her excellent care.

• Kip lives in a suburban neighborhood with one other dog, Yuki. The dogs get along well and get several off leash runs and on leash walks daily. Kip is obsessive over tennis balls.

How would you describe your pet's personality? .Confident and driven to do his best. He is very cooperative and friendly. He is sure he is the smartest dog alive.

Medical History

Normal Medical History.

Education History

How many dogs have you trained? Have always had dogs, this is the second one that I am training for competition.

What is your training experience? I'm working on it!

Do you have any competition titles? My other dog, Yuki, has a CD and a RN.

Age when you started lessons/training with this dog: As soon as I got him home. We started group and private lessons right away.

How was daily living with this dog? As long as he gets enough exercise and gets to display his knowledge of obedience on a daily basis he is a joy to live with. Kip (and my other dog, too) get three walks a day, and I take them to a nearby forest and park area to run daily.

How did obedience training go? Kip is eager to learn and learns so quickly, who wouldn't be pleased? I just have to be careful to give distinct and correct cues.

If I get frustrated at all if he responds incorrectly he gets upset.

What kind of technique was used? Positive Reinforcement

Anything else you would like to tell me about your dog's training? Numerous repetitions are required to acquire desired behavior. Your cues must be really consistent. I cannot be sloppy.

Behavioural History

Can you take food or toys from your dog? Yes. But other DOGS cannot take toys without a confrontation. He doesn't look for a disagreement, but if the dog tries to steal toys he is playing with he will protest.

Have you ever been uncomfortable because you thought that your dog might bite you or someone else? No.

List any behaviours that were of concern to you. How long had this behaviour been occurring or at what age first observed: No particular behavior, I just wanted Kip to be happy as a pet and I wanted to do competition obedience and rally with him.

Has the frequency or the intensity of the occurrence of the behaviour changed since the problem started? Situation dependent. Like at shows or when he gets stressed. Stays have always been very difficult for him.

Presenting Issues (from Brenda's point of view)

When Andi wanted to add a second dog we found her a rescue Border Collie. Because Andi is so active and spends so much time with her dogs I knew she would be up to the task of handling the active mind and body of a Border Collie. Because Kip is a rescue dog and has not been trained other than basic house manners he is an excellent candidate to try the Get Connected work. He is a bit "checked out" around a tennis ball (okay, he is uncontrollable) and since Andi wishes to compete in Obedience, this will rear it's ugly head over and over.

Like most dogs, Kip likes being touched as long as it is his idea, but is uneasy with other touches. He is never in the least aggressive, but his discomfort is obvious with certain touches. The Be Still Switch will help make Kip comfortable and prepare him for the Stand For Exam. The Move Into will prepare him for Heel work and make walking two dogs at a time possible.

Kip is a very bright and kind dog. The ideal Border Collie, really - one of my questions to myself is: Will there be enough improvement to this nice, normal dog to warrant doing the work.

Protocols & Management (Brenda's instructions to the client)

- The Be Still Switch to prepare Kip for the Stand For Exam and to make grooming easier. On the Stand, the "Judge" comes up and uses the Be Still Switch as does the handler, who has pivoted directly in front of the dog. Once this is going well, the handler will stand one step back from the dog, while the "Judge" does the Be Still Switch. Any foot movement or fidgeting on the dog's part causes the handler to walk directly towards the dog and have him back up a couple of steps, then the handler repeats "Stand" and moves carefully back into position a step away. As the handler moves back into position it must not look like a Back Away or the dog will surely follow. This can be accomplished by having the handler turn their body slightly laterally to the dog as they move back into position. This is to be approximated until the handler is at the requisite six feet away and the "Judge" has faded the Be Still Cue to a stroke from head to tail or the three touches that Judges often use: one on the head, one on the back and one near the tail.

- Working on the Follow The Feel will help both with loose leash walking and his competition style Heeling.

- Move Into for inattentive behaviour while doing competition style Heeling and for loose leash walking.

- Get Between, Mirror & Switch games (exercises) and Move Into in preparation to teaching Kip how to ignore tennis balls when working.

- Back Away for use as attention getting cue when distractions are present.

Recheck & Brenda's Conclusions at 30 days

- The Be Still Switch made the Stand For Exam a piece of cake. I love it when a plan comes together as expected. I am really starting to trust this protocol as a sophisticated teaching tool, not just for big problems. In addition, it did make Kip more comfortable with a variety of touches, important both for his comfort and for giving the handler many more ways to get information across to the dog. I use luring as a technique, but prefer to limit its use and use it very carefully for competition dogs (it can be time-consuming to fade the lure out of the picture). Because Kip is comfortable now with a variety of touches, we can model him into place or physically guide him very gently into position with no resistance and no tension. Therefore, the communication loop remains open and information can get to the dog efficiently. The Follow The Feel work really helps with this aspect of training, too, as it further reinforces no resistance and to follow guiding by the handler instead of becoming tense or resistant about it.

- The Get Between, Back Away and Move Into gave us a way to gently correct Kip in a way he understands when working with his tennis ball distraction. Since I want to be able to use the tennis ball as a reinforcer and to "pep" up his competition Heeling, it is important that this work is done carefully and with consideration for the terminal response: a dog who knows when the tennis ball is available and when it is not.

- Follow the Feel gave us a way to teach loose leash walking very effortlessly to Kip. In addition, we can use this exercise to get focused, fast and straight recalls. I find that a lot of Border Collies tend to put an arc in their recall, which they should never be punished for because it is hard-wired herding behaviour. Restrained, short distance recalls can really help teach the dog that the arc is inappropriate in this context. Instead of doing the typical "restrained" recall where the collar and leash is tight, I can put two fingers on Kips chest to restrain him. It works just like placing a horse in collection - the energy is all there, but instead of me physically containing it to increase the "force" of the release, the animal "mentally" contains it himself. The results are far superior to the traditional picture of the dog straining forward, pulling mightily against the collar - I get a quick, strong explosion forward without any physical stress to me or the dog. In addition, instead of a Hind Brain, non-thinking response we get a Front Brain awareness of the exercise.

Owner's Input After Using Protocol

Was there a specific or precipitating reason for using the Get Connected protocol? The techniques worked well with my other dog, so it seemed natural to use them with Kip. Kip is also manic about tennis balls, and will become absolutely "checked out" and Hind Brain. He would fixate on the ball and you couldn't get his attention.

What Exercises did you use?

- Move Into.
- Follow The Feel (Pressure on the collar causes the dog's feet to back up).
- Work with a dowel to back up. (This is advanced work that is not covered in this volume, but will be in Volume 2.)
- Switching exercises, using the Get Between Leave It and Move Into.

Which exercises did you feel helped your dog the most? What makes the most difference to this dog is the repetition and rhythm of precise body movement and cues. When signals, cues or body language is ambiguous he panics because he gets confused. He gets nervous if he thinks he is wrong. We have been very careful teaching this dog the Stand For Exam for Obedience. I have not allowed him to move forward at all, even after the exercise is completed in order to keep this friendly beast from deciding to move forward to greet the judge. We used a dowel to teach Kip to back up really well, (Dowel work is advanced and will be covered in Volume 2) then when I stand in front of him for the Stand For Exam, if he moves forward at all I can ask him to back up easily. This helps him to understand that he is not to move forward during this exercise. The Move Into and the Get Between help when practicing Switching exercises with the tennis ball. (Brenda's Note: Refer to the *Mirror & Switch Games* on page 284.) If Kip fixes on the ball (or I should say "when" he does) I use a Move Into or a Move Into and a Back Away to get his attention back to me, or I can use a Get Between combined with a Back Away to get his focus, then check to see if he is committed to me instead of the ball. When he gives me good attention, then he is rewarded by going to get the ball or I get another ball out and play with him.

Changes observed after Get Connected protocol work. Kip is much easier to handle when he is distracted. Working on the Mirror & Switch exercises really keep him attentive to me. The Move Into exercises teach both of us how to have a good relationship about personal space. Any spooky behaviour will be discovered as you do this exercise, and if your dog is afraid of something it is very good to know, so that you can begin to help the dog past any uneasiness he might have about his personal space. Move Into also is a great tool for competition dogs, as it gives a way for the handler to gently and unobtrusively (with a little practice!) divert the dog's attention from a distraction back onto me.

Changes In Your Dog & You Interaction?

Was your relationship with your dog ever nervous, tense or did you feel the relationship was under strain? No, this dog really wants to be connected and stay connected. I do have to be careful with my cues, as I have mentioned. I stay body aware because Kip really watches every move your body makes.

Did you notice any adverse changes in your dog's behaviour After the Get Connected protocol? No.

Did you feel your dog was placed under excess stress during this protocol? No, he is a very confident dog. He just became more attentive around the tennis ball!

Do you think that this protocol changed any ways that you think and interact with your dog?. Yes, I am more aware of his body language and he is more aware of mine. I am now able to be more consistent with my body language as a result of this awareness.

the
Brenda
ALOFF
c o n n e c t i o n

Merlin

Owner: Rachel
Australian Cattle Dog mix
male, castrated
DOB: 2001

Photograph by Dave Schrader

Social & Environmental History

- I got Merlin when he was approximately 2 years old from the shelter, and have had him 4 years now.

- I live in a suburban neighborhood and work at a Doggy Day Care. I can take dogs to work with me and often do. I have a fenced yard where the dogs can get adequate exercise. I also do some on leash walks and take the dogs to various "doggy" functions, like pet fairs and other social gatherings. I have worked with Merlin and Brenda doing private lessons for a couple of years.

How would you describe your pet's personality? When I got him he was very hyper-active. He is smart and shows his anxiety with increased activity levels.

Medical History

Normal Medical History. Castrated at about 2 years old, after I got him. We did start Merlin on Fluexotine after we worked with the Get Connected protocol for about a year.

Education History

How many dogs have you trained? Many. I have taught pet obedience classes, work as a groomer and at dog day care centers. I have worked as a veterinary technician.

What is your training experience? I have done rescue of mixes and Boxers for several years. I foster dogs, evaluate them, train them and then re-home them. I have worked with many problematic dogs, including aggression. I instruct group classes and do private lessons.

Do you have any competition titles? No.

Age when you started lessons/training with this dog: As soon as I got him home. He was approximately 2 years old. He had no apparent training prior to me getting him that I could tell.

How was daily living with this dog? Miserable! He was way too active, over the top. He was frantic and if I allowed him to be loose indoors with the other dogs he kept things in a constant uproar unless I was immediately supervising him, or kept him tied to me on a leash or tied to a piece of furniture. I made sure he got lots of running in my fenced yard, played games with him and walked him (which was also a nightmare), but because he was so difficult he had to be crated, confined behind a dog gate or tied when I could supervise him in the house. Otherwise he just ran from one "bad" to the next, keeping himself and all the other dogs in a state of constant agitation. It was difficult to get him to retain lessons.

How did obedience training go? Slowly, I was not pleased with the progress and could see he was not going to be a dog I could re-home (I do a lot of rescue work). So I was just coping with him as best I could.

What kind of technique was used? Positive Reinforcement, specifically Clicker training.

Behavioural History

Can you take food or toys from your dog? Yes. Never a problem.

Have you ever been uncomfortable because you thought that your dog might bite you or someone else? No. Thank goodness he is super friendly. Sometimes too active for some dogs, he can be overwhelming, but he is friendly with other dogs.

List any behaviours that were of concern to you. How long had this behaviour been occurring or at what age first observed: The hyperactivity, the lack of being able to settle down. He was indifferent to me, which is surprising because my other dogs are all very loving. He had lots of anxiety, which exhibited as super-active, couldn't settle down and listen.

Has the frequency or the intensity of the occurrence of the behaviour changed since the problem started? The indifference was always about the same. Interesting to me was that Clicker training and using food intensified the hyper-activity. I have taught clicker classes and clicker trained other dogs. But with Merlin, it seemed as if his agitation got worse the longer I worked at it, over about a year.

Presenting Issues (from Brenda's point of view)

Rachel is a very experienced dog handler with problem dogs. She has done extensive rescue work and has fostered and placed many dogs of many breeds as well as mixed breed dogs. She has a multi-dog household of rather complicated characters which she manages and trains.

I have seldom seen a dog who is tougher than this dog. Some days working with him for a lesson is so frustrating and requires so much patience that I cannot imagine living with him. His activity levels are off the charts, he cannot seem to sit still and has selective attention raised to an art form. He has been taught to be still and quiet in his crate and will lie down on leash next to the owner at home in the evening. We do not know his past, but if I had to guess - and this is a guess - he presents like other dogs I have known who spent their first year or so chained to a dog house. This is so incredibly frustrating for some dogs that they continue to sensitize and get ever farther from a "normal" chemical state because of the chronic stress. Thus, the anxiety becomes ever further ingrained the longer it is "practiced." This dog is also physically very tough and finds humans quite irrelevant. He is far from stupid and learns things, when you can get his attention for any five-second time frame, quite rapidly. He is always wagging his tail and happy, looking as if he wants to interact, but is so inappropriate and rough when you try that it is like trying to have a sensitive conversation with a fast-moving freight train. Thank goodness he is totally non-aggressive with humans and dogs. Inappropriate, yes, but I cannot imagine what it would take for him to bite a person.

Rachel is understandably frustrated and the dog is very stressed, although at first glance many people would find him "too happy" and really active, having "too much fun." If you look closely, he shows classic, but subtle stress symptoms - dander on the top of his coat that appears as his activity level ramps up. The increased activity level with very little stimuli is also an indicator of stress.

The client has been using Clicker training with this dog. After I watched for a few minutes, I decided that he had associated the clicker with his over-the-top anxiety and activity levels. As soon as Rachel would begin clicking and treating, you could see his activity levels increase by another 50%, making him even more like training the Tasmanian Devil (the cartoon character from The Roadrunner Show. Am I dating myself?).

When allowed off leash in the house he goes from dog to dog irritating each one in turn. When he is not busy doing that he moves from one naughty thing to the next naughty thing.

The client wishes to eventually do Agility with him, competitive perhaps, or non-competitive and just for fun.

I want to make a difference for these two, take the frustration out of the relationship and determine if the dog is normal or abnormal. This dog desperately needs to learn coping mechanisms and how to calm himself. He also needs to learn how to communicate with humans in a more effective way. Once he has learned that, we can teach him how to be more functional and comfortable in his daily life.

Protocols & Management (Brenda's instructions to the client)

- A verbal Marker was installed, and the clicker entirely discarded with this dog.

- I recommend that this dog be moved backwards a lot. In horses it is well known that backing up makes their going forward much, much better. This needs to be used judiciously with horses because some horses will then learn to resist the rider by backing up and this can lead to rearing up and throwing themselves over backwards on the rider (I used to own one of these.) However, one can apply some critical thinking to this problem, and my thinking is like this: A dog can be moving forward and still be in a Hind Brain state, such as when they are leash pulling and in pursuit of prey. But backing up and going sideways require higher order thinking, as they are not such "natural" states of locomotion. At first glance I could not even detect Front Brain activity in this dog. Well I guess he had learned to hold a sit stay for one entire second. Okay, so a couple of neurons are occasionally firing. When walking he would rush forward, turn, rush back, snatch the cookie, vibrate, rush forward; and if no Click & Treat was available he would just rush forward. His forward locomotion patterns were out of control. Therefore, I told the client that I wanted this dog to move backwards as much as possible.

- The Basic Boot Camp exercises (refer to Basic Training Boot Camp on page 120). chapter)

would be re-installed using the verbal Marker. In the process of retraining instead of focusing on getting a position, such as a Sit, the focus will be shifted to the *emotional state of the dog*. That is teaching the dog that calmness is important, in addition to the position. The Front Brain state being of much more importance than the position itself. As time goes on, precision about the position will be ever more important, as it will give the dog something to concentrate and focus on.

- The Be Still Switch and a lot of work with the dowel (This is advanced work that is not covered in this volume, but will be in Volume 2.).

- Follow The Feel exercises, Move Into and endless Mirror & Switch games.

- This dog is so smart and so quick to identify patterns and take advantage of them I feel we just need the right approach to get our foot in the door. We currently do not have efficient means of communication and the dog has such a disregard for personal space it is difficult to be around him sometimes.

- This is getting adequate exercise, but I wish to increase the amount of "thinking" exercise he gets, using obedience exercises and/or tricks.

Recheck & Brenda's Conclusions at 30 days

- At 14 days there was marked improvement. When I asked Rachel how much she was able to back him up, and if she thought it made any difference, she told me that if he was with her and on leash, he was backing up to get anywhere. I was so delighted that she was so dedicated and took this suggestion seriously. He was allowed to get out of the crate, then he was backed up to the door, allowed to go out and exercise and relieve himself. Sometimes she would play appropriate games in the fenced yard also. Then she would put the leash on and he was backed up through the door of the house and backed into his crate, or backed into another room of the house where he would be allowed to lie down and chew on bones, etc. To walk Merl, Rachel would back him out of the house and back him around the block. Sometimes she was in front of him backing him up and other times she would have Merl in Heel

position and both of them would back up. She did confess her neighbors asked some questions about her behaviour. By golly, it did help, too! She could see a difference and so could I when she walked him into the building. She backed this dog everywhere for 2 full weeks. Then we started allowing him to go forward as well as backwards on walks. He was allowed to go forwards between 3 and 7 steps, then he was asked to back up from heel position, Rachel would turn into him and ask him to back up or Rachel would use a Back Away. I advised using this strategy for another 8 to 12 weeks.

- Merlin was now able to lie down and sit and do sit and down stays after 2 weeks. After one month, he could do 2 to 3 minute stays and longer with minor distractions. Merlin's recalls are improving and his hyper-active behaviour is still exhibited frequently, but is now easy to interrupt with a verbal cue, followed up by a Move Into if required. The Move Into is acquired behaviour and works even when Merlin is off leash and playing in the yard.

- The Get Between has been a mainstay and improved this dog's impulse control by approximately 80%. This is according to the client's observations at home and to my observations on the weekly private lessons I do with this Rachel and Merlin.

- At the 30 day mark there is still a very long row to hoe, BUT the progress is quite clear and I am very pleased. The improvement in this dog is attributable to the correct exercises and new understanding on the dog's part about personal space and the relevance of humans. More than usual credit goes to the handler, because this was a very frustrating dog who required more-than-usual levels of patience and expertise to be applied. A streak of stubborn (persistence) was also required.

- Follow the Feel helped with the loose leash walking, but Merlin still had a tendency to ignore cues on a sort of random basis. (We began dowel work for loose leash walking and it was extremely effective. This exercise is included in Volume 2.)

- The Be Still Switch and other desensitization was helpful, although Merlin was not body sensitive in any way. I am hoping that the awareness gained from this will facilitate and increase the efficacy of the Move Into.

- The Move Into did wonders. Merlin learned a lot about how to keep his body in his space and allow you to have your body in your space without constant violations. This awareness helped make his company tolerable. He did not just improve his personal space manners around people, after these exercises Rachel says she sees improvement with his interactions with other dogs, too. They are calmer and he pays more attention to the body language of the dogs, and is not so invasive.

- Mirroring and Back Aways taught Merlin to come into personal space only when specifically invited to do so, and to ask politely (by hanging around and waiting for an invitation) to come into your personal space.

- Rachel has persevered admirably and her handling skills are smoother. She recognizes instantly when to release pressure.

- Update: Rachel and I started Merlin doing some agility work. In private lessons he is now sequencing and learning to work away from Rachel and learning front and rear crosses. Rachel took him to an agility class and the instructor commented on how well behaved, under control and on his ability to pay attention to Rachel. We rather felt like we'd gotten a gold medal, as well as having a good chuckle at the irony.

Owner's Input After Using Protocols

Was there a specific or precipitating reason for using the Get Connected protocol? None in particular. I was getting really frustrated with my current training efforts. Particularly so since I had trained lots of rescue dogs who had problem behavior and had gotten different responses from them. I knew how to train a dog, but the techniques that had worked with other dogs just didn't seem to work well with Merlin. None of them acted like Merlin. He acted like he would get it, but was so hyper-active that he was hard to control or get his attention for any longer than 2 seconds.

What Exercises did you use?

- Desensitizing the dog to touch using the Be Still Cue.

- Move Into.

- Follow The Feel (Pressure on the collar causes the dog's feet to back up).

- Work with a dowel to back up. (This is advanced work that is not covered in this volume, but will be in Volume 2.)

- Walking on a loose leash by keeping his toes behind my toes.

- We walked backwards - literally EVERYWHERE. This helped him to engage his Front Brain.

- Switching exercises, using the Get Between Leave It and Move Into.

Which exercises did you feel helped your dog the most? All of the leash work and the Move Into. The impulse control exercises, such as the Get Between. Teaching Merlin that he didn't have to charge everywhere we went.

Changes In Your Dog & You Interaction?

Was your relationship with your dog ever nervous, tense or did you feel the relationship was under strain? Yes, the dog was constantly agitated, causing me to be also, even when I was trying to be patient. I was frustrated about the training, too. Merlin was impossible and incorrigible to live with! He would go non-stop and trash the house and irritate the other dogs.

After we worked with Merlin about a year, there were amazing changes in his behaviour. He was calmer, could concentrate and do Stays. I could interrupt his horrid behaviors and his obedience was getting good. He could heel and we could walk in the neighborhood, he was more compliant with me and his interactions with the other dogs were better because if he got rough or was too active inappropriately I could stop it and have him lie down. He could be loose in the house.

Merlin was still having trouble concentrating sometimes, especially when we tried to do agility work, he would get over-excited. His training began to plateau. At this point Brenda recommended fluexotine. The meds made the last bit of difference. His house behavior improved even more and his training moved ahead at a rapid rate again. It would have been hard to establish a baseline for his behavior without the training,

because I didn't want the worry of medicating Merlin if he didn't need it.

Did you notice any adverse changes in your dog's behaviour After the Get Connected protocol? No.

Did you feel your dog was placed under excess stress during this protocol? Life was excessively stressful for Merl. He was certainly placed under stress, but during each training session, even though he got stressed, he would calm down as we worked with him. Finally he was habituating instead of getting more and more agitated.

Do you think that this protocol changed any ways that you think and interact with your dog?. Yes, awareness of each other's personal space. Merlin learning how to identify what my personal space was! We have now started agility classes and he is doing great, even if the other dogs are running around and the class is chaotic.

Wilson

Owner: Rachel
Great Dane/Hound mix
male, castrated
DOB: August 2006

Photograph by Dave Schrader

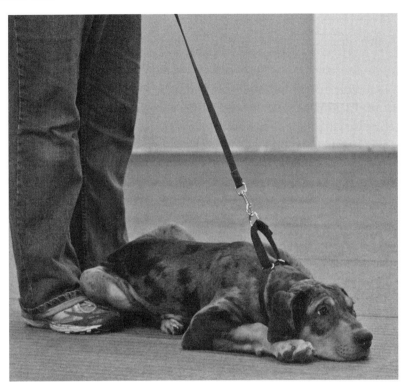

Social & Environmental History

- I got Wilson when he was approximately 10 weeks old from the shelter. I have had him about four months now. I work at a Doggy Day Care and Wilson goes to day care on some work days to get socialization with dogs and people. Other than this he gets regular walks and outings.

- I live in a suburban neighborhood with a fenced yard. I have a multi-dog household. (See Case History for "Merlin").

How would you describe your pet's personality? .Pushy. Mouthy. Uncooperative. Very hyperactive. Dominating with other dogs.

Medical History

Normal Medical History. Castrated after I got him.

Education History

How many dogs have you trained? Many. I have taught pet obedience classes, work as a groomer and at dog day care centers. I have worked as a veterinary technician.

What is your training experience? I have done rescue and fostered rescue dogs for the past several years.

Do you have any competition titles? No.

Age when you started lessons/training with this dog: As soon as I got him home. It was apparent that his pushy behavior with dogs was going to get him into trouble. Even at this young age he was also pushy with people and if you tried to restrain him at all, he would

get excessively mouthy. He was a bizarre mixture of anxious and pushy.

How was daily living with this dog? Fine. He requires the same amount of work as other puppies.

How did obedience training go? Good

What kind of technique was used? I started right away with the Get Connected protocol Bodywork and personal space exercises.

Behavioural History

Can you take food or toys from your dog? Yes. Never a problem.

Have you ever been uncomfortable because you thought that your dog might bite you or someone else? He did bite me as I was bending over him doing basic husbandry work, grooming, about a week after I got him home. He came right up off the floor at me and bit me in the neck. This was alarming from such a young dog. It was not in the least playful, he meant business. Since I had been handling him from day one, it had the appearance of a correction-type bite he would administer to another dog. This was definitely not good.

List any behaviours that were of concern to you. How long had this behaviour been occurring or at what age first observed: Extreme anxiety at handling, observed at 7 weeks; pushy with other dogs, observed at 10 weeks; pushy with people, observed at 10 weeks.

Presenting Issues (from Brenda's point of view)

When an experienced handler comes to me and says they are concerned about a dog's behaviour, I sit right up and take notice. Wilson, on first appearance was a goofy, floppy little hound puppy. But as soon as you started to touch him and ask him to do something his resistance was palpable. He displayed extreme reactivity when you touched him; he would get super wiggly and lie down if you persisted, roll on his back and then begin to bite at your hands. His activity levels would increase drastically when you approached and touched him, clear signs to those experienced in reading body language that the dog is very anxious and resistant about touch. This dog was also using his activity level and size to move the handlers feet in a controlling way. At twelve weeks

old this dog already weighed about 40 pounds, so we had to get control of him quickly.

The bite he administered to Rachel rather terrified me, she is not the type of personality that dogs usually try to move and take charge around. The client's concern with how pushy and rude this young puppy was with other dogs was also of great concern to me and made my prognosis on the initial evaluation of this dog to be guarded to poor.

This dog's overall behaviour matched the behaviour I have observed time and again when puppies are removed from their mother and litter mates too early. Too early is anytime before 8 weeks of age, which is, of course, my own humble opinion. This puppy presented like other dogs I have worked with who I know have been removed from their mother between 4 to 6 weeks of age. What we do know is that this puppy was brought to the dog shelter by the time he was 6 to 7 weeks of age. He left his mother much too young, and this leaves gaping holes in a dog's social development.

This dog is very pushy, in a deliberate way, with other dogs. It is not frantic or hectic, but a slow and deliberate approach and escalation of shoving the other dog and pressing on boundaries, both physical and mental. Of course, if it is an adult dog who immediately corrects him, he submits quickly and without resistance and learns in one or two trials not to push that dog again.

This is an excellent chance for us to see how frugal we can be with treats and still get the job done properly, with a happy and willing dog. Because he has problematic behaviour, but is very young, I was very eager to try the Get Connected protocol and see what sort of difference they would make. I am hopeful, but dubious that this set of protocol will make enough difference for this dog to be considered for placement into a home other than Rachel's, which is her goal at this time.

Protocols & Management (Brenda's instructions to the client)

- Restraints, both Sit Restraints and Down Restraints. (These are detailed in *Aggression In Dogs*.)

- Be Still Switch.

- Follow The Feel.

Wilson

- Move Into.

- Walk Nicely.

- Wilson's bullying behaviour with other dogs is to be minimized. If he persists past two or three interruptions he will be removed from the play groups at Day Care. At home, the client must watch carefully and monitor his interactions with her own dogs. Any dog that will not hurt Wilson should be allowed to correct him - let them work it out. Any dog that is inclined to carry a correction too far, will of course be stopped. If Wilson bullies any house mates, he is to be put on leash and placed in a Down Stay or to be crated until he is less adrenalized and then allowed to try again. Handling of this must be 100% consistent. The client is a very experienced handler so she will be capable of carrying this out without causing further frustration and harming the dog to dog relationships.

Recheck & Brenda's Conclusions at 30 days

- I am extremely pleased with Wilson's response, which occurred even with minimal work both because of the client's work schedule and also because this is a multi-dog household. There is only so much time in a day, and Rachel currently has 3 problematic dogs that we are actively working with who are not on maintenance behaviours. (All are rescue dogs that she did not feel were candidates for re-homing.)

- The Be Still Switch is fantastic: he quiets immediately. The client reports that using the Be Still Switch on approaches is holding up quite well, and has been generalized more quickly than she expected. We did approaches in work session 1 (on the DVD included with this book) and work session 2 (also included on DVD). Then Rachel took the behaviours out on the street a little bit, which would be in week 3 of beginning this protocol. The three initial training sessions done with Wilson are to be seen on the DVD that is included with this book. You get to see Wilson at his worst! And his best!

- Without doing any Eye Contact work or impulse control work, which I generally insist is done first, we started this dog on the following specific exercises of the Get Connected protocol, taught in this order:
  1. Be Still Switch
  2. Follow The Feel
  3. Move Into
  4. Walk Nicely, "keep your toes behind my toes."

- Rachel agreed that those four exercises were to be done for 4 weeks before other work (other than house-training and other house manners, like stay off the counter tops) will be introduced. This gives me a very good chance to see what sort of results I would get with a dog that has had no prior training. Get Between and Move Into exercises were used at doorways to teach Wait at the Door.

- After this Get Connected work was done, the Basic Boot Camp exercises will be introduced (refer to *Basic Training Boot Camp* on page 120). I would still recommend that 99% of the time the Basic Boot Camp exercises are started before beginning the Get Connected protocol, but with this dog, doing it the other way round was a resounding success. I felt it was important to gain this dog's respect and work on the personal space issues first. Because he was not timid or cautious, but a rather bold and pushy puppy, this worked well. For the majority of dogs, it is important that they are not intimidated by Eye Contact and understand Get Between so they build confidence and have many successes under their belt before I would ask them to handle the mentally and physically more demanding work of the Get Connected protocol. In addition, I wanted very much to experiment and see how the Get Connected protocol would work on a dog that had no prior training.

- The quantity and quality of the Eye Contact you get from this dog is surprising, because to date the dog has not been "fed" for this behaviour. The Back Away was taught as a part of the Move Into exercise, as a release of the pressure caused by the Move Into.

- I was most pleased with how calm Wilson was with restraints, touching and bending. He now met this with no resistance and no anxiety. Walking him on a Loose Leash was an absolute treat. When distracted by items, either indoors or out, a subtle step towards him followed by a Back Away drew him from the distraction and

right to the handler. This worked with Rachel, me and another handler that he had not seen, but who has used some of these techniques with her dog.

- After Session 3, and at 30 days, I decided I liked this dog quite a bit. Rachel says that he is still pushy with dogs who will allow it, but she is monitoring this carefully, and he is not allowed to play with any dogs at Day Care that he could bully. He is promptly interrupted and after two to three interruptions if he is not appropriate, Rachel removes him from that play group. We have discussed this at length and have decided this is the best way to manage and teach Wilson, without causing other dogs to be made uncomfortable by him.

- At the end of 30 days this dog could easily be placed with a person who had some dog experience, although a person who is of a very permissive temperament will not be appropriate. However, this dog is quite handleable and cooperative with people who are clear with communication and give him known cues.

- Update: After 6 weeks Rachel started mentioning teaching competition style Heel work because Wilson's attention and loose leash walking are so good.

Owner's Input After Using Protocol

Was there a specific or precipitating reason for using the Get Connected protocol? . Anxiety about handling and his biting. On a first evaluation, Brenda and I discussed euthanasia because of the early onset and intensity of Wilson's pushy behavior and willingness to use his teeth. This dog needed to learn how to relate to people properly and fast!

What Exercises did you use?
- Desensitizing the dog to touch using the Be Still Cue.
- Move Into.
- Follow The Feel (Pressure on the collar causes the dog's feet to back up).
- Work with a dowel to back up. (This is advanced work that is not covered in this volume, but will be in Volume 2.)
- Walking on a loose leash by teaching "Keep Your Toes Behind My Toes."

Which exercises did you feel helped your dog the most? Desensitization to touch of all kinds reduced his anxiety. Be Still made him approachable (he is a very large dog). The Move Into made a huge difference immediately in the way he understood personal space.

Changes In Your Dog & You Interaction?

Was your relationship with your dog ever nervous, tense or did you feel the relationship was under strain? I felt indifferent to Wilson. He was not particularly friendly and was pushy. He was difficult to feel close to.

Did you notice any adverse changes in your dog's behaviour After the Get Connected protocol? No.

Did you feel your dog was placed under excess stress during this protocol? No.

Do you think that this protocol changed any ways that you think and interact with your dog?. Wilson was much improved and more responsive all the way around after two hour-long sessions which were a week apart. I was able to work with him a limited amount in between - maybe ten minutes a day. He is calm when greeting people now, and even though he is pushy as he is entering adolescence, it is minor and easily and quickly controlled. He walks on a loose leash amazingly well - better than other dogs I have trained. I took him lure coursing and he kept a loose leash even though he was very excited by the other dogs and the opportunity to chase the lure (a rag). This means that he gets to do more because he is fun to take. I like him now and that is good.

the
Brenda ALOFF
connection

Weaver

Owner: Victoria
Border Collie
male, castrated
DOB: May 2003

Photograph by Pierette Daigle

Social & Environmental History

- I got Weaver when he was approximately 18 months old. He had at least one other prior owner. I have now had Weaver for 2 1/2 years. Weaver is my first Border Collie, and I got him from a rescue group.

- When I first got Weaver we lived in town, but have since moved to a rural area with a fenced yard. Weaver lives in a multi-dog household.

How would you describe your pet's personality? complex, abnormal, intelligent, loves to work, driven, sensitive.

Medical History

Normal Medical History. The dog was castrated before I got him, I believe it was done at around 6 months of age.

Education History

How many dogs have you trained? Lots.

What is your training experience? I have worked at a Humane Society as the Director, as well as training many of my own dogs.

Do you have any competition titles? Yes, ADC, AADC & CL-1, all agility titles.

Age when you started lessons/training with this dog: Immediately when I got him home.

How was daily living with this dog? Daily living with Weaver started very rough. He had not been handled much at all and was easily spooked and unpredictable. I remember the first night I brought him home, it was quite a trip. I went and picked him up, I thought he was gorgeous and could see such potential in him, but he hardly noticed me at all even when I was trying my best to interact with him. He refused my treats and looked away each time I tried to talk to him.

I took him to a fenced in area at a friend's house to try to get to know him some and to introduce him to my other dogs in a neutral territory. I had him in one car and my other dogs traveled in another car with a friend.

Weaver got out first and I had some time with him in the fenced area. I brought an orange ball to initiate some play with him, it worked...but I couldn't get him back, he ran circles around in the fenced area. My friends and I kind of herded him into an area and as he passed by one of us, she reached out to take his collar and he turned and bit her. Not a horrible breaking skin

type of bite, but more a warning bite, enough that she was startled and felt it.

Eventually we got him and put him on a leash...the rest of the first night was on a leash. It took two of us and several minor bites later to actually get him into the car (even with a leash). He was terrified of the car and drooled and panted until we got home.

It quickly became apparent that Weaver had not been handled much at all. For weeks he bit me every day for one reason or another out of fear. He also bit when he was forced to do anything he didn't want to do...whether it was coming in from outside, getting into the car, changing rooms, etc. Even though I went slowly with him he still had trouble. I think it is important to note that these are not bites that required any medical attention nor did they leave any lasting damage to the skin: they were minor marks and bruises.

I got really good at expecting the bite each times so I could stop reacting badly when it happened. It was good to expect it because then I could plan a way to not let fear and surprise make me jerk my hand away in retreat or better yet, avoid the situation altogether. I became very good at reading his body language. I got bit less.

After several months he finally began to trust me more and stopped biting. We started to bond. Agility was a huge help in this area. We were both able to have fun and relax doing something as a team. It was a long process nonetheless...we worked on nothing but trying to get his attention in agility class for the first 2 groups of classes. He couldn't think or participate in the classes, as he was completely unfocused and scattered. He had absolutely no impulse control at all.

Weaver had been tied out most of the time with his prior owner and even when something was really great and fun right under his nose, he still longed for whatever he might be able to see in the distance. It was almost like he was so used to watching things and being stimulated from afar and frustrated that he couldn't concentrate on what was close. Most times it took two of us to work with him. One person would hold on for dear life and the other would work really hard at getting his attention. I think I accepted an ear flick in my direction as the first criteria of attention.

How did obedience training go? Obedience training was rough to say the least. Although he got so

he was great at home in times of no distraction, the second there was something, anything other than us in the room, he would lose his mind. Weaver would become over stimulated, out of control, frantic and so very reactive in a nanoseccond. His reactivity level was so high that if I placed it on a scale of 1 to 10 he could go from 1 to 10 and skip all the steps in between in the blink of an eye. At times, he didn't acknowledge that I existed; I was just this annoying thing in his way that he needed to look around to see what was really of interest to him. It was like he couldn't hear me, see me or even feel me right there with him.

My thoughts were to get him out to as many places as I could to try to work on appropriate behaviour and social skills. We joined many different trainers classes and attended sessions several nights a week for about a year. When we joined these classes I had no expectation of being able to participate in what the class was doing. I just wanted a corner furthest away from them so I could to start working my own curriculum on trying to get his attention. Getting this attention was most times impossible.

After working with Weaver for about a year of this training using common traditional techniques and treats we had some progress and his social skills were improving some. for example, in group situations, I could get a fleeting moment of acknowledgment. Those tiny bits felt huge to me at the time. Keep in mind that in order to get this I had to have someone use all their strength to just hold him on his leash while I hustled around trying to break through that indifference.

We tried lots of different methods ranging from Clicker training, active play engagement, punishment to any other attention getting song and dance you can possibly imagine. We attended impulse control seminars - of which we could only participate for about 5 minutes at a time before he lost complete control of himself. He could not keep himself under control at all, even his voice would change and he would sound like I was killing him, he would struggle against any restraint and literally scream. After his 5 minute working sessions, he would go back to the car (which he still hated) and have some alone time for about an hour. Then I would bring him out and start all over again. After all this time, though better, he still be over stimulated and frustrated at the slightest event, such as someone walking across the room or by someone standing in the distance.

I guess you could say most of obedience training was not really obedience at all. It never took less than 2 people at a time to hold him. He would dig and twist and scream and carry on like he was a wild animal. People were afraid of him, understandably, since he would be lunging and looked ferocious. I saw more: in our time alone at home was when I got to see a glimpse of who I felt Weaver really was.

His agility training did improve. Somehow we were able to connect, at least a little bit, around others. After many, many classes where we didn't participate, months of them, we started taking controlled turns at the exercises.

By the time 8 months had passed Weaver was doing well in agility training and able to participate in fairly regular doses of agility class (of course with alone rest time in the car during other people's turns). We entered our first competition at our home club trial. I felt fairly confident that he would stay with me on course, because there were no other dogs running at the same time, as there was only one ring, and once he saw the equipment he was able to focus on the job at hand for a short time. I still had a strategically placed team of people placed around the ring to intercept any quick change of plans to leave me. I couldn't risk his safety, or the other dogs at the trial, so I took as many precautions as possible. I spoke to the judge ahead of time to let her know what I was doing. Luckily she was understanding and allowed us a try.

Weaver did very well during his turns at that trial and had a couple of qualifying scores! He stayed with me like glue, he was able to focus even at the distractions of the trial. Once we got in the ring it was like a light came on in his head. Making our way to the ring through the chaos was another story altogether. He was frantic on the way, but then so oddly peaceful once we got in the ring.

Daily living remained very difficult through all of this. Weaver was a nightmare to take anywhere in public, such as a pet store or walking down the street.

We were stuck on a plateau, making minor and slow progress and were not moving forward. I couldn't find a way to raise the criteria and still have success.

One year after getting Weaver I attended our first seminar with Brenda Aloff. It was a seminar for aggres-

sion. I was nervous because we had a working spot. Any new experience with Weaver was challenging and unless among friends, quite embarrassing. Although it was an extremely emotional weekend, I felt both hopeful and exhilarated at the same time. I had finally found someone that understood and could help us work through to the next level. That weekend was really pivotal for us and has enabled us to strengthen my relationship with Weaver. His self control and overall comfort level has grown immensely since we started using Brenda's techniques.

The techniques made instant sense to me and I was able to adopt that train of thinking quite easily. The practical part was not always easy; it was a lot of work. However, the improvements I was realizing with Weaver daily were enough to keep me going. At times, of course, we had set backs, but we just kept working through and trusting the methods. We carried on with our intensive training regime, except now we were working on different things. I think people thought we were crazy. We would join someone's class, go into the corner and do nothing but massage and body work and relaxation for the first half of the class then move to nothing but attention work for the last bit. Followed by more relaxation and body work. That has paid off big time. We were finally able to stay throughout an entire hour of class without a melt down.

Behavioural History

Can you take food or toys from your dog? Yes. Hard as that is to believe, this was never a problem.

Have you ever been uncomfortable because you thought that your dog might bite you or someone else? Yes. I have seen him bite someone else on two occasions. These both occurred during the first week I had him, when he had absolutely no social skills at all. The first bite was in the fenced yard that first day. That same week I hired a behaviourist to come to the house to help with Weaver and Weaver bit him during the visit.

When he bit that second time he was so aroused and terrified that his anal glands released. The bite caused some redness, but did not break the skin at all.

Of course, he bit me many times whenever he didn't want to do something or when he was uncomfortable. These bites were more startling than painful, sometimes not painful at all, but his teeth still contacted my

skin. They were warning bites or tantrum-related bites: a firm pressure to the skin but not at all damaging.

There are conflicting stories about what happened before he came to me. I have heard that he bit someone who was passing by on the street. He apparently had broken the chain and rushed out and bit a lady in the calf. Some people say he did bite her, others say he just nipped at her pant legs. It is impossible to know what actually happend.

Overall, I am very careful with him, as I fear that in his anxiety and in his reactivity he has the potential to bite, so I give him no opportunities to do so. Management is meticulous and thoughtful. I never let him get close enough to bite anyone, and always read his body language carefully. He sometimes is accustomed to someone approaching in as little as 30 seconds to several minutes, depending on the situation. After that he is comfortable and very safe around that person.

When walking through the crowd to agility he is fine now getting him to the ring.

The other times he is likely to bite is when he gets frustrated. If he is reactive to something and someone passes by within his range he will reach out to nip or grab at them. He is especially reactive around boys of a certain age group.

List any behaviours that were of concern to you. How long had this behaviour been occurring or at what age first observed: His extreme reactivity, the lack of ability to handle him at all, the biting and guarding behaviours were all evident from the first day I got Weaver. Several trainers recommended euthanasia. His previous owners were going to euthanize him when I got him.

Presenting Issues (from Brenda's point of view)

I first observed Victoria and Weaver at a clinic in Nova Scotia. He was easily the most problematic dog in the room, in fact one of the most ill-behaved dogs I had seen. His owner seemed proud of the progress she had already made, which was a frightening fact. When we had our first work session with dogs, controlling Weaver was like trying to control a whirling dervish. Vic did not have good control of him at all. I made sure he had a Halti head collar on and told Vic to begin working on the Be Still Switch. I told her to get right down on the ground with him and

squish him to her own body if she must, but to continue rubbing his body until he stopped moving his feet. He was twisting and vocalizing. I had the other students do various exercises during this session, but I explained to Victoria that her dog was not ready to move on, and she was to do the same thing, persistently until she outlasted him. It was pretty clear to me that this dog needed to learn how to lose a battle gracefully - and soon.

By the end of the second work session, Weaver was doing marginally better. At least he had stopped screaming like an idiot and was vibrating rather than twirling. I discussed with Victoria to keep the criteria simple. At this point in time I did not know the entire extent of Weaver's erratic behaviour, but at that moment it wouldn't have mattered anyway, there was so much wrong and I figure you need to begin somewhere. I wondered about the sanity of working with a dog that was this bad, and when she told me she showed him in agility I was rather shocked, but could visualize this dog getting engaged in work. He had plenty of intensity but absolutely no impulse control. By the end of the second day, and many emotional scenes later, he was markedly better. I discussed with Victoria dropping in on classes and using a Halti to control where Weaver was looking, and working on only attention and body work and relaxation for at least two to three months before any new criteria would be added. I could see she was devoted to this dog and perhaps stubborn enough to make a difference. Weaver's only saving grace at this point was that he had good inhibition concerning the force of the bite, rather more than one would expect given his impulse control overall. Even though this was obviously very emotional for Vic, she kept working and trying whatever I asked her to do. Maybe there could be hope for this pair, although my prognosis on that first encounter was guarded to poor. Well below poor actually, but I have seen stubborn accomplish a lot (I have a dose of it myself). The real question was how normal was this dog as far as hard-wiring goes and how much of his hectic behaviour was due to environmental factors. Only time and the right kind of work could give these answers.

We also did restraint work with Weaver, which was a struggle, but he finally acquiesced, although it took both of us to initiate the exercise. Then I was able to show Victoria an easy Shiatsu massage technique that would help change Weaver's breathing. He was constantly holding his breath, never a good sign! The

brain requires huge amounts of oxygen to work well and his brain needed more than it was getting.

What struck me most was his resistance. He resisted everything that was presented to him with an appalling tantrum, fury and intensity. Thank goodness he was not so ready to use his teeth and by the case history it appeared as though he had quite an amazing amount of bite inhibition. The bite inhibition was the only thing that saved him from my point of view. It was surprising the intensity and lack of impulse control this dog exhibited coupled with the bite inhibition. It was the only encouraging thing I could see other than Vic's refusal to give up.

On day 2 he was able to stand still for up to a few seconds at a time. Well, that was progress. Weaver was allowed to learn the Follow The Feel exercise. Yessirree, another tantrum. Victoria and I persisted, with me offering physical help occasionally as well as instruction. After the first work session he was moving backwards, only a small foot movement, but that was way better than the tantrums.

The client was very emotional and we discussed this. I have empathy for the amount of frustration and how embarrassing this dog is to take anywhere. The tears I saw were, I think, a combination of past frustration and a release of having at least something new to try. If people have not worked with difficult animals they do not necessarily know the scope and intensity of the emotions that come with this kind of territory. It is confusing and frightening and relief all at the same time. I did not get involved with this at the time other than to tell her I understood her emotions and that she needed to put them in the closet while working the dog. I have stood in those shoes myself a time or two.

Once, after all the work of a successful work session, I observed the client allowing her dog to walk over and visit with people that he was friendly with without Victoria having given him permission to do so. I was incensed. This is inconsistency for the dog - with this kind of dog you are either in control all the time or you are not. You cannot be wishy-washy or casual or relaxed about the way you handle the dog. I trotted over and said pointedly, "Victoria you cannot have it both ways. Figure out what you are going to be, grey or black & white." If this handler were to succeed with this dog, if she took nothing else home, she needed to take this home and live by it. She took

this very well and continued to be 100% consistent the rest of the clinic. I quite admired her tenacity with this dog and hoped she would be successful in spite of the guarded prognosis I would have given if asked at this point in time. Sometimes a dog is just too damaged by past treatment to operate in a functional way. Would this be the case for Weaver? Only time would tell.

Protocols & Management (Brenda's instructions to the client)

- Restraints, both Sit Restraints and Down Restraints. (These are detailed in *Aggression In Dogs*.)

- Be Still Switch.

- Use a Halti Head Collar to help enforce attention. This dog needs to have endless Eye Contact and impulse control (Leave It) exercises. They should be done sporadically as many times a day as possible in very short sessions. Then the same behaviours were to be worked on in every room in the house, the back yard, the front yard and then finally on very short walks.

- Once the Be Still Switch and body work was getting results in the above situations, Weaver and Victoria were to go to class and do the exact same work.

- I showed Victoria how to do some Shiatsu massage, a very simple technique to help Weaver change his breathing patterns. Change the breathing patterns, change the position of the dog and you can change the emotional state of the dog.

- The emotional state was to be emphasized and reinforced, using treats during times when Weaver was not too stressed to take treats. This means treats would only be useful in very few and limited circumstances.

- Follow The Feel will help this dog to learn to cope with his incredible frustration and the low thresholds exhibited for frustration of any kind. Tying this dog out on a chain created a monster. He was so desensitized to tightness and pressure, and had learned to resist for very long periods of time. He was accustomed to feeling adrenalized, and this chronic stress really had him out of balance. Whatever coping skills he had tried had not worked, no matter what he did, the only constant was frustra-

tion. The tight pull on his collar had been associated with the extreme frustration, so anytime he felt any pressure on the collar at all, the frustration was evoked. This would have to be changed if Weaver was ever going to be comfortable.

- Move Into will teach Weaver to let go of his incredible resistance. It will gain Victoria respect and make both of them more comfortable with personal space. It will place this team in the situation of carrying out a negotiation and Victoria "winning." This gives Weaver a chance to "lose," and then Victoria has the opportunity to heavily reinforce "losing." Losing is merely a euphemism for the dog becoming submissive and taking Victoria's suggestion instead of being so constantly resistant.

- Victoria is to work on being calm and in control. This will happen for her as she finds the techniques do-able and gains confidence in her dog's ability to respond appropriately.

- The handler is to work on having 100% attention from this dog in all contexts that involve others. It will not always be pretty, but that must be the goal. At home he can be a dog. In public he needs to attend to Victoria - end of discussion.

- Boot Camp exercises (refer to *Basic Training Boot Camp* on page 120) to be started in conjunction with all others, with special emphasis on Eye Contact and Impulse Control exercises.

- The handler is encouraged to be patient with herself and to understand that the dog has to help, too. Relationships mean that both members work at it - you cannot carry on a relationship all by yourself and bear the entire burden no matter how much you want to. This is just never going to work. We must set up situations so that the relationship can thrive and make sure that communication lines are open. It is up to the handler to set these situations up and to be "available" for the relationship. It is up to the dog to try and to pay attention. When the dog understands that he will not be asked to do anything that he does not have a skill set for he will begin to trust. When he can trust and respect, then he will negotiate. Part of developing this trust and respect is having realistic expectations, clear criteria and excellent boundaries.

Recheck & Brenda's Conclusions at 30 days

- I went back home to the States after the two-day working clinic, with instructions to Victoria to: "Call me, for goodness sake, if you think I can offer you any help. Work on the easy stuff and don't worry about anything but his emotional state." I did not know what to expect because humans can be extremely unreliable.

- However, Victoria did call and wrote to me, and said that Weaver was improving in leaps and bounds, with the occasional frustration and plateau. This sounded like a very normal learning curve to me, and I told her so. The overall picture was improving as evidenced by the fact that Weaver was now able to go to class and remain there for the full hour with no melt-downs. Victoria could now handle him by herself too, since it no longer took two people to hang on to him.

- As time went on, Victoria kept in touch with me to keep me updated and to do an occasional telephone consultation. Weaver was getting more stable as time went on.

- Update: I saw Weaver a year later at another working clinic. I was very pleased with the progress made. Weaver could walk into a room of dogs and people and stay connected with Victoria. They were doing well in agility. An approacher could walk up without it turning into chaos. I had been most concerned about the relationship and was gratified to witness how it had flourished. I no longer saw a dog that looked miserable, anxious and frustrated with a devoted but equally miserable and frustrated handler. Weaver is still very intense, but much more comfortable and happy. People can approach him now and he knows Vic will keep him safe. He walks nicely on a loose leash and if pressure is applied to his collar he readily backs up. His concentration and impulse control skills are improved by 200%. Okay, that is not very clinical, but he has hardly any resemblance at all to the wacko (that's a technical term) that I had seen a year earlier. Victoria's easy confidence as she handles Weaver is in great contrast with her handling of a year ago. It tells me all I need to know about the improvements in the relationship.

- Update #2: In 2007 at the CPE Nationals in Canada (Canine Performance Events, which is an international agility organization). Weaver got High In Standard Level 2 and CPE CL 1 & 2. He got Master Gamblers Dog of Canada (MGDC). I went to New Brunswick to do a clinic and was able to stay with Victoria at her home. Weaver was delightful, and looked like a different dog: he was so relaxed. He still has a quirk or two, but he and Victoria have certainly exceeded everyone's expectations in every way. I am so glad these two have succeeded on every level. The closeness and connection between Victoria and Weaver is a lovely thing to behold.

Owner's Input After Using Protocol

Was there a specific or precipitating reason for using the Get Connected protocol? . Extreme reactivity, you couldn't handle him or touch him without a temper tantrum. His biting of me and others was much reduced, but I wanted more tools and ways to work with Weaver to ensure that the biting would become a behaviour that would disappear. I had tried pretty well everything else and it was not working very well. I was searching desperately for something that would turn Weaver around.

What Exercises did you use?

- Desensitizing the dog to touch using the Be Still Cue.
- Move Into.
- Follow The Feel (Pressure on the collar causes the dog's feet to back up).
- Endless body work and massage.

Which exercises did you feel helped your dog the most? Body work and the Be Still Cue. This was huge for us! Not only did it desensitize Weaver to touch, but it also enabled him to relax - just as important, I got more relaxed during this work, too.

It offered an acceptable option that I could be doing when we went somewhere and he felt stressed - which for him was 99% of the time. He grew to enjoy the touch and the massage and was better able to breath and cope with the surroundings. Before we learned this technique, people often told me it was painful to watch Weaver and I togehter. He was frantic and I was trying too hard to help him. It was not uncommon to see him twisting and writing at the end of his leash, while I frantically tried to think of something...anything to get his attention.

This exercise was very easy and peaceful to use. The criteria I had for him was very clear and easy to recognize so when he had it our time was peaceful and enjoyable. For Weaver his basic criterion was that he just had to stay in whatever position I put him in and accept the massage. To some that might sound easy, but for Weaver that was the most difficult thing in the world to ask of him. He wasn't familiar with just being and doing nothing. He found it hard to just stay in position and not react to everything, or at the very least run through over and over his repertoire of tricks I had taught him at home. One thing about Weaver is that he is very easy to shape because he was very experimental - sometimes to our detriment. Before learning these techniques, I often would contribute to his frenzy inadvertently. I thought that perhaps making him work and do tricks was a way to get his attention. Actually, it added to the chaos and the stimulation. I have since learned that there are some things that are just not acceptable for experimentation and simply cannot be left to chance, they must be meticulously controlled.

The massage and body work and the Be Still Cue has helped out a lot in our agility training, especially in a trial situation. Not only has it taught me to keep all emotion (as best as I can) out of my training, but it has allowed us to relax right before a run. We have a routine as we make our way to the ring now that always includes several minutes of the Be Still Cue. I try to get him into a Zen like state so he can think. A thinking dog on the line is far more successful than a reacting dog, no matter how fast he reacting dog is, he will make mistakes.

In the past as I prepared for our run, I would use toys, tugs, treats whatever I could to wind him up for his run. If you have ever competed much, you will have seen most people taking part in this ritual of really winding the dogs up and then going to the start line. For us, this had a very detrimental effect - Weaver couldn't think and I was contributing to this state. I learned that he doesn't need my help to wind up; he needs my help to unwind and think.

Now I use every second I can to use the Be Still Switch and connect with Weaver before we enter the ring. I do this until the last possible moment when they are calling our name to enter.

It has worked for both of us, he and I both relax and it allows us to focus on each other and what anxiety I have about his behaviour and the anxiety he has about his surrounding disappears and we are able to enter the ring as a confident team.

Thinking of Eye Contact as an emotional anchor and not just attention was another "Ah ha" moment. Using treats for Eye Contact is requisite, but the Move Into helped with the Eye Contact, too. If Weaver was too stressed or preoccupied to want treats I still had a learned behaviour I could call on instead of standing there helpless when treats wouldn't work.

Changes In General Activity Levels?

Before the Get Connected protocol: If things went 100% Weaver's way in familiar situations he was relaxed and normal acting. In all social situations and if ANY changes occurred to his routine his activity level would range from hyper-active to off the charts reactivity. He was also wary and fearful frequently.

After the Get Connected protocol: Weaver is now more accepting of changes and able to cope better. He is not perfect, but the daily living is now possible without constant chaos and stress. His wary and fearful behaviour is improved. He has a lot more trust in me now and follows my lead better. In times of higher stress he still gets wary, but the threshold is much higher. This means he is more relaxed, therefore his activity level is definitely that of a Border Collie, but a more relaxed one. He is more trusting and calmer in social situations and looks to me now. This is good, he can use me as an anchor and if he is looking at me he can stay calmer and I have a chance for input.

Changes In Your Dog & You Interaction?

Was your relationship with your dog ever nervous, tense or did you feel the relationship was under strain? Yes, and on a daily basis. His overwhelming social ineptness combined with his reactivity and total disregard for me was unbelievably frustrating and sometimes made me feel helpless in the face of it. I was trying everything I knew and researching trying to find answers, trying to find a way to connect with him.

Did you notice any adverse changes in your dog's behaviour After the Get Connected protocol? .No. I realized that his behaviour was not personal, he physically could offer nothing more with the tools we had at the time. Once I "got" this I was able to offer him what he needed, which was a big "Ah ha" moment.

Animal reaction to strangers entering the room, noises in the room, being left alone in the room, other pets in the room, etc. Weaver is very reactive and protective of his turf. If a stranger enters he becomes very upset. Once he has met someone and gotten calm around them and they use his name he is fine.

After the Get Connected protocol: Now when there are changes in the environment Weaver is much better. He recovers from the reactivity faster. I have more control.

Did you feel your dog was placed under excess stress during this protocol? Never. It was not always easy, but was always humane and anything done was done with serious thought and consideration to the dog's well-being and the relationship between the dog and handler.

Do you think that this protocol changed any ways that you think and interact with your dog? Yes, my thinking and my interaction with Weaver has changed dramatically since learning this protocol. The most important thing I have learned that the training starts with myself. I have to make sure I am grounded, centered and prepared to support Weaver through whatever may come.

I have a much deeper understanding of what is happening to him and with him and myself. I feel confident and in control during stressful situations now because I have effective tools. No matter what challenges presented along our journey I feel empowered and have alternatives to the frantic, frenzied behaviour of the past. Brenda's methods have touched both Weaver and I in a way that is difficult to describe. We are definitely more of a team now, I more in tune with his subtle changes in demeanor and the signals he provides to let me know he is having trouble coping. He is also very in tune with me, he feels everything I feel, so I must be careful to present him with a calm, focused and yet sensitive presence. When I am stressed he really feels and mirrors it. These methods have somehow allowed me to release some of that tension and live in the now rather than the past. I try to be very aware of what I am feeling during my training sessions. If there are days when I am particularly wired - those are the days where I try to not put us in situations of potential additional stress. I have learned that this is crucial to our training and our relationship. I have also learned that when something is not working for me to look deeper and get to the root of the issue rather than just treating the symptoms of the behaviour - I want to find the source of the issue and work on that.

At times our relationship is still difficult, but I understand him so much better now. Teaching the protocol step by step taught me about him and him about me. As we concentrated on doing tasks that were within our range we grew closer and can trust each other more. His social improvement has eased our relationship considerably.

I have also learned that my relationship with Weaver will be something I will always need to be aware of and work on. That is okay, I love him just the same. A lot of Weaver is about management and not always about cure. Although we work for cure always, some things work out and improve and others do not and will have to be managed for his entire life.

Brenda has used her methods and taught me to be patient not only with Weaver, but also with myself. I now have fewer expectations of both of us. This is not to say I do not have high hopes and lofty goals, but more like being comfortable going at what ever speed we need to in order to gain ground. The confidence these methods have given me, along with Brenda's guidance have made all the difference.

In summary Weaver and I both cope better with his stress. He has come to enjoy touch and being handled, now he comes looking for it. He is more easily focused and less reactive. He is able to concentrate and relax with some levels of distraction. His Eye Contact is better and more meaningful rather than just another trick in his bag. He can easily fool a person into thinking he is offering an honest look into your eyes and really he was still reactive inside and working out of his Hind Brain. Now I am more certain of the intent when I get Eye Contact.

Weaver can ignore some distraction without losing his mind. He is more in control of himself and happier. Overall the Get Connected protocol has changed our lives. We still have lots to work on using the same types of exercises, but looking back I am amazed we have come this far. There was a time when I worried I would never be able to reach him. Weaver and I are still a work in progress, but progress is a wonderful word.

the
Brenda
ALOFF
connection

Raven

Owner: Carol
Great Dane, female, spayed
DOB:2005

Photograph by Rhonda Kibbey

Social & Environmental History

- I bought Raven at 5 weeks of age, from a breeder.

- We live in a Suburban neighborhood. Raven gets plenty of exercise, walking and running in the yard. If she is not getting enough exercise, she lets me know!

How would you describe your pet's personality? Loving, spooky, easily over stimulated, controlling, a friendly monster.

Medical History

Normal Medical History in general, with the exception listed. Spayed at almost 2 years of age. She had a false pregnancy at around 19 months of age, and she started showing aggressive tendencies just before that. During and after the false pregnancy the aggression escalated. Since spaying her health has been fine and all veterinarian check ups have been normal.

Education History

How many dogs have you trained? 3.

What is your training experience? I consider myself an inexperienced trainer. I have not done any showing or competition with dogs.

Age when you started lessons/training with this dog: 8 weeks.

How was daily living with this dog? Exhausting! She was obviously intelligent but everything was a power struggle. She brought me to tears on many occasions from frustration. I was also physically bruised and sometimes felt quite battered because she jumped on me so much.

How did obedience training go? The regular obedience classes I attended with Raven did very little. She would do some very basic behaviours, but her general demeanor was the same.

What kind of technique was used? I tried everything that trainers I saw suggested. Some things made minor improvement but my confidence level was at an all time low with Raven. I had tried obedience training, treats, choke collars and shock collars. The shock collar was a big mistake and did not have the results that I was led to believe would occur.

Behavioural History

Can you take food or toys from your dog? Yes, with the one exception of when Raven was in her false pregnancy and had adopted a toy as her substitute puppy. She guarded the fake puppy with fervor.

Have you ever been uncomfortable because you thought that your dog might bite you or someone else? Yes, I was worried about her behavior with the small dogs that live in the house. The one she had a particular problem with was Amigo, a terrier mix.

List any behaviours that were of concern to you. The most frightening and serious problem was when she picked up Amigo and shook him. We were able to pull the dogs apart, but it was awful. This happened three times. In addition, Raven was constantly jumping up on everybody and mouthing people's hands. She was often disobedient unless she felt like doing what you asked and she pulled on the leash. She is way too big to be pulling on the leash and jumping. It hurts!

How long had this behaviour been occurring or at what age first observed: Raven was always uncooperative and stubborn, but she didn't show serious aggression toward Amigo until she was about 19 months old.

Has the frequency or the intensity of the occurrence of the behaviour changed since the problem started? The disobedience and not listening got much worse when Raven was 18 to 19 months old. The jumping, mouthing and pulling was consistent and constant.

Presenting Issues (from Brenda's point of view)

Carol and Rhonda live together and have Raven, a Great Dane and Amigo, a small male terrier mix. They also have two Shih Tzu's. Raven clearly came home much too young, and she presents very much as the many other dogs I have worked with that have left their mother between 4 and 6 weeks of age. These dogs tend to have extremely low tolerance for frustration and tend to be extra "mouthy." Their bite inhibition is generally poor and they have non-existent impulse control. This combination of no impulse control and low frustration thresholds is not good.

Carol and Rhonda were both clearly very caring and very frustrated dog owners. Raven is large and was extremely unruly. Carol tried to put boundaries on Raven, but was struggling. Raven showed her frustration and anxiety by jumping on the client every time she was told to do something or that she would not be allowed to do something. Rhonda reported that at home, Raven would frequently come over to Rhonda when she was in a chair and mount her. Rhonda could not even begin to walk Raven on leash. Raven also mounted or, alternately, flung herself at me when I took the leash to work with her. Thank God she was not human aggressive was my only first thought.

At this point in time, Raven and Amigo and their altercations are my primary concern. Currently, the client is keeping Raven muzzled whenever they have the dogs together. This was keeping the small dogs safe, but Raven was increasingly frustrated. There was a lot of barking, started by the small dog, Amigo, who was not present at the consultation.

Protocols & Management (Brenda's instructions to the client)

- I educated the client about bringing home a puppy who is too young (under 8 weeks of age), and the inherent problems that are associated with this. This helps the client gain understanding into the dog's behavioural patterns. It also prevents future error.

- No more barking at the door and barking at the window. When this occurs the clients are to interrupt the behaviour immediately. They may call the dogs, place the dogs on leash and put them in a Down or crate the dogs for a few minutes until they are more easily controlled. An additional strategy is to use the Be Still Switch to help calm the dogs. These techniques may be used together, or one time and the other another time, whatever works for the individual. The bottom line is: I do not want the dogs practicing arousal behaviours.

- Eye Contact and Get Between work. This will help Raven to learn how to concentrate, and also begin to teach her some much needed impulse control. While Carol is the primary owner, it is crucial that Rhonda get better control over Raven as well.

- Raven gets stressed very easily and refuses treats. This has made it very difficult to use treats with her. Still, the Eye Contact and Impulse Control work can be used with treats at home, where Raven is more relaxed and therefore likely to take treats. She has never taken treats in a training class or when they are out walking, and customarily refuses treats in those circumstances.

- Use the Be Still Switch at home frequently under low level distraction, or when the dog is already comfortable. After a couple of weeks use the Be Still Switch everywhere Raven goes. Hopefully we can get her to relax in a bigger variety of circumstances. It would be good if we could get her to take treats in more situations.

- Move Into will be used for inattentive behaviour that is difficult to interrupt. If Raven even thinks about violating Carol's personal space, she is to use a Move Into. Carol is not to give way to Raven and allow her to move Carol's feet when she is jumping or mounting. Instead use a Move Into.

- Gaining control when Raven gets excited and pulls while on leash will be accomplished by using the Walk Nicely technique. It is important for Rhonda to do this work also, so she can gain more respect from Raven.

- I cannot address the dog to dog issue unless Amigo is also under control. Therefore, even though Amigo is not present, Rhonda should do all the same work with Amigo. Especially important is to get the barking under control. Barking is a good place to practice getting an aroused dog to attend to and prioritize the owner.

- Sit Restraints (refer to Aggression In Dogs) and the Be Still Switch is to be used for mouthing behaviours.

- Use a Halti for all walking and if needed, for the long Down in the house.

- The clients are to have Raven and Amigo on leash and just have them hang out in the same room under controlled circumstances. Liberal treats may be used for appropriate and calm acceptance of the other dog in the room. I want to address Amigo's growing fear and Raven's control mania. I would like this to hap-

pen for as many minutes per day as possible. Hopefully, in the evening when reading or watching television, the dogs could be brought in and practice Down's while on leash. The leash can be placed under the handler's foot and held in a hand; this way if the dog moves, the handler is quickly alerted and can place the dog back into the Down position.

- Scheduled Feed.

- Notes: I worked the dog for the first hour of our session. She refused all treats, so I was not able to begin where I like to, which is with Eye Contact and Get Between. Raven was too big and strong for me to handle on a flat collar, so I put a Halti on her in order to even up the odds a bit. Then I started with the Be Still Switch, which initially looked like a rodeo. After about 15 minutes, Raven would sit in response to being touched. I needed to quickly address the frustration and anxiety this dog was exhibiting. Once Raven accepted my touch with the Be Still Switch, I began working on Move Into. Raven was quite fond of leaping towards you the moment you looked at her or stepped in her direction. Every time she jumped at me or attempted to mount me, by climbing up my leg (and my body) I would slowly, carefully and deliberately step into her personal space until she showed any signs, no matter how slight, that she was going to restrain herself. Within a half an hour, she was quietly yielding to me moving towards her and allowing me to touch her and bend over her. By this time, she was becoming attentive to me and giving me lots of voluntary Eye Contact. Then I began with Follow The Feel and spent another ten minutes working on loose leash walking utilizing Move Into and other Walk Nicely techniques. By now Raven was no longer airborne. Her resistance and mounting and assault behaviours had changed so much that even I was surprised. She was walking nicely by my side, she was attentive and she was trying to cooperate instead of seeking conflict. Her anxiety was down. She was far from perfect, but it was a very good start. Then I had Carol take Raven through each step of each exercise that I had done. Then we had Rhonda do the same thing. By the end of the marathon second hour, she was behaving wonderfully for all three of us.

Recheck & My Conclusions at 30 days

- At the end of 30 days I was able to see Raven again. Carol reports that Raven now listens 95% of the time and the other 5% it is easy to interrupt unwanted behaviour. She no longer jumps up on Carol, so no more bruised and battered owner. The mouthing of the hands is pretty much eliminated, she will occasionally have an incident of spontaneous recovery, but the mouthing is easily interruptible.

- She is walking beautifully on a leash.

- There have been no further incidents between Amigo and Raven. We are far from being out of the woods yet, but the dogs are now much more comfortable in each other's presence. Carol said they were now having the dogs together, and the muzzle is no longer necessary. If Amigo starts looking at Raven, he is put in a crate or told to "go to his room," whereupon he goes into Rhonda's bedroom and stays on the bed. Raven is much calmer, especially since the barking has been under better control.

- Raven is no longer mounting Rhonda, either in or out of the chair. Rhonda has even walked Raven a few times and said it was a pleasure.

- I am extremely pleased at the drastic difference in this dog's behaviour. She is much more attentive to Carol, and is visibly relaxed and letting Carol be in charge. There is no more evidence of the conflict and anxiety I first observed.

- It is a relief that Rhonda and Raven have a healthier relationship, with Rhonda in control.

- I was quite impressed with the amount of work and the number of behaviour changes the clients made. They had to totally change the way they were living with their dogs; and that means they had to change the way they perceived their dogs and the relationships they had developed. This is very hard work and not always fun to do. The proof is in front of me - they have succeeded beyond any expectation in a very short amount of time.

Owner's Input After Using Protocol

The specific or precipitating reason for using the Get Connected protocol? Regular obedience was not working. I either had to find the right help, or I was going to have to get rid of her, which would be devastating to me. We came to Brenda as an act of desperation. I love this dog and didn't want to give up on her. But she had shaken the two small dogs. While they were not seriously hurt, more scared than anything, it could have easily been horrible, unspeakable. The use of the Halti was great in the training. I highly recommend them to anyone with a large dog (or any dog!). I thought I had been a good owner: when obedience didn't work I tried other methods: choke chain, shock collars - anything I could to save my dog. The shock collar was a big mistake. Almost immediately upon the Get Connected protocol being put in place, Raven knew where her limits were and it made her a happier dog. It gave her natural intelligence the ability to shine. She is a joy to walk now and fun to live with. I am not so worried now that she will hurt our smaller dogs, but I still manage and restrict her. It hasn't been very long and I want to make sure she doesn't return to the old behaviours.

What Exercises did you use?

- Be Still Cue: This calms Raven down and we use it at various times, whenever she gets aroused. It works when we are practicing with Amigo in the room.

- Move Into - This exercise got Raven's attention and helped me to gain authority.

- Follow The Feel (Pressure on the collar causes the dog's feet to back up) - Walking Raven is now fun, and Rhonda can easily handle her, too. This changed the way that Raven sees us in the environment, she can be less stressed and she has a job to do.

- Walking on a loose leash by teaching "Keep Your Toes Behind My Toes." - See #3.

- The long Down, with the help of the Halti worked so well. Enforcing that she will lie down where I tell her and for a long time really helped her relax! She knows when I tell her Down that she will be there for 30 to 60 minutes, so she quickly relaxes and is much more patient. This also really helped her realize that I was the one in control, not her.

Which exercises did you feel helped your dog the most? Move Into. Walk Nicely exercises. Long Downs.

Changes observed after Get Connected protocol work: The obvious changes, no longer jumping on me, so no more physical damage (bruising, etc.) would be expected. But the added bonus of being calm with company now is very nice. Another less obvious expectation is that she no longer hauls the cat around or instantly chases the cat all the time. Raven is more cooperative and I feel our relationship is better. We are both less frustrated.

Changes in General Activity Levels?

Before the Get Connected protocol: The just not listening when you asked her to do something was maddening. She was very over-active.

After the Get Connected protocol: She is still excitable, but much easier to get under control. The longer we work the better she is at getting herself under control. I don't let her have her way on things just because it's easier or I don't want to make it difficult for her. I make her wait (for instance) and give Eye Contact before she can go outside. She has to stand and wait and not barge by me. I am much less frustrated, she is calmer and I am more in control.

Changes In Your Dog & You Interaction?

Was your relationship with your dog ever nervous, tense or did you feel the relationship was under strain? Yes, we loved her, but were puzzled and frustrated with her sometimes. Yes. I was concerned that I would have to re-home Raven, because she was a danger to the small dogs.

After the Get Connected protocol. This protocol gave us many extra tools to get Raven to listen to us instead of follow her "reactive side." Raven now respects me enough to do as I tell her to (at least a much bigger percentage of the time!).

Animal reaction to strangers entering the room, noises in the room, being left alone in the room, other pets in the room, etc. Raven and Amigo used to agitate each other. Raven would be out of control with company. She chased the cat all the time. She could be so uncontrollable and I worried that

Raven 371

she would seriously hurt Amigo or the other small dogs.

After the Get Connected protocol: Quite relaxed with company now. Better with the cat. Ignoring Amigo. The dogs get along so much better now. I don't feel like something is going to happen at any moment. We manage carefully, are proactive and never leave them unsupervised, but it is so much easier because we can have the dogs in the room with us, relaxing. I am no longer embarrassed to have company over.

Did you notice any adverse changes in your dog's behaviour After the Get Connected protocol? No.

Did you feel your dog was placed under excess stress during this protocol? No, she did struggle with the control issue, but when it was determined it wasn't her, she was much more relaxed. She clearly felt a relief that she did not have to be controlling everyone around her all the time.

Do you think that this protocol changed any ways that you think and interact with your dog? I am so aware now of arousal levels and have the tools to control the arousal. Raven is so much more pleasant and I am less frustrated. It is also nice that Rhonda can control Raven now, too. I know how important it is to explain structure to the dog in a way that she can understand it. It is such a relief to know that I do not have to give Raven up.

Amigo

Owner: Rhonda
Terrier mix, male, castrated
DOB: August 1997

Photograph by Rhonda Kibbey

Social & Environmental History

- I got Amigo at 6 weeks of age from a friend.

- I live in a suburban neighborhood. Amigo gets daily attention and exercise, which is moderate due to his age.

How would you describe your pet's personality? Lovable, but very stubborn. Likes to do things his own way.

Medical History

Normal Medical History. Castrated at 6 months of age. His tail was docked by his breeder at 2 days old.

Education History

How many dogs have you trained? 2.

What is your training experience? I am not an experienced dog trainer. Amigo is my second dog. I have never done any showing of dogs.

Age when you started lessons/training with this dog: Training began immediately upon bringing Amigo home. We did not do any formal lessons.

How was daily living with this dog? Amigo is a very spoiled little boy! He was frustrating because he would not do as he was told, even though I had done my best to teach him what I wanted. He was irritating and obnoxious, barking a lot and would not be still. My roommate has a Great Dane and we had started to have some trouble between the two dogs. It was difficult to control Amigo sometimes and he was also becoming fearful of the Great Dane, making the situation ever more tense.

Behavioural History

Can you take food or toys from your dog?. Yes
This has never been a problem.

Have you ever been uncomfortable because you thought that your dog might bite you or someone else? No. .

List any behaviours that were of concern to you: Dominating and bossy behaviour toward the Great Dane that we have.

How long had this behaviour been occurring or at what age first observed: This started when Amigo was about 8 years old, ever since Raven (the Great Dane) came into the house. It started out him being bossy, but as Raven got bigger and they got into a few altercations, he was alternatively bossy and then would act afraid of Raven.

Has the frequency or the intensity of the occurrence of the behaviour changed since the problem started? Yes, it was becoming steadily worse.

Presenting Issues (from Brenda's point of view)

This was a very interesting case history for me, because I have never seen Amigo in person. Originally Rhonda and Carol called and made an appointment for their Great Dane, Raven. I worked with Raven and the clients, so both people who were living with the dog were using the same cues and techniques. Rhonda, the owner of Amigo, asked me at the session if I thought Amigo would benefit from the same exercises. I replied in the affirmative and so Rhonda faithfully practiced the exercises with Amigo as well as Raven. When I saw Raven the second time, Rhonda said that Amigo was like a different dog after using the Get Connected exercises that I had prescribed for their other dog.

Protocols & Management (Brenda's instructions to the client)

- No more barking at the door and barking at the window. When this occurs the clients are to interrupt the behaviour immediately. They may call the dogs, place the dogs on leash and put them in a Down or crate the dogs for a few minutes until they are more easily controlled. An additional strategy is to use the Be Still Switch. These techniques may be used

together, alternately, whatever works for the individual. I do not want the dogs practicing arousal behaviours, especially since the dogs have had some fights occur.

- Use the Be Still Switch to help Amigo feel calm, and to teach him how to have some control over his emotional state.

- Encourage Amigo to ignore Raven, and reinforce him heavily for doing so. It may help to have a "place" for Amigo to go, such as your room, where he already tends to go when he needs a break from Raven.

- Gaining control when Amigo gets excited and pulls while on leash will be accomplished by using the Walk Nicely technique.

Recheck & My Conclusions at 30 days

- Client reports that the uncontrolled barking is now easily interruptible and much reduced.

- I am most pleased with the increased awareness on the handler's part and how much more quickly she reads the dog. Also improved is the handler's proactive behaviour in noticing and gaining control of arousal in the dog.

- The altercations between Amigo and Raven have not reoccurred. We discussed further management, which will be required indefinitely. Continue to reinforce the dogs for ignoring each other and continue to keep arousal levels low.

- The client reports that Amigo is generally much calmer in daily living, and he is more comfortable in general now that she is controlling the environment.

- Using Positive Reinforcement, teaching the client to be pro-active and using body work reduced the dog's anxiety. Adding structure helped the dog and the owner to live together peaceably.

Owner's Input After Using Protocol

The specific or precipitating reason for using the Get Connected protocol? The aggressive incidents he started with Raven, the Great Dane. This resulted in injury to him and Carol and I were so worried, because of the size difference, that Amigo would be seriously injured or even killed. We love both dogs and have raised both from puppies. They are our fam-

Amigo 373

ily, so we are responsible to resolve this and keep both dogs safe.

What Exercises did you use?

- Be Still Cue: This calms Amigo. Within a few days of starting this, we could use the Be Still Cue to calm Amigo when he got too excited.

- Follow The Feel (Pressure on the collar causes the dog's feet to back up) - helps with walking.

- Walking on a loose leash by teaching "Keep Your Toes Behind My Toes." - helps get him under control and so I want to walk with him more. It is less embarrassing in public.

- Get Between for the constant barking and arousal around the house.

Which exercises did you feel helped your dog the most? Desensitizing. There is a big difference between a dog who is emotional and reactive and a dog who is thinking and able to listen to you. Having a plan to reduce Amigo's stress made all of us feel better. Even though you are doing the best you can, if you do not know what to do and in what order, it is frustrating for everybody.

The biggest change was getting control of the barking, which we did by using Get Between and then using cookies and praise when Amigo was quiet. He now stops right away on a verbal cue and is quiet and calms down quickly. What a relief!

Changes observed after Get Connected protocol work: Amigo is calmer, in general. He no longer darts out the door and runs around the neighborhood, with me in pursuit and feeling helpless. It seemed amazing to me that controlling the barking, making it clear that he could not pull on the leash and changing my daily relationship with him so that it was more structured resulted in a dog that now comes when called! He follows my commands now, instead of ignoring me. I really worked on being consistent and it paid off.

Changes in General Activity Levels?

Before the Get Connected protocol. Often tense and nervous, wouldn't settle down.

After the Get Connected protocol. I am more aware of arousal levels of the dogs and provide more

structure. This makes for a much calmer dog, who shows self control after a couple of months of training.

Changes In Your Dog & You Interaction?

Was your relationship with your dog ever nervous, tense or did you feel the relationship was under strain? Yes, Amigo was so easily over-stimulated and then was difficult to get him to be calm and quiet again. He would ignore commands. Sometimes he would slip out the door and run around until I could catch him.

After the Get Connected protocol. He is easier to calm down and now I know what to do to get him calm. I didn't realize that lack of structure could make a dog nervous.

Animal reaction to strangers entering the room, noises in the room, being left alone in the room, other pets in the room, etc. Sometimes Amigo would look very stressed and tense.

After the Get Connected protocol: Amigo's social skills have really gotten better. He knows that he can ignore things that bother him and that I will take care of the environment.

Did you notice any adverse changes in your dog's behaviour After the Get Connected protocol? No

Did you feel your dog was placed under excess stress during this protocol? No

Do you think that this protocol changed any ways that you think and interact with your dog? This protocol changed ways I think and interact with Amigo. I learned that old dogs can learn new tricks. I know now that he can change and learn. He is more relaxed when I am in control and take away his stressors. I make sure that he feels safe and that I am protecting him and managing him. He is much more pleasant and is very happy being "a dog," and he no longer has the pressure of me expecting him to be a little person in a fur coat.

References

Aloff, Brenda. (2004). *Aggression In Dogs.* Washington:Dogwise.

Animal Behaviour, Cognition and Welfare Research Group, Department of Biological Sciences, University of Lincoln, Riseholme Park, Riseholme, Lincoln LN2 2LG, UK. *Clever Hounds: Social Cognition In The Domestic Dog (Canis familiaris).* www.sciencedirect.com

Appleton & Lange. (1995). *Essentials Of Neural Science And Behavior.* USA: Simon & Schuster.

Belasik, Paul. (2001). *The Essential Paul Belasik Omnibus: Riding Towards the Light, Exploring Dressage Technique, The Songs of Horses.* Vermont: Trafalgar Square Publishing.

Burch, Mary R. & Bailey, Jon S. (1999). *How Dogs Learn.* New York: Howell Book House.

Carey, Joseph, Editor. Managing Editor: Dawn McCoy. Society For Neuroscience.(revised 2006) *Brain Facts: A Primer On The Brain And Nervous System.* Fifth ed.

Catania, A. Charles. (1992). *Learning* (3rd ed.). Englewood Cliffs, NJ: Prentice Hall.

Chance, Paul. (1994). *Learning and Behavior.* Pacific Grove, CA: Brooks/Cole Publishing.

Clothier, Suzanne. (1996). *Body Posture & Emotions: Shifting Shapes, Shifting Minds.* Stanton, NJ: Flying Dog Press.

Donaldson, Jean. (1996). *The Culture Clash.* Berkeley: James & Kenneth Publishers.

Flaherty, Charles F. *Animal Learning And Cognition.* 1985. McGraw-Hill, Inc.

Gacsi, Topal, Csanyi, Gyori, Miklosi, Viranyi and Kubinyi. "Species-Specific Differences and Similarities in the Behavior of Hand-Raised Dog and Wolf Pups in Social Situations with Humans." *Wiley Periodicals, Inc.* (2005).

Gladwell, Malcolm. (2000, 2002). *The Tipping Point: How Little Things Can Make a Big Difference.* New York: Little, Brown and Company

Glenbrook South Physics Home Page, csep10.phys.utk.edu/astr161/lect/history/ newton3laws.html. Accessed December 2006.

Gray, Lendon and the Editors of Practical Horseman. (2003). *Lessons With Lendon.* Vermont: Trafalgar Square.

Grandin, Temple and Catherine Johnson. (2005). *Animals In Translation: Using the Mysteries of Autism to Decode Animal Behavior.* New York: Scribner.

Griffin, Donald. (2001). *Animal Minds: Beyond Cognition to Consciousness.* Chicago: University of Chicago Press.

Jago, Wendy. (2001). *Schooling Problems Solved With NLP.* London: J. A. Allen.

Johnson, Steven. (2004). *Mind Wide Open: Your Brain And The Neuroscience Of Everyday Life.* New York: Scribner.

Lit, Lisa. (2002). *Cognitive Canine II.* Bloomington WA

Martin, Garry & Pear, Joseph. (1996). *Behaviour Modification: What It Is and How To Do It.* Upper Saddle River, NJ: Prentice Hall.

McGuire, W. and Hull, R.F.C. (editors). (1977). *C. G. Jung Speaking: Interviews and Encounters,* Bollingen Series XCVII. NJ: Princeton University Press.

Miller, DVM, Robert M. and Lamb, Rick. *The Revolution In Horsemanship And What It Means To Mankind* (2005).

McConnell, Ph.D., Patricia B. (2005, 2006). *For The Love Of A Dog: Understanding Emotion in You and Your Best Friend.* New York: Ballantine Books

Nelson, Leslie, Pivar, Gail & the staff of Tails-U-Win™. (1997). *Management Magic.* Manchester, CT: Tails-U-Win.

References

Peace, Michael and Lesley Bayley. (2005) *The 100% Horse: How To Create The Go-anywhere, Do-anything Horse.* UK: David & Charles.

Pryor, Karen. (1985). *Don't Shoot the Dog!* New York: Bantam Books.

Rugaas, Turid. (1997). *On Talking Terms With Dogs: Calming Signals.* Hawaii: Legacy By Mail, Inc.

Siegel, Daniel J. (2007). *The Mindful Brain.* New York: W. W. Norton & Company, Inc.

Society For Neuroscience.(revised 2006) *Brain Facts: A Primer On The Brain And Nervous System.* Editor: Joseph Carey. Managing Editor: Dawn McCoy. Fifth ed. Printed and bound in Canada. www.sfn.org

Swift, Sally. *Centered Riding 2: Further Exploration.* 2002. Trafalgar Square

Tellington-Jones, Linda & Hood, Robyn. (1994). *The Tellington TTouch for...Dogs & Puppies: Step-By-Step.* *La Quinta,* CA: Thane Marketing International.

Resources

As complete a collection of **Dog Books and Videos** as you will find anywhere; great customer service; some training aids:

Dogwise
701B Poplar
Box 2778]
Wenatchee, WA 98807-2778
1.800.776.2665
1.509.663.9115
www.dogwise.com

From Dogwise you will find a variety of books on Positive Reinforcement training and other relevant topics. Some of my favorites are by authors: Karen Pryor, Patricia McConnell, Linda Tellington-Jones, Sue Sternberg, Morgan Spector, Stephen Lindsay, Kathy Keats, Suzanne Clothier, Ali Brown and Trish King .

Martingale Collars, cotton & leather training leads, & great environmental enrichment toys:
Premier
800.933.5595

Great Leather Tug Toys:
www.Eurosportk-9.com

List of Quoted References

A

Anderson, Clinton (2004) *Downunder Horsemanship.* p. 1. 49

Anderson, Clinton. Any film, clinic or book by Clinton Anderson will contain this phrase. www.downunderhorsemanship.com has a list of all of his materials and clinic dates. 60

Animal Behavior, Cognition and Welfare Research Group. *Clever Hounds: Social Cognition In The Domestic Dog.* Department of Biological Sciences, University of Lincoln, Riseholme, Lincoln UK. p. 236 www.sciencedirect.com 41

B

Belasik, Paul. *Exploring Dressage Technique. (1994). London*
    J.A. Allen. p. 22 21

C

Carey, Joseph, Editor. Managing Editor Dawn McCoy. Society For Neuroscience.(revised 2006) *Brain Facts: A Primer On The Brain And Nervous System.* Fifth ed. p. 5. 40

Carey, Joseph, Editor. Managing Editor, Dawn McCoy. (revised 2006) Society For Neuroscience. *Brain Facts: A Primer On The Brain And Nervous System.* Fifth ed. p. 5 41

F

Flaherty, Charles F. (1985) *Animal Learning And Cognition.* p. 265. 108

Flaherty, Charles F. (1985)*Animal Learning And Cognition.* p. 265. 107

G

Gacsi, Topal, Csanyi, Gyori, Miklosi, Viranyi and Kubinyi. (2005)"Species-Specific Differences and Similarities in the Behavior of Hand-Raised Dog and Wolf Pups in Social Situations with Humans." *Wiley Periodicals, Inc.* 89

GaWaNi Pony Boy quotation. Miller, DVM, Robert M. and Lamb, Rick. *The Revolution In Horsemanship And What It Means To Mankind* (2005) page 64. 185

Glenbrook South Physics Home Page, csep10.phys.utk.edu/astr161/lect/history/newton3laws.html. Accessed December 2006. 182

Gray, Lendon (2003) *Lessons With Lendon.* p. 31. 76

L

Lit, Lisa (2002) *Cognitive Canine II: Exploding The Myths.* p.27 27

Lit, Lisa *Cognitive Canine II: Exploding the Myths* (2002) p. 19. 87

Lit, Lisa *Cognitive Canine II: Exploding the Myths* (2002) p. 4. 82

M

McConnell, Ph.D., Patricia B. (2005) *For The Love Of A Dog: Understanding Emotion In You And Your Best Friend* p. 78. 193

Miller, DVM, Robert M. and Rick Lamb. (2005) *The Revolution In Horsemanship And What It Means To Mankind* p. 74. 185

P

Peace, Michael and Lesley Bayley. (2005) *The 100% Horse.* p. 22. 60

S

Swift, Sally. (2002) *Centered Riding 2: Further Exploration.* p. 39. 285

Swift, Sally. (2002) *Centered Riding 2: Further Exploration.* p. 41-42 285

Index

Index

D

About The Author:

BRENDA ALOFF is a professional dog trainer. In addition to working with owners on the rehabilitation of fearful and aggressive dogs, Brenda also teaches puppy socialization, fundamental to competition obedience, conformation, tracking, back-packing, musical freestyle, and agility classes at Heaven On Arf Behaviour and Training Center, LLC, in Midland Michigan.

Brenda's childhood love was training and showing horses. Watching animal behaviour has always been a favorite activity. Her first Smooth Fox Terrier sparked culture shock and a fascination in dog behaviour.

As a natural progression of working with dogs with aggression and other behaviour problems, Brenda learned a lot about observing dog body language - the dog's own Native Language and primary means of communication. Brenda's understanding of canine language and social systems provides dog owners with effective means of communicating with their dogs and modifying their behaviour.

Brenda is currently sharing her living space with: Maeve, a rescue German Shepherd Dog (deceased during the writing of this book); Rylie, a Border Collie; and beloved Smooth Fox Terrier Zasu (aka Zoomer). Abbey, her daughter, is currently studying creative writing in college.

Brenda's first book, *Positive Reinforcement: Training Dogs in the Real World*, was published in 2000. In 2001, this book was a finalist for the prestigious Dog Writers Association of America Award. She has also authored several magazine articles on dog training, produced a television program about canine behaviour, and been a guest on radio talk shows dealing with canine issues. Brenda's second book, *Aggression In Dogs: Prevention, Practical Management and Behaviour Modification*, was published in 2002. Canine Body Language was a Maxwell Award winner.

She is a member of The National Association of Dog Obedience Instructors (NADOI), the International Association of Dog Behavior Counselors and several other breed and training organizations.

Brenda travels all over the United States and Canada, doing working clinics on canine aggression and learning theory, from short lectures to intensive week-long workshops. Body Language is always included, whatever the topic. People also travel to spend a week in Midland, and do a week of private and group sessions with dogs who have problem behaviour.

Photograph by
Dave Schrader.